Understanding the
Paragraph and Paragraphing

Understanding the Paragraph and Paragraphing

Iain McGee

SHEFFIELD UK   BRISTOL CT

Published by Equinox Publishing Ltd.

UK: Office 415, The Workstation, 15 Paternoster Row, Sheffield, South Yorkshire
       S1 2BX
USA: ISD, 70 Enterprise Drive, Bristol, CT 06010

www.equinoxpub.com

First published 2018

British Library Cataloguing-in-Publication Data

A catalogue record for this book is available from the British Library.

ISBN 978 1 78179 287 2 (hardback)

Library of Congress Cataloging-in-Publication Data

Names: McGee, Iain, author.
Title: Understanding the paragraph and paragraphing / Iain McGee.
Description: Sheffield, UK; Bristol, CT: Equinox Publishing Ltd, 2018. |
  Series: Frameworks for writing | Includes bibliographical references and
  index.
Identifiers: LCCN 2017022685 (print) | LCCN 2017042631 (ebook) | ISBN
  9781781795897 (ePDF) | ISBN 9781781792872 (hardcover)
Subjects: LCSH: English language—Paragraphs.
Classification: LCC PE1439 (ebook) | LCC PE1439 .M315 2018 (print) | DDC
  808/.042—dc23
LC record available at https://lccn.loc.gov/2017022685

Typeset by S.J.I. Services, New Delhi
Printed and bound by Lightning Source Inc. (La Vergne, TN), Lightning Source UK Ltd.
(Milton Keynes), Lightning Source AU Pty. (Scoresby, Victoria).

Contents

Dedication

To SAYS – the four girls in my life

Editor's Preface

Iain McGee's *Understanding the Paragraph and Paragraphing* is a monumental work of scholarship incorporating historical and state-of-the-art perspectives on the nature of the paragraph and the factors involved in making paragraphing decisions when constructing written text. Within its comprehensive scope, it includes discussion on the origin of the paragraph and its nature as explored in centuries past as well as in recent work in discourse analysis and corpus linguistics, with implications drawn for pedagogy and future research. The author's wide-ranging and in-depth scholarship has resulted in a book that will, I believe, be recognized as the definitive treatment of the paragraph and paragraphing for some time to come.

McGee profiles the work of key figures who helped to set traditional notions of the paragraph, and then turns to recent and contemporary empirical research and theorizing on paragraph structure and on writing process activity related to paragraphing decisions. A notable feature is the author's comparative and critical perspectives, as fed by his practical and theoretical interest in paragraphing and by his own empirical research. The extensive review and close analysis of sources, combined with the author's knowledge of research traditions and methodologies, provides a strong foundation for McGee's probing study of the paragraph and the resulting enlightened understandings of it that the book provides.

Most readers will find that almost every page offers a new angle or insight on paragraphs, a topic which has long been clouded in vague and inaccurate information, leading to overly general pronouncements and prescriptions, and to unhelpful or faulty teaching. Given that what the general public and indeed most teachers know about paragraphs and paragraphing does not represent actual paragraph structure or paragraphing practice, this is a timely book which anyone wishing to have a better understanding of how written text is organized would benefit from reading. It stands as an exceptionally rich study on a topic of key importance to writing theory and practice, and I am pleased to have had a role in its publication in the Equinox Frameworks for Writing series.

– Martha C. Pennington
Series Editor, Framework for Writing

Preface

It may well help the reader better appreciate what this book is about if I explain, at the outset, my reasons for writing it, elaborate on why it contains the material that it does, and clarify why it is organized as it is.

The key stimulus for writing this book was my own frustration in teaching paragraphing, and my dissatisfaction with the educational materials I was using. In saying this, I do not mean to dismiss the educational value of prescriptive approaches to paragraphing. Rather, it is an honest admission (perhaps confession) that as an applied linguist and educator, I did not believe in what I was teaching in my classes, and, quite frankly, neither did I know what I actually believed about paragraphs and paragraphing. Accordingly, my overriding goal in writing this book has been to address my own curiosity to understand the paragraph and paragraphing through a consideration of the relevant theories, ideas, and research.

Secondarily, I have tried to consider what such a research- and theory-driven understanding of the paragraph might mean for myself and other practicing writing instructors (whether working in schools, colleges, or universities). This additional motivation, accordingly, has been to write a book which not only informs, but also helps writing instructors discuss paragraphs and paragraphing intelligently with their students. Researchers and applied linguists should also find material in this book to stimulate their interests, and I close the book with a number of suggestions for future research in Chapter 9.

Given the above-noted motivations for writing this book, I have attempted to position the text, in both content and style, at the juncture of teaching practice and scholarly research into paragraphing. It is my hope that such positioning will satisfy the interests of both educators and scholars. While some of the chapters have a more obvious pedagogical orientation (particularly Chapters 3, 4, and 9), others are not so oriented: Chapter 2 is historical, Chapters 5 and 6 essentially linguistic, Chapter 7 psychological, and Chapter 8 is concerned with actual writing practice. However, because this book is published in the *Frameworks for Writing* series, even the chapters which are not primarily pedagogically oriented contain some discussion about what the various research findings and theories might mean for the teaching community.

In terms of reading the text, although the reader may be particularly interested in one area of research in this book (e.g. early paragraphing practice in Greek, computational linguistic research into the paragraphing, or contrastive work on paragraphing) and may wish to dip into the book to find out more about a particular area, the text should, ideally, be read cover to cover. This is because the material considered in any one chapter builds on discussion in previous chapters. In Chapter 9, I seek to bring all of the discussion together in offering new definitions of the paragraph and paragraphing and a descriptivist pedagogy of paragraphing.

This book has benefited greatly from the generous input of the series editor, Martha Pennington. Not only has Martha added significantly to the quality of the written text, she has engaged with me and the subject matter throughout the writing of the book, and I (and the resulting final manuscript) have profited immensely from her comments and questions as a result. I feel honored to have worked with Martha on this project. I would also like to express my sincere thanks to Marti Hearst and Gilbert Youmans for permission to reproduce diagrams from their work, and also to MIT Press. Thanks are also due to Louisa Buckingham, Anthony Berber-Sardinha, Shane Butler, Richard Enos, Jukka Hyönä, Debra Myhill, and Matthew O'Donnell. Errors and oversights are solely mine (and I hope they are few in number).

– Iain McGee
Majan University College, Muscat, Oman

1 Paragraphs and Paragraphing: An Overview of the Issues

Introduction

In this chapter, I seek to set the stage for what follows, by highlighting areas of tension and uncertainty about what the paragraph is, what it does, and how paragraphing should be taught. This overview is intended to provide perspective, a bird's eye view of a quite diverse and complex body of research, theories, and ideas which are discussed in more detail throughout the book. In Chapter 9, I return to a number of the issues introduced in this chapter and, in light of the detailed analyses conducted in Chapters 2–8, put forward three new definitions of the paragraph, and also attempt to distill the critical essence of a descriptivist paragraphing pedagogy.

What is a Paragraph?

The English word "paragraph" is derived from the Greek παράγραφος (*paragraphos*) meaning "beside writing," a mark that was placed in the margin of ancient Greek alphabetic text, and described in more detail in Chapter 2. We still have a paragraph mark which is put "beside writing" in English, and which indicates the beginning of a (new) section of text – the pilcrow (¶).[1] Although this symbol is not used by many writers today, it is present in the tool bar of some word processing programs.

Historical lexicographical treatment of the English word "paragraph" suggests that the "marker" meaning (i.e. the pilcrow) and "the thing so marked" meaning (the indented textual unit)[2] existed side by side since the early 1700s. For example, *The English Expositor improvd*, by John Bullokar (Bullokar, 1719 / 1616) defined the paragraph as both a mark and a section of text:

> It properly signifieth any mark set in a margin, to note the different discourses in a book, or long chapter…wherefore such divisions in writing are commonly called *paragraphs*.

Some lexicographers continue to give a marker sense to the word "paragraph," perhaps for etymological or historical reasons. However, while the *American Heritage College Dictionary* (4th edition, 2002), *Merriam Webster's Collegiate Dictionary* (10th edition, 2002), and *World Book Dictionary* (1995) all give these two meanings, the first meaning under the entry for "paragraph" in each of these dictionaries is the "unit of text" meaning – suggestive of the increasing importance of this meaning of the word over time. The *Concise Oxford Dictionary* (10th edition, 2002), in contrast to the dictionaries noted above, reserves its definition of "paragraph" for a block of writing "…a distinct section of a piece of writing…," and has a separate entry for the pilcrow, which it treats under "paragraph mark." Perhaps aware of the ambiguous or indeed conflicting meanings of the term "paragraph," the editors of *The Shorter Oxford English Dictionary* (6th edition, 2007) differentiated the meanings by placing "more fully **paragraph mark, paragraph sign**" (original emphasis) before their comments on the second meaning (i.e. the "mark" meaning) of "paragraph" in their dictionary. The *Chambers Dictionary* (9th edition, 2003) similarly terms the pilcrow a paragraph mark, rather than a paragraph. Most contemporary corpus-based dictionaries omit any reference to the marker meaning of *paragraph*, and learner dictionaries (e.g.

Longman Dictionary of Contemporary English, 5th edition, 2009;
Cambridge Advanced Learner's Dictionary, 4th edition, 2013)
define the paragraph only as a block of text, making no reference to
the pilcrow, a symbol which, I suspect, many people today would
be unable to name.

Throughout this book, I will, following the *Concise Oxford
Dictionary*, use the term "paragraph mark" to refer to the pilcrow
and the word "paragraph" to mean an indented block of text, in
line with contemporary usage. It is important to note, however,
that some scholars have used the term "paragraph" for a section of
text which is not necessarily indented, and this usage is discussed
further below. More comprehensive definitions of the paragraph
are provided throughout the book as necessary (see Chapter 6),
and I provide three new definitions (from textual, reader and writer
perspectives) on the basis of the research considered throughout
the book, in Chapter 9.

Before moving on, it is important to reflect a little on this "dual
identity"[3] of the paragraph as a block of text and as a marker, the
shift towards a particular meaning – the sense of a unified block of
text – over time, and the effects of this shift on educators.

As will be discussed in Chapter 3, it was the block of text (rather
than indentation) which captured the imagination and interest of
scholars in the late 19th century. The profound impact of this work
on generations of writing instructors and educators in the Western
world cannot be overstated. The indented section of text was
considered to be a mini-essay, a discrete unit of text that could
be theorized, was subject to certain rules, and could be assessed
against the gold standard paragraph – which for a long time was
considered to be the Bainian (1866 / 1890) deductively organized
paragraph, as we will see in Chapter 3.

It was not until the 1960s that a difference in opinion arose as
to where the focus of paragraph theorizing should be. This was
evident in a series of exchanges held in 1966, in the *Symposium
of the Paragraph*. In this historically important exchange (to be
discussed in more detail in Chapter 4), a well-known scholar,

Francis Christensen (Christensen, 1966: 63) observed that Paul Rodgers (Rodgers, 1966a) focused on the writer's decision to indent rather than his own focus on the internal characteristics of the paragraph. In some aspects, at least, Christensen and Rodgers, though using the same word "paragraph," were actually talking about, and attempting to explain, different things – though at the same time vigorously attacking each other's work.

Being aware of the dual identity issue at the outset of our quest to understand the paragraph and paragraphing is important. This is because some scholars have focused on the unit of text, and others the unit of text as it exists within the overall discourse (i.e. they have considered not just the paragraph unit, but paragraphing, also). It is essential to balance academic interest in the textual unit with the paragraph's incompleteness, and its connectedness within the whole text, and consider the reasons for, functions of, and constraints put on the placement of a paragraph marker – or, today, the decision to indent or to start a new paragraph block – not just the discrete paragraph unit entity. An exclusive focus on the textual paragraph will tend to isolate it from the preceding and following text with which it co-occurs – its *co-text* in other paragraphs – and also isolate it from the writer's overall purpose and the reader's comprehension of that purpose. It is a basic premise of this book that to understand paragraphing, both ways of looking at a paragraph – the two different "identities" of the paragraph, as it were – need to be considered (together). I will therefore consider research both on the paragraph unit and the paragraph break or *juncture*, and how neighboring paragraphs connect or relate to each other.

A Taxonomy of Paragraphs

Laurent Heurley is one of the few writers to classify paragraphs (Heurley, 1997), not in the sense of providing a taxonomy of paragraph types (e.g. "inductive," "descriptive") which a number of scholars have done, but from a wider theoretical academic perspective. He suggested that the paragraph could be studied as either a linguistic unit or a processing unit (Heurley, 1997: 181). He believed that within the first perspective, that of linguistic unit, there are three possible understandings or approaches to studying the paragraph: as an orthographic unit (i.e. an indented unit of text); as a structural unit (a textual unit having certain formal and semantic features,[4] with no necessary relationship to the indented unit); and as a "mixed unit," defined by Heurley as one in which the orthographic and structural units agree, or map onto, one another. Eric Paltridge suggested that this latter perspective on paragraphing (Paltridge, 1978: 169) was espoused by Christensen (1965), whose work is discussed in more detail in Chapter 4. Most of the discussion which follows in the first section of this chapter will consider these three linguistic perspectives on the paragraph (i.e. orthographic, structural, and mixed orthographic / structural). Viewed not as a linguistic unit but as a processing unit (the second major classification he provided), Heurley considered how readers read paragraphs and how writers compose them, subjects covered in Chapters 7 and 8, respectively.

Heurley's approach to considering paragraphs is a useful one, particularly when the linguistic product is considered in the context of the psycholinguistic and cognitive processing constraints surrounding the production and understanding of paragraphs. Generally speaking, historical interest in the paragraph was product-focused and linguistic in orientation, and the issue of text management (whether writer- or reader-focused) was hardly considered. Recent technological developments (described in detail in Chapters 7 and 8) have facilitated research into understanding how paragraphs are processed, making new kinds of data available for analysis, and highlighting the importance of paragraph processing.

While I utilize Heurley's basic taxonomy in what follows, I add one more category to his linguistic classification, what I shall term the "co-textual paragraph." By this I mean perspectives and research on the paragraph unit which have considered it primarily within its larger co-textual environment, as seen, for instance, in the work of Rachel Giora (Giora, 1983a,b , 1990) and Michael Hoey (Hoey, 2005), rather than as a discrete unit, as seen in the early paragraph work of Alexander Bain (Bain, 1890) as well as that of Christensen (1965, 1966) and Alton Becker (Becker, 1966). The focus on the discrete unit has tended to result in theories of the paragraph, but not of paragraphing. As noted earlier, it would seem necessary to consider both the unit and the unit's textual connectedness to understand what paragraphing is and does – hence my reasons for adding a fourth linguistic perspective.

Below I consider in more detail the various linguistic perspectives noted by Heurley (1997) – *structural, orthographic*, and *mixed*, in addition to the *co-textual* perspective mentioned above. I also briefly touch on the *oral paragraph*. Although such a unit is not, strictly speaking, of relevance to the focus of this book, this unit has been discussed in the literature, and a number of interesting connections have been made between oral and written paragraphs. Processing considerations (reader and writer experiences of paragraphs) are dealt with in a later section of the chapter.

Linguistic Perspectives on Paragraphing

Few linguists or grammarians have made the (orthographic) paragraph a focus of study,[5] and when the term "paragraph" has been used by them it has not, typically, been used to refer to the typographic or orthographic unit – my focus in this book. In a chapter entitled "The Paragraph as a Grammatical Unit," Robert Longacre opened his study by defining his interest in a unit which was "structural rather than orthographic" (Longacre, 1979: 115) in nature – a critical distinction which has not always been appreciated by others citing his work, such as Stanley Porter (Porter, 2009: 179). For Longacre, the orthographic paragraph could not be the subject of meaningful grammatical analysis because he saw it to be influenced by a variety of nonlinguistic factors such as page look and length of material, rather than purely linguistic considerations.

Longacre (1979) believed that the structural paragraph was open to systematic analysis, and he theorized the form of this unit on the basis of his analyses of various languages. He argued that two characteristics were fundamental to such units: thematic unity and closure. The idea of thematic unity is fairly self-explanatory, and Longacre believed this could be either participant-oriented or theme-oriented; also relevant here is the work of Joseph Grimes (Grimes, 1975[6]). By closure, Longacre meant the existence of a functional slot at the beginning and ending of a paragraph which could be filled by certain *particles* (i.e. formulas), noting that some languages had (oral) paragraph-specific opening formulae. Longacre believed that a paragraph could begin with specific types of sentences (e.g. setting, orienting), and also end in certain predictable ways (e.g. with a verb of movement, such as *go away* or *go off*). Just as a clause can be embedded in a clause, he believed that a paragraph could be embedded in another paragraph – that is, recursion could occur – and a paragraph could be embedded in a functional slot within another paragraph.

In his *Grammar of Discourse* (2nd edition), Longacre (1996: 101) expanded on the semantic dimension of his view of the paragraph: "It is assumed that any two or more sentences which are semantically related constitute a paragraph." He provided a taxonomy of nine paragraph types, subject to stylistic variation, as given below:

1. Conjoining (coupling and contrast)
2. Alternation
3. Temporal (simultaneous and sequence)
4. Implication (conditionality, causation, warning, inference)
5. Paraphrase
6. Illustration (simile and exemplification)
7. Deixis (identification and comment)
8. Attribution (quotation and awareness)
9. Frustration (i.e. non-expected relationship)

If recursion (i.e. embedding of a paragraph type in a functional slot within the above units) is taken into consideration, Longacre believed the above classification would cover all paragraph types; Shin Ja Joo Hwang provides additional discussion on paragraph recursion (Hwang, 1989). Below I provide just one example put forward by Longacre, a contrast paragraph:

> *Thesis*: I got on a bus, traveled around an hour or two, got off and went through the municipal museum, and altogether had a delightful time.
> *Antithesis*: Tom, on the contrary, stayed home and felt sorry for himself all morning. (1996: 104)

Longacre's paragraph types may or may not correspond to orthographic paragraph units. Indeed, one can easily imagine indentation separating thesis and antithesis in the example above (or indeed any contrasting textual unit). If, however, the structural unit is also indented, then it would be a "mixed" example (using the terminology of Heurley, 1997), that is, one in which the indented (i.e. orthographic) unit and the semantic unit map onto each other. If, on the other hand, indentation occurs between the thesis and antithesis, it is necessary to distinguish the structural unit (here, two semantically related sentences) and the orthographic units (the two resulting indented units).

Interest in theorizing the existence of a discourse unit between the level of the sentence and the whole text is common among many text linguists, and Longacre's attempt is just one of many. In the same volume that Longacre discussed the idea of the paragraph as a grammatical unit, John Hinds likewise used the term "paragraph" for a unit of text which may or may not correspond to the orthographic unit: "a unit of speech or writing that maintains a uniform orientation" (Hinds, 1979: 136). Hinds believed that paragraphs comprised *segments* (clauses and sentences) which have a common bearing or orientation, and he termed these "the structural building blocks of the paragraph" (p. 146). Segments are specific to the discourse type; for example, a segment in expository discourse might have different functions: "introductory, highlight, motivation, or unexpected twist" (p. 149). He provided an example of a text from a *Time* magazine article in which a piece about Teng Hsiao-ping is broken down according to the above functions. Moving within the segment, Hinds believed that each segment, likewise, has "internal structure" (p. 150), and the structure within a segment might include peak sentences having a full noun phrase being syntactically marked, and non-peak sentences playing a semantically subordinate role. Accordingly, Hinds was able to develop a discourse grammar tree with the (non-orthographic) paragraph unit at the highest level of the tree.

Teun van Dijk, writing in the same era as Hinds and Longacre, preferred to use the word "episode" for suprasentential textual units, though he considered this term synonymous with the (non-orthographic) "paragraph" as this term was used by his peers (van Dijk, 1981: 177). He believed that episodes may (or may not) be signaled by indentation, in other words, that an episode may also map onto the orthographic paragraphs within the text, and he provided examples of cases where this was so.

Another paragraph term was coined by John Lackstrom, Larry Selinker, and Louis Trimble (Lackstrom et al., 1973), and also used in work by Selinker and Trimble with colleague, Mary Todd-Trimble (Selinker et al., 1976): the "conceptual paragraph." Lackstrom et al. (1973) distinguished this unit from the "physical paragraph" (their term for the orthographic unit) by defining it as, "a group of organizationally – or rhetorically – related concepts which develop a given generalization in such a way as to form a coherent and complete unit of discourse" (p. 130). They believed that in the field of English for Science and Technology, this unit was "the basic unit of discourse" (*ibid.*), rather than the physical paragraph.

Above I have considered a number of attempts to theorize various suprasentential units of text – all of which used the term "paragraph" for the textual units (whether considered primarily semantic or grammatical in nature). Stepping back from the terminological variations reported above, there are, I believe, two key issues to be noted. Firstly, there is an assumption underlying much of this work that the orthographic paragraph is an unsatisfactory unit for theorizing. It is too complex, one might say too whimsical for serious linguistic study, as suggested by Longacre (1979). One result of this belief has been the almost total absence of serious research into the orthographic paragraph in educational contexts over the last 50 years, as pointed out by Mike Duncan (Duncan, 2007). Gillian Brown and George Yule's plea not to discard the orthographic unit, and to consider orthographic paragraphing in different genres with a view to identifying regular textual features within these (Brown and Yule, 1983: 99, 100), has gone largely unheeded. Secondly, it is clear that there is an uneasy tension when "mixing" (Heurley, 1997), or mapping, does not occur. Why is it that mapping of the structural paragraph onto the physical or orthographic paragraph is not automatic? Why does it occur sometimes (perhaps often) but not always? When it does not occur is the result a poor or weak orthographic paragraph, or what Brown and Yule (1983: 99) termed "a deviation from the [Longacre-defined] 'true' paragraph"? The reinterpretation of the meaning of the term "paragraph" by Longacre was without historical precedent; in driving a wedge between a text's linguistic message and its formatting, he solved some problems, but he created many others.

The Orthographic and Mixed Paragraph: Some Different Perspectives

In this book, my main interest is the orthographic paragraph (as opposed to the structural paragraph or the mixed unit). One of the key orthographic identity issues has already been noted above, which is whether the paragraph is best considered as a break in text or as a unit of discourse. Below I provide a brief overview of more specific views within these two broad approaches, focusing on what different scholars have considered to be the characteristics and functions of the break or the textual indented unit.

The Paragraph Break

The paragraph break: A big period

As will be elaborated on in Chapter 2, one of the earliest functions of the paragraph mark in Greek and Latin seems to have been for rhetorical prosodic purposes (rather than grammatical considerations[7]). The relationship between punctuation and prosody was elaborated on by Randolph Quirk, Sidney Greenbaum, Geoffrey Leech, and Jan Svartvik, who described punctuation as "a surrogate and a rather inadequate substitution for the range of phonologically realized prosodic features at our disposal" (Quirk et al., 1985: 1445). The pilcrow has been considered by a number of scholars to be a significant punctuation mark. For example, Geoffrey Nunberg compared paragraph indentation with spacings between words and spacings between sentences (Nunberg, 1990); Quirk et al. (1985: 1611, 1612) put the pilcrow at the highest level of their hierarchy of punctuation marks; Martin Nystrand, Anne Doyle, and Margaret Himley included the pilcrow as a punctuation device (Nystrand et al., 1986); and Paltridge (1978) labeled indentation an "ally of punctuation." If the pilcrow, or indentation, is considered as a break like that between sentences, but on a larger scale – that is, like a big period – the contrast between the sentence and the paragraph is simply one of degree: prosodically, the paragraph is associated with longer pausing and greater tone shifts than seen around the sentence unit; and semantically, just as there is always some kind of shift in meaning from one sentence to another, the decision to indent can be interpreted as a signal of a bigger shift in meaning than is seen between neighboring sentences within the same paragraph. In this view, the difference between the period and the pilcrow, or indentation today, is one of scale (whether prosodic or semantic).

The paragraph break: A discourse-managing technique

A discourse-managing view of paragraphing was put forward by Dionysis Goutsos (Goutsos, 1997). Rather than drawing an analogy between the period and the pilcrow, Goutsos considered indentation one of seven topic shift and continuation tools available for use by a writer. These seven tools are: orthographic markers (including the paragraph break and brackets); metadiscourse markers (e.g. *at this point, to sum up*); prediction pairs (e.g. a question followed by an answer); discourse markers (e.g. *but, therefore, of course*); cohesive devices (e.g. pronominal reference, shell nouns); time framing (i.e. change of tense); and sentence structure (e.g. initial adverbials) – see Chapter 5 for a full discussion of these. Goutsos believed the paragraph break to be the strongest indicator of topic framing and closing (alongside metadiscourse markers) in expository text, with the other tools often needing reinforcement from another signal to help indicate the continuity or shift: for example, a writer might utilize a discourse marker together with time framing to make a topic shift signal clear. Goutsos' work on topic shift and continuity is interesting in a number of ways, and I mention just two here. Firstly, Goutsos found the paragraph break to commonly co-occur with one or more of the other tools (though, strictly speaking, this is not absolutely necessary, because of its primary position in the hierarchy). This points to a degree of redundancy in discourse management, an issue of relevance in reader segmentation studies as will be discussed in Chapter 7. As Brown and Yule (1983: 99) commented, when there is such reinforcement (e.g. an adverbial clause being used in paragraph-initial position) there is "overwhelming evidence that the writer is marking a 'topic shift' in his discourse." The fact that the different tools tend to combine would suggest the need to consider instances of paragraphing alongside other discourse management techniques, if one wishes to come to grips with a full understanding of what paragraphing is and does. The second key issue I would like to note in the work of Goutsos is his proposed discourse-managing tool hierarchy for different genres. For example, he argued that the paragraph break is not such a strong indicator of topic framing or shift in journalistic writing as it is in expository writing. This is an interesting suggestion, though one which requires further investigation, and is discussed in more detail in Chapter 5. Goutsos' view of the paragraph is rather unique in that he considered it as (just) one tool among many that a writer may utilize to help manage text.

The paragraph break: A highlighting technique

Another rather unique perspective on the function of the paragraph break (though one with ancient precedent – see Chapter 2) is that provided by Hoey and Matthew O'Donnell (Hoey and O'Donnell, 2007). Hoey is one of the few discourse / corpus analysts to consider the paragraph in any detail co-textually, as already mentioned. Some of Hoey's (2005) research involved manipulating text (e.g. changing a noun for a pronoun, or the position of a lexical item in a sentence or paragraph) and then comparing the paragraphing segmentation decisions of participants to different versions of the deparagraphed text. He found that principled manipulation of the text (e.g. changing the subject's name for a pronoun, changing the position of an adverbial) affected segmentation decisions, and this led him to question the idea that the paragraph is a topical unit, with the break indicating topic shift.

Hoey's main interest in the paragraph was psychological, and he argued that readers seem to be primed to expect certain phrases to occur in specific positions within sentences and paragraphs, these patternings being termed "textual colligation." In their reader-oriented psycholinguistic view of the paragraph, Hoey and O'Donnell (2007) suggested that the function of the paragraph is to underline or highlight a particular point in the text. That is, the writer's decision to indent should be seen as comparable to a reader marking a text with a fluorescent marker: its function is to draw attention to something important within the text.

The significance of the first and last sentences within a paragraph for the reader was noted in the late 19th century, and the idea that paragraph-initial and paragraph-final sentences are read rather differently than other sentences within the paragraph has more recently been confirmed with eye-tracking technology (discussed in Chapter 7). In Hoey and O'Donnell's view, indentation is related to emphasis. It is important to note that such highlighting may or may not correspond to the beginning or ending of a thematic or functional part of the text, in the sense that one might choose to highlight, through paragraph indentation, *any* part of a text. For example, one might indent at a point in the text that shows a logical link which is often overlooked or indent at a point that challenges a commonly held view. Such decisions should be differentiated from the more predictable constraining, and possibly redundant, role of indentation in (simply) mapping, and as a consequence enforcing the structural (i.e. formal and semantic) paragraph unit of Longacre or Hinds mentioned above. According to the highlighting view, the paragraph break places extra focus on a particular location in the text where the writer wishes the reader to focus, and as such gives a writer an opportunity to highlight a particular point, as discussed by Andrew Chesterman (Chesterman, 1998: 170), Nicola Owtram (Owtram, 2010: 219) and George Gopen (Gopen, 2004: 233).

The paragraph break: An aesthetic device

Paragraphs have been considered in terms of their spatial presence on the page in several studies in the last two decades, including those of Martin Fischer (Fischer, 2000), Thierry Olive, Ronald Kellogg, and Annie Piolat (Olive et al., 2008), and, most recently, a study by Olive working with Jean-Michel Passerault (Olive and Passerault, 2012). Previously, Sandra Bond and John Hayes had pointed out that segmentation decisions are influenced by page look (Bond and Hayes, 1984), and Quirk et al. (1985: 1624) suggested that short paragraphs "…provide…aesthetically pleasing contrasts between print and white space." Page look considerations related to paragraphing was a factor believed to influence indentation decisions, as noted by a number of educators in the late 19th century, as will be seen in Chapter 3. As mentioned earlier, aesthetic factors influencing the decision to indent have been considered to militate against linguistic interest in the orthographic unit (e.g. as argued by Longacre, 1979); however, it is suggested here that aesthetic considerations cannot simply be sidelined as insignificant.

The possibility that the decision to indent can be made at any point in a text, as suggested by Leo Rockas (Rockas, 1964), and hence may be *purely* aesthetic, is not a commonly held view, as paragraphing is usually considered to be somehow related to prosodic, formal, semantic, or pragmatic textual considerations. A less radical view is that aesthetic considerations may work alongside, though possibly preceding, these other factors. Accordingly, a long piece of text is not cut arbitrarily in two by its author when revising. Rather, the felt need to indent (related to spatial considerations such as balance and relative length among paragraphs) may prompt a search for suitable locations within the text where indentation would be considered appropriate on principled grounds (whether semantic or otherwise), and possibly at points in the text which would require minimal textual revision resulting from indentation. Unfortunately, little is known about aesthetic considerations in relation to paragraphing practice.

The Paragraph Unit

The paragraph: A formal grammatical unit (a big sentence, or a little essay)

Various analogies have been drawn between the paragraph unit and the sentence. Bain (1890), Christensen (1965, 1966), and Becker (1965, 1966) all believed the sentence to provide the blueprint (in miniature) for the paragraph, though drawing different analogies. Bain drew an analogy between the lower-level relationship of subject and predicate of the sentence, and the higher-level relationship of the topic sentence and supporting sentences of the paragraph. Christensen drew an analogy between the base clause of a sentence and its modifiers, at the lower level, and the topic sentence of the paragraph and its supporting sentences, at the higher level. Tagmemic paragraph theory, as advocated by Becker (1965,

1966), also viewed the paragraph unit from a sentence perspective, with the tagmeme[8] slots of the sentence becoming the slots in the larger textual unit (the paragraph). Some theorists have appealed to reader segmentation studies, as discussed in more detail in Chapter 7, as providing support for their formal perspectives of the paragraph.

An alternative direction from which the formal nature of the paragraph can be approached is by analogy from the essay to the paragraph. Such a view was common in the 1890s, and is still found in pedagogical materials today. For example, Adrian Wallwork recently stated: "Each paragraph is like a microcosm of a paper – it has its own title (the topic sentence), the intermediate sentences are like the sections of the paper, and the last sentence is like the conclusions" (Wallwork, 2011: 56).

The paragraph: An aid to text structuring

Those who believe that the orthographic paragraph should map onto the rhetorical structure of the text (e.g. Christensen) – that is, who believe mixing (or mapping) should be the norm – typically argue that the function of the paragraph unit is to support the structure, being a supplementary helping, orienting, and guiding tool which can be used by an author to help the reader in the reading process. Some research into Rhetorical Structure Theory, notably, that of Daniel Marcu (Marcu, 2000a,b), has interpreted the paragraph break as a signal of rhetorical shift, such as indicating a shift from *background* information in one paragraph to *elaboration* information in another. The idea that texts can and should be "reader-considerate," with indentation supporting the textual shifts and helping convey the writer's message to the reader has been made by a numbers of researchers and educators, as will be noted in Chapter 7. Whether (so-called) *inconsiderate paragraphing* (i.e. paragraphing which does not map onto the rhetorical structure of a text) is a problem or not is an issue discussed at various points throughout the book.

The paragraph: A cohesive unit

The concept of paragraph unity was an important aspect of 19th century educational work, as will be discussed in Chapter 3. A textually instantiated notion of unity was proposed by Michael Halliday and Ruqaiya Hasan (Halliday and Hasan, 1976), who discussed a text's lexical cohesion in terms of "reiteration relations" (specifically, repetition, synonym, superordinate word, and general word) and "collocation" (i.e. which words co-occur with each other). This perspective was, in turn, taken up and exploited by computational linguists such as Marti Hearst, who found that by identifying and mapping the lexical cohesive links within a text, software could fairly accurately guess where the paragraph breaks occurred originally in a deparagraphed text (Hearst, 1994a). That is, an algorithm could be created to identify the textual units within text, with breaks in lexical cohesion patterns being considered likely locations for a paragraph break. This research (described in more detail in Chapter 6) suggested, inter alia, that topicality (as evidenced by lexical cohesive links) is a key characteristic of the paragraph in expository text, and that the paragraph is best understood as a semantic unit.

Another semantically oriented view of the paragraph is that indentation serves to indicate which sentences should be considered together (i.e. processed and comprehended as a related set). Quirk et al. (1985: 1624) interpreted the paragraph break as a writer tool to indicate the closeness of relationship between a sentence and one particular set of sentences, rather than another set, arguing that all paragraphs "have in some sense a self-contained unity" (p. 1492).

The Co-textual Paragraph

In both structural and mixed paragraph research interest has been shown in subordination and coordination relations between sentences, intersentential cohesion patterns (grammatical and lexical), together with formal and semantic considerations. The co-textual environment of the paragraph has often been neglected, with a few notable exceptions, which I mention here. Giora (1983a,b, 1990), examined how writers might link their paragraphs through what she called "topic foregrounding," in which the to-be-developed topic is mentioned at the end of one paragraph and then becomes the linguistic theme at the beginning of the next paragraph (this often being achieved through lexical repetition across the paragraph juncture). She found this to be a fairly common writer strategy in her analyses of passages in a textbook of readings. Hoey (2005) also considered the relationship between paragraph units and how certain lexical and grammatical elements link paragraphs or not – for example, pronominal anaphora (typically not crossing the paragraph break) and general nouns (sometimes termed "shell nouns"), which are often used anaphorically in paragraph-initial position to refer to material in a previous paragraph (see Chapter 5 for further discussion of these). In addition, it should be remembered that the presence of discourse markers such as *but*, *therefore*, and *of course* in paragraph-initial position can only be understood within the wider co-textual environment. Finally, the idea that a topic sentence may cover (or control in some way) the material in more than one paragraph (such a sentence termed a "major topic sentence" by Braddock, 1974) strongly suggests that some paragraphs can only be properly understood within their larger co-textual environment.

The work referred to in the previous paragraph should be seen to balance Quirk et al.'s (1985: 1445) belief that, "…a paragraph has on the one hand a relatively strong sense of internal coherence and on the other a relatively loose linkage with the textual material before and after it." While this comment might be true for the specific example those grammarians were discussing, it is not universally so. Indeed, Quirk et al. (1985: 1492) themselves seemed to acknowledge this point in commenting on the "exceptionally close linkage" they noted between a paragraph-final and paragraph-initial sentence in another example they discussed. The textual linkage that a paragraph unit has to following or preceding units may be explicit and strong (in terms of the presence of repetition links, anaphoric reference, and / or discourse markers), or implicit (i.e. not signaled by any explicit lexis) – for example, when a new subject opens a paragraph. Why these differences exist is discussed in more detail in Chapter 5.

Oral Paragraphs

Although speech (obviously) does not contain orthographic paragraphs, as noted by Julian Warner (Warner, 1994: 25), it does have what can be considered "speech paragraphs," variously referred to as "oral paragraphs" by Rose Nash (Nash, 1973) and Mari Lehtinen (Lehtinen, 2010), among others; as "paratones" by Gillian Brown (Brown, 1977); or simply as "paragraphs" by Hinds (1978, 1979) and others such as Wallace Chafe (Chafe, 1979, 1992, 1994). Four factors have been proposed to support the existence of paratones or (oral) paragraphs in conversation and monologue: thematic considerations, pauses, tone patterns, and speed variation. In what follows, I consider each characteristic in turn.

Chafe (1979: 162) pointed to the existence of hesitation and pause fillers in speaking as evidence for the existence of discourse episodes, and he believed these to be related to recall and planning activities. Chafe (1979: 176) also reported research in which readers' judgments regarding paragraph segmentation of de-paragraphed written texts correlated significantly with the pause duration of speakers. He found speaker pausing to be influenced by space, time, and character shifts, as well as new event orientation. James Gee likewise focused on pauses and how they indicated the presence of what he termed "stanzas" (rather than paragraphs) in speech (Gee, 1986).

Concerning prosodic, rather than pause data, the term "prosodic paragraph" was coined by Gisbett Keseling (Keseling, 1992: 41). He found that when readers read a text (a fairy tale) out loud, the long pauses (often associated with oral paragraphs – see above) were preceded by a falling tone; and Brown and colleagues Karen Currie and Joanne Kenworthy observed that the beginning of a paratone unit is signaled by an initial high pitch (Brown et al., 1980). Leo Noordman, Ingrid Huntjens-Dassen, Marc Swerts, and Jacques Terken conducted research which showed that the prosodic characteristics of spoken discourse are related to its rhetorical discourse structure, and that as a consequence a listener will be helped to identify the structure of spoken discourse by the prosodic features, such as pause and pitch, used by a speaker (Noordman et al., 1999: 147). Swerts (1997) reported on an investigation into paragraph boundary marking of monologues comparing written paragraph identification (of the de-paragraphed text) with the segmentation decisions of participants given the spoken monologues, as a way to investigate the facilitating role of prosody in the judgments of those participants who heard the monologue. He found that the segmentation decisions were more consistent in the audio task, and that pause length and pitch were important elements influencing the judgments (though these were not the only factors affecting the performance of the participants). The accuracy of the decisions in the two experimental conditions was similar, but different in that there was more variation among the decisions of participants given the written text.

Finally, research has indicated that the speed of speaking or reading is also related to the discourse structure of the text, with initial speech of a new text segment being slow, and becoming faster when completing a segment, as noted by Julia Hirschberg (Hirschberg, 1993) and Johanna Neeltje den Ouden (den Ouden, 2004).

As I will show in Chapter 2, there is strong evidence to suggest that early paragraphing (in Greek) was added to an already transcribed text as an aid to the reader in reading the text aloud. Today, written paragraphs are usually read silently, and written paragraphing is rarely considered from a prosodic perspective (though see Chafe, 1994). The idea that prosodic considerations *may* play a part in how we read paragraphs has recently been suggested as a possible reason for pausing in reading at the paragraph juncture by Victor Kuperman, Michael Dambacher,

Antje Nuthmann, and Reinhold Kliegl (Kuperman et al., 2010). From a processing perspective, there are some interesting parallels between oral and written paragraphing in terms of how cognitive demands (for review, planning, consolidation, and execution of the message) are managed, and how a pause, or indentation, may help with these subprocesses of textual production or performance.

The Paragraph Break and Unit: A Cognitive-Easing Device for Writer and Reader

The need to consider the paragraph from processing perspectives (of both reader and writer) was the second broad perspective of paragraph classification provided by Heurley, and research into reader and writing orthographic paragraph processing has been facilitated by technological advances in recent years. While historically some of the research on writing paragraphs was carried out by having writers reflect on their writing experience after the fact or having them think aloud when writing, a more direct way of examining what writers do when composing has been facilitated by keystroke logging, that is, recording writer behavior as the keys of the computer keyboard are depressed, with all of the pauses, explosions of activity, and revision involved in this activity being recorded and made available for analysis. A key finding in this research is the relationship between pauses and the paragraph juncture. This finding has given additional support to the idea that a main reason for paragraphing is not merely or even primarily to help the reader, but rather to help the writer manage the complex task of writing, as John Colby had noted (Colby, 1977: 20) and also Heurley (1997) after him. Simplistic notions that paragraphing is an exclusively previsional activity which is primarily considered during the planning stages of writing, before writing begins (e.g. as suggested by Wendell, 1891), do not seem to square well with writers pausing between (and indeed within) their paragraphs. Although direct, in-process writing data is now relatively easy to obtain, interpretation of that data is not necessarily straightforward, as discussed further in Chapter 8.

Running parallel with technological advances enabling researchers to track writing behavior is the use of eye-tracking devices facilitating research into how readers experience text and the effect of topic sentences and paragraph breaks on reading behavior. Considerable evidence suggests that paragraph beginning and ending sentences are key locations in a text – at least according to readers' attention patterns at these points, as measured by eye fixation duration. These data have, in turn, spawned psychological theories to explain them, most notably Morton Gernsbacher's Structure Building Framework theory (Gernsbacher, 1991, 1996), which is discussed in more detail in Chapter 6.

Reflections on Different Views of the Paragraph

The reader will note the similarities, inherent contradictions, or possible contradictions between some of the perspectives reviewed above. For example, the formal understanding of the paragraph may be considered to be at odds with the semantic unit perspective, and the idea of paragraph unity seems to go against Hoey and O'Donnell's (2007) highlighting perspective of indentation, or instances of topic foregrounding across the paragraph juncture, which may involve bridging lexical cohesion links. One might feel, intuitively, that there is an element of truth in some or all of the opposing views: for example, the paragraph unit may be a topical one, but is not necessarily so; a paragraph may bear a certain similarity to a sentence in some contexts, but not in others. A key reason for some of the above-noted differences lies in genre differences.

The need to make genre-specific analyses and comments would seem to be a necessary first step in coming to grips with paragraphing (e.g. as argued by Brown and Yule, 1983). Although some writing manuals (and possibly teachers as well) can be quite dogmatic in their advice about how to paragraph, the reality is that paragraphing practice is not only genre-constrained and genre-specific; it is also positionally constrained. Thus, an introductory paragraph in a particular genre may be quite different from the conclusion paragraph within that same genre – not just in its function, but in the typical patterns of movement between the sentences within these paragraphs, how the sentences are linked, the cohesive patterns present, and other differences as indicated by Scott Crossley, Kyle Dempsey, and Danielle McNamara (Crossley et al., 2011).

An example of insensitivity to genre distinctions in relation to paragraphing can be seen in James Reinking, Andrew Hart, and Robert von der Osten's *Strategies for Successful Writing* (Reinking et al., 2005). One chapter of the book addresses paragraphs, and the other chapters focus on different types of writing: narration, description, argumentation, etc. The rationale implicit in such organization is that the "characteristics of effective paragraphs" (Reinking et al., 2005: 78) – given as unity, topic sentence, adequate development, organization, and coherence – are the same in each genre / text type. The problem is that this is clearly not the case if one studies paragraphing patterns in stories, academic writing, and newspaper editorials. Even if the same terms could be applied to different paragraphs, it would soon become clear that the realization of the concepts is different in different genres: unity in a story paragraph, for example, is different from unity in a newspaper editorial paragraph. Part of the reason for differing views of the paragraph and paragraphing is that scholars have, at times, been talking about different kinds of paragraphs, and they have not always been careful to delimit their comments to the specific kinds of paragraphs they were examining (a tradition which I believe started with Bain, 1866, 1890; see Chapter 3).

With regard to the reader–writer processing issue mentioned above, this might also be considered an area of tension. Some researchers have argued that paragraphing may (at times) simply be a trace of the writing process, with little or no reader-oriented consideration (e.g. Heurley, 1997). At other times, it is clear that writers do consider their readers very carefully in their paragraphing decisions. I am not aware of any published research investigating writers' segmentation decisions when reparagraphing a deparagraphed version of part of their own writing. However, some of my own preliminary work in this area suggests that authors do not always reparagraph their texts according to their original decisions, suggestive of the complexity of writer-reader considerations in paragraphing, and the difficulty of replicating decisions made when a writer is juggling multiple considerations during the writing process. Is the degree of textual redundancy the key issue in affecting such reparagraphing decisions? Do paragraphing decisions play a significant role in conveying meaning, and do they really matter? These are some of the questions I seek to answer in Chapter 7.

The complex picture painted above is, I believe, largely responsible for some sectors of the educational community finding solace in simple prescriptivist approaches to paragraphing pedagogy, and it is to this issue I now turn. In what follows I provide a brief overview of the paragraph as considered by various sectors of the educational community. I elaborate on this work in Chapters 3 and 4, but introduce the reader to some key foundational issues here.

Prescriptivism, Laissez-fairism, and Paragraphing Pedagogy

As Debra Myhill observed, approaches to the teaching of paragraphing are quite varied (Myhill, 2009). Within the United States some educators, influenced by testing criteria, curricula considerations, and possibly their own classroom experience, might value and prescribe formulaic approaches to paragraphing, such as the five-paragraph essay. Supporting such practice are numerous composition books and writing manuals on the market in the United States, in which prescriptivist approaches are common. Karen Bennett, in her review of writing manuals (Bennett, 2009), reported quite traditional and formulaic approaches to the teaching of paragraphing (discussed in more detail below), and prescriptivist approaches to paragraphing also seem to be common in books written for second language learners, such as those of Joy Reid (Reid, 1994) and Keith Folse, April Muchmore-Vokoun, and Elena Vestri Solomon (Folse et al., 2010).

Myhill (2009) argued that in the UK and Australia less prescriptivist approaches to paragraphing are probably more common. In her brief overview of these two different approaches to paragraphing, Myhill made a direct connection between marking rubrics and teaching practice. In discussing the situation in the English school context, she observed that the lack of rigid views of paragraphing in marking criteria tended to result in the absence of tight pedagogical approaches to teaching paragraphs.

Three key American (NCTE) journals (*College Composition and Communication*, *College English*, and *English Journal*) have published articles on the paragraph over the last six decades. However, voices from the United Kingdom and Australia are rarely heard – in part, because the above-noted journals are U.S.-focused, and also because composition classes are not compulsory in higher education in these countries, and so there is probably less interest in paragraphing in these contexts. This being so, approaches to paragraphing in educational settings around the world are rather different: prescriptivism centering on very basic paragraph structure, and what may be described a "laissez faire" attitude in which paragraphing is not a major focus, or considered in a principled manner.

Up until the 1960s, the orthographic paragraph was the unchallenged suprasentential unit of discourse taught in classrooms around the world. This was probably due to the effect of late 19th century theorizing of the paragraph in the United Kingdom and the United States (as we will consider in Chapter 3). If paragraphs could be considered little essays, then they would be a valid focus for learner-writers, and a more manageable one for teachers to handle, when compared to essays. During the 1960s, however, the first cracks in this formal, linguistic-product approach to paragraphing began to appear, and for two different reasons. The first was a reaction against 19th century product-focused work. Christensen (1965, 1966) and to a lesser extent Becker (1965, 1966) wanted to help students write; their concerns were essentially practical, and they were interested in the process of writing. The second was the voicing of a truly descriptivist perspective, seen in the work of Rodgers (1965, 1966a,b), who vigorously argued for the importance of a variety of factors influencing the decision to indent: Rodgers was highly critical of attempts to argue that the paragraph was a formal grammatical unit. Arguably, Rodgers' work paved the way for some of the alternative terminology (e.g. "conceptual" paragraph) noted at the beginning of this chapter, and he put forward his own term for the basic suprasentential text unit – "the stadium of discourse" – discussed in detail in Chapter 4. However, descriptivist work in the 1960s and 1970s did not result in a satisfactory descriptivist pedagogy of paragraphing being developed, although Willis Pitkin's work (Pitkin, 1969, 1977), discussed in more detail in Chapter 4, could be considered an attempt to fill this gap.

After the 1960s and 1970s, the paragraph as an orthographic unit was still important, but it had taken something of a battering, and it had lost credibility: as a subject of serious academic enquiry in the field of education, it moved into the shadows and has remained there until the current time (see Duncan, 2007). Educators in the United States in the 1970s were put into a difficult position, and I believe that there were three options open to them concerning possible approaches to teaching paragraphs:

1. Focus student attention on the new units within text (stadia, structural paragraphs, etc.) and put the discourse-level writing focus there, and leave the orthographic units to one side.
2. Ignore descriptivists (e.g. Rodgers) and text grammarians (e.g. Longacre), and maintain a focus on the orthographic

paragraph. This could be done by either continuing to draw on prescriptivist work from the late 19th century and / or focusing on what Heurley termed the "mixed" unit, drawing on work published in the 1960s and 1970s (e.g. as propounded in Christensen's and Becker's writings).
3. Develop a descriptivist paragraphing pedagogy which would be accessible and useful for teachers and students.

The teaching profession in the United States chose the most realistic option open to it: number 2. Text grammarian work was never really developed with educators in mind, and few sought to make the connections between textual analytical work and education, perhaps with the exception of Pitkin (1969, 1977) and the later contribution of Richard Coe (Coe, 1988). However, this work did not stand the test of time, and is now largely forgotten. Concerning choice number 3, not enough was known about actual paragraphs to make this a feasible proposition: discourse analysis was in its infancy, and corpus linguistics had barely been born. In reality, there was no choice: tight prescriptivism had something to offer teachers; there was an allure about the orthographic unit that teachers could not resist. The very nature of teaching, one might argue, is to simplify and generalize: pedagogical statements may not always be true, but since the mixed unit exists, why not make it the pedagogical focus? As such, some teacher-educators papered over the cracks created by Rodgers, who provided evidence to show that orthographic paragraphs did not always develop as prescriptivists argued, and reverted to traditional paragraphing pedagogy, or more practical "how to" versions of this earlier work – Christensen's generative rhetoric, in particular.

Today it seems that advice on paragraphing is typically prescriptive. My justification for claiming this comes, in part, from Bennett's review of academic style manuals. Bennett (2009: 46) commented (neither critically, nor uncritically) that "…there is great uniformity concerning the advice given. All of the authors agree that the structure of the paragraph should mirror that of the text as a whole, with a Topic Sentence functioning as introduction, giving a general idea of what is to come, followed by a middle section providing supporting evidence or developing the idea further, and a concluding sentence." One might argue that teachers do not follow textbooks blindly; however, it seems reasonable to believe that the traditional concepts of topic sentence, support, concluding sentence, and the like are the staple notions used by teachers engaging in paragraph instruction around the world today. If Bennett is accurate in her appraisal, it would also be fair to say that not much has changed over the last 100–150 years with regard to paragraphing pedagogy (at least in terms of the materials analyzed in Bennett's overview), as it seems that scholars from the late 1800s onwards were essentially saying the same things that are found in today's manuals. Below I provide some quotes to support this claim.

> The opening sentence, unless so constructed as to be obviously preparatory, is expected to indicate with prominence the subject of the paragraph. (Bain, 1890: 108)
> Devoted, like the sentence, to the development of one topic, a good paragraph is also, like a good essay, a complete treatment in itself. (Scott and Denney, 1895: 1)
> [The Paragraph is a] connected series of sentences containing the development of a single topic. (Hepburn, 1875: 247)

Bennett (2009: 52) noted that the academic style manuals she reviewed have been influenced by developments in Text Linguistics and Discourse Analysis. However, one has to question how much influence there really has been from these two recent disciplines on pedagogical paragraph theory if it is (still) presented in ways which our 19th century forebears would recognize as their own.

The need to reconsider paragraphing pedagogy should be viewed alongside changes and developments in language teaching over the last twenty or thirty years. There has been an increasing awareness among language educators that models of language presented to students can be measured and assessed, and found wanting, largely due to insights gleaned from corpus linguistic studies. Paragraphing pedagogy (up to this point largely untouched by research findings) should likewise be updated: just as newer approaches to teaching grammar and vocabulary sit more comfortably alongside research insights and understandings, so too paragraphing pedagogy needs to be realigned, despite the "devilishly difficult" (Duncan 2007: 471) obstacles in the way of such endeavors.

Some educators may not be convinced by the above argument. After all, pedagogy is a much larger concern than language description, and how, when, and if research data (corpus-based or not) can or should influence what goes on in the classroom remains an open question – largely because of the multifaceted nature of the pedagogical enterprise and the narrowness of the strictly academic one. As Arn Tibbetts and Charlene Tibbetts have noted (in discussing the pedagogy of composition rather than paragraphing per se), "Our impression…is that in recent years research has had little permanent effect on either textbooks or teaching" (Tibbetts and Tibbetts, 1982: 857). This might be because of the delayed trickle-down effect of research findings into educational practice. However, it may also be because of the different concerns and priorities that teachers have as compared with scholars. Teachers draw on practice-based experience, in addition to theories and research-based findings. They can therefore take the moral high ground and might say to scholars, "Well, you come into my classroom and see how your ivory tower ideas play out in reality with a class of 30 demotivated students!" This is a challenge, I believe, few scholars would relish.

However, it should not be assumed that educators are satisfied with current prescriptivist approaches to paragraphing either, and are unwilling to accept new ideas. On the contrary, just as in the 1960s there were rumblings about the dominant paragraphing paradigm, since 2000 there have been new rumblings (see Myhill, 2009, for an overview of some of these).[8] Elizabeth Hayes' attack on Bainian paragraphing was an articulate and focused one: not only was she highly critical of the continued adherence to prescriptivist tenets which do not match actual paragraphing practices, she also suggested that some prescriptivist practices were educationally damaging (Hayes, 2003). Lil Brannon et al. (2008) believed that the five-paragraph essay persists only because of its entrenched nature in books and other materials in the United States, not because of any inherent value. They also maintained that the formulaic nature of paragraphing in some contexts disempowers students: "Students learn that writing means following a set of instructions, filling in the blanks. Such writing mirrors working-class life, which requires little individual thinking and creativity combined with lots of monotony and following orders" (Brannon et al., 2008: 18). Jeanette Miller, writing from a high school perspective (Miller, 2010), suggested that students might find comfort in the five-paragraph essay, but that its effects are probably detrimental in the long term. She also suggested, implicitly at least, that for teachers the actual product resulting from tightly prescriptivist practices is predictable, unimaginative, and even depressing to engage with. Her solution to this state of affairs was to encourage teachers to "convey the idea that there are many ways to develop an effective piece of writing, depending on audience and purpose" (Miller, 2010: 100).

Prescriptivist antagonists have tended to either criticize certain practices or point to rather general alternatives. With regard to the latter approach, Melinda Reichelt, Natalie Lefkowitz, Carol Rinnert, and Jean Marie Schultz recommended that teachers indicate to their (U.S.) students that the five-paragraph essay is a strictly American way of doing an essay, an approach which would not be valued or acceptable in France, for example (Reichelt, 2012: 27). Other writers have encouraged creativity, offered constructivist views of education, or made observations similar to those provided by Miller above. Such views, I believe, are valuable, but they cannot be considered to constitute a feasible challenge to prescriptivist approaches.

The content of this book offers such a challenge and in the last chapter of this book, I provide a descriptivist pedagogy of paragraphing based on my analyses of the research data provided in Chapters 5–8, and also a reconsideration of educator thought on the paragraph as documented in Chapters 3 and 4. The approach is, I believe, a feasible third option for teachers to follow (see earlier on the three choices idea). Given developments in linguistics and psychology over the last 50 years, I believe that choice 3 is now a more realistic option than it was in the 1970s, once the relevant research data are collected, analyzed, and filtered for educational purposes. Research is still needed in a number of key areas (as I note throughout this book), and my proposals in Chapter 9 should be seen as a work in progress which needs to be trialed in classrooms. I believe that educators who currently adopt a laissez faire attitude to paragraphing (whether in the United Kingdom, Australia, or elsewhere) may benefit from a more principled approach to paragraphing, and it is hoped that the simple framework I propose may help facilitate more intelligent discussion about paragraphs with students in these contexts. I also hope that writing instructors who currently adopt a prescriptivist approach, and are not entirely satisfied with their current practice, or their students' writing, may benefit from some of the ideas I put forward.

Conclusion

In this chapter, I have sought to provide an overview of various ideas about and perspectives on the paragraph and paragraphing, and have also briefly considered the problematic issue of pedagogy. In the chapters that follow, I seek to take up issues raised in this chapter one by one and examine each in more detail. All of the separate topics dealt with in the chapters that follow could fill entire books in and of themselves. However, my goal in writing this book has been to bring together research and ideas from a wide range of disciplines (education, linguistics, and psychology) within the same volume, centered on paragraphing. Therefore, discussion is not exhaustive, but should give a reasonable overview of past and ongoing work on paragraphs and paragraphing. The approach I adopt in reporting and discussing previous work is to present ideas and analyze them as necessary, and then to consider their possible pedagogical implications. Rather than critiquing writing manuals, my approach is to focus primarily on research data, and consider how these may be of value to educators, and learner-writers.

Notes

1   Walter Skeat rather ingeniously traces the etymology of "pilcrow" to *paragraphos* (actually from the Latin derivation of the Greek) as follows: from *paragraphus* (Latin) to *paragraphe* (French), and then to *paragraffe, pargraf, pargrafte, pergrafte, pelgrafte, pilgrafte, pilcrafte, pilcraf*, and finally to *pilcrow* (Skeat, 1901). He notes, however, that a number of the above forms are not attested (p. 216). The etymological development is further complicated by the fact that the above terms (at least the attested ones) may actually refer to different things. Lewis (1894), for example, notes that the *pylcrafte* was defined as *asteriskus* in 1440 but after Caxton (England's first printer), it was used to refer to an index. We must therefore allow for not only etymological development, but also functional development or multi-functional development, in addition to changes in the graphical form of the symbol used.

2   See Andrew Haslam (Haslam, 2006) for some alternatives to the traditional indent (e.g. hanging indent, drop lines, etc.).

3   Strictly speaking, the word "paragraph" does not have only two meanings. Other meanings in dictionaries refer to a piece in a newspaper, a stretch of music, or a complete individual entity (as opposed to part of a larger text); but the key meanings discussed in this book are just the two mentioned above, though the isolated paragraph (i.e. the individual entity) is also noted.

4   At its most basic, a formal understanding of the paragraph is one which considers the paragraph, like the sentence, to have a discernible form: whether this be the presence of initial formulas, tagmemes (see footnote 8, this chapter), a topic sentence and supporting sentences, or other formal features. A semantic view of the paragraph is essentially concerned with its conceptual "aboutness," typically the topic or theme

of the paragraph. Longacre (1979, 1996), as we will see, combined both formal and semantic elements in his theory of the paragraph.

5   Notable exceptions are Elena Padučeva (Padučeva, 1974) and Edward Crothers (Crothers, 1979). Padučeva's work, rather ambitiously entitled "On the Structure of the Paragraph," focused only on initial paragraphs, particularly descriptive ones, in the work of Chekhov. In her study she sought to identify the structural regularities that occurred (in typographical paragraphs) in Chekhov's work. Crothers' (1979) work offered a way to move from the text surface to its deep structure through inferences based on connectives, propositions, and elements in the text.

6   Grimes (1975: 238) combined semantic and structural considerations in his understanding of the non-orthographic paragraph, believing that it, like the sentence, has "a kind of semantic unity on the one hand, and embodies certain characteristic structural signals that define its nuclei and boundaries on the other."

7   See Edward Levenston (Levenston, 1992: 63ff) on the relationship of punctuation to rhetoric, and the change of the functions of punctuation to clarifying syntax over time. See also Malcolm Parkes (Parkes, 1992) and David Olson (Olson, 1996) on this subject.

8   In tagmemics, the basic units of language are called tagmemes, which are considered to be slots which certain fillers can occupy – e.g. the noun filler can occupy the subject slot.

9   It should also be pointed out that the five-paragraph essay has been defended as well: see, for instance, Byung-In Seo (Seo, 2007) and Kerri Smith (Smith, 2006). Matthew Nunes (Nunes, 2013) considered both sides of the five-paragraph essay debate, mentioning the possible strengths of that essay form along with possible abuses.

2   Paragraph Genesis

Introduction

In this chapter, I seek to provide a brief historical overview of the paragraph, starting with early Greek usage, moving on to Latin paragraphing, and ending with paragraphing practice in various historical forms of English, up to the end of the 19th century. I then provide a summary and critique of Lewis' (1894) book *A History of the English Paragraph*, which is the only text to have been written tracing the historical development of the English paragraph.

From an educator's point of view, this chapter may not seem strictly necessary. After all, an understanding of ancient Greek paragraphing may not strike one as being particularly relevant to teaching writing in a composition class. However, I suggest that the material discussed in this chapter is relevant to anyone interested in understanding the paragraph, because it helps us see why we have some of the ideas about the paragraph that we do, and implicitly challenges us to reconsider our ideas.

The first scholars to have taken any interest in the English paragraph were rhetoricians and educators during the late 19th century, as noted by Duncan (2007) and also by John Brereton (Brereton, 1995) and Robert Connors (Connors, 1997). Foremost among these scholars was Alexander Bain, whose well-known work *English Composition and Rhetoric* (Bain, 1866 / 1890) is considered the seminal text of the era, having a wide-ranging impact on both his contemporaries and future generations (see

Connors, 1997; Hayes, 2003; Rodgers, 1965). Bain's work will be considered in more detail in the next chapter. To preview that work, Bain argued that the paragraph should, typically, be a deductively organized unit of text, and he emphasized its unity (non-digression), early notification of purpose, inter-sentential connectivity, internal grammatically parallel construction, consecutive arrangement, and the signaling of importance of ideas through non-subordination and the actual amount of text devoted to dealing with an idea. Up until the 1960s, the Bainian paragraphing model remained largely uncriticized, and in Chapter 4, reasons for the emergence of those criticisms are discussed.

From where did Bain get his ideas of the paragraph? When scholars have discussed the possible influences impacting the writings of the father of the paragraph, Bain's academic background, the educational context within which he wrote, and his view of the sentence are regularly mentioned – for example, in Rodgers (1965) and Hayes (2003), as well as in the work of Arthur Stern (Stern, 1976), Andrea Lunsford (Lunsford, 1982, 1998), and Shelley Aley (Aley, 1998). However, one looks in vain for reference to awareness of historical developments in paragraphing informing his work, or discussion of such developments within his writings.

The unfortunate consequences of this neglect are compounded by the methodological approach adopted by the only scholar of the 19th century to study the development of the English paragraph – Edwin Lewis. Lewis' Ph.D. thesis on the English paragraph (Lewis, 1894) is an invaluable source of information on English paragraphing practice in English prose. However, the problematic issue with Lewis' methodological approach was that he did not study historical English texts from the position of a disinterested spectator, but rather as an avowed Bainian apologist. Consequently, he viewed historical paragraphing through the lens of Bain's work. Rather than trying to *understand* historical paragraphing and paragraph organization, Lewis was more interested in establishing where a particular piece of writing (or a writer) lay on the paragraph evolutionary scale, Bain's (1890) loose (deductive) paragraph being the *super-paragraph*, the culmination and apex of the evolutionary process. Lewis' gold standard measuring rod, has, in turn, become the one used by many educators today, who at times, like Lewis, condemn certain paragraphing practices without really trying to understand them. If, as has been claimed, Bain's "long shadow" (Hayes, 2003: 1) still influences paragraphing pedagogy, it may well help us to change our own position vis-a-vis his work, and consider paragraphing before his writing and without reference to it. Therefore, in this chapter I provide an overview of historical paragraphing, before engaging with Bain's work in Chapter 3.

The questions I seek to address in this chapter are:

- What do we know about early paragraphing in Greek and Latin?
- What does recent research reveal about historical English paragraphing?
- What did Lewis say about the development of paragraphing in English?
- What are the strengths and weaknesses of Lewis' work?

What We Know about Early Paragraphing in Greek and Latin

Following the demise of Greek syllabary (a syllable-based writing system), and a hiatus in Greek writing, the early Greek alphabet was invented, typically dated 10th–8th centuries BC. Received wisdom[1] suggests that early writing practice was letter-cluttered when compared to textual formatting today, as Paul Saenger observed (Saenger, 1997). With no spacing between words (such text being termed *scriptura continua*), together with initial *boustrophedon* writing style (left to right, then right to left), followed by the exclusively left to right practice with which we are familiar today (termed *stoichedon*), reading of ancient Greek must have been quite a different skill than what reading is today, though how different is a matter of debate, as noted, for example, by Jocelyn Small (Small, 1997: 17) and Shane Butler (Butler, 2000: 177).

Even before the invention of the Greek alphabet, a kind of text division mark existed: Greek syllabary text has been found to contain spaces or horizontal lines between discourse units, as documented by Richard Enos (Enos, 2006: 229). However, very little has been said about this textual feature in the literature.

In what follows I focus on ancient and later Koiné Greek, and Latin paragraphing practice and comment on developments of function (primarily), paragraph-opening formulaicity (secondarily) and changes in the paragraph marker form, only briefly. The reason for the focus on Greek and Latin is because of their direct historical influence on English, and also because Lewis largely overlooked (or perhaps more accurately, minimized) the possible influences of paragraphing in these languages on the English paragraph in his own research.[2]

Before proceeding, a cautionary point must be made. There is a fairly commonly held view that early punctuation was sporadic, idiosyncratic, and emergent in the ancient world.[3] Indeed, the initial "lack of procedures for transferring *writing* into *text*" noted by Ken Morrison (Morrison, 1987: 244, original emphasis) means that, at times, it is quite difficult to know what the initial writer (or a later scribe) intended by inserting a *paragraphos* (or other paragraphing mark), why he did so along with other punctuation marks (or without them), or why he indented / outdented (see below) or left a space. Indeed, the question arises whether there was any overarching rhyme or reason behind initial punctuation practice, and this already difficult state of affairs is made more complicated when one considers clearly errant scribal markings on existing texts. Parkes (1992: 19) believed that the legacy left to us by the punctuation markers of antiquity is "a fruitful source of confusion." While there is undoubtedly a lot of truth in this assessment, this point of view may be a little too pessimistic. In recent years, there has been quite a strong rejection of the belief that medieval English punctuation (which has traditionally been considered similarly unfathomable) cannot be understood. It is possible, therefore, that further study of ancient Greek and Latin punctuation practice may, similarly, reveal greater systematicity and less confusion than is commonly supposed. Having made these observations, we now turn to consider some of the key data from antiquity, and their various interpretations.

As mentioned in chapter 1, the English word "paragraph" comes from the Greek παράγραφος (*paragraphos*), an ancient Greek punctuation practice of inserting a marginal horizontal line between two lines of text. The *paragraphos*, the earliest punctuation mark in Greek, appeared at a transitional time, a time when a predominantly oral communication culture was shifting to an oral and written culture, as noted by Small (1997) and also by James Murphy (Murphy, 2012). According to Walter Ong, the relationship of writing to speaking was one of subservience: "Writing served largely to recycle knowledge back into the oral world..." (Ong, 1982: 119). It seems that writing was not alone in serving oral needs – punctuation did also. Both Aristotle (see later) and Aristophanes[4] suggested an oral support function of punctuation in their writings, and contemporary scholars, with a wide knowledge of punctuation practice in the ancient world, have concurred. Enos (2006: 227), for example, characterized the early paragraph as "...an oral delimiter, a graphic instrument to facilitate verbal expression...."

It is, however, important to remember the word "largely" in Ong's quotation above ("Writing served *largely* to recycle..."). Naomi Baron noted how early writing was valued for providing a "durable record," not just for providing oral support (Baron, 2001: 22). In addition, some academics have suggested that text in the ancient world was read silently and not only out loud, including Bernard Knox (Knox, 1968), Aleksandr Gavrilov (Gavrilov, 1997), and Alessandro Vatri (Vatri, 2012). If such was the case, then it would seem reasonable to expect paragraphing practice in these two different text types (text as a record, and text for silent reading) to be rather different from that found in material to be orally recycled.

Three Functions of the Early Paragraphos

The oral function

It was in the 4th century B.C., in the context of Greek alphabetical writing, that one of the earliest mentions of the *paragraphos* is found. In his famous *Rhetoric* (Book 3, 8: 1409), Aristotle (c. 384–322) made reference to the term in a section prefaced with the subheading "Of Rhythm" in Theodore Buckley's translation (Buckley, 1857: 226). In writing of rhetorical diction, Aristotle stated that it should have harmony or rhythm, but not meter or regular measurement. He went on to speak of particular types of Greek rhetorical rhythm, before making the key reference:

> ἀλλὰ δεῖ τῇ μακρᾷ ἀποκόπτεσθαι καὶ δήλην εἶναι τὴν τελευτήν, μὴ διὰ τὸν γραφέα, μηδὲ διὰ τὴν **παραγραφήν**, ἀλλὰ διὰ τὸν ῥυθμόν.
> (copied from the edition by Edward Cope and John Sandys; Cope and Sandys, 1877: Book 3, section 8, with emphasis added on *paragraphein*)

A translation of this extract is given below:

> "But it is right to break off with a long syllable, for your conclusion to be clearly marked, not by means of the *amanuensis*, nor merely by **annotations on the margin**, but by means of the *rhythm*."
> (Buckley, 1857: 229, original italics on *amanuensis* and *rhythm*; emphasis added in bold for the translation of *paragraphein*).

Other translations, or comments, on *paragraphein* in the Aristotelian reference are: "a marginal annotation (marking the end of the sentence)" (Cope and Sandys 1877: 91); "The 'marginal annotation'…would answer to the full stop" (Welldon, 1886: 251); and "paragraphical marks or punctuation" (Gillies, 1823: 393).

Clearly, there is some variety in the above translations (perhaps more strictly speaking, interpretations) of Aristotle's meaning. However, what is clear is that the *paragraphos* was used to close or end a section of oral rhetoric in Aristotle's time, and the thrust of Aristotle's meaning seems, simply enough, to have been a warning that a mark alone indicating closure (namely, the *paragraphos*) was not enough – the rhythm of what was being said needed to close properly. In the words of Enos (2006: 232), the *paragraphos* served "to isolate critical ideas in the phonology of texts."

Other punctuation marks co-existed with the *paragraphos* mark referred to by Aristotle, and according to William Johnson, there are many texts in which additional punctuation marks indicating a pause or closure co-occur with the *paragraphos* (Johnson, 1994). After discussing various possible explanations for this dual marking, Johnson arrived at the rather simple, yet practically satisfying, conclusion that a clear indication of a textual break on the left-hand side of a text aids in the reading out loud of a manuscript: a person giving a speech can easily look up, gesture, pause, and then depend on the mark in the margin to help return to the right place in the text and so help ensure a smooth delivery of the speech.

The fact that Greek punctuation (including paragraphing) in certain texts was related to its oral delivery suggests quite a different view of punctuation than the one that is normally held today, in which it is often seen to play a largely grammatical role (i.e. to separate sense units). However, as mentioned in Chapter 1, there are some interesting links between oral paragraphs and written ones, and paragraphing prosody has not been discounted as playing a role in how we read (silently) today.

With regard to Latin, Butler (2000), initially at least, offered a similar (i.e. orally rhetorically motivated) explanation of *capita* (singular form *capitulum*), that is, text "outdenting," also termed "edenting," occasionally marked by uppercase *K* (for *Kaput*, i.e. Head) as found in Cicero's (106BC–43BC) writings. Butler (2000: 305) came to the conclusion that while edenting alone did not give enough oral support to future reciters of Cicero's text, it gave some support (see also Gotoff, 1979). For non-Ciceronian Latin Eulogies (*laudationes*), Butler (2009: 24) also suggested that the paragraphing function would have been orally motivated, necessitated by "rhetorical or thematic divisions of some sort, triggered by shifts in sound or sense."

The psychological function

Butler adjusted his position somewhat between 2000 and 2009. He considered, in some detail, the function of capitulation and the *kaput,* in Ciceronian text. Did it indicate "the main thrust of an argument" (Butler, 2009: 17), that is, was edenting motivated by the actual message, or was the *kaput* just a descriptive term for the edent – a term used because the actual edent looks like the *head* of a nail? The first interpretation, i.e. *kaput* referring to the semantic head of a section of text could be viewed as a precursor to the "topic sentence" concept articulated in the 19th century; the other view, however, appears more descriptive – one which says nothing, per se, about the material so headed, or the reason for the edenting.

Based on his analysis of Ciceronian text, Butler (2000: 301) believed there was little support for the thematic head under-standing. He noted that capita coincide with full sentences and that as a consequence there is some kind of shift sense involved with the beginning of a new capitulum. He nonetheless argued that there is little evidence for the idea that the edent indicates a larger shift than that indicated between words coming before and after a period / full stop, a point also made by E. Otha Wingo (Wingo, 1972: 52). Butler appealed to later editorial paragraphing of Cicero's work to challenge the legitimacy of the traditional head view of the caput (i.e. the idea that a capitulum occurs at the beginning of a new point or at a point of major semantic shift). He argued that if this were the case editors and translators of Cicero's work would have paragraphed his writing in the same way, but they did not.[5] On the basis of his analyses, Butler suggested that the *capitulum* was only unit-like in that it had been capitulated – not for any thematic divisional reasons. In saying this, Butler rejected a key tenet of paragraphing in Bain's work: the topicality of the paragraph.

So why capitulate at one point and not another? Having rejected the semantic head argument, the only other reason would seem to be oral support. However, Butler (2009) was also skeptical about this (despite his initial adherence to this view), because of how he believed the texts to have been commonly read. As noted earlier, the traditional idea that early Greek text was exclusively written for out-loud reading has been called into question by a number of scholars (e.g. Gavrilov, 1997; Knox, 1968; Vatri, 2012), and Butler believed that Cicero's work was largely read in private. If this was the case, we are left to look elsewhere than oral rhetorical support for capitulation. Then why were certain sections of Cicero's writing edented? Struggling to put forward any other data-based view, Butler suggested that the reason for capitulation can only be provided by cognitive psychologists, who can investigate and understand the differences between reading, speaking, and listening, arriving at the conclusion that, "…capitulation structures the space and thus the experience (an admittedly vague term) of reading" (Butler, 2009: 33). Butler's explanation is indeed vague – and yet his suggestion that the edenting practice may be linked in some way to reader psychology, is quite reasonable, as we will consider in more detail in Chapter 7.

The reference function

Turning our attention to other types of writing in the ancient world, various comments have been made about the use of the *paragraphos* and the *kaput*. With regard to the *paragraphos* in law, Enos (2006: 235) observed its presence in a number of specific contexts: "a special or counter plea," "a point of admissibility," "an exception or emendation," "a legal objection," and "a stipulation in a contractual agreement." In dramatic text, Johnson (1994: 65) documented its function in indicating a change of speaker (in "tragedy, comedy, or Platonic dialogue"); in lyric, separating a metrical group; as a divider of sections in poetry; in documents separating sections or members in a list; and in separating the main text from a *subscriptio* (i.e. a response to an indictment).

Turning to Latin, Butler (2009: 19) provided evidence to show that the *paragraphus*[6] was used to separate one legal clause from another in legal writings – dating this to at least 101 BC. In this and other uses, Butler did not see Latin paragraph practice as signaling a great departure from Greek practice, but suggested that the Latin practice of dividing legal texts spread to a wider variety of text types than was seen in Greek paragraphing practice. With regard to the function of the *kaput* in these text types, Butler (2009: 24) believed that it played a role in facilitating reference in those cases when one might need to refer to only one part of the whole text.

It would seem, therefore, based on the brief overview provided above, that paragraphing practice in the ancient world served three functions: oral support, a little understood function related to reader psychology in silent reading, and enabling a reader to more easily find what s/he was looking for in a text. The different functions seem to be dependent on the text type, which in turn is related to how the text was read (out loud, silently) or used (e.g. as a reference to find a particular item within the text, rather than as a speech read from beginning to end). I discuss the concept of text reception in more detail later in this chapter.

The Form of Greek and Latin Paragraphs

Most of the interest in Greek and Latin paragraphing has focused on the paragraph marker (rather than the text so marked), perhaps because the initial *paragraph* was a mark. However, some recent research has focused on the language of the separated (i.e. outdented) body of text and I refer to a couple of studies below, which considered paragraphing practice in Greek New Testament texts.

Porter (2009) investigated the paragraphing of the Gospel of Mark and The Epistle to the Romans in *Codex Sinaiticus* (typically dated 4th century). In terms of the mechanics of paragraphing, he noted that it is achieved by a marginal line together with outdenting

– which he terms *ekthesis* (cf. Butler's use of the term "edenting," for the Latin practice of outdenting). Porter observed the presence of recurring paragraph-initial formulae in Mark's Gospel. Of the 310 paragraphs, 172 began with initial καί ("and," "also," "even"), 54 with initial δέ (often untranslated, but possibly weak *but*), four with ἀλλά ("but"), four with γάρ ("for," "because"), one ἰδού ("look," "behold"), one with ὅταν ("whenever"), and five with verbs of speaking. This means that 241 of the 310 paragraphs begin with formulaic configurational elements which, Porter suggested, might well indicate a formal treatment of paragraphing, rather than a topical, semantic one. Indeed, like Butler (see earlier), Porter provided indirect evidence against the topical paragraph, namely, that paragraphs in sequence may, at times, develop the same subject or theme. Porter went on to suggest that a hierarchy of features was used when beginning a new paragraph: opening conjunctive elements being the most important (as noted above), then participant factors, word order, topic, and additional cohesive devices.

Porter (2009) found that the Sinaiticus version of the Epistle to the Romans was quite different from the Markan gospel referred to earlier, in terms of paragraph length and openings. He found a tendency for shorter paragraphs to be used in Romans[7] with only 28% of paragraphs opening with conjunctive elements (cf. 78% for Mark). The shift from Markan narrative to Roman epistle has clear paragraphing implications (at least with regard to length of the paragraphs and the paragraph-initial elements).

But what of an oral rhetorical function? In concluding his study, Porter (2009) commented that the relatively short paragraph length in Mark and Romans (relative to paragraphing practice today) may have been because of recitational needs (i.e. there may well have been some kind of oral rhetorical reason underpinning the paragraphing practice). However, he observed that length of text alone does not seem to have dictated paragraphing practice: Romans 1: 21–25, for example, is longer than other paragraphs within the epistle. This would tend to suggest that oral support was *a* factor in paragraphing, but not *the only* factor affecting paragraphing practice.

Matthew O'Donnell further extended Porter's paragraph-initial language analysis of the Sinaiticus text (O'Donnell, n.d.). He compared the frequency of paragraph initial position words in certain New Testament books with their occurrence elsewhere in text, thus creating a *keyness* statistic (i.e. a measure indicating how common it was for these items to occur in paragraph-initial position rather than elsewhere in text). This showed, inter alia, that while καί is indeed a very common paragraph opening element, this is not, statistically speaking, a particularly interesting fact, since it is a very common word used elsewhere in text, and as such, not a distinctive paragraph-opening element. However, O'Donnell found that for other conjunctions, namely, δέ, ούν ("therefore," "consequently") and γάρ ("for," "because") there was a strong statistical tendency for them to open paragraphs. O'Donnell documented other important paragraph-initial opening elements in the NT books he studied as being different nominative forms of definite and indefinite articles, names of people, personal address, and salutations.

With regard to Latin, Butler (2000, 2009) did not analyze Ciceronian writings for paragraph-initial formulae. However, Lynn Fotheringham, in her comments on the structure of Cicero's *Pro Murena*, hinted at the possibility of certain expressions or lexical items being common in paragraph-initial position (Fotheringham, 2007: 60). It is possible that more detailed research along these lines may hold the clue (or at least a clue) to a better understanding of capitulation practice in Cicero's writings, if indeed thematic and / or rhetorical oral support functions are inadequate explanations for it, as noted earlier.

The research of Porter, O'Donnell, and Fotheringham echo key findings in Longacre's (1968) work on oral paragraphing in languages of the Philippines, in which he observed the presence of formulaic paragraph opening markers (see Chapter 1), and also more recent work by Hoey (2005) on textual colligation and the paragraph in English, in which he argued that readers are primed to expect certain lexis or phrases to open up new paragraphs. The idea that paragraph-initial phraseology is distinct and identifiable as such is a subject that writers of the 19th century never really considered, and this issue is discussed further in Chapters 5 and 7. Further, the idea that paragraphing conventions are genre-specific (as seen above in the Mark vs. Romans analyses) was almost totally overlooked by both Lewis and Bain.[8]

Changes to the Form of the Paragraph Mark

How did we get from a horizontal line in the margin, dividing two lines of text, to our modern pilcrow? This is a disputed area, and one which is not of great importance to our focus in this book. However, for the sake of completeness, in this section I provide a brief summary of different views about how these changes occurred.

In addition to marginal underlining (Aristotle's *paragraphos*), other, different, text division practices (larger than the period) existed in antiquity: edenting / ekthesis, and also space between sections. Additional marks, possibly related to paragraphing are the κορωνις (coronis, a symbol like a number 7), and the διπλη (dipli, a wedge >). In later English paragraphing double *virgules* (//) appeared, upon which *paraph* symbols (single or double CCs, often present in texts from the 15th century onwards – perhaps indicating *caput*) were sometimes placed.

Lewis (1894: 10) believed that the κορωνις became the capital gamma mark (Γ), over time and that this, in turn, spawned numerous other markings, indeed referred to a form which he suggested may have further mutated to become the pilcrow.[9] However, against this possibility he noted the co-existence of a gamma form alongside early pilcrow variants. St. Isidore of Seville (c. 560–636), in his famous *Etymologies* (Barney et al., 2006: 51) also referred to the capital gamma form – terming it the *paragraphus*, commenting on its function in opening a piece of text, and the mirror image of this form, the *positura*, closing the paragraph (these symbols look a little like our modern parentheses symbols of today).

Lewis (1894) suggested that a *P* symbol was used as an abbreviation of *paragraphus* by Latin scribes (less familiar with the Greek *gamma*), and that the form was reversed over time – possibly to distinguish it from the letter, or for ease of producing the left curve of the pilcrow. Lewis was skeptical about the argument that indentation was introduced for the purpose of leaving a space for the insertion of a *Littera notabilior* (capital embellished letter), a practice which fell out of use with the development of the printing press. However, other writers (e.g. Baron 2001: 37) believed that this is a reasonable explanation for indenting (as opposed to outdenting), which is commonly found in English writing from the 17th century.

Some scholars believe that the *K* (rarely) found in the margin of Cicero's writings, between two sections of text, and mentioned earlier, was an important transitional form of the *paragraphos* before its later transformation into the pilcrow. Baron (2001: 37), observed the presence of *K*'s in early *insular* manuscripts (i.e. texts dated 6th–9th century), and believed that the *K* became a *C* in the 12th century (*C* for *capitulum*). She suggested that the final stage in the formation of the pilcrow was the addition of a vertical bar to the *C*, added to indicate the need for a *Littera notabilior* to be inserted.

What Recent Research Reveals about Historical English Paragraphing

General Comments

Perhaps the greatest push towards more, rather than less, punctuation was when Latin spilled over its geographical borders, into lands where it was a foreign language. When Latin was encountered by monks in Ireland, for example, they needed much more language support assistance (especially reading support) than did their counterparts living in Rome (see Charles Briggs, 2000: 411–412). In time, as early forms of English began to be written down, scribes no doubt borrowed Latin punctuation marks, and these were to become the "foundation" of English punctuation, as Baron (2001: 31) stated. One such mark which was introduced into Early English was the *paragraphus*. As Parkes (1992: 20) commented, within this changing context punctuation practice was not simply transferred, but adapted, partly to establish a "grammar of legibility." This is not to say that oral rhetorical considerations were considered irrelevant, but rather that grammatical considerations began to play a more important role in punctuation, for readers for whom Latin was a foreign language.

Functions of Paragraphing in Different English Medieval Texts

As Teresa Marqués Aguado observed, punctuation in English in medieval times has been a rather neglected subject, and she suggested that this is probably because of the emerging, non-standard nature of punctuation during this era, together with the multi-functional nature of punctuation marks (Aguado, 2009: 55). However, and as noted earlier in this chapter, in recent years there has been renewed interest in punctuation in this and earlier periods. In what follows I provide a brief overview of five studies indicating various roles of paragraph markers in medieval English. This overview is necessarily brief,[10] and the texts summarized are deliberately taken from a variety of writings: religious, historical, medical, mathematical, and scientific.

A religious text

Elizabeth Zeeman examined the punctuation of a 15th century manuscript, *Mirror of the Blessed Life of Jesu Christ*, a well-known English-language text in its time that had been translated from the Latin by Nicholas Love (Zeeman, 1956). She observed that its author was aware of the "mixed media reception" that his work would receive, addressing the recipient as both reader and hearer: "every devoute creaour that loveth to rede or to here this book" (p. 12). Zeeman stressed that the paragraph marks do not function as would our modern paragraph mark, in that they segment less material, perhaps just one or more sentences. She saw the function as rhetorical, to mark a significant pause, perhaps prompted by the need for reflection on what has just been read / heard, or to heighten anticipation for what follows. She believed that these pauses are sense-related, in that they close part of a narrative or argument, and help develop stages in the text (p. 13).

A historical text

Ruth Carroll, Ruth, Matti Peikola, Hanna Salmi, Mari-Liisa Varila, Janne Skaffari, and Risto Hiltunen believed that the *paraph* (a variant form of the *paragraphus*, mentioned above) in the *Polychronicon* (a late medieval history of the world) started a new section of text (Carroll et al., 2013). They suggested that the *paraph* functioned at three different discourse levels: on the *textual level* operating as a frame shift initiator; on an *interactional level* separating structures which could cause grammatical or discourse ambiguity; and at an *authorial stance* level, where it is inserted alongside the naming of an authority to support a point being made. The idea that the same mark was playing quite distinct roles in the same text indicates a multi-functionality which is quite at variance with more narrowly construed functional perspectives.

A medical text

Aguado (2009) examined the punctuation practice in a medieval medical text (the *Antidotary*), which she dated to the middle of the 15th century. She described the function of the paragraphing as "macro-textual," namely, that the paragraph markers "highlight relevant sections from the point of view of the subject matter dealt with" (p. 59). Specific examples of this function include introducing a recipe, a new feature, or a new condition. However, Aguado also observed sentential level functions, namely: marking independent sentences, marking off asyndetic coordination (i.e. coordination omitting conjunctions), and separating main from subordinate clauses. It is important to note that when used in these latter contexts, Aguado believed the *paraph* to have been inserted to highlight key following information.

A mathematical text

Javier Martín and Antonio Garcia investigated punctuation in a 15th century arithmetical treatise, *The Crafte of Nombryge*, and made a number of comments about the presence of the *paraph* within it (Martín and Garcia, 2005). Specifically, Martín and Garcia (2005: 33) believed it was used to:

- "…mark off the beginning of a section or subsection," which they believed to be quite widespread, and also to "single out the sentence which follows";
- "…separate the English and the Latin pieces", and also to separate Latin verses (which they termed a grammatical function);
- "… separate the different units of an enumeration";
- "…introduce direct speech," co-occurring with the word *questio*, which they suggested played a distinctly rhetorical function, relating to intonation;
- "…introduce a conclusion";
- "…introduce a coordinate clause," though noting that the *punctus* (a symbol like a comma) was more typically used to do this and suggesting a highlighting function when the paraph was so used;
- "…introduce logical connectors" (e.g. *also*).

Again, the variety of functions of the *paraph* is self-evident from the analysis of this text.

"Popular" scientific writing

Unlike the scholars noted above, Elizabeth Tebeaux's research on popular scientific, self-help, and how-to texts from the late 15th century onwards was conducted with the goal of identifying early instances of the characteristics of the Bainian paragraph in use, rather than simply documenting and trying to understand paragraphing practice (Tebeaux, 2011). Tebeaux observed that these texts were aimed at English-speaking middle-class readers, for whom a new "non-Latinate" style of paragraph, in which topic sentences, shorter sentences, and a more direct, clear style were considered appropriate.

A particularly interesting type of writer analyzed by Tebeaux (2011) is the author who had a foot in two camps, writing both classical humanist as well as practical texts. She observed that Sir Thomas Elyot's style in *The Boke called the Gouernour* contained paragraphs, but with no Bainian correspondence. However, the same author's practical text, *The Castle of helth*, written for a very different audience, contains lists, facilitating easy reference, as well as headings and paragraphs with clear topic sentences. Commenting on Elyot's ability to write different text types for very different audiences, Tebeaux (2011: 237) stated: "Elyot apparently understood that reading for information or for instruction differed from contemplative reading."

In concluding her analyses, Tebeaux (2011) argued that the Bainian paragraph was present during the late 15th century in technical writing, though the topic sentence was not always utilized. She believed that Ramist logic (a theory of logic developed by Petrus Ramus), with its emphasis on sequence, access, and memorability, was a driving force affecting the form of the early technical paragraph, in which organizing, partitioning, and dividing made the resulting textual material clear and memorable.

In documenting areas of correspondence between early (technical) text paragraphing and Bain's prototype paragraph, Tebeaux's (2011) work serves as an important counterbalance to the observations of Lewis (1894), noted below, who believed that the Bainian paragraph came to be exemplified in the writings of the essayist William Temple (1628–1699) discussed in more detail below – in other words, at a much later date than the texts considered by Tebeaux. However, as will be mentioned, Lewis saw traits of the Bainian paragraph (e.g. unity) many, many years before the medieval period. As such, there is, perhaps, an issue of *degree* of similarity between Bain's (1866 / 1890) prototypical paragraph, and that of paragraphs before Bain, which Tebeaux did not consider. There is a clear need for large-scale comparative analyses to be conducted to explore this issue further.

From this admittedly brief overview, based on a consideration of several different text types from a similar historical period in English, a number of points are evident. The paragraph marks clearly played a number of different functions: definitely oral-rhetorical at times, but also macro-textual, in addition to more narrowly grammatical. The highlighting role of the paragraph – not simply to segment, but also to stress – is an interesting thread evident in a number of the comments above, and one which seems to differentiate it from other punctuation marks of the period. The fact that different functions seem to be more or less present in different genres is suggestive of genre adaptations and authors' treatment of paragraphing as a flexible authorial interpretational tool. It can be assumed that authors considered how their paragraphing decisions would (potentially) affect their readers and, while a number of the earlier functions have died out, it is clear that a number remain.

Lewis' Scholarship on the Development of Paragraphing in English

Lewis' Ph.D. thesis on the English paragraph (1894) is an invaluable source of information on English paragraphing practice in English prose. Lewis had a very strong admiration for Bain, describing him as "perhaps the ablest writer on rhetoric since Aristotle" (p. 29). Lewis not only admired Bain's work, he embraced his theory of the paragraph unreservedly. His book combines careful empirical quantitative analyses of paragraphs from a wide range of writers and books, though it is rather lacking in qualitative analyses.[11] Lewis utilized a Bainian-inspired evaluation framework to critique the writings he considered, and he sprinkled his research with dry wit and humorous asides about the writing styles of the writers he considered.[12] In what follows I discuss Lewis' research under three headings, before going on to evaluate his work:

- The single-sentence paragraph and paragraph length;
- Key historical developments; and
- The contributory factors to the evolution of the paragraph.

The Single-Sentence Paragraph and Paragraph Length

Whether or not a single sentence could also be a paragraph was an issue of some contention among educators in Lewis' day, as he documented. In terms of its usage, analyses of his data suggested that in the latter part of the 19th century it was used less often than in the 18th century, and much less so than in the 17th century.[13] He suggested that the main reason for the decrease in usage of the single sentence paragraph was because sentence length was reduced over this period of time, citing other research indicating that sentence length in English halved over a period of 300 years. Lewis (1894: 26) commented that writers of his own era used the single sentence paragraph in specific ways, namely, as: "transitional, preliminary, and directive single-sentence paragraphs."

Lewis (1894) considered and investigated whether the historic reduction in English sentence length may have had an influence on paragraph length. His conclusion was that it did not, though he did document a considerable variety in paragraph length among the writings he considered (ranging from 50 to 700 words). In reviewing the developments, he commented "the great changes in the structure of our prose have taken place *within* the paragraph, and have not, in four hundred years, materially affected the *length* of the paragraph" (p. 37; emphases added).[14] In one of the very few comments he made throughout the whole of his book showing any awareness of genre variation, Lewis suggested that the wide variety evident in paragraph length in the different texts he studied can, in part, be explained by reference to genre conventions. Another reason for differences in paragraph length, Lewis believed, related to the "mental power" (p. 43) of the writer, suggesting that some writers thought in larger "nebulous masses" than others, though he believed that these masses were sometimes broken down by the writer into smaller units for the less able reader.

The brief overview of Lewis' (1894) work which follows provides the context for an evaluation of his theses regarding the forces he believed to have influenced changes in the English paragraph.

Key Historical Developments

9th century to 16th century

Lewis (1894: 66–67) suggested that initial paragraphing in early English performed four functions:

(1) noting a logical section;
(2) noting an emphatic point;
(3) distinguishing sacred names; and
(4) ornamenting and distinguishing titles and colophons (i.e. printing or publishing information).

The above observations overlap and concur (to a certain extent) with the findings of the earlier paragraphing studies summarized in the previous section, though it should be noted that Lewis (1894) made these observations in relation to Old English as well as the medieval form of the language, Middle English. Lewis suggested that all of the above functions were present in most Old English manuscripts (though he believed that paragraphing was employed to a greater or lesser extent in different writings from this period).

He argued that, on the whole, "unity of subject" (p. 67) was the norm in Old English paragraphs (despite the function delimited in b above), though in Lewis' opinion, much of the writing was not coherent, well-massed (i.e. key information placed in a prominent position) or proportionate (i.e. a balance existing between mixing of sentence types).

16th century to late 17th century

Lewis (1894: 75) described paragraphs before William Tyndale (1494–1536), the famous Protestant reformer and bible translator, as lacking in "structural character," but suggested that the two hundred years between Tyndale and William Temple (1628–1699) saw a growing tension between the principles of the "modern unit" (i.e. the Bainian paragraph) and "Latin paragraph style" (details discussed later). In the writing of Temple, Lewis saw the dawning of the Bainian paragraph (cf. Tebeaux, 2011, noted earlier, who saw this much earlier in the how-to books of the late 15th century).

Lewis (1894: 81) made numerous critical remarks about the paragraphs of this era. Of Stow, he believed that he "confounds the sentence with the paragraph," and concerning Ascham, he was critical of the excessive use of connectors (so too Walton). Concerning Lyly, he criticized his use of excessive illustration, and complained about the difficulty of finding his topic sentences among his heavy-going paragraph introductions. He went on to criticize a number of writers for having poor or no unity in their paragraphs (e.g. Lodge and Sidney), and others for having sentences which are too long (e.g. Clarendon). Concerning Hobbes, he suggested that his paragraphs are not long enough to hold his long sentences, and, regarding Bacon, he criticized the "stiff monotony" (p. 91) of his paragraph openings and closings (discussed in more detail below). At the same time, Lewis made numerous positive comments. He commended Burton and Bunyan for their short sentence length, and Ben Jonson for his mastery of the isolated biography paragraph (i.e. a single paragraph treatment of a subject).

Late 17th century to early 19th century

There is a shift towards a more positive evaluation of the paragraphs that Lewis (1894) reviewed throughout this period, and I focus on the positive comments, essentially because the negative observations are largely the same as those noted in earlier periods. It should be mentioned, however, that although Lewis generally saw development in the paragraphing of this period, he also documented how some writers were not moving with the times – most notably, Defoe.

Lewis (1894) commended Dryden for how his word order helps create coherence and therefore does not need or depend on sentence connectors, and he also approved of Samuel Johnson's writings for not depending on connectors to help create cohesion and development. Sir William Temple and Lord Bolingbroke were evaluated as being skilled in paragraph transitions, and Swift was commended on his placement of key words (i.e. important ideas or themes in his texts) in opening and closing paragraphs. Concerning Shaftesbury and Lamb, Lewis observed how they give the topic in the opening of their paragraphs. Hume's paragraph unity was termed "impeccable" (p. 118), and Burke was similarly commended for the unity of his sentences.

Early 19th century to late 19th century

Lewis (1894) believed that De Quincey's (1785–1859) work was a watershed in English paragraphing (though arguing that within the same historical period there were poor paragraph practitioners – Bartol being the prime offender). Lewis was positively eulogistic about De Quincey, and his emotions seem to outrun his analytical approach in discussing his work at times. He commended Dickens for his emphasis, Macaulay for his rhetorical unity, some of Carlyle's work for its orderliness, and Arnold for his parallel constructions. He summarized the period as follows:

> In the nineteenth century the paragraph is organized as in the eighteenth, but acquires greater concentration. The emphasis of the

short sentence is more keenly felt and more effectually employed. The unity is more organic. The coherence depends less and less on formal connectives. The question of mass receives its first serious attention. (Lewis, 1894: 137)

The Contributory Factors to the Evolution of the Paragraph

Having provided the brief historical overview above, we are now in a better position to be able to understand how Lewis (1894) arrived at his theses concerning what he believed to be the contributory factors to the evolving English paragraph. I note his points below, and comment on each of them in turn.

Thesis 1: "The growing idea that the paragraph 'distinguishes a stadium in thought' / 'stadium of thought'"[15] *(pp. 44, 172)*

By this statement, Lewis seems to have had in mind the idea that writers began to conceive of the paragraph as embodying one idea, or one idea leading from / to the next – as opposed to the sentence being the key vehicle for expressing the thought. Lewis did not like digression, and he commended paragraphs which focused on one point and within which everything contributed to this thought.

Thesis 2: The demise of the Latin influence of paragraphing (p. 44)

Regarding what he termed the "Latin influence," Lewis suggested that this was the main factor working against the four evolutionary contributory factors noted in this section. It is important to mention, however, that Lewis did not trace these influences directly to historical Latin, but rather to influences from the 14th to 16th centuries, exemplified in the works of Hooker and Milton. By Latin influences, Lewis meant three things. The first of these was the long sentence. Lewis was critical of long "clause-heaped" sentences. He believed that the reason why some writers confused the role and function of the period and the paragraph (specifically, Lord Brooke and Spenser) was because of the clash of Latin influence, the "large unit of thought" (p. 44) in the sentence, with new developments in writing, among which the shorter sentence was critically important. The other types of "Latin influence" were the almost total absence of paragraphing in some of the writings of Hooker and Milton, or paragraphing solely for the sake of emphasis (specifically noting this in Milton's *Eikonoklastes*). The decline of the Latin influence, Lewis believed, came with the realization that the "unit(s) of thought" (note thesis 1 above) of the writer could not be contained in one sentence in English.

Thesis 3: The "natural genius of Anglo-Saxon structure" (p. 44)

Lewis termed this "Anglo-Saxon structure" "favourable to the paragraph" (p. 172), though he never really spelled out what he meant by this. However, holding up Tyndale and Latimer as proponents of Anglo-Saxon structure style, his comments about these writers may help us understand his meaning. In their writings, Lewis observed the use of short, easily comprehensible sentences, with a logical consecutiveness between them, ordered in what he called a "loose" (i.e. deductive) manner. It is unclear whether he saw parallelism as an Anglo-Saxon trait (noting the Hebrew influence in Tyndale), though he commented positively on it in referring to Arnold, which would suggest that this feature, too, was a part of the (borrowed) "genius" to which he referred.

Thesis 4: The adoption of an "oral style" of writing (p. 44)

It is easy to be confused by Lewis' "oral style" (p. 44) reference here. He did not mean the incorporation of what we typically consider to be "oral style" characteristics in writing today, such as repetition and redundancy. Lewis understood the term to refer to a style using a large proportion of short sentences with clear connections between them (though he was keen to stress that good style would resist the use of connectors to signal these connections). One of the key reasons for a writer adopting this style, Lewis believed, was to make the writer's thought easier and clearer for the reader to follow. He commented, however, on the possible problems resulting from the overuse of such a style, when its effect would result in it being "terse and intense" (p. 65) upon the reader. He suggested that the oral style encouraged the thought of the paragraph to be spread equally throughout the propositions being advanced.

Thesis 5: "the study of French prose" (p. 44)

Lewis (1894) believed that the relatively late-coming influence of French prose style worked alongside the Anglo-Saxon and oral styles noted above. What Lewis had in mind concerning the effects of French prose style can only be gleaned by various off-hand references that he made throughout his book. French prose was characterized by Lewis as using short paragraphs (pp. 114, 118, 119) and short sentences (p. 148), lacking connectors between sentences (p. 105), and possessing "lucidity" (p. 118). He termed this style a more suitable vehicle for clear, straightforward thought than Latin style paragraphs (see Thesis 2 above).

Strengths and Weaknesses of Lewis' Work

Lewis' (1894) work, as noted earlier, is a valuable resource for anyone wishing to study the historical English paragraph: his largely empirical approach stood in stark (and refreshing) contrast to that of his peers, and his analyses covered a tremendous number of writers and texts. It is easy to be critical of Lewis' study in the light of new developments and new research, but that is not my intention here. Rather, it is to assess the work *within its own context*, and, accordingly, point out its contextual shortcomings.

Lewis' Approach

The most obvious limitation of Lewis' (1894) work, as noted earlier in this chapter, was his approach. His historical evaluative approach used the modern model of the paragraph of the time

– Bain's paragraph – as the gold standard against which to compare all other historical prose paragraphs. Lewis failed to appreciate the dangers in reviewing the past in the light of the present – rather than considering the past in terms of *its* past (see Ong, 1944: 349). In so doing, Lewis did not take into account the possible *irrelevance* of the modern model as an aid to understanding past paragraphing practice. To impose one's own "good paragraphing" framework upon older paragraph practice (as Lewis did) was to fail to consider or understand the contexts of the times of the writers, and this was a serious flaw in Lewis' methodological procedure.

Concerning notions of what is, or is not, appropriate paragraphing, as mentioned in the first section of this chapter, some editors of classical works (specifically, those of Cicero and Horace) have reparagraphed key texts differently (note also different paragraphing of the Bible[16]). At least *part* of the reason for differences in paragraphing of the same text (over periods of hundreds of years) is, doubtless, changing ideas about what constitutes good paragraphing practice. The fact that reparagraphing occurs, and that we are not unduly troubled by such a practice (at least when it comes to older texts), suggests that "appropriate paragraphing" is a relative term.

Changes in Philosophical Orientation

Lewis' (1894) theses concerning the five evolutionary points seem reasonable enough – though they are not, perhaps, as clear-cut as he portrayed them to be (due to overlap). There are, however, a number of points not noted. One of these is the influence of Ramist logic – particularly from 1555 onwards (see Tebeaux, 2011) which, one can safely hypothesize, spilled over into other types of writing, not just technical writing.[17] William Temple (whom Lewis noted to be a good Bainian paragrapher) is called "Ramist" by Ong (1968: 65), and Lewis did not consider that Temple's view of logic and philosophy may have played a role in influencing his approach to writing.

Purposeful Digression

Lewis (1894) believed the main destroyers of unity to be digression and run-on paragraphs. Regarding the former, digression can be intentional or accidental: a (deliberate) literary device or an (unconscious) straying in one's train of thought as pen is put to paper. Steven Belletto commented that digression in literature can be significant to a writer's purpose, but that some modern literature critics have failed to recognize this, regarding digressions as blemishes working against the main plot, which can only be recovered by a process of suppressing the distracting elements (i.e. the digressions) in a text (Belletto, 2011), a view similar to that of Lewis.[18] To argue that digression works against the development of one's topic, as Lewis suggested, is, logically, to argue that a writer's reason for digressing is against his or her own overall purpose (whatever that may be). This makes little sense – unless the writer really does lose his / her train of thought for a time. To view digression as aesthetically pleasing, or as a focus on what is not normally the subject of focus, or as a tool to challenge a reader to consider what is or is not important, is a positive and purposeful understanding of digression, and one which ultimately seeks to incorporate it into, rather than exclude it from, a writer's purpose or purposes.

Complex / Alternative Paragraphing Models

Lewis (1894: 142) claimed that Milton "had no paragraph sense" – while noting his occasional use of paragraphs for emphasis. In a very detailed and quite complex study, James Whaler proposed that Milton's "epic paragraphs" were, far from being insensitive to paragraphing patterns, rather the product of the mind and pen of a brilliant poet, mathematician, and musician all rolled into one (Whaler, 1971). Milton's paragraphs, Whaler (1971: 162) claimed, incorporate "the rhythmic method of contrapuntal music" and combine mathematical progressions and symmetry. Whether

Milton or his original readers believed the paragraphs to possess or not possess paragraph sense is the real issue that Lewis failed to address. In his evaluations, Lewis seems to impose or transpose his own paragraph-wrought frustrations onto the original readers of the various writings which he criticized. I suggest, however, that it is highly unlikely the original readers groaned at the sentence and paragraph length or the paragraph organization of the "Latin style" writers whom they chose to read: this was, after all, the type of writing that they were used to.

Genre Differences

With the exception of a comment on paragraph length, Lewis (1894) said very little about genre differences in his analysis of paragraphs. This is, perhaps, because all of the writings that he considered are, broadly speaking, "prose." However, the legitimacy of drawing together the wide range of text types that he considered under this single heading, and measuring them all against a super-paragraph prose style was a highly questionable research approach. If different paragraph functions are present in a medical text, a mathematical text, a religious text, and a historical text from the 15th century (as seen above), it would seem wise to allow for a similar legitimate variety in sermons, biographies, philosophical writing, and other genres from similar and later historical periods. In grouping these text types together, Lewis ignored issues of purpose, the discourse community, and, to use more modern terminology, discourse community genre-specific norms.

Another genre-related issue concerns who was reading or listening to the written material. As noted earlier, Tebeaux (2011) suggested that the 15th and 16th century witnessed the appearance of a new class of reader: the middle-class readership of the English Renaissance. The how-to books of the Renaissance period (as observed by Tebeaux) were paragraphed rather differently as compared to the belletristic, contemplative literature and rhetoric traditionally taught to clergymen in universities. The relationship between paragraphing and readership was, however, barely considered by Lewis (1894), with the exception of a comment concerning how large a paragraph might be, and the ability of a reader to get to grips with it.

Historical Developments

Changes in paragraphing were not happening in a vacuum, but Lewis (1894) seems to have largely overlooked two practical developmental changes in his evaluation. The first of these was the absence of any consideration of how paragraphing may have differed according to the medium upon which texts were written or printed. It is not unreasonable to assume that scribes or printers considered the psychological impact of the visual organization of the page, and the paragraph mark or paragraphs within these, when making paragraphing decisions. Factors such as text type (manuscript versus printed book), font size, the actual paragraphing technique employed (pilcrow, indentation, use of *Littera notabilior*), may well have affected paragraphing decisions.

The second historical development overlooked by Lewis (1894) was the standardizing effect of punctuation from Caxton and printing onwards, as documented by Ben McCorkle (McCorkle, 2005: 44). The wide availability of printed books (formatted in a similar way) may well have affected other writers' ideas about paragraphing, and may have molded practice over time – something that could never have happened before the advent of the printing press. As McCorkle (2005: 30) pointed out, print technology, empiricism, and the industrial revolution all happened at once; changes in paragraph writing were not happening in a vacuum, but Lewis did not seem to consider this interdependency in his analyses.

Changing Reception Format

A key issue which links the earlier review of Latin and Greek paragraphing with work on the English paragraph is the subject of reception format, which is how the text was received (read aloud and heard, or read silently). Lewis (1894) began his work on the paragraph by referring, inter alia, to Aristotle's *paragraphos,* but not to its oral support function in reading prose out loud (as described in some detail earlier in this chapter). This major oversight, it is suggested, had an unfortunate consequence for Lewis' resulting analyses of English paragraphing: nowhere does Lewis consider the possibility that a writer might paragraph differently according to whether the text was to be read privately and silently or read out loud.

In discussing reception format, Brita Wårvik noted that a text can be written solely for the writer, for a silent reader, for a listener or listeners, or to be read aloud in a large or private group; or a text can be written with a combination of these audiences and purposes in mind (Wårvik, 2003). On the basis of the earlier observations concerning early Greek paragraphing, it is not unreasonable to suggest that knowing how one's writing is to be received will affect paragraphing practice.

The paragraphs that Lewis (1894) considered were written over a number of centuries, and they were undoubtedly composed for a variety of reception formats (see also comments on this in *Mirror of the Blessed Life of Jesu Christ* as referred to above). Wårvik (2003: 20) noted, for example, that Malory "clearly writes for his listeners" and that the "rule of St Benedict required texts to be read aloud to monks during meals" (*ibid.*). Ruth Crosby similarly believed that the authors of Chaucer's time wrote primarily for the public *ear*, not just the public *eye* (Crosby, 1938: 414, 432). Even during Caxton's era (the time of the advent of the English printing press), Wårvik suggested that writing (and so printing) for listeners was still common – indeed, she believed this was so up until the 17th century.

Certain oral features, Wårvik argued, were common in "aural" texts: additive structuring, formulaic language, repetition and redundancy, certain types of discourse markers, and direct address. Lewis (1894), however, simply adopted a negative evaluative stance when he encountered such features within the paragraphs he considered, as observed in the overview provided earlier. A couple of specific examples help illustrate this point. Concerning paragraphing in *Ayenbite of Inwyt*, a Christian tract on morality, written for a non-educated audience, Lewis (1894: 70) stated that it is "systematic to the extreme, each section being introduced by a set phrase (usually a numerical one) and forming one step in the long list of virtues and vices." But might not this repetitive style have been an aid to a *listener*? Similarly, with regard to Bacon, Lewis commented, "There is a stiff monotony in Bacon's way of opening a paragraph with, 'Now as to the first point,' and closing it with, 'Thus much for the first point'" (p. 91). Again, we must consider whether this might not have been an intelligent and purposeful formulaic paragraphing device (for listeners) rather than the "stiff monotony" of a writer who structured his paragraphs in a rather uninteresting way. As George Saintsbury commented, "…repetitions [and] stock phrases…have a certain attraction, in matter orally delivered" (Saintsbury, 1897: 49; see also Ong, 1982: 24). Lewis seems to have been largely unaware of the fact that he was, in part, documenting how reception format was changing, and how writing style was adapting accordingly. To criticize writing produced for listeners, on the basis of criteria valued by certain kinds of readers when engaging with certain written texts, does not make much sense.

It would appear, therefore, that a more detailed and careful consideration of changes in paragraphing practice indicate Lewis' (1894) theses, to be partial, and incomplete explanations for changing paragraphing practice in English. Focusing on the changes in paragraph organization Lewis failed to step back and consider why these were happening: historical context, philosophical orientation of writers, varying functions, genre differences, changes in text format, the value of paragraph-initial formulaicity in certain contexts, and differing reception formats. The theses he advanced were rather narrower than these wider concerns.

Conclusion

Written words leave much unsaid, or un-communicated, whether engraved on stone, inscribed on copper, written on parchment, or printed on a mechanical press. From ancient times, punctuation, whether provided by the original writer, or a later rewriter or reader, has sought to assist readers and / or hearers, or to affect, manipulate or guide them in some way.

As noted in the first section of this chapter the *paragraphos* (or *paragraphus*) did not only play an oral rhetorical function in the ancient world. Writers (or inscribers) of texts of different genres employed the *paragraphos / paragraphus* for a number of reasons: to facilitate reference, to influence the experience of the reader (in some way), in addition to aid a future reciter. In later medieval English, the paragraph mark seemed to be similarly multi-functional, and to have had both narrowly grammatical and more broadly macro-textual functions, as well as supporting oral delivery. In the overview on Greek usage it was observed that in NT Koiné Greek the paragraph break did not occur in a vacuum, but rather that certain paragraph opening formulae accompanied it in specific text-types: certain conjunctions in a narrative text, and other elements in an epistle. Early English paragraphing, as referred to earlier, also appears to have utilized certain paragraph opening elements, possibly for an aural support function. The pause associated with the paragraph break did not occur alone. More recent work on paragraph-initial language conducted by corpus linguistics supports the idea of multi-signaling, and is discussed further in Chapter 5.

Lewis (1894), in his diachronic work on the English paragraph, did not really consider the variety of different functions that the paragraph mark could play, or the different forms that the paragraph could take. As the overview provided in this chapter has made clear, paragraphing was a dynamic, multi-functional tool until the time of Lewis. Clearly, some of its earlier functions had died out by the late 19th century, but Lewis (following on from Bain) focused on one specific type of paragraph, and, in a sense, immortalized it for future generations. It is suggested here that had Lewis adopted a different approach to his historical analyses and appreciated the role of wider concerns affecting the form of the paragraph, this would not have been the case. In the next chapter I consider in more detail the problems which resulted from divorcing various kinds of context from the Bainian form of the paragraph. In one of those unfortunate accidents of history, post-Bain scholars (whether in education or applied linguists) developed a rather too narrow view of the paragraph, a view which underemphasized its multi-functionality, and dynamic and complex nature. In saying this, I do not mean to be overly critical of Bain. Rodgers (1965) and Stern (1976), two of Bain's biggest critics, have, I believe, misrepresented Bain in a number of ways, by oversimplifying his work. Rather, I am considering what Bain *might* have written, and how future scholars *might* have inherited a very different view of the paragraph, had objective historical diachronic work played a role in Bain's theorizing and a wider approach to understanding historical changes in paragraphing practice informed Lewis' approach. The issue of readership, paragraph-initial formulaicity, purpose, and genre variation were never adequately addressed by Bain or Lewis. Lewis tended to divorce the paragraphs he studied from the wider contexts within which they were written. Why? One possible reason is that Lewis may have been influenced by standardization practices in other areas of language. Just as sentence grammar and then at a later date punctuation became more standardized over time, Lewis and Bain may have been motivated to follow this tradition of standardization with the paragraph.[19]

I suggest that awareness of the issues largely overlooked by Lewis (1894) – changing types of readers, changing media, changing reception formats, changing or emerging genres, formulae, and other matters raised above – may well help us understand developments in paragraphing practice today, much of which bears no relation to Bain's (1866 / 1890) prototype. Indeed, we can go further, and suggest that contemporary developments in paragraphing largely mirror the changing English paragraph up to Bain, being shaped by broadly similar factors.

Notes

1   This has been challenged by Shane Butler, who argues that Saenger's work overlooked well-punctuated texts in antiquity (Butler, 2000, 2009). See also the work of Edward Thompson, who argued that *scriptura continua* was not a universal Greek phenomenon, mentioning a text pre 154 BC not written in this style (Thompson, 1893: 67). However, he suggested that *scriptura continua* was the norm.

2   Other scholars have looked at early paragraphing practice in Biblical Hebrew – for instance, Johannes de Moor and Marjo Korpel (de Moor and Korpel, 2007) and Wilfred Watson (Watson, 2007) – and Quranic Arabic – notably, Salwa El-Awa (El-Awa, 2006).

3   At times, punctuation (of any kind) seems to have been done away with altogether – for example, *Codex Vaticanus* (a fourth century Koiné Greek New Testament manuscript) contains no original punctuation, as observed by Thomas Husband and Margaret Husband (Husband and Husband, 1905: 14). Both Thomas Brown (Brown, 1974) and Baron (2001: 21) suggested that Aristophanes' punctuation system (see note 4) was not commonly used, though Steven Fischer argued that it was used extensively up until the first few centuries AD (Fischer, 2001: 262). He also commented on Roman scribe confusion over the function of the different punctuation points. Codex Sinaiticus, dated at around the same time as Vaticanus, includes various punctuation markings, and this text is discussed later in this chapter.

4   Aristophanes differentiated three types of marking on a text, directly related to the length of pausing, and as such provided for the benefit of the reading-out-loud reader of the text: the comma, the colon, and the periodus (see Baron, 2001).

5   Specific details regarding various paragraph edits of Cicero are noted by Fotheringham (2007, footnote 2, p. 40). Regarding the differences, she commented: "That there are more paragraphs in translations than in scholarly editions may be attributed to the desire to appear more 'user friendly'" (*ibid.*). Note also footnote 22 in the same article. Robert Petzinger also commented on the variety in the paragraphing decisions

of editors of Vergil's Aeneid (Petzinger, 1967), and Roy Watkins' book *A History of Paragraph Divisions in Horace's Epistles* (Watkins, 1940) documented not only the great variety of paragraphing adopted by editors of Horace's work, but also the fact that the same editor (in different editions) chose to paragraph the text differently.

6   I use *paragraphus* rather than *paragraphos* to distinguish the Latin form from the Greek, following Skeat (1901).

7   At an average of 24.8 words per paragraph, the paragraphs are shorter than those in the Gospel of Mark, where the average is 36.5.

8   Bain (1890) did not consider it inappropriate to subject literary writers to the same paragraphing criteria as writers of scientific texts on dialysis (p. 109), and plant descriptions (p. 115), though he did acknowledge that narrative would have different topic sentence patterns.

9   Thompson (1893: 71) similarly believed the pilcrow to be derived from the Γ.

10   I do not comment here in any detail on the different forms of the paragraph marker used.

11   Lewis (1894) did not provide many examples of paragraphs to support a number of the more general claims he made. For example, the following evaluative comments are made with no textual support: "The melody of Dickens's prose is equable and flowing, with a tendency to metre now and then. He has no right feeling for the paragraph as a rhythmic whole" (p. 156); "We may say that George Eliot's paragraphs have unity, barring an occasional philosophical digression. We may say that they show logical coherence, excepting now and then where a remote conclusion is introduced before it is analyzed" (p. 157). However, balancing this criticism are occasions when Lewis did provide examples to support his points – for example, the Alfred paragraph (p. 68), Tyndale's Hebrew inspired parallelism (p. 76), and examples of Burke's short, "crisp" opening and closing paragraph sentences (p. 122).

12   Indeed some of his comments about writers are not just humorous, but bordering on the libelous: "If excessive variability in stylistic averages goes to show mental irregularity, then Burton's paragraph-length would prove him mad" (p. 93). Concerning Macaulay he wrote "Now I do not wish to be understood as maintaining the existence of any very close connection between paragraph-length and heart-disease. But a tired man is likely to be loquacious, if he tries to talk, and when a writer has incomplete control of his brain he is likely to be at first diffuse in his composition, and later, incoherent" (p. 50).

13   It is important to note that Lewis was careful to document when single sentence paragraphs were due to dialogue change, and to exclude these from his analyses.

14   For example, Milton had both long sentences and long paragraphs.

15   It should be mentioned that Lewis (1894) used both expressions in referring to the same thing. They are, however, capable of being interpreted rather differently – the "in thought" (p. 44) reference as a "step on the way," the "of thought" (p. 172) reference, a "block." The former seems to indicate development of an idea, while the latter does not, indicating instead a completed idea.

16   Frederick Scrivener, the editor of the Cambridge Paragraph Bible (1873), described the paragraphing in the King James version of the Bible (KJV) as "unequally and capriciously distributed," observing that paragraphing came to an end after Acts 20: 36 (Scrivener, 2010: 128). Lewis (1894: 90), similarly, believed that in the KJV, "There is nothing necessary in these divisions" concerning the paragraph divisions.

17   Tebeaux (2011) did not discuss this possible cross-over from Ramist-driven technical writing to Ramist-driven prose.

18   Of De Quincey's writings, Lewis (1894: 138) commented: "We may say of his longer paragraphs that the best show unity in somewhat wide variety, while in all cases he returns consciously, from digressions within the paragraph, to the topic."

19   In Robert Lowth's *A Short Introduction to English Grammar*, Lowth (1799) illustrated violations of *his* rules by great writers, and Bain (1866 / 1890) did essentially the same thing in commenting on the paragraphing practice of great writers who broke the rules of his paragraphing model.

3 Teaching and Learning Paragraphing (I): The Late 19th Century

Joseph Angus

A paragraph is a combination of sentences, intended to explain, or illustrate, or prove, or apply some truth; or to give the history of events during any definite portion of time, or in relation to any one subject of thought. (Angus, 1862: 401)

Alexander Bain

[The paragraph] is a collection, or a series of sentences, with unity of purpose. (Bain, 1890: 91)

John F. Genung

A paragraph is a distinct division of the discourse, related indeed to preceding and following, as a link in a large chain, but complete in itself, and exhaustive of its topic. (Genung, 1891: 194)

Barrett Wendell

A paragraph is to a sentence what a sentence is to a word (Wendell, 1891: 119)

Fred N. Scott and Joseph V. Denney

A paragraph is a unit of discourse developing a single idea. It consists of a group or series of sentences closely related to one another and to the thought expressed by the whole group or series. Devoted, like the sentence, to the development of one topic, a good

paragraph is also, like a good essay, a complete treatment in itself.
(Scott and Denney, 1895: 1)

Introduction

The period between 1862 and 1895 was the formative era for the theorizing of the paragraph, and the most significant work of this era was undoubtedly that produced by Alexander Bain.[1] Before considering the writings of Bain, and some of the other key rhetoricians and educators of the time, it is worthwhile considering the historical context within which they wrote, for as Kathryn Flannery argued, one cannot really understand a particular development in education or rhetoric without appreciating the context within which it is born (Flannery, 1995: 6).

Hayes (2003) suggested that the Scottish context within which Alexander Bain wrote influenced his approach to the theorizing of the paragraph, and adds that a similar context in the United States provided the right conditions for the widespread acceptance of his rules there. What were these contexts? The new students of Aberdeen, Scotland, in the late 19th century were not particularly well read, and Hayes believed that Bain designed his rhetoric (including his paragraphing rules) to fast-track these students up to satisfactory academic levels. She noted that following the American Civil War (1861–1865), American colleges were facing a similar situation: the need to accommodate a large number of a new type of student aspiring to become middle-class citizens, and who did not have training in classical rhetoric. During this period in the United States, as James Berlin has recorded (Berlin, 1984: 60), student teacher ratios ranged from 1–100 to 1–300, and this situation called for a simplified way of teaching and evaluating student writing. Bain's work on both the paragraph and the four modes of discourse (*description, narration, exposition*, and *persuasion*), together with contributions from his peers facilitated this. Hayes (2003) believed that the Harvard Reports of the 1890s played an important role in spreading the Bainian approach to writing in schools. One of the results of the reports was for universities and colleges to tighten up the writing requirements in their entrance examinations, and Bain's work provided a suitable marking rubric for this purpose. Scott and Denney's (1895) hugely popular work on the paragraph grew out of their experience as teachers and, according to Donald Stewart, in direct response to the calls of teachers needing help (Stewart, 1990: 168).

The relationship between theory, pedagogy, and assessment is not a simple one, and different educational stakeholders with varied priorities and agendas filtered, in various ways, the theoretical work on paragraphing for their own purposes – a point to which we shall return later in the chapter.

The Era of Terminology

If I were to assign the late 19th century work on paragraphing a particular label, it would be *The Era of Terminology*. Different laws, explicated under simple headings, were the order of the day. While Bain (1866) had six laws governing the paragraph (*explicit reference, parallel construction, topic sentence, consecutive arrangement, overall unity*, and *marking of subordination*),[2] Scott and Denney (1895) had five (*unity, selection, proportion, sequence, and variety*), Andrew Hepburn (Hepburn, 1875) had four (*unity, continuity, proportion, and variety*), and Wendell (1891) just three (*unity, mass, coherence*).

The terms most commonly associated with paragraph pedagogy today ("unity," "emphasis," and "coherence") are an amalgam or simplification and renaming of the different terms employed by the various writers of this era. In what follows, I survey the contributions of the theorists under these three terms and discuss what they had to say about them, or their 19th century equivalences or partial equivalences. In addition, I document a number of issues elaborated upon by these same scholars which have not filtered down to later generations, and consider the consequences of this selective filtering for contemporary academics and writing teachers. The chapter concludes with a discussion of the value of terminology in writing classes today.

Unity

"Unity," a word utilized by nearly all of the 19th century writers in their discussions of the characteristics or requirements of a paragraph, is the only term which didn't change during the era and hasn't changed since. Graphologically or typographically, the paragraph is a unit, and this is beyond dispute. However, in surveying the relevant work of this era it becomes apparent, very quickly, that the 19th century theorists meant rather different things by the term.

The definitions of unity

Joseph Angus , the first writer on the paragraph of the era, spoke of paragraph unity in terms of one subject of thought, or one theme: "Properly a paragraph has *one* theme" (Angus, 1862: 401, original emphasis), and he saw the role of the sentences within a paragraph as illustrating and explaining or expounding this one theme. Angus differentiated theme from purpose, saying that a writer may begin a theme without specifically announcing the purpose, the purpose being made clear later by the theme being variously proved, illustrated, or applied, or by its contrary being stated.

Bain (1890), on the other hand, suggested that unity related to the purpose of the paragraph, rather than its theme. Bain (1890: 92) believed that the paragraph has "unity of purpose," explaining this as "a sustained purpose, [which]…forbids digressions and irrelevant matter" (p. 112). He noted several violations: the first being the "run on" paragraph, where a paragraph break rather than a sentence break should have been made, the possible consequence being that the reader loses the sense of unity of purpose of the writer. Good paragraphing style, Bain (p. 91) argued, requires that, "sentences [are] properly parted off." Another, though less common, problem impinging on unity of purpose according to Bain is when paragraphs are too short, resulting in a disjointed sentence – that is, where the paragraph break is reduced, in effect, to the sentence break. A third (and more serious) violation for Bain was digression or irrelevance within the paragraph itself.

Scott and Denney (1895: 4) characterized unity as "The most important" of their laws: their understanding relating to "thought and purpose," tying together Angus' and Bain's rather different emphases. They listed the standard breakers of unity mentioned by earlier writers: digression, inclusion of irrelevant material, and the run-on problem. Further, in defining a paragraph as "a unit of discourse developing a single idea" (Scott and Denney, 1895: 1), their understanding suggested a dynamic unity, stressing, as it does, movement.

For Genung (1891), unity could be tested, namely, abstracted or summarized into a sentence expressing the main idea. Like Genung, Wendell (1891: 124) argued that the test for paragraph unity was being able to "state its substance in a single sentence." Like Bain, Wendell believed that paragraphs which are either too small or too long can threaten unity.

The problem of unity

The term "unity" (however understood) is a problematic one, when discussing the paragraph. Regarding unity of purpose (Bain's focus), it is clear that a writer can have more than one purpose in writing[3] (as a speaker can have in speaking). Regarding unity of theme, or substance, this focus seems rather incomplete: it would seem necessary to mention the reason for discussing the theme in order to have a clear understanding of the paragraph. Defining unity in terms of thought and purpose (as Scott and Denney did) seems more reasonable, but even here there are problems: what are the implications for unity when one has two purposes and one theme, or two themes and one purpose, for example? Problematic, surely, is the use of the term "unity" when one has in mind two distinct concepts (thought and purpose), neither of which loses its individual identity.

The threats to unity

One of the threats to unity noted by Bain is internal (i.e. related to the subject matter within the paragraph) – the threat of digression. The other two relate to the external form of the paragraph (i.e. the actual length of the paragraph): one is the run-on problem, which is when a paragraph is too long, going beyond its focus, and the other is the undeveloped paragraph, which is when a paragraph is too short. In what follows, I look at each of these threats in turn.

Digression

As commented on in Chapter 2, digression can be intentional or accidental: a (deliberate) literary device or an (unconscious) straying in one's train of thought as pen is put to paper. In discussing digression, the scholars noted above provided examples from published written works (rather than their students' writing), which begs the question whether they may not have conflated the two types, and failed to recognize the former (legitimate) use of digression in certain types of writing.

Does digression destroy unity? As suggested in Chapter 2, digression can, or perhaps should, be incorporated into notions of paragraph purpose. The following paragraph by Twain has been termed "rambling" by Carol Aikman and Michael O'Hear, who believed that the paragraph begins in one direction and then takes another (Aikman and O'Hear, 1997: 192). They suggested that Twain's humorous purpose plays an important role in his digressions, and that this is responsible for "his comparatively large number of paragraphs without main ideas" (*ibid.*).

> *The country schoolhouse was three miles from my uncle's farm. It stood in a clearing in the woods and would hold about twenty-five boys and girls. We attended the school with more or less regularity once or twice a week, in summer, walking to it in the cool of the morning by the forest paths, and back in the gloaming at the end*

of the day. All the pupils brought their dinners in baskets – corn dodger, buttermilk, and other good things – and sat in the shade of the trees at noon and ate them. It is the part of my education which I look back upon with the most satisfaction. My first visit to the school was when I was seven. A strapping girl of fifteen, in the customary sunbonnet and calico dress, asked me if I "used tobacco" – meaning did I chew it. I said no. It roused her scorn. She reported me to all the crowd, and said: "Here is a boy seven years old who can't chew tobacco."

But does the paragraph above have no "unifying" main idea? It can be summarized as "These are some of my humorous reflections on boyhood schooling in the South," or something similar. If it passes the paragraph summarization tests of Genung and Wendell, does the paragraph not exhibit some kind of unity? As I discuss in more detail later on, tests of unity seem to raise more problems than they solve.

The run-on paragraph

The second challenge to paragraph unity was posited to be the run-on: when a paragraph break would have been more appropriate than a sentence break, that is, when the paragraph goes on past where the unified part ends. One way to resolve some instances of run-on is to appeal to the existence of other discourse units (larger than the sentence) and not aligned with the paragraph within a text (see the structural paragraph concept discussion in Chapter 1). Although not specifically developed to deal with this kind of problem per se, Scott and Denney's (1895) concept of the "stadium of discourse" (discussed in more detail below) is helpful. If one admits the existence of such stadia (i.e. thoughts) in discourse, a writer may break a paragraph at a "substadium" level (i.e. smaller discourse unit), or a larger "stadium" level of thought within the text, according to the subject matter and the writer's perception of the reader's needs. This being so, if a particular reader were to argue that a paragraph break would have been more appropriate than a sentence break at a particular point in a text (i.e. after a substadium), a response to this could be that the paragraphing within the text was decided upon for a different type of reader, who may not agree that the paragraph is too long: a paragraph may contain a number of substadia, if they are all related under a larger stadium of thought, in which case the indentation can be defended.

The short or one-sentence paragraph (the undeveloped paragraph)

Whether or not a single sentence could be a paragraph was something of a contentious issue for the writers of this era, with views expressed on both sides, as noted by Lewis (1874: 22), and mentioned in Chapter 2. Angus (1862) seemed to reluctantly allow it, while Bain (1890) excluded it in his definition (see chapter-opening quote), and Scott and Denney (1895) did not mention it. Today, no-one really doubts that the single sentence can be paragraphed to dramatic effect in literature. It may also be used to highlight key points in other forms of writing as well, and its more mundane usage, in such genre conventions as the closing move in a letter, should not be forgotten. In new e-texts, the single-sentence paragraph has been exploited extensively (see Chapter 9 on this), and one need only casually glance over the BBC News website for plentiful instances of such paragraphs. In the late 19th century, however, the single-sentence paragraph was somewhat problematic, and it is easy to understand why: it did not conform to what paragraphs were typically conceived to be, or should be. For this reason, it was largely overlooked or sidelined.

Testing unity

Can we subject a paragraph to a test of unity? What are we to term a paragraph if its unity cannot be summarized in a single sentence? A defective paragraph? A purely orthographic paragraph? I suggest that one can create a nonsensical piece of writing that defies a summary sentence; yet the number of paragraphs which cannot be meaningfully summarized, are, I suggest, very few indeed. The two examples provided below are both hypothetical, and were drawn up by their respective creators to illustrate non-unity in relation to the paragraph. As such, one would assume that they would establish their arguments fairly convincingly; however, I suggest that they do not.

Herbert Smith provided a hypothetical example of a student paragraph about tennis, produced below, and commented that the paragraph is "devoid of unity…to the orderly adult mind" (Smith, 1920: 393).

I am especially fond of tennis because there is so much exercise connected with it. On a frosty winter afternoon, sunshiny and windless, nothing is so refreshing as a game of tennis. Not only under this favorable condition, but at any time of the day or year, I find tennis just the sport I would most enjoy. My ambition is to be able to serve and receive swiftly. I think a tantalizing occurrence is to find yourself in this position: to be near the net with your opponent near the back and to drop a ball just over the net, out of your opponent's reach, and find it have landed out. I think it is very interesting to watch two good players indulge in a set of singles. Each is ready for any trick the other might play on him, and at the same time tries to catch his opponent unawares. (ibid.)

This paragraph certainly contains some odd expressions, but is it devoid of unity? On the one hand one might say "yes," and for various reasons. For example, the first sentence does not guide the reader concerning what follows. Further, one might argue that the relationship between the sentences is disjointed, or just list-like as there seem to be a number of possible themes touched on, but not developed, namely, tennis as exercise, tennis and the seasons, tennis as a spectator sport. But what if we apply the tests noted above? Can the student paragraph be summarized in a single sentence? Yes. Does it cover one theme, purposefully? Yes, broadly speaking, the above paragraph can be summarized as: "There are a lot of things I like about tennis." However, for Smith (1920: 393), the paragraph "focuses on no one proposition" and it is not a logical unit – it fails the unity test. However, crucially, the test criteria that he employs to make this judgment are never spelled out, though

Smith did discuss *relevance* and the need for every sentence to be related to a topic sentence, in addition to noting the importance of "orderly thinking" (p. 400) when writing.

Leon Mones, on the other hand, writing at the same time as Smith (Mones, 1921), appeared to have had very different ideas about unity and students' writing. He argued that students rarely violate unity, characterizing (perhaps more accurately caricaturing) students as having "a single-track mind," making the rather quotable comment that "Youth is the age of monotheism" (p. 459), that is, different views and ideas are not problematic for student writers, as they see the world rather simply or narrowly. Indeed, Mones saw non-unity as more typically a problem with "the frenzied creations of [certain] textbook writers who seek new illustrations for scholastic vanities" (p. 459). Presumably, what he meant by this was that made up examples, rather than actual student writing, formed the basis of textbook writers' advice and pedagogical guidance to students. Although Mones may have over-reached himself in making this point, his ideas do balance those of Smith's.

Another example of a "unity-free" paragraph is provided by Richard Warner:

> *Patience is often considered a virtue. Many people have patience, but some do not. Job learned patience through adversity. Patience is not common in an industrial society. Patience means different things to different people.* (Warner, 1979: 152)

Warner noted – approvingly – that "most of [his] students have been able to observe that [it] fails to be a paragraph because this set of sentences, although sharing a common topic, seem to be saying a great many unrelated things about that topic That [*sic*] is, a paragraph must have a common theme as well as a common topic" (*ibid.*). Perhaps the real issue with this paragraph is not so much the absence of a common topic and theme, but poor cohesion: the relation of one sentence to another is not sufficiently spelled out to be clear, and the underlying point unifying the sentences is not actually stated, but is, rather, implied. However, if one were to rewrite the above to make the connections between the sentences more explicit, connections which a reader may actually endeavor to make in his / her mind in the absence of any specific guidance provided by the writer, as considered by Walter Kintsch and Doris Monk (Kintsch and Monk, 1972), one wonders whether the students whom Warner refers to would also reject its unity. In my rewriting of the above paragraph, I have attempted to fill in the gaps,[4] though other readers might develop rather different directions for this particular piece of writing, perhaps by developing the topic sentence in different ways:

Patience is often considered a virtue. Many people have patience, but some do not. One famous example of a patient person is Job who learned patience through adversity. However, patience is not common in an industrial society – adverse though it may be. Patience means different things to different people: though considered virtuous it is also contentious.

What becomes clear when we actually look at paragraphs, and consider unity (in more concrete terms), is that tests of paragraph unity are not clear-cut: different readers may agree or disagree about whether a paragraph displays such a quality; and, if defined broadly enough, few (if any?) real paragraphs would seem to fail the unity test. This possibility seems to have been largely overlooked by Genung (1891) and Wendell (1891). They do not appear to have considered instances when a paragraph might be summarized differently by different readers (especially so when the readers may be from different cultural or educational backgrounds), or scenarios in which the paragraph could be summarized solely with reference to content or to function (rather than both, together). Further, they nowhere commented on the legitimacy or plausibility of the summary sentence provided, solely the ability to give one.

The construction of unity

Different unities are, in reality, constructed by readers of the same paragraph. The tests of Genung (1891) and Wendell (1891) are not so much tests of textual paragraph unity (as they purport to be), as they are of three related factors:

- The reader's reading skills (e.g. differentiation of main from supporting ideas, sensitivity to purpose of the paragraph, relation of purpose to theme);[5]
- The reader's knowledge (both textual and background);
- The reader's writing skills (in crystallizing the subject matter clearly, in writing the summary sentence).

With regard to the second of these factors (reader knowledge), Stephen Witte discussed the inadequacy of a view of discourse topic[6] which fails to take into account the reader, and the reader's knowledge (Witte, 1983). As he commented, "…discourse topic – is not derived from the text alone, but from the interaction of the text with the reader's prior knowledge"[7] (p. 316). Such prior knowledge may be built up within a text, be external to it, or be a combination of the two.[8] If built up within a text, then the reader's ability to summarize a paragraph well is logically dependent on his / her cumulative reading of both previous and later paragraphs.[8] All of these points may help explain why it is that different readers summarize paragraphs differently: Charles Knoblauch has noted that "subtly different conclusions" (Knoblauch, 1981: 57) are drawn by different readers about a paragraph's unity and emphasis.

To contextualize the above discussion, an example provided by Witte (1983) is helpful. Witte (1983: 317) provided the following paragraph concerning Mathesius' work on theme, rheme and discourse:

…From his work during the 1920's, Mathesius attempts to explain the relationship of individual sentences within the context of extended texts…. He hypothesizes that the themes of the sentences usually appear first in English sentences, expressing old or given information that provides a semantic link with the preceding sentence and hence the preceding elements of the discourse… Mathesius also hypothesizes that new information introduced into the text typically occurs near the ends of the sentences as the rheme.

Witte (p. 317) believed that on reading this paragraph, different readers may produce different discourse topics (largely dependent on prior knowledge), two possible summaries[9] being:

1. "Mathesius' contributions to a theory of functional sentence perspective" (prior knowledge high);
2. "Mathesius' view of the relationship between sentences in a text" (prior knowledge low).

As can be seen, these summaries are, in terms of their content, quite different, though both are legitimate summaries according to Witte. Witte (1983: 317) believed that the existence of a topic sentence may well guide and limit a reader's view. However, when there is no such clear indicator, and thought and inference is required, there is the possibility of quite different summary sentences being produced by different readers.

How valuable is the concept of unity when discussing paragraphs? Wendell (1891: 122) suggested that the term, as explained in textbooks, was of little value, terming attempts at definition "pedantically lifeless." As I suggest at the end of the chapter, the term may be of value, so long as one recognizes that it is not static, but rather might be interpreted differently in different genres (perhaps looser and tighter versions of unity could be differentiated). Further, it may be more or less valued by the writer, due to the fact that unity is not the sole characteristic of writing that might be considered of importance. The relationship of unity to emphasis and coherence (both concepts discussed in the next two sections) has been understood differently: it is probably not best to consider these abstract characteristics to be independent and unrelated (see later). Perhaps the fact that the paragraph was a textual unit blinded scholars of the 19th century into thinking that unity was somehow a given, but it is clearly a more complex notion than was generally understood, and the tests of unity, in particular, seem to be of questionable value.

Emphasis

In discussing emphasis, the second paragraph characteristic, Bain (1890) extrapolated the sentence-based concept of principal and subordinate components (and their relative importance) to the paragraph: what is principal should not be presented as subordinate, and vice-versa. Further, what is principal, or important, "should have bulk and prominence" (p. 121). He suggested that not just quantity, but also mechanical means (e.g. the use of footnotes), or a statement employed to indicate the comparative importance of what is being written (e.g. *But this is after all, a matter of secondary importance*), can be utilized for the same purpose.

Regarding what he termed "mass," Wendell (1891: 126) referred to the "external form" of the paragraph, namely, that the main parts of the composition are, "so placed as readily to catch the eye" (p. 127), commenting that these are the beginnings and endings of paragraphs. He argued that if one can intelligently skim a paragraph, then it is "well massed" (p. 128), and believed that the summary of the opening and closing sentence of a paragraph should function as subject and predicate, respectively. Albert Kitzhaber termed this requirement "far too rigid and unequivocal" (Kitzhaber, 1990: 169), observing that Wendell's own paragraphs miserably failed his tests. However, the ideas that the first sentence should state what the paragraph is about, and the last sentence should summarize its contents were to become important prescriptivist requirements, as can be seen in various pedagogical volumes today. For Wendell (1891), not just the number of words about a point, but also their specific location in the paragraph, was important, and this issue is discussed in more detail in Chapters 6 and 7.

Genung (1891) referred to the length of the paragraph, and also considered its effect upon the reader. He suggested that "paragraphs of over a page in length should be avoided" (p. 193), solely on the grounds that they are difficult for the reader to cope with. Possibly as a consequence of this belief, he recommended that "the subject proposed in a paragraph may sometimes be so comprehensive as to require more than one paragraph for its treatment" (p. 200). In making these comments, Genung not only acknowledged the existence of discourse units within the text which were larger than the paragraph (see comments above and below on stadia), he also seemed to recognize the psychological-cognitive needs for paragraphing, a subject discussed in more detail in Chapter 7.

In writing of the law of proportion, Scott and Denney (1895) stated that what is written in the paragraph should be sufficient for the purpose of the paragraph. They believed that the importance of an idea is best served by its being amplified, while also noting over-amplification of a simple statement to be poor practice. They believed that it is not good practice to write a paragraph containing more than 300 words, because more than this may challenge the reader's ability to manage the information – a view of paragraphing which incorporated processing considerations.

The topic sentence

The topic sentence concept is probably best considered under the characteristic of emphasis, though relevant to both unity and coherence. Regarding the placement of the statement of the theme of the paragraph, Angus (1862: 401) observed that it "...may be stated in the margin, or at the beginning, or at the close, or at both beginning and close: or which may be implied only and not stated." He went on to suggest that placing the theme at the end is "most appropriate in closing or commencing a narrative" (p. 404). Regarding instances in which the theme was (only) implied, rather than stated, Angus felt that this would result in a paragraph which would be "generally defective in clearness" (p. 401).

Bain (1890: 108) believed that the opening sentence of a paragraph "unless obviously preparatory" should "indicate the scope of the paragraph," though commenting that this is more applicable to expository and descriptive text than to narrative. He went on to observe, however, that "frequently the opening sentence is so constructed as to throw the subject of the paragraph to the end" (p. 109), and reflected that a possible reason for this "may be to suspend the interest of the reader" (*ibid.*), a technique which he suggested to be most commonly used in beginning a new text, or chapter.

The one main idea of the paragraph, Scott and Denney (1895) maintained, is usually found in a topic sentence within the paragraph. However, they suggested that it may be only part of a sentence, or implied, rather than stated, that is, it may exist in the mind of the writer as a "working theme" (p. 19). They noted four possible placements of the "formal statement of the theme" (*ibid.*):

- Stated First (typical when proving a principle, expanding an idea or treating a formal proposition);
- Stated First and Last (giving roundness to a paragraph, when such an emphasis is justified);
- Stated Last (a strategic decision – when the idea may not be accepted by the reader if stated at the onset);
- Implied (occurring in "a large number of cases" [p. 23], though the reader can still articulate the theme, this being "the test of a good paragraph" [p. 19]; in narrative and description, the theme may not be explicitly stated, though unity of effect will still be maintained).

Regarding the development of the idea or theme of the paragraph contained in the "germ-idea" (Scott and Denney, 1895: 25) of the topic sentence, Scott and Denney argued that the other sentences within the paragraph "bring out and develop" (*ibid.*) this by repeating or defining the topic, stressing that the writer should choose which means of development best serves "the nature of the thought discussed" (*ibid.*). They also believed that the topic statement "may mean more or less than the writer intends" (p. 26), thereby requiring "restriction or enlargement" (*ibid.*) by the sentences which follow. This comment suggests that the topic statement, by its very nature (i.e. just a statement, and hence possibly ambiguous), cannot always be so precise as to clearly guide the reader concerning the direction that the text will take.

The topic sentence problem

A lasting legacy of the writers of this era is the concept of the topic sentence, the term first used by John McElroy (McElroy, 1885). Such a sentence, typically placed up front in the paragraph and indicating to the reader what is to follow, has become an extraordinarily inflexible writing requirement in some contexts (as noted, for example, by Bennett, 2009).

It should be noted that Bain showed a flexibility on this point which his detractors (e.g. Rodgers 1965, 1966a,b; Stern 1976) largely failed to acknowledge, though he did stress that in exposition it was a virtual necessity for a topic sentence to occur in sentence-initial position. As is clear from the above, Bain's peers also showed stylistic awareness concerning the placement of such a sentence, a point endorsed by more recent scholars (e.g. Aikman and O'Hear, 1997). There has been considerable research and discussion concerning the existence and use of topic sentences in paragraphs since the 1970s, and I seek to summarize the key findings below.

Some research, most notably that of Richard Braddock (Braddock, 1974) and James Baumann and Judith Serra (Baumann and Serra, 1984), has suggested that the majority of paragraphs do not have topic sentences, and that the paragraph-initial topic sentence is actually quite rare. Braddock's corpus consisted of essays in popular quality American magazines and newspapers, and Baumann and Serra's corpus consisted of social studies textbooks written for school children. Braddock began his study by expressing his frustration in identifying what is actually meant by a topic sentence, and he then went on to provide his own taxonomy of topic sentence types:

- Simple topic sentence (i.e. within one T-unit);
- Delayed completion topic sentence (extending two T-units);
- Assembled topic sentence (collected from around the paragraph);
- Inferred (not actually found in the text per se).

(Braddock, 1974: 293–295)

In his analyses, Braddock (1974: 295) observed the presence of a "major topic sentence" – a term he coined for a topic sentence covering more than one paragraph. He found that only 13% of the paragraphs in his corpus opened with a topic sentence and that only 55% of the paragraphs in his corpus had an identifiable topic sentence anywhere in the paragraph. He did, however, suggest that the essays would have been easier to read if they had employed topic sentences more often. Baumann and Serra (1984) set out to discover whether the Braddock (1974) findings could be extended to different texts, written for a different audience. They found that 27% of the children's social studies textbook paragraphs opened with a simple topic sentence, and that 44% of the paragraphs contained an explicit topic sentence. They suggested that textbook writers should increase the number of sentence-initial topic sentences to make the texts more accessible to their readers.

What is particularly interesting about both Braddock's (1974) and Baumann and Serra's (1984) work is the conservative conclusions they reached on the basis of their analyses of the data; namely, they did not argue, on noting their absence, that topic sentences are unnecessary but rather that they would have been helpful in cases where they did not occur. However, other writers, such as Stern (1976) and David Moore and John Readence (Moore and Readence, 1980), interpreted their data as challenging the received wisdom concerning the need for a paragraph to have a topic sentence.

Other research seems to have contradicted the Braddock (1974) and Baumann and Serra (1984) findings. A study by O'Hear with Richard Ramsey and Valli Pherson of composition and sociology texts revealed that both had sentence-initial main ideas within the paragraphs over 50% of the time (59.5% and 52.9%, respectively), with only 11.4% of the paragraphs in the composition texts not having a stated main idea, and just 4.6% of the sociology texts not having one (O'Hear et al., 1987). In a study of various 19th century American authors (of different types, e.g. scientists, social scientists, and popular writers), Aikman and O'Hear (1997) found that 65.8% of the paragraphs contained main idea propositions, and that first-position topic sentence placement ranged from 40.5% to 83.9%, noting that the first, second, or last sentence within the paragraph typically provided the main idea clue. Randall Popken, in a study of academic research articles, provided an alternative, function-based, classification of topic sentences to the one noted by Braddock (1974), believing that such sentences could be:

- Proposition carrying;
- Announcement; or
- Metadiscursive. (Popken, 1987: 211–212)

Like Braddock (1974), Popken (1987) differentiated the paragraph-specific topic sentence (the minor topic sentence) from the major topic sentence, which can extend over two or more paragraphs. He found that 54% of the paragraphs in his corpus had minor topic sentences, noting interesting differences between the different disciplines. For example, 71% of the literature paragraphs contained minor topic sentences, whereas just 34% of civil engineering article paragraphs utilized them. Popken (1987), like Braddock (1974) observed that a major topic sentence can control the development of following paragraphs, noting that when this occurs the need for a minor topic sentence in the following paragraph may be obviated.

Craig Smith, in a meta-analysis of research (Smith, 2008), observed the skewing effect of the short paragraphs in the corpora, and hence the findings, of both Braddock (1974) and Baumann and Serra (1984). Smith preferred to analyze topic sentences from the perspective of chunks or blocks of discourse, rather than from the perspective of the orthographic paragraph, and in so doing, found that in his corpus of American magazines, 95% of the blocks had a topic sentence, and paragraph-initial position was by far the most common location for the sentence. He argued that the relevance and importance of the topic sentence needs to be reestablished.

While those with an interest in the paragraph and paragraphing might be tempted to throw their hands up in the air at these apparently contradictory findings, these studies have, in reality, considerably refined the late 19th century views of the topic sentence. Rather than just presenting data which tells a different story, Popken (1987) and Smith (2008), in particular, attempted to explain the reasons for differences in the presence and specific location of topic sentences in the various texts studied by different researchers. I seek to summarize these explanations below, in particular, in relation to the *absence* of a topic sentence in a paragraph.

Popken (1987: 222) commented that headings may well play the role of "para-topic sentences," in research articles (see also Angus' (1862) comments above, on the various locations of the topic sentence – including *outside* the body of the text). It has also been noted that certain types of paragraph (specifically, introductory or example paragraphs) may not need a main idea statement, as O'Hear et al. (1987) stated. Popken (1987) suggested that certain discipline-specific short paragraphs may not need such a sentence, operating as they may do under the influence of a preceding paragraph's major topic sentence. Finally, Popken (1987) commented that conventional text schemata may make the use of a topic sentence redundant. He observed that a paragraph making reference to research shortcomings in the conclusion of a research article, seems not to require a topic sentence indicating such, as readers know that conclusions often contain such information.

The research into topic sentences carried out since the 1970s indicates that the 19th century view of the topic sentence was overly rigid. One can trace this rigidity, in part, to the focus on the paragraph itself – specifically, the prototypical deductively organized paragraph, together with the general failure to consider the role of the orthographic paragraph within the wider discourse, and its relation to other textual units. This latter failing is particularly evident when one considers the more recent differentiation made between major and minor topic sentences, as described above. As Smith (2008: 88) noted, making the paragraph the "base unit" of topic sentence textual analysis does not really make sense. Stern's (1976) main criticism of Bainian paragraphing was this very issue: he argued that teachers and learners need to focus on the discourse rules, not the rules governing the paragraph per se. This is a good example of research findings indicating how structural and orthographic paragraphs do not always map onto each other, or create the mixed unit, using Heurley's (1997) term, and as mentioned in Chapter 1.

Having made the above observations, it is important to mention here that there is something to be said in favor of the paragraph-initial minor topic sentence from a psychological point of view (as opposed to a discourse-organizing perspective), a matter which is discussed in more detail in Chapter 7.

Coherence

Coherence, as mentioned earlier, is the third of the tripartite characteristics of paragraphs, according to some scholars. Today, more commonly than not, the term "cohesion" is used in applied linguistics to refer to textual relations as shown in specific linguistic devices, and the term "coherence" to whether a text makes sense to the reader (e.g. as discussed by Patricia Carrell; Carrell, 1982; see also Brown and Yule, 1983). However, this was not so in the late 19th century, when the term "coherence" was employed to describe textual organization and stylistic elements, as made plain in the overview which follows.

Regarding the internal structuring of the paragraph, Angus (1862: 405) recommended to his readers a combination of the "fullness" of the German style, and the "brevity" of the French style: "Brief sentences give force and clearness; full sentences add impressiveness and weight." In terms of the development of the theme in a paragraph Angus believed that sentences within a paragraph may be "easily separable" (p. 408), appealing "now to memory, now to reason, and now to fancy" (*ibid.*). He also suggested that there might be tight cohesion between sentences, where the writer "makes each sentence after the first originate in some word or turn of thought in the preceding" (p. 411). Angus discussed the connection of paragraphs to each other, not just their internal structure, commenting on the importance of logical ordering for writers and of transitioning between paragraphs – through either a restatement of the theme or by the use of connectives.

Bain's (1890) concept of coherence entailed three points: explicit reference, parallel construction, and consecutive arrangement. Regarding the first of these, Bain wrote, "The bearing of each sentence of a Paragraph on the sentences preceding needs to be explicit" (p. 94), at the same time commenting that this need not be explicitly stated as such: "In many instances, no connecting words are used" (p. 98). He mentioned the role of conjunctions (cumulative, adversative, illative, subordinating); demonstrative phrases (e.g. *in this case*) and expressions (e.g. *On the contrary, In a word*); repetition; and finally the "mode of arrangement" (p. 100) in creating cohesion between sentences. Cases in which no explicit reference was needed were:

- when to use a conjunction would be to "encumber the composition";
- when a sentence following iterates, or explains what has preceded;
- in succeeding cumulative statements (which are assumed "to have a common bearing");
- to state a consequence (expressing "special energy"); or
- when the thoughts to be connected are either too close, or too distant. (Bain, 1890: 98–100)

Concerning the second of his coherence elements, Bain (1890: 105) defined parallel construction as follows: "When several consecutive sentences iterate or illustrate the same idea, they should, as far as possible, be formed alike." He explained this by reference to sentence logic, in which the principal subject and principal predicate are clearly indicated. However, he also argued that the principal subject, may, for the sake of emphasis, actually come last in the sentence (particularly when introducing a subject), though after this, "it must take its proper position" (p. 106).

With regard to the concept of consecutive arrangement, the final element of coherence in Bain's thought, Bain (1890: 114) summed this up in the maxim: "Proximity has to be governed by Affinity," essentially meaning that an idea should be followed by its connected proofs or arguments before another subject or point begins. Bain went on to state that both the nature of the subject, together with the regularly adopted style of its development (e.g. as seen in the description of plants in natural history texts, or the description of people in popular composition), enables both easy comparison (to other similar texts), and memorability.

Wendell (1891: 134) observed that coherence controls the internal structure of the paragraph, that is, the relation of each sentence to its contextual surroundings. Concerning the order of sentences, he maintained that "[m]atters closely connected in thought should be kept together" (p. 135). He also believed that coherence can be brought about by the use of similar constructions: "Phrases that are similar in significance should be similar in form" (p. 137). The third and final aspect of coherence for Wendell was the use of connectives. He reflected that these may not be needed in certain cases, namely, when the relations within the text are clear (p. 145).

In discussing cohesion, Scott and Denney (1895) referred to sequence and variety. The first of these is related to the ordering of the sentences, such ordering serving the thought of the paragraph. They commented that different orders are followed in different types of text, such as chronology in narration, or movement from the least to the most forcible point in expository or argumentation discourse. Concerning variety, Scott and Denney allowed that this was desirable, but must be balanced by the purpose of the paragraph and evident in structure, phraseology, ordering, and the method of paragraph construction utilized.

Scott and Denney (1895) believed that certain types of sentence (introductory, transitional, and summarizing) have very specific roles: for example, to introduce the topic sentence, to act as a bridge (internally within the paragraph), or to summarize one part before proceeding to another. They went on to state that the theme of the paragraph controls which sentences are emphasized through the use of connectives, word order, position of phrases, sentences, and higher discourse units. They pointed to the tools of inversion, parallel construction, repetition, subordination, and punctuation in serving the theme.

There does not appear to be anything too contentious concerning the above comments, particularly as cohesion was considered not only semantically, but also syntactically and contextually; Robin Markels offers some supporting discussion (Markels, 1983). There are however, three points which should be made before closing this section. Firstly, lexical cohesion and its role in creating textual cohesion was not given a particularly strong emphasis in the work noted above, there being a much stronger focus on grammatical cohesion. Halliday and Hasan (1976), in particular, stressed the lexical aspect of textual cohesion, and this subject is discussed in more detail in Chapter 6. Secondly, although the writers did mention connectives between paragraphs, as well as cohesion within the paragraph (their main focus), they did not differentiate these two types of cohesive patterns, or recognize that they might be quite distinct – indeed that certain types of cohesion are typically used either within or between paragraphs within the same genre. This subject is discussed in more detail in Chapters 5 and 6. Finally, there are potential terminological problems with the concepts of subordination and coordination, as used by these writers, as we will discuss in Chapter 4.

Bain (1890) and Scott and Denney (1895) did, at times, though tentatively, seem aware of register and genre differences between texts, in mentioning typically recurrent patterns in paragraph organization in certain kinds of text. However, I believe that the importance of this aspect of their work was neither fully appreciated by themselves, nor by later educators, who, too often began to prescribe a fixed inflexible unit, regardless of genre, purpose or readership when guiding learner-writers.

Overlooked Aspects of the 19th Century Work

It would be wrong to think that a consideration of the three terms "unity," "emphasis," and "coherence" fairly represents what writers of the 19th century were saying in relation to the paragraph. In what follows, I review three key issues, noted by one or more of the writers of this era, that seem to have been lost, over time. I suggest that the neglect of these points has had a negative effect on our understanding of the paragraph.

The Bigger Overarching Goal in Writing

What is the writer's goal in writing? What is the desired effect one is seeking? A theorist who considered this question, and did so in the light of the three characteristics of the paragraph was Wendell (1891). I believe Wendell (1891: 146) was the first among his 19th century peers to allow for the breaking of prescribed paragraph rules (on principled grounds) when an effect other than "firm precision" (i.e. clarity) for the reader was sought by the writer, citing the literary output of Heinrich Heine[10] as an example. Wendell (1891: 148) argued that Heine occasionally disregarded unity to create the effect he was seeking on his readers. The key goal or consideration in writing, Wendell argued, is the effect that one desires to make upon one's reader: simple adherence to a set of principles which produce "firm precision" is not enough. This is an astute comment, and possibly the first time in which the terms of the era were perceived as serving a higher governing maxim (namely, "firm precision" for Wendell). The recognition that this higher maxim may not be best served by simple adherence to certain predetermined criteria was an extension of this observation. Wendell was aware of the "dangerous dogmatism" (p. 130) implicit in his triad and stressed the importance of principles being guides (only), and that "fine good sense" (p. 131) was even more important in the composing process. There is some evidence that Wendell was actually quite disturbed at how his *unity*, *mass*, and *coherence* ideas were taken up and (ab)used by his colleagues (as reported by Robert Connors, 1997: 286).

In most academic writing the overarching principle of firm precision may well be the key driving force that affects how one writes. However, there was a tacit assumption among nearly all of the writers of this era that this was the only possible overarching principle that one may have in writing. Such a view is clearly inadequate. Digression, for example, was roundly condemned by scholars as it seemed to work against firm precision. I suggest that later generations have isolated the terms "unity," "emphasis," and "coherence" from the wider purpose which they were typically envisaged to serve. In effect, the terms have been cut from their moorings, and the concept of the overarching principle needs to be reconsidered again in our classrooms.

*Different Readers, Different Paragraphs, and
Discourse Awareness*

Many of the writers of the era related the paragraph to the sentence (as seen, for example, in some of the opening quotations of this chapter) and failed to seriously consider the paragraph in relation to the wider discourse, as mentioned earlier in the discussion about the topic sentence, and also as discussed in Chapter 1.[11] Perhaps the most important contribution of Scott and Denney (1895) in relation to the paragraph (and seen only with the benefit of hindsight) is found in the last chapter of their book, following from the discussion of their classifications and rules summarized above. In a comment that strongly echoes that of Johnson (1994) provided in Chapter 2 concerning the function of the *paragraphos*, Scott and Denney (1895: 93) made the point that the paragraph aids the reader in returning to the text: "The indented lines serve as landmarks for the reader's eye, enabling him to find his place again if he should happen to turn aside for a moment." However, they believed that this was not a sufficient reason (in and of itself) to explain paragraphing. In what is perhaps the clearest explanation up to this point in time of larger discourse organizing principles, and the role of the paragraph within these, Scott and Denney argued that the subdivisions of the thought of the essay may or may not correspond to the paragraph junctures, stating that the writer can choose to indent at smaller, or larger thoughts, as illustrated in the diagram below.

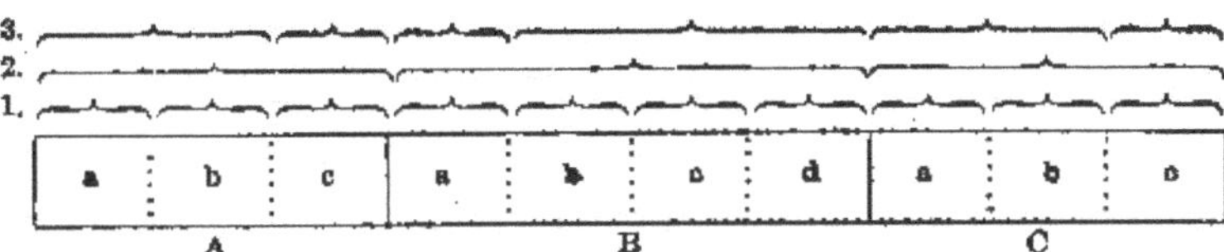

Figure 3.1. Diagrammatic Representation of Divisions of Thought within an Essay (Scott and Denney, 1895: 97)

Scott and Denney (1895) termed the larger and more important parts of the developing thought of the discourse "stadia" – represented here as A, B, and C. The three paragraphing options open to the writer are:

1. To paragraph "at every joint" – i.e. each and every substadia (a,b,c);
2. To paragraph "at the larger joints" – the stadia (A,B,C); and
3. To paragraph one time at the smaller, and another at the larger joints (for which only one possible instantiation is provided above). (Scott and Denney, 1895: 96)

They went on to take a stretch of discourse and divide it by each of the three methods they proposed, concluding that, "Each of the arrangements…is correct, and each may be called for by the nature of the work in which it occurs, or by the character of the readers to whom the writer is addressing himself" (p. 100). Problems in paragraphing, they state, occur when "a main articulation is brought into the middle of a paragraph" (*ibid.*), that is, when paragraphing occurs in the middle of a substadium, or combining a stadium and a substadium.

The concept of the stadium used by Scott and Denney (1895) is a positive and lasting legacy of their work (for further discussion on this and related terms, see Chapter 4). The idea that the same text can be paragraphed differently, but also acceptably, seems almost revolutionary if one reads some of the style manuals produced today. While Scott and Denney broke new ground in making these observations, this aspect of their work was never seriously considered by their peers, and I believe it has largely been forgotten by later educators. A key issue to note here is that Scott and Denney considered readers in the making of paragraph decisions – an issue largely overlooked by Lewis (see Chapter 2), and also by theorists of this era, who, like Lewis, focused on the written text, rather than why it was written, or for whom.

Product Prescriptivism versus Process Prescriptivism

The third issue which needs to be remembered is the focus of Bain. Was Bain (1890) prescribing practice, prescribing a product, or describing a product? Although some writers have suggested that Bain was more descriptivist than prescriptivist in his orientation, this is a difficult case to argue. Lunsford (1982: 297), for example, suggested that Bain's work contained only latent prescriptivism. However, one can hardly rewrite and reorder swathes of sentences from well-known writers and criticize their style,[12] and be considered only *latently* prescriptivist. In his chapter on the paragraph, Bain (1890) employs the word "should" in critically discussing the work of others 15 times. For example, in discussing a paragraph by Macaulay, he says "The second and third sentences should have run thus" (p. 115), using the same word another nine times in making general prescriptive statements – for example, "related topics should be kept close together" (p. 114). Bain was certainly not averse to applying his rules, and it seems almost incredible to us today that he attempted to edit the work of literary figures – as opposed, for example, to scientists who were not making a point clearly or students who were straying from a main idea. Making literary figures targets was to overextend the reach of his prototype paragraph, and thereby to expose his work to legitimate criticism.[13]

If we accept that Bain's work was prescriptivist in orientation, the question arises whether his focus was on the writing process or the writing product. Bain stated that he wanted his students to read the writings of well-known authors and to critique them: "I know of no better method than to prescribe passages containing good matter, but in some respects imperfectly worded, to be amended according to the laws and proprieties of style" (cited in Brereton, 1995: 317–318). Bain was quite against the giving of written assignments to his students:[14] his English classes were not writing classes; they were thinking classes in which he encouraged his students to apply various rules and maxims to different types of writing (Aley, 1998: 214). Further, as Lunsford (1998: 226) observed, Bain was totally against composition examination questions as we currently think of them, combining as they do thought and writing: Bain argued that exams should only test what has been taught. Therefore, the statement above, that Bain was prescriptivist, must be carefully delimited to his prescriptivist *analysis* of the written product, rather than taken to refer to the prescription of rules for writing. As observed by Lunsford (1982: 297), Bain conceived of his paragraph rules as "practical analytical tools." Whether or not Bain believed that his principles could be usefully employed by a writer in drafting written work is not really clear.

Lunsford (1982: 299) blamed later educators for misusing Bain's work, and it is fair to say that textbook writers coming after Bain have not been averse to applying his principles, or gross simplifications of them (rather rigidly) to the process of paragraph writing. Using an analogy, I suggest that Bain's rules were rather like a thermometer: they could be used to measure (or assess) a particular paragraph. A student, for example, might, by employing Bain's rules, notice that a particular writer had too many unnecessary cohesive connections between the sentences, and the *reading* on the thermometer would be affected accordingly (i.e. a defect or abnormality noted in the *health* of the paragraph). However, I believe that well-intentioned educators went on to misuse his rules as a water heater (continuing the analogy) to actually produce text. I suggest that one of the misreadings of Bain has been to use his rules (i.e. the thermometer to measure the health of a paragraph) to help students write composition (i.e. as a water heater to bring a paragraph up to the required temperature). This does not seem to have been Bain's intention.

What Should be Done with the 19th Century Terminology?

Is the terminological triad useful? Would teachers or students be any the poorer if we were to lose the three terms "unity," "coherence," and "emphasis" that have been discussed in this chapter? Some scholars have suggested that the terms be abandoned. In what follows the views of two terminology critics, Kitzhaber (1990) and Connors (1997), are noted, and their contributions to this debate analyzed.

Kitzhaber (1990: 139) criticized the concepts of unity, coherence, and emphasis as "static abstractions…[which]…substitute mechanical for organic conceptions, and therefore distort the real nature of writing." He went on to argue that abstractions oversimplify, particularly when viewed as ingredients of a composition, and that focusing on them minimizes the view of language as communication and the role of rhetoric in meeting social needs. Adherence to abstractions, Kitzhaber argued, is to reduce composition to an academic exercise, existing in a social vacuum (which, unfortunately, is what school and college writing often is).

Connors (1997: 270) used the same term, "static abstraction," in a very similar way to Kitzhaber, though he discussed it in far more detail. Connors believed that the abstractions are static in the sense that they are theoretically contextualized, paradigmatic, and absolute, and in the sense of being merely a label on the final product. They are abstract in that they are general. Connors argued that the concepts, in being both static (non-dynamic) and abstract (non-specific), are not helpful in composing paragraphs, though he vacillated about their value in editing, as discussed below.

Connors (1997: 291) suggested that the appeal of static abstractions has been for teachers, not students, essentially because they sounded impressive, and provided some structure to what is, otherwise, a content-less subject area (written composition). Whether teachers are so swayed is, of course, debatable! He built his argument against the value of the static abstractions by making four observations. The first of these is the same as a point made earlier on, namely, that the meaning of a static abstraction is actually the response of the reader to the text. Summarizing, approvingly, the views of Louis Milic (Milic, 1967), Connors (1997: 294) pointed out that "static abstractions are based in the subjective responses of the reader rather than being in the affective domain of the writer." Secondly, he argued that in composition, "[r]eal writers do not process their intentions through such abstract and isolated items" (p. 294), referring to empirical work to support this. Knoblauch (1981: 56) had also remarked that unity may emerge through the writing process, rather than being a controlling factor affecting writing from the outset. Thirdly, the idea that the three abstractions (unity, coherence, and emphasis) can be viewed independently of one another, Connors (1997: 294) argued, is problematic, appealing to work by Henry Lathrop

(Lathrop, 1920) in support of his skepticism. In fairness to Bain (1890), it should be remembered that he did make an effort, at times, to connect the three notions. For example, in referring to a paragraph by Dryden, he commented that "Explicit reference and Indication of the Theme tend to secure the Unity of the Paragraph" (p. 114). Lathrop (1920) went one step further, and argued that students cannot apply first a test of unity, then a test of coherence, and then a test of emphasis to a piece of writing, as to do so is to view these concepts as somehow independent of each other. Lathrop suggested that they are, in fact, interdependent: emphasis being an aspect of coherence, and coherence an aspect of unity. Finally, Connors argued that the generality of an abstraction such as *unity* makes it, in reality, "useless as prescription" (p. 292). He is not alone in holding this view. The problem is, as Knoblauch (1981: 54) realized, if one defines a concept such as unity broadly, it loses "descriptive utility"; and if it is defined narrowly, then too many (good) paragraphs seem to fall outside the borders, in effect challenging the need for and value of the concept.

While Connors (1997) was fairly absolute in his condemnation of the value of static abstractions as useful concepts to guide the writing process, he seemed to vacillate on their value when discussing them as aids in evaluating text and in editing, as the following quotations make clear:

> Quotation 1: *"I am not proposing that good writing does not have the qualities of Unity, Coherence and Emphasis. Of course it does. I hope this book does."* (p. 291)
> Quotation 2: Static abstractions may *"describe good writing."* (p. 291)
> Quotation 3: *"Static abstractions…do not help students…edit their own work."* (p. 295)

In the first two quotations, Connors suggests that static abstractions are not solely created by the reader, that is, that they are not only a matter of reader response. Clearly, the idea that the reader *creates* abstractions (regardless of textual considerations) can be carried too far; otherwise, Connors could not expect or hope that the readers of his book would respond to it in certain preferred ways. Connors seems aware of the danger of the pendulum swinging too far over to an exclusively reader-orientated interpretation of the abstractions, in making these comments.

Having made these observations about the inherent qualities of text, one would have expected Connors to have left the door open for the abstractions to be useful in editing, as this seems a logical development of his point. So why did he exclude their value in editing, as he does in the third quotation? Connors went about justifying this position in the following way. He argued that (historically) the abstractions had meaning (for students), but they no longer did so at the time when he was writing. Commenting on the pre-1970s era, Connors stated: "So long as most students had read a few books and could vaguely grasp what Unity or Coherence looked like in practice, static abstractions were at least defensible" (p. 294). In saying this, Connors was arguing that an abstraction has meaning when it is contextualized; and specifically, in this case, he is suggesting that the models (i.e. texts) to which students from a previous era were exposed helped them contextualize the same or similar meaning of an abstraction such as unity. However, he then went on to argue that after the 1970s abstraction-based pedagogy was less tenable, essentially because students were reading less complex materials, such as *Jaws, Peanuts*, high school textbooks, and *TV Guide*.[15]

It is probably true that Peter Benchley's paragraphing of *Jaws* or the paragraphing of *TV Guide* or any other popular magazine, not to mention the paragraphing of textbooks, is less varied and complex than the reading material studied by students of previous generations. However, in stating that the paragraphs of textbooks do not embody a characteristic such as unity or coherence is hard to follow, as is Connor's implicit argument that the collective reading of such texts does not contextualize these terms for a group of readers, who can then draw upon them in editing or assessing writing.[16] To believe that the writing of a different era helped students of that era better appreciate the abstraction of unity is to tie unity to specific exemplars. I suggest it would be safer to argue that the concept of unity is shaped by experience, rather than by a specific model, as educated readers and writers of English today will surely have different ideas of paragraph unity than would educated readers and writers in the 19th century. Indeed, as mentioned earlier, the concept of unity should probably be understood rather differently in different genres and historical contexts.

Is there a place for the terminological triad in editing? Tentatively, I would argue that there is, though with the following reservations. Firstly, and following on from the point made in the previous paragraph it must be acknowledged in our classrooms that these terms may be understood differently by different writers and readers, at different times and in different contexts. Indeed, such variety of interpretation makes this area a potentially fruitful one for classroom discussion with our students, as they come across various texts: old and new, fact and fiction, classic and popular. Secondly, I would argue (following Wendell) for the need for the terminological / conceptual triad to be grounded, and in addition, considered interdependently, not independently (following Lathrop, 1920), that is, considered in relation to the overarching purpose of the writer when "firm precision" is the goal in writing, and also in relation to each other. Finally, I would suggest learners be encouraged to consider how other, different, abstract terms may be more appropriate measuring tools to evaluate paragraphs when writers have different goals to the creating of "firm precision" for their readers. In such cases, the terms can be set aside, when it seems that they are not relevant, and other characteristics might be seen to be suitable substitutes for them.

Conclusion

The influence of the 19th century paragraph theorists on later generations of students, teachers, and academics has been immense. William Coles, Jr.'s definition of the paragraph in the *World Book Encyclopedia*, for example, looks, to all intents and purposes, to be a 19th century creation:

> A paragraph is a section of written work that consists of one or more sentences constructed and arranged to function as a unit…. An effective paragraph must be unified, ordered and complete. A paragraph is unified when all the sentences contribute to creating a single idea…. (Coles, 2002: 15)

As regards the wide-ranging influence of Bain's work on the paragraph, Connors (1997: 248–249) claimed that, "There is literally no textbook during the period 1895–1950 that does not use some recognizable version of [his]…organic model," and Rodgers (1965) believed that the work of most of Bain's peers was (simply) to elaborate and enforce Bain's work (both on the paragraph and his famous modes of discourse). More recently, Hayes (2003: 2) has argued that "Bain's [paragraphing] rules have become our rules, and most contemporary freshman rhetorics restate them in more or less the same fashion."

It is clear that the theorists of the 19th century were logic-oriented and text-focused, paying little attention to the writer's purpose in writing the text, or to reader expectations: the fact that Bain was a logician, rather than a rhetorician, was not lost on his critics (see, e.g. Rodgers 1965). As documented above, both Scott and Denney (1895) and Wendell (1891) made insightful comments concerning the reader, the wider discourse, and the writer. However, their comments were tentative in many ways, and rather undeveloped. For example, while Scott and Denney (1895) attempted to place the paragraph within the wider discourse, they did not consider how different paragraphing decisions performed at different stadia levels would impact the inclusion or exclusion of particular phrases or cohesive tools or lexis, or the presence or absence of a minor topic sentence in any particular paragraph. Further, though Wendell (1891) recognized that terms needed to be anchored to a governing principle, he did not consider, in any detail, what these different principles could be, or how terms may be more or less valuable in serving these principles.

Over time, Bain's (1890) product-prescriptive terminology began to be used by materials writers and teachers as an aid to paragraph writing, as opposed to paragraph product evaluation. This adaptation was highly questionable, but went largely unchallenged until the 1960s (as discussed in the next chapter). While the abstract terms associated with the 19th century can certainly be misunderstood, and misapplied, I have argued in this chapter that they may still be of some value for students and teachers today, though only if handled carefully, and contextually. We can safely conclude, nonetheless, that the terminological triad cannot be the mainstay of paragraphing pedagogy.

Notes

1   Angus (1862) was the first writer to discuss the paragraph, and his views are therefore discussed in some detail within this chapter. However, as Tebeaux (2011: 222) observed, his work quickly fell under the shadow of Alexander Bain's more comprehensive study (Bain, 1866), published just a few years after his own.

2   Bain actually had seven rules, but the first of these is, essentially, a definition. In his later and expanded discussion of the paragraph, Bain (1890) provided 25 points, or rules, which he discussed typically, though not always, by exemplification through the provision of an example paragraph, part of a paragraph, or a series of paragraphs. In this book, I typically refer to this updated and enlarged text when discussing Bain's work.

3   For example, a writer may wish to inform and persuade, *infomercials* being a good example of this dual purpose writing. Arthur Walzer believed that multiple purpose writing is the norm in writing: "all texts pursue multiple purposes" (Walzer, 1991: 121).

4   This is, admittedly, my own personal and subjective interpretation of the writer's original intention.

5   On the relationship between reader skills and awareness of main idea, see the discussions of James Coomber (Coomber, 1975: 265) and Dan Donlan (Donlan, 1980: 135).

5   Witte (1983: 316) defined this as "a topic which controls or governs the meaning of the topics of individual sentences."

6   Paul Butler suggests that concepts such as cohesion may be in our responses, rather than in the writer's text as such (Butler, 2008).

7   With regard to prior knowledge, Witte (1983) notes that this is particularly important when more inferencing is required in understanding a text, that is, when the topic itself may not be explicitly stated.

8   This is an interesting point hinted at by Knoblauch (1981), who argued that a paragraph from Neil Postman may be understood somewhat differently depending upon whether one reads the opening sentences of the following paragraph before summarizing the previous paragraph.

9   Admittedly, these are title summaries, rather than summary sentences, but they could be changed to sentences quite easily.

10   Heinrich Heine (1797–1856) was a German literary figure.

11   Although some writers considered the paragraph to be a composition in miniature, there was still a tendency to consider the paragraph without reference to the larger discourse.

12   Writers criticized include Macaulay, Dryden, Channing, and Tennyson. One example of Bain's criticism is: "In Tennyson's Duke of Wellington, there is an occasional dislocation of topics, that impairs the influence of the Ode as a whole" (Bain, 1890: 120).

13   George Gopen's comment concerning Bain's revision of a piece of writing by Bacon is wry and to the point: "Bain assumes there exists a 'best' way of arranging Bacon's words. He predicates that on the assumption that he knows the truth behind what Bacon was trying to say" (Gopen, 2004: 126).

14   Bain, as cited by John Harned, stated: "the composition of themes involves the burden of finding matter; and belongs rather to classes of science or other departments, than to a class of English" (Harned, 1985: 48).

15   Connors (1997) specifically mentions each of these text types.

16   If Connors (1997) had meant to say that students do not read, then all well and good, as this would have helped establish his case; but he did not say this.

4 Teaching and Learning Paragraphing (II): The 1960s

Introduction

It was not until the 1960s that the first serious rumblings against the adequacy of the terminological triad to help understand or write paragraphs were felt. The most significant shift in orientation of the era was, doubtless, the move away from a focus on the *what* of the paragraph (in terms of its abstract qualities) towards a consideration of the pedagogical *how* (in helping students write paragraphs), in addition to a consideration of the *why* of paragraphing and an interest in writer paragraphing decisions. Alongside these developments, the 1960s and 1970s witnessed the first serious attempts by scholars to consider the paragraph's identity within the larger discourse within which it occurs, and in relation to other supra-sentential textual entities.

While the 1960s witnessed significant developments in paragraphing pedagogy, it should not be forgotten that a number of traditional 19th century orientations to its study were maintained. Foremost among these was the attempt to relate paragraphs to sentences, as is clearly evident in Becker's (1965, 1966) and Christensen's (1963, 1965, 1966, 1967, 1968, 1973) work. Secondly, the overtly prescriptivist orientation to the paragraph remained dominant, particularly in treatments by John Lord (Lord, 1964) and Christensen (1965, 1966). Becker (1965, 1966) however, focused more on the reader than the writer in his work on the paragraph, and Rodgers' (1966a,b) work was the first descriptivist approach to paragraphing.

Before looking at the ideas and evaluating the work of four of the most important writers of the era, it is worth highlighting a point noted above – the focus on the *how* of paragraphing during the 1960s. This significant shift in emphasis marked a move away from what Richard Young (1978: 31) termed the "vitalist" assumptions of composition, the idea inherited from the Romantics, that little could be said about teaching good style in composition classes, style being dependent on the "natural powers of the mind and the uniqueness of the creative act...." Some of the writers of the 19th century mentioned in Chapter 3 hinted at their vitalist assumptions in casting doubt on the adequacy of the rules they put forward to actually help develop writing skills. For example, Angus (1862: 413) commented that adherence to his rules was insufficient: an "earnest heart," reading good models, and practice were also needed; and Wendell (1891: 131) argued that "fine good sense" was actually more important than the paragraph principles he discussed. The educational context of the 1960s and 1970s was clearly anti-vitalist, and Lord, Becker, and Christensen were all determined to take the mystery out of paragraph writing, and to replace it with practical guidelines and support for learner-writers.

Lord: The Paragraph: Structure and Style

Lord's (1964) contribution to paragraphing pedagogy in the 1960s has been almost totally forgotten,[1] but needs to be documented in this book. Lord was interested in considering and developing students' exposition or argumentative paragraphing, and increasing their understanding of the role of the paragraph in indicating "a new unit of development" (p. v) within text. His pamphlet on paragraphing contained some new ideas, particularly in relation to reader interest, along with his three dimensional view of the paragraph (explained below). There are a number of similarities between Lord's work and that of the three key paragraph figures of the 1960s, though it is impossible to know whether his work influenced them.[2] In terms of influences on Lord's work, it was argued by Rodgers (1966a) that he took the concept of vertical movement (abstract / particular) within the paragraph, discussed in more detail below, from Wendell Johnson (Johnson, 1946).

Lord (1964) considered paragraphs from two perspectives: structure and style. In what follows, I summarize his ideas.

In his discussion of structure, Lord differentiated the integrity of the paragraph from its movement. By "integrity" he meant the features of good paragraphs,[3] including the presence of topic sentences, transitions and the like. Paragraphs which did not exhibit integrity, as Lord (1964: 5) understood it, were termed "informal," and considered to be only paragraph-resembling units. By "movement," Lord meant the steps (e.g. general to specific) by which the thought in a text was developed. He believed that integrity and movement are interdependent, though can be studied separately.

Regarding movement, Lord (1964) differentiated the "analytical" paragraph (typically following a *topic sentence–developers–terminator* pattern) from the "synthetic" (usually following a *developers–topic sentence / terminator* pattern). The key difference between these two types was the direction of movement, governed by the movement of thought. Lord noted that synthetic movement is particularly appropriate if one expects some resistance to what one is writing (e.g. in argument), analytical movement being more common in expository writing. He analyzed various paragraphs and commented on their coherence, the role of lexical repetition, substitution (i.e. use of grammatical reference, and synonyms) and function words in helping a paragraph hang together. He also described how subordination contributes to the movement of a paragraph, a key aspect of Christensen's (1965) theory (see below). Lord (1964: 30–31) believed that a synthetic or analytical treatment of a subject may be executed rationally or emotionally, which in turn may be oriented by time and space.

In discussing style, the second major perspective of paragraph analysis in his thought, Lord (1964: 46) considered grammar, rhythm, diction, and interest. He believed that tone (an aspect of diction) is achieved through careful choice of lexical items (including the choice of words with particular connotations), and considered it to be related to subordination: "...a shift in subordination probably will alter the tone" (*ibid.*). Regarding rhythm, Lord argued that this is created by grammatical choice, expansion (i.e. elaboration), punctuation, and word choice (i.e. choosing a word for its particular rhythm). In discussing diction and interest, Lord observed how abstract words and abstract thought and concrete words and concrete thought are related to each other, and how mixing between these creates interest. He commented, "...all good writing is a constant weaving up and down between the concrete and the abstract, as well as a constant forward movement from a beginning through a middle to an end" (p. 73).

For Lord (1964: 74) the paragraph had three dimensions: length (i.e. the purpose being developed); breadth (i.e. tone, attitude); and height (the movement between abstract and concrete). This "dimensional" view of the paragraph is perhaps the most original contribution of Lord to the theorizing of the paragraph. Lord's mapping of an example paragraph according to its "height" is provided below.

> *Experts in classical anthropology, like experts in other fields, dispute* **innumerable questions** *of fact and of interpretation which the layman can only pass over in respectful silence.* **One of the thornier questions** *seems to be* **whether myth or ritual came first.**

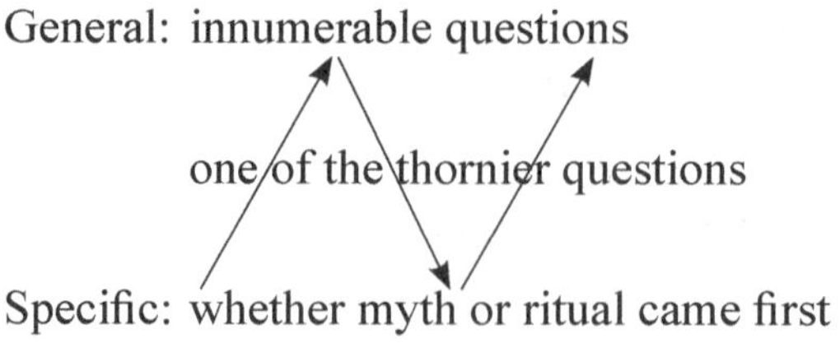

General: innumerable questions

one of the thornier questions

Specific: whether myth or ritual came first   (Lord, 1964: 76–77)

According to Lord's (1964: 77) description, the arrows in the above diagram "...represent the thought processes in alternating flow of current between these two extremes; they are what we mean by 'interest'; they represent mental activity." His belief that such movement between general and specific is critical to the development of reader interest is a rather unique suggestion.

Lord (1964) concluded his treatment of the paragraph by discussing how paragraphs may be linked by certain transitional words or expressions and how different types of paragraph are related to each other: a paragraph may be introductory, serve as a conclusion, be subordinate to other paragraphs, or coordinate[4] with other paragraphs. He believed (p. 88) that the use of certain expressions (e.g. *so much for X; now, as for Y*) may indicate these relations. He also commented that paragraphs can be combined if they cover the same thought.

We cannot say that Lord's work heralded the renaissance of interest in the paragraph in the 1960s since it received such little attention, critical or otherwise. However, he touched on certain issues (specifically, subordination, lexical cohesion, and the interplay of form and style) that were all felt to be important, to a greater or lesser extent, by one or more of the better known writers of this period.

Three key articles on the paragraph appeared within two years of Lord's (1964) work, followed, in turn, by a valuable symposium piece in which the authors of these articles elaborated on their own theories, defended them from various attacks, and interacted with the views of others.[5] In what follows, the three key theories are summarized, criticisms of each are noted in turn, and comments are made on their uptake and impact.

Christensen: A Generative Rhetoric of the Paragraph

"The typical paragraph is but a cumulative sentence writ large."
(Christensen, 1973: 169)

Christensen's generative rhetoric, has, occasionally, been confused with Noam Chomsky's generative grammar (e.g. Chomsky, 1957, 1965), and for obvious terminological reasons. However, as observed by Philip Cook (Cook, 1968: 1168–1169), the term "generative" for Christensen meant "productive," in the sense that grammatical forms can generate content (explained in more detail below). This understanding of "generative" must be differentiated from that as used in Chomsky's generative grammar, where the term "generate" means "enumerate," in the sense that all the sentence patterns of a language can be generated from a small set of grammatical rules specifying core patterns and how these can be expanded, reduced, or otherwise transformed in allowable ways. Christensen sought to marry grammatical form and rhetoric, that is, he postulated that grammatical form generates rhetorical possibilities. Christensen applied his theory first to the sentence (Christensen, 1963) and then to the paragraph (Christensen, 1965). It was further extended by Richard Larson (Larson, 1971), Michael Grady (Grady, 1972), and Frank D'Angelo (D'Angelo, 1974) to full texts, that is, to the composition. In what follows, Christensen's (1965, 1966) paragraph theory is summarized, and then various responses to it are noted. In keeping with the focus on the paragraph, it is not my intention to elaborate in any detail on his work on the sentence. However, a basic understanding of this work is required, and therefore given, because of the sentence-to-paragraph orientation of his theory.

Christensen's theory of the paragraph was (unapologetically) extrapolated from his view of the sentence, and such an approach (sentence to paragraph orientation) is strongly reminiscent of Bain's (1890) perspective, along with some of the other early composition rhetoricians' work documented in Chapter 3. However, Christensen drew a sharp distinction between his approach and Bain's, and legitimately so. In his symposium piece on the paragraph Christensen (1966: 61) acknowledged that both theories were sentence-based. However, while Bain's paragraph theory extrapolated the role of subject and predicate in the sentence to topic sentence and supporting sentences in the paragraph (respectively), Christensen's own theory was quite different. The relevant extrapolation for him was: "the topic sentence of a paragraph is to the supporting sentences what the base clause of a cumulative sentence is to its free modifiers" (Christensen, 1966: 61). Christensen (1963: 156) defined a *cumulative sentence* as one in which additions to the main clause modify it, explicate it, or exemplify it. These additions may appear in initial, medial, or final position of the sentence, though his preference (stylistically) was for final position of these free modifiers.[6] The subject of a sentence must have a predicate: however, a simple or main clause can stand on its own, and so too can a topic sentence (though when alone it is not considered to be, or called, a topic sentence). It is the possibilities for expansion that are generative in Christensen's model. Bain's sentence–paragraph analogy, Christensen would have contended, did not contain this generative element, having as it did *only* an obligatory element.

It is useful at this point to consider an example. In the model cumulative sentence below, which is an abbreviated form derived from one written by Sinclair Lewis,[7] Christensen (1963) exemplified his generative rhetoric of the sentence. The base clause is labeled 1.

Model Cumulative Sentence
    1 He shook his hands,
      2 a quick shake,
        3 fingers down,
          4 like a pianist.

Obviously, the writer could have placed a period at the end of the simple clause, and the result would have been a simple sentence: *He shook his hands.* However, the author added a number of free modifiers in final sentence position: *a quick shake* is a noun cluster, *fingers down* a verb cluster (with its own subject), and *like a pianist* a prepositional phrase. The numbering and indentation pattern signify multiple levels of addition: the third element being unlike the second (i.e. not coordinate to it), is labeled 3, and the fourth element is subordinate to the third – related only to the first clause through the second and third elements. As there is no parallelism between the additional elements, each is added at a different grammatical level (hence the sequential numbering), also indicated through the indentation pattern. The additions elaborate the meaning of the initial clause, and Christensen (1963: 160) argued that it is the knowledge of such possible additions that can give the student "...insight into that elusive thing we call style." As James Green observed, Christensen saw writing quality as a "...function of the relationship between form and content" (Green, 1969: 893).

The four principles which Christensen developed in relation to the sentence were, he argued, also applicable to the paragraph (1965: 145). These principles are noted below.

1. Addition
   Addition to the topic sentence results in a paragraph being formed.
2. Direction of modification / movement
   The writer (and later on the reader of the text) discerns the relations between sentences (a backward and forward movement).
3. Level of generality
   Developmental sentences usually operate at a lower level of generality (i.e. a higher level of specificity) than the sentence added to.
4. Texture
   Addition of more sentences to the topic sentence makes the texture of the text denser.

Christensen (1965: 146, 147) provided the two paragraphs below as exemplars of two different (pure) types of paragraph, though observing that the most common paragraph sequence is mixed (i.e. combining both coordinate and subordinate sequences).

Coordinate sequence paragraph[8]

1 *This is the essence of the religious spirit – the sense of power, beauty, greatness, truth infinitely beyond one's own reach, but infinitely aspired to.*

  2 *It invests men with a pride in a purpose and with humility in accomplishment.*

  2 *It is the source of all true tolerance, for in its light all men see other men as they see themselves, as being capable of being more than they are, and yet falling short, inevitably, of what they can imagine human opportunities to be.*

  2 *It is the supporter of human dignity and pride and the dissolver of the vanity.*

  2 *And it is the very creator of the scientific spirit; for without the aspiration to understand and control the miracle of life, no man would have sweated in a laboratory or tortured his brain in the exquisite search after truth.*

Subordinate sequence paragraph[9]

1 *The process of learning is essential to our lives.*

  2 *All higher animals seek it deliberately.*

    3 *They are inquisitive and they experiment.*

      4 *An experiment is a sort of harmless trial run off some action which we shall have to make in the real world; and this, whether it is made in the laboratory by scientists or by fox-cubs outside their earth.*

      5 *The scientist experiments and the cub plays; both are learning to correct their errors of judgment in a setting in which errors are not fatal.*

      6 *Perhaps this is what gives them both their air of happiness and freedom in their activities.*

Christensen (1965) began his treatment of the paragraph by observing that textbook coverage at the time at which he was writing was essentially Bainian in its orientation, namely, the provision of the topic sentence followed by its development through utilization of one of the methods of paragraph development. He criticized this method as being unrealistic: firstly, it is not how writers go about writing; and secondly, actual paragraphs utilize a variety of methods of development (p. 144). After drawing the parallelism between the sentence and paragraph, noted above, he went on to make the following nine claims concerning the paragraph. I number these for convenience and summarize them in the next section, before commenting on them in more detail in the section that follows.

Christensen's Claims

1. "The paragraph may be defined as a sequence of structurally related sentences." (p. 145)

The sentences within a paragraph may be related to one another by coordination or subordination, and if a sentence is not so related, "The paragraph has begun to drift from its moorings, or the writer has unwittingly begun a new paragraph" (*ibid.*).

2. "The top sentence of the sequence is the topic sentence."
(p. 146)

In Christensen's characterization, the topic sentence is the sentence on which the other sentences depend relationally (these being subordinate or coordinate to it).

3. "The topic sentence is nearly always the first sentence of the sequence." (p. 146)

While recognizing the existence of inductive and deductively organized paragraphs, Christensen believed, based on his own analysis of "many scores of paragraphs" (*ibid.*), that the topic sentence is very typically placed at the beginning of the paragraph.

He suggested, however, that it may be more or less explicit, possibly only "a mere sign" (p. 146), and it may not even be a full sentence. The key issue for Christensen is that "...the reader gets the signal and the writer remembers the signal he has called" (*ibid.*).

4. "Simple sequences are of two sorts – coordinate and subordinate." (p. 146)

It is on this subject, Christensen argued, that the parallel between the sentence and paragraph is particularly clear. The two-level cumulative sentence can be compared to the coordinate sequence paragraph, where each sentence following the topic sentence is coordinate to it, this often being clearly indicated by structural identity at the beginning of the sentence, though the sentences "need only be like enough for the reader to place them" (p. 148). The multilevel cumulative sentence, on the other hand, is analogous to the subordinate sequence paragraph, in which each sentence is subordinate to the previous sentence. In such a case, there is no structural parallelism, and each following sentence is only related to the topic sentence through all of the interposing sentences. Different structural methods of development are used when adding subordinate sequences (rather than coordinate sequences), thereby making the identification of unity, coherence, and emphasis more difficult in these types of sequence, when compared to coordinate sequences.

5. "The two sorts of sequence combine to produce the commonest sort – the mixed sequence." (p. 148)

It is here, in Christensen's view, that the term "generative" finds it fullest meaning in his theory: "The teacher can, with perfect naturalness, suggest the addition of subordinate sentences to clarify and of coordinate sentences to emphasize or to enumerate" (*ibid.*). Christensen proceeded to analyze five paragraphs, all following the mixed sequence pattern he describes, going on to offer suggestions as to why writers adopted the particular pattern or approach to the subject that they did.

6. "Some paragraphs have no top, [sic] no topic, sentence."
(p. 152)

This point must be taken as an exception to points 2 and 3 above. Christensen elaborated on two types of paragraph in which there may be no topic sentence. The first is where there is no level I – no superordinate sentence. The second is where the topic sentence is to be found in the previous paragraph (arbitrarily so), or where the previous paragraph is, in fact, the topic sentence.

7. "Some paragraphs have sentences at the beginning or at the end that do not belong to the sequence." (p. 153)

Reminiscent of Bain's (1890: 108) "unless obviously preparatory" comment (see Chapter 3), regarding material that may occur in paragraph-initial position but not be the topic sentence, Christensen allowed for introductory or transitional sentences to precede the sequence of the paragraph, these sentences operating, as it were, outside the body of the paragraph. Similarly, he allowed for extra-sequential material to follow on from the paragraph sequence, in a conclusion. He suggested that such an ending may function as a conclusion to a series of paragraphs, not just for the one in which it occurs. Noting that the conclusion typically operates at a higher level of generality to preceding sentences, he considered that it may be thought of as a topic sentence and that in such as case there may be two topic sentences, one at the end and one at the beginning of the paragraph.

8. "Some paragraphing is illogical." (p. 154)

Christensen commented that some paragraphs may be compound (i.e. having two level 1 sentences), and that others are "simply illogical" (p. 155), breaking a sequence at a point which is very difficult to justify (within his theory).

9. "Punctuation should be by the paragraph, not by the sentence." (p. 155)

Christensen was critical of cases where coordinating material that occupied the same level within the paragraph (e.g. two propositions at level 2) had the same form and intent but were punctuated differently (e.g. one proposition was a compound sentence and the other was a simple sentence). Accordingly, Christensen argued that the structure of the paragraph should determine the punctuation of individual sentences within it.

Christensen (1965: 156) concluded his discussion by stating that the identity of the paragraph as a logical unit jostles with its identity as a visual unit, and that the possible lack of concordance between the two is problematic and "...has kept us from making sense of the paragraphs we encounter in our reading." He cautiously added that his paragraphing claims are real, but he did not claim, though he admitted that he would have liked to, that his structural model covered good paragraphs (alone) – and only good paragraphs.

Critique of Christensen

Christensen's generative theory attracted many favorable, and also critical comments, though most of these (whether favorable or not) were made in relation to the sentence theory, not the paragraph theory, and so not directly relevant to our focus here. In what follows, I survey some of the more critical responses to Christensen's paragraph theory, before commenting on uptake of his model.

What generates?

Christensen (1963: 156) claimed that "the mere form of the sentence generates ideas" and, as mentioned previously, with regard to the paragraph, "The teacher can, with perfect naturalness, suggest the addition of subordinate sentences to clarify and of coordinate sentences to emphasize or to enumerate" (p. 148). The form of the paragraph (for Christensen) generated ideas: the possibility of adding coordinate and subordinate sentences is generative. He has been challenged by a number of writers over this idea.

Firstly, Rick Eden and Ruth Mitchell observed that the orienting sentence – the sentence upon which other sentences depend in some way in Christensen's model – is often discovered as a writer writes: "In rough drafts the sentences which would work best as orienting sentences of paragraphs often turn up last" (Eden and Mitchell, 1986: 422). In making this comment, Eden and Mitchell strike at the very heart of Christensen's generative theory: if the orienting sentence is not fixed at the beginning, but comes to be in the course of writing, then one must, of course, question its fundamental role in the development of the paragraph. Rather than seeing the paragraph form as generative, Eden and Mitchell (1986: 422) preferred to see paragraphing as a tool to be used in revising written work.

Secondly, David Stevens questioned the idea that the form (itself) generates, arguing that it does so only secondarily, likening form to a carpenter's tools (Stevens, 1967: 174); see also Vivian Horn who argued essentially the same point (Horn, 1972: 413). While the presence or absence of tools certainly affects what a carpenter and a writer can do, Stevens (1967: 176) argued that it is the writer, and his / her "close observation" or introspection that generates – not the form itself. Clearly a writer needs to be aware that sentences can be added to existing sentences (at different levels of generality as per the Christensen theory) and to consider their placement in the paragraph. However, to argue that this form, or knowledge of the form, in and of itself, *generates* is certainly a contentious claim: the writer must, after all, have something to add. Rodgers (1966b: 76) called *generative* in Christensen's theory "opaque," adding that he was unsure as to whether it referred to a logical generation or psychological generation.

This observation leads on to another issue. Put simply, what stops generation? There seems to be nothing in Christensen's model to halt the (possibly) never-ending addition of free modifiers (to base clauses) or coordinate and / or subordinate sentences to a topic sentence within a paragraph. The fact that sentences and paragraphs do end has to be accounted for, and in this sense the model is incomplete.[10] If the decision to end a paragraph is dependent on either the writer's capacity to generate, or the reader's capacity to assimilate the information, then clearly something outside the *form* of the paragraph is affecting the process of generation. If, though, it is specific paragraph discourse constraints and discourse norms that affect such decisions, then it would appear more reasonable to argue that it is the *specific discourse form of the paragraph* which both generates and stops generation – rather than the form of the paragraph per se.

Subjectivity, the choice of model, and its relevance to other text types

Christensen (1966: 66) argued that professional writing is the only valid source for the appreciation of rhetorical principles, and that inductive study of paragraphs will turn up some "odd fish," that is, examples which are not helpful in an educational context and which teachers may wish to discount as good models for their students. His decision to reject certain paragraphs as precedents, and accept others as models, was, he argued, based on their effectiveness in "...accommodating the writer's subject to the situation and the reader – and what is aesthetically satisfying – as orderly, proportioned, and architectonic" (p. 66). The problem with this view is that what is aesthetically satisfying is a largely subjective judgment. His dismissal of the long clause, which he termed the mark of an "inept style" (Christensen, 1968: 576), and his identification of a mature style with the extensive use of free modifiers – particularly in final position – attracted serious criticism.

Sabina Johnson argued that the whole of Christensen's theory was tied to what Christensen believed to be quality writing, in short, that it was subjective (Johnson, 1969). Further, when this subjective preference was applied *carte blanche*, beyond the specific type of writing that Christensen derived his model from, Johnson stated, the model becomes untenable. To support her argument, Johnson (1969: 161) produced a paragraph by James Baldwin (containing many subordinations), which she referred to as "sandwiching." She commented favorably on the style: "Sandwiching creates a parenthetic style, one that gives the illusion of approximating well-turned speech. **It does not flow as Christensen would like sentences to**" (*ibid.*, emphasis added). If Christensen had had different tastes, Johnson (1969: 163) argued, his rhetoric would, accordingly, have been different.[11] She believed that Christensen's theories were presented in more absolute terms than warranted by his specific observations and his limited stylistic preferences. Johnson was not alone in expressing these concerns. With regard to the choice of a prototype, Coe (1998: 135) commented on the favored status given to a particular style of writing by Christensen, and Anthony Wolk, in a detailed statistics-based analysis of paragraphs (Wolk, 1970), observed that David Halberstam (the writer whom Christensen lauded as an excellent model), is quite extreme in his writing style (when compared with other published writers), and as such perhaps not the best model upon which to build a theory.

Regarding Christensen's (1963: 160) extension of his theory from fiction and description to other types of writing, Joseph Schwartz commented on the dangers of extrapolating a fiction-based analysis (and model) to a non-fiction style: "Fiction raises hosts of problems which are not relevant to the writing of non-fiction" (Schwartz, 1968: 41). Schwartz (1968: 42) also observed the dangers of making the modifier the focus of the sentence model, arguing that such could lead to "a crippling dependence upon qualifiers when precision may call for better word choice in the first place." This comment can easily be extended to the paragraph as well: an unhealthy focus on coordinating and subordinating sentences may detract from careful consideration of the thought and wording of the topic sentence (if there is one), or making one's meaning very specific in the first place. Susan MacDonald suggested that one of the problems in extending Christensen's model to other text types was that it generalized the concept of specificity, which, she argued, varies across time, place, and different types of writing (MacDonald, 1986). She observed how, in sentence development, Christensen's preference for subordination is for increasing sensory specificity (MacDonald 1986: 196). However, this development, she argued, cannot be assumed (by default) to be desirable in other types of writing: the type of supportive evidence present in a novel is different from that in college writing, for example (pp. 197–198). This being so, MacDonald stated, militates against the broad-brush application of Christensen's generative rhetoric, built as it is on fiction writing and the particular types of development that might be used in such text. She suggested that the real need for writing teachers is to consider context when thinking about textual development, that is, to "teach specificity in relation to audience, purpose and the writing situation" (p. 202).

Christensen, while recognizing the prevalence of mixed-sentence paragraphs (i.e. paragraphs which contain both coordinating and subordinating sentences to the topic sentence), did not consider whether different combinations or types of sentence arrangement are more or less appropriate or common in different types of writing, whether that variation be in the relational patterns between the sentences or the number of sentences so generated (see also Larson, 1967: 20). A sentence-based model when extended to the paragraph is insensitive to discourse norms and typical discourse patterns, which severely limit, constrain, or guide the generative element of writing (see also Coe, 1998: 134). It is perhaps not too contentious to claim that Christensen left too much generative freedom to the writer in his theory, freedom which, in reality, the writer does not have, even in fiction-writing. One does not – indeed, one cannot – *generate* (in the Christensen sense) in a discourse vacuum.

Coordination and subordination within the paragraph

Perhaps the most significant criticism of Christensen's work by a number of his critics was in relation to his understanding and use of the terms "coordination" and "subordination." Some writers (e.g. Rodgers, 1966b: 76) commented on their difficulty identifying whether a sentence was coordinate or subordinate using Christensen's model. Eden and Mitchell (1986: 422) observed that the same rhetorical marker (e.g. *however, on the other hand*) may coordinate or subordinate, and Ardiss Mackie and Chris Bullock described the levels numbering system of Christensen as "cumbersome" (for both teacher and student) to apply (Mackie and Bullock, 1990: 69). Dennis Packard believed that particular problems arose when trying to align embedded units, whether coordinate or subordinate (Packard, 1986: 60). He argued that Pitkin (1969) helped overcome this problem, though he believed that Pitkin's theory was too complex to be a useful classroom tool (Packard, 1986: 65). Christensen himself acknowledged that he was not always able to work out subordinate or coordinate relations within his model (cited in Rockas, 1966: 151), and in a specific type of writing he seemed to suggest that his paragraph theory was not applicable: "In *pure* narrative, the sentences are all at the same level; there is no shifting of level from sentence to sentence. In narrative the sentence, not the paragraph, is the basic unit..." (Christensen, 1967: 188, original emphasis); see also the discussion of David Karrfalt (Karrfalt, 1968: 216).

In addition to those who struggled to implement the Christensen system (as it stood), other writers challenged Christensen's understanding of subordinate and coordinate relations. Rodgers (1966b: 78) argued that all following sentences in a paragraph (i.e. those following on from the topic sentence) are subordinate in the sense that they support, comment on, or develop a sentence at the next higher level, and that they may or may not be coordinate to the topic sentence as well. Karrfalt (1966) believed that Christensen's model failed to incorporate sentence relations which were neither coordinate nor subordinate. He pointed out that a sentence in a paragraph may stand at a higher level of relation to preceding sentences (i.e. be superordinate to them). Further, he argued that Christensen only dealt with vertical structures (i.e. coordination and modification) in his model, not horizontal ones (i.e. predication and complementation). He provided an example of a paragraph with such horizontal structure as evidence of this patterning, where following sentences add to the existing ones, not being subordinate to or coordinate with them (i.e. completing them). He suggested that the relationship between sentences in such a case is analogous to predicate and subject, and in making this observation, one is reminded of Bain's sentence-based paragraph model, which Christensen distanced himself from, and yet which in this modified form as developed by Karrfalt, may be seen to complement Christensen's model.

Pitkin (1969) also saw problems with Christensen's understanding of coordination and subordination.[12] Regarding coordination, he observed that in Christensen's view this could be either repetition or a relation of co-hyponymy. However, he pointed out that related items such as question–answer or cause–effect[13] should also have been included in the coordinate class. Accordingly, Pitkin combined this type of complementation relation with simple coordination (referring to repetition, or co-hyponyms to a superordinate) and termed these "horizontal relations." Concerning subordination in the Christensen model, Pitkin believed that it was understood too widely, containing all relations not covered by simple coordination. He believed that the term itself was problematic, as it included its opposite (superordination). He preferred, therefore to use the term "vertical relations" for these two types of relation.

In terms of his own adaptation, Pitkin (1969: 139) suggested that discourse comprised "discourse blocs" which could be related to each other vertically (i.e. through subordination and superordination) or horizontally (i.e. through coordination and complementation). He defined "discourse blocs" as functional units. He argued that these blocs are the basic units of discourse, rather than sentences or paragraphs, and that certain language, what he called "bloc signals" (p. 142), may signal the actual relationship between two blocs (e.g. *it follows*). He went on to elaborate on the "discourse bloc" concept in a later article, as discussed further in the next paragraph.

Pitkin (1977) differentiated three understandings of the term "hierarchy" in text: structural (i.e. relationships between words, paragraphs, and complete texts), semantic (i.e. (*general – specific* relations within text), and functional (i.e. operational relations, e.g. *cause – effect*; *fact – consequence*). He proposed that while the first two views of hierarchy had some merit, only a functional view of hierarchy could satisfactorily explain discourse. Pitkin argued that Christensen never fully differentiated the structural and the functional hierarchy of discourse in his own model, asserting that Christensen had incorrectly assumed the functional integrity of the paragraph. While the paragraph exists within a structural hierarchy – in the sense that it is a unit which has a relation to the larger text and the smaller sentences within it – Pitkin argued that in the discourse hierarchy the paragraph which he called a structural unit (a rather different meaning for the same term used by Heurley, 1997) may or may not be a functional unit within the complete discourse. Pitkin maintained that discourse contains functional "discourse blocs" which are of different structural unit sizes, including parts of sentences, sentences, parts of paragraphs and paragraphs. I believe his key contribution to the paragraphing debate was his argument that the structural unit may not map onto a functional unit – indeed may be at odds with it (Pitkin, 1977: 657). This was his main criticism of Christensen's thought. In his own words "…the structural (formal) hierarchy is often at odds with the operational (functional) hierarchy" (pp. 658, 659). As such, the strong sentence and paragraph focus in Christensen's work, Pitkin argued, could, ultimately, only confuse, rather than enlighten or add to our understanding of discourse.

As a student of Christensen, Pitkin saw himself as advancing Christensen's work, but he arguably did more than this: he challenged it and modified it to the extent that what he proposed was not really a version of Christensen's model, but his own. Pitkin's viewpoint, in some ways, was similar to the linguists mentioned in Chapter 1, who argued that the orthographic paragraph was not what it seemed to be – a complete unit (howsoever understood), and as such, could not be a valid unit for linguistic analysis. The difference is that Pitkin adopted a functional hierarchical understanding of discourse, and retained the word "paragraph" for the orthographic unit, and coined the term "discourse bloc" for the functional unit.

Impact

Christensen's approach was radically new, detailing as it did subordinate and coordinate relations, and postulating that an understanding of these took the mystery out of good paragraph style. In connecting form and style, he moved into new ground (though note the comments of Lord, 1964, who had touched on some of these points).

The Christensen theory offered hope to many writing teachers and learner-writers: it provided them with a principled way of developing paragraphs, a technique which promised a resultant positive impact on style. The experimental data advanced to support Christensen's method was impressive, both in terms of student writers' sentence-level rhetoric development (as seen in increased T-unit length and the use of a greater number of free modifiers) and paragraph model development, as indicated in the studies of Charles Bond (Bond, 1972) and R. Craig Hogan (Hogan, 1977: 277). Christensen's work certainly impacted composition practice during the 1960s and 1970s. His own program (*The Christensen Rhetoric Program*) was popular, and his paragraph theory was later taken up (in a revised form) by Coe (1988) in *Toward a Grammar of Passages*. His influence is also clearly evident in more recent texts, in Connors and Cheryl Glenn's *St. Martin's Guide to Teaching Writing* (Connors and Glenn, 1995) and Erika Lindemann's *A Rhetoric for Writing Teachers* (Lindemann, 1995: 147–157). Thomas Pace believed, however, that the treatment of Christensen's ideas in these two texts is lacking in various ways, arguing that the former text interpreted Christensen in an overly prescriptive manner, failing to investigate and appreciate "the tension between form and content" (Pace, 2005: 11). Interest in the Christensen model declined over time, and this was traced to various objections: the lack of a meaningful rhetorical context within which exercises were conducted, in addition to attitudes among some writing specialists of anti-formalism, anti-behaviorism, and anti-empiricism (see Robert Connors, 2000). In addition, some research indicated only short-term gains in stylistic advancement when using his method (as noted by Coe, 1998: 134).

Rodgers' Discourse-Centered Rhetoric of the Paragraph

Rodgers' (1966a) work on the paragraph signaled a radical departure from existing paragraph theories, being characterized by Duncan (2007: 480) as "the first full-fledged functionalist theory of paragraphs." Central to Rodgers' theory was a concept which had been used by both Lewis (1894) and Scott and Denney (1895) many years before him – "the stadium." I consider this term in some detail in the next few paragraphs, before discussing Rodgers' contribution.

Lewis (1894: 22) introduced the term "stadium / stadia" casually, suggesting that beginning writers, when they are taught to write paragraphs, might fail to "distinguish the larger stadia of the thought from the smaller." He further believed that authors usually attempted to ensure that their paragraphs were stadia (p. 26), and he differen-tiated a "logical" stadium paragraph from a "rhetorical" stadium paragraph (*ibid.*), the latter being a thought "raised to the dignity of a paragraph by its artistic value in the general development" (*ibid.*). As an example of the latter, Lewis commented on a particular author (Laurence Sterne) who employed rhetorical paragraphs in some of his writing, and reflected that: "Sterne was analysing, not logically, but rhetorically; fastening attention on these small stadia simply for the imaginative suggestions involved in their pregnant brevity"

(Lewis, 1894: 120). He also acknowledged that a single sentence may be paragraphed as a logical stadium (p. 27). The idea that a paragraph was a stadium in or of thought was seen by Lewis as a key factor in the crystallization and historical development of the paragraph concept (as discussed in Chapter 2).

As described previously in Chapter 3, Scott and Denney (1895) also used the term "stadium." They believed that in the process of thinking, "the thought-process consists of a series of leaps and pauses" (p. 94) and as such, the essay mirrors these movements, with pauses between the thought processes becoming the subdivisions within the essay. They argued that the "articulations of the thought" (p. 96) within the overall essay form the basis of paragraphing. However, they were careful to observe that actual paragraphing does not always map onto a larger subdivision in the thought, as mini-thoughts (i.e. substadia) can be grouped together into a larger paragraph (though still constituting a unified thought); that is, paragraphing may occur at either the substadia or stadia level of thought.

Although Rodgers (1965, 1966a,b) nowhere cited Lewis (1894) or Scott and Denney's (1895) references to notions of stadia, it seems reasonable to assume that he was influenced by their work (in referencing both texts in 1965), though using the term "stadium of discourse" rather than just "stadium" or "stadium of / in thought." However, unlike Lewis, or Scott and Denney, Rodgers refined the concept and theorized it more comprehensively, indeed made it the cornerstone of his theory, though only defining it in his later work. I discuss this later work first, before proceeding to detail his work on the paragraph.

Rodgers (1967) set the stage for defining the stadium of discourse by differentiating simple and complex statements. The former he defined as single independent clauses with any modifying material, noting that these are often sufficient for the writer's purpose: "...one independent clause does the job" (Rodgers, 1967: 179). The other type of statement (complex) is one in which another clause, or maybe more than one,[14] is added to the first, extending the thought, and resulting in a "mental amalgam" (p. 179) being formed in the mind of the reader, that is, a single idea is formed by more than one clause. He called this blending "accretion" (*ibid.*), which he differentiated from "adjunction," in which the second clause may simply support the first claim, but not add to it, or extend it, or not be essential to the argument (pp. 179–180). Rodgers argued that accretion may be a product of inexactitude, or a consequence of an idea needing two clauses. After discussing these terms, Rodgers went on to define a "stadium of discourse" as a "unit...containing a single topic, together with any accrete extensions or adjunct support..." (p. 184). Such units, he argued, are "the basic rhetorical constituents of prose" (*ibid.*). These discourse stadia may or may not be paragraphs: if they are not, it is possible that part of a stadium can become one, "providing that structural relationships remain clear" (*ibid.*). Further, he stated that a series (i.e. two or more) stadia may join together to form a paragraph "...providing the resulting bundle of material constitutes an acceptable blend" (*ibid.*). Rodgers (1967: 184) argued that Rockas (1964: 6), who suggested that a paragraph break can be made before almost any sentence in "sophisticated prose," failed to appreciate the existence of these "larger rhetorical units" in adopting his view. While Rodgers believed that many places in a text *could* be legitimately indented (many more than Christensen, for example), he believed that stadia of discourse play an important role in affecting paragraphing decisions.

Turning now to his earlier work, it is not surprising, given his focus on a discourse unit larger than the sentence, that Rodgers (1966a) began his *Discourse-centered Rhetoric of the Paragraph* by rejecting Bain's (1890) sentence-based approach to the paragraph. Rodgers stated that disquiet was expressed concerning the Bainian model in the late 1950s and early 1960s, but no substitute had been offered. He therefore sought to develop a theory which could describe all paragraphs – not only some – arguing the need for a "...flexible open ended *discourse-centered* rhetoric of the paragraph" (1966a: 4, original emphasis). This was a radically new approach to the paragraph, one which readily embraced a much wider recognition of the factors affecting the decision to indent than had been considered up to this point in time, and a theory which was not seeking to place some paragraphs on pedestals as models, or deem others "bad" (unlike Christensen, 1965,1966; Lord, 1964 referred to earlier), though it should be noted that he did describe some paragraphs as "good" (Rodgers, 1966a: 6) and came close to calling some bad.[15]

A substantial part of Rodgers' (1966a) article is taken up with a detailed commentary on a series of paragraphs written by Pater, and the level of detail discussed in his analysis is not of relevance here. Below, I attempt to summarize the essence of Rodgers' theory.

Rodgers believed that traditional models of the paragraph were concerned primarily with only one aspect of movement within the paragraph – the horizontal, forward movement, though Johnson (1946) and later Lord (1964), added the idea of vertical movement, as mentioned earlier. Rodgers commented that the peaks of abstraction in the vertical movement are usually understood to coincide with the topic sentence, the beginning of a new paragraph. However, he argued that neither a horizontal or vertical movement shift necessitated the beginning of a new paragraph; they were, for example, also characteristic of movements between some sentences within discourse as well. Having said that, he observed that new paragraphs do often indicate significant horizontal and vertical phases, which, he commented, often coincide with each other (Rodgers, 1966a: 5).

The heart of Rodgers' model was that an author inserts a paragraph break to mark off a section of the discourse as a stadium of discourse: "all good paragraphs are distinct stadia" (Rodgers, 1966a: 6). Paragraph indentation is a stadium marker: it is a punctuation marker available to the writer, indeed "the most emphatic" (p. 5), indicating the completion of a stadium. The decision to indent may be made for one specific reason or for a number of different reasons, and it is here that Rodgers' thought was much more flexible than other writers of this time. He argued that while most stadia are "logical" divisions, they may also be influenced by other considerations: editorial requirements; reader effect; variety for its own sake; "prose rhythm"; tone shift; and formal reasons (*ibid.*). Consequently, he defined the paragraph as:

> an autochthonous pattern in prose discourse, identified originally by application of logical, physical, rhythmical, tonal, formal and other rhetorical criteria, set off from adjacent patterns by indentations, and commended thereby to the reader as a noteworthy stadium of discourse (Rodgers, 1966a: 5–6).

He went on to comment that the different considerations (noted above) may "tug against" the logical requirement of the paragraph (Rodgers, 1966a: 10), citing as an example of this a section of a Pater text where "rhetorical criteria ... take precedence over logical..." (p. 9). Like Scott and Denney (1895) before him, Rodgers (1966a: 6) suggested that while all paragraphs are distinct stadia, this does not mean that all stadia are paragraphs: some may be "potential" paragraphs only. Rodgers believed, therefore, that the decision to indent is not (purely or solely) formally determined: it is author determined. Thus the Christensen student *how?* became the Rodgers' author *why?*[16]

Rodgers (1966b: 73) believed that structure is (probably) a defining quality of the stadium of discourse (see above), not the paragraph per se,[17] though in a later article he wrote that "the paragraph ... must always reveal the boundaries of a unit of structure" (Rodgers, 1967: 185) – which may indicate a shift in his thinking. However, in stating that only *part* of a stadium may become a paragraph in his later work (referred to earlier) Rodgers seemed to weaken the relationship he was trying to create between a stadium of discourse and the paragraph. In fact, he seems to contradict himself, since he had earlier stated, speaking of all paragraphs, that "their authors have marked them off for special consideration as *stadia of discourse*" (Rodgers, 1966a: 6, original emphasis), thus implying that a paragraph is always a *complete* stadium of discourse (or a combination of smaller stadia). Rodgers

(1966b: 73) argued that the theories of Christensen and Becker were actually theories of discourse structure, not paragraph structure per se. The difference was, in part, due to starting point: Rodgers started with the stadium of discourse, which he theorized and placed the paragraph within and around,[18] whereas Christensen started with the paragraph,[19] moving out towards the larger discourse units.

For Rodgers (1966a: 6), paragraphs are not created: they are discovered; the decision to indent is interpretative, not creative. Consequently, Rodgers believed that normative statements about the qualities of a paragraph are of no value; hence his total rejection of Bain's work and his suspicion of Christensen's, though he did believe that Christensen's theory and Becker's theory would cover most paragraphs that one would normally read in an essay (Rodgers, 1966b: 75).

Critique

Although, as described above, some aspects of Rodgers' theory were not very clear, his work did not receive much attention of a critical nature. It is, though, interesting to observe that Pitkin's discourse bloc concept has been referred to by scholars far more often than Rodgers' stadium of discourse, and it is possible that a reason for this may be the clearer explanation of blocs as compared to stadia. In their symposium pieces, Christensen (1966) and Becker (1966) made several critical comments about Rodgers' work, though not so much in relation to the theory, but rather in relation to its assumptions and its value.

Concerning assumptions, Christensen raised two major concerns about Rodgers' work. The first of these was in relation to how people write. Christensen (1966: 64) stated that his own writing practice did not follow Rodgers' ideas about how paragraphs come to be, that he wrote "by paragraphs," contrary to Rodgers' idea (and presumably practice) that paragraphs come into being editorially, after the writer has composed his / her stadia, and considered which stadia or group of stadia warrant indentation, given the writer's purpose, emphasis, and other decision criteria.

D'Angelo (1974: 389) suggested that Christensen and Rodgers occupied two different poles of writing practice, commenting: "Surely the truth lies somewhere between. We invent paragraphs, and we discover paragraphs." Although Rodgers largely eschewed making normative comments on the structure of a paragraph, he did appear to make normative comments about paragraph writing practice, and he can be criticized for doing so. Not only did his views on revision and editing lack empirical justification, he paid too little attention to how the writing task, the writer, the genre and the mode of writing affect the decision to indent (see Chapter 8 on this). For example, a student writing an essay by hand in an exam cannot easily edit paragraph structure, and yet in drafting this chapter I have reworked and reparagraphed many sections of the text.

The second assumption-based criticism which Christensen voiced concerning Rodgers' work was in relation to prescriptivism. Christensen's work was unashamedly prescriptivist: "I would not have written and published the studies I have if I had not believed that composition and rhetoric are arts and as arts are necessarily prescriptive and that at this time and in this place we are sorely in need of sounder prescriptive standards" (Christensen, 1966: 66). Rodgers (1966b: 73), on the other hand, was attempting to construct a theory to explain all paragraphs and not pass judgement on any (though, as noted earlier, I believe he was a little inconsistent on this point): he wanted to try to understand the various factors (formal and non-formal) affecting the decision to indent, not to provide a pedagogical theory. Becker (1966: 68) also added to the criticism made by Christensen on the matter of pedagogy, and asked what the value of Rodgers' theory was in an educational context: "The question is, what can we do with his observations?" He criticized Rodgers' theory for not making general statements, arguing that any model will fail to approximate reality, but that this does not stop the work of scientists or devalue the importance of generalizations. Becker (1966: 69) argued that "useful generalisations are possible in discussing paragraphs," contrary to Rodgers, whom, he claimed "sees only variation" (*ibid.*) in paragraphs. Duncan (2007: 481) thought Becker's criticism of Rodgers "a bit facile"; and yet, from an educational point of view, Becker had a point. The business of pedagogy is, in many ways, the art of simplification: "real" language can be messy, as Rebecca Hughes and Michael McCarthy have amply demonstrated (Hughes and McCarthy, 1998), and students expect simplification and guidance. To simplify is not a crime: even some corpus linguists such as Michael Barlow (Barlow, 1996: 30) have argued for the presentation of simple example sentences, to help in learning, as opposed to real examples of usage. As Henry Widdowson noted, teachers of all disciplines recognize the fact that effective pedagogy requires being "economical with the truth" (Widdowson, 1991: 21) or, in the specific situation under consideration here, teachers value paragraph models which do not necessarily cover all paragraphs. The fact is that educational texts on paragraph writing look to make generalizations, and such being the case, they found little in Rodgers' theory to exploit.

Summing up, from a pedagogical perspective, while Rogers did make the occasional normative comment on the paragraph and paragraphing, it is not entirely clear what teachers could do with his comments, other than inform students that indentation may occur for a number of reasons, or possibly introduce them to the stadium of discourse concept. Additionally, it is worth remembering that a number of the non-formal considerations which Rodgers wrote of in relation to paragraphing are not relevant in much school or college writing (e.g. column width or physical restriction considerations affecting the decision to indent).

Becker: A Tagmemic Approach to Paragraph Analysis

Tagmemic theory, formulated by Kenneth Pike in the 1950s, was an ambitious attempt to explain linguistic (and non-linguistic) phenomena. At the heart of the theory was a 9-cell heuristic matrix which can be applied to any language unit, including the paragraph. Young and Becker (1965: 456) believed that three aspects of a linguistic unit must be specified to understand it completely: "its contrastive features, its range of variation, and its distribution in sequence and ordered classes." In addition to this, tagmemics advanced a trimodal perspective of language units in which items could be viewed as "particles (discrete contrastive bits), waves (unsegmentable physical continua), or fields (orderly systems of relationships)" (Young and Becker, 1965: 459). Therefore, a 9-cell matrix could be developed from these 3x3 classifications. Discourse tagmemic theory was an extension of sentence tagmemic theory, and not nearly so developed as sentence tagmemics, a point which Becker (1965) himself acknowledged in his work on the paragraph.

In opening his article, "A Tagmemic Approach to Paragraph Analysis," Becker (1965: 237) discussed the tagmeme from the perspective of sentence grammar, defining it as "...the class of grammatical forms that function in a particular grammatical relationship." The example he provided to illustrate this concept was that of sentence subject, serving a grammatical relationship or function, and realized by certain forms – for this case, noun phrases and pronouns. He explained that another way of considering a tagmeme is to view it as a "spot" or "slot" in a substitution-based system which included the spot / slot and the forms that can be substituted in that spot or slot. A key part of tagmemics, according to Becker, was the connection of meaning and form, this constituting the *particle perspective* of the theory, the primary focus in his work on the paragraph. The other two structural features which needed to be considered for a comprehensive theory were: "continuity or concord between the parts" (Becker, 1965: 238) – i.e. the *wave* perspective – and "a system of semantic relationships in which the reader's expectations are aroused and fulfilled" (*ibid.*) – i.e. the *field* perspective. Becker argued that tagmemic theory could be usefully extended from the sentence to the paragraph, and his writing focused on the expository paragraph, though he believed that narrative, descriptive, and argumentative paragraphs could be analyzed in the same way, despite having different structures. Becker acknowledged that his theory of the paragraph ignored rhetorical field structure (p. 242), further stating that its primary focus was the particle perspective (p. 238). As such, it is clear that he did not intend his theory to be a comprehensive tagmemic theory of the paragraph.

Becker believed that there are two main paragraph patterns utilized in exposition: the T (*topic*) R (*restriction*) I (*illustration*) pattern, and the P (*problem*) S (*solution*) pattern.[20] In the TRI pattern paragraph, the three functional slots are filled, respectively, by the stating of the topic, its restriction (i.e. narrowing), and its narrowed description or illustration. He argued that the three slots are typically associated with different levels of generality: T might be a proposition (i.e. the most general element), R a more specific (i.e. less general) restatement of the proposition, and I an example. In such a paragraph there are, therefore, three tagmemes, and he suggested that the shift in the level of generality was indicative of a shift in function.

The example paragraph which Becker provided to illustrate this idea is given below, though I note only the first clause of the (I) tagmeme.

> *(T) The English constitution – that indescribable entity – is a living thing, growing with the growth of men, and assuming ever-varying forms in accordance with the subtle and complex laws of human character. (R) It is the child of wisdom and chance. (I) The wise men of 1688 moulded it into the shape we know...*[21]

In the PS pattern, the P slot may be filled with a question, or it may state a problem or an effect requiring explanation. The S slot deals with the solution, or explains the cause of the problem. Becker believed that an extended S may actually have an internal TRI structure. He also stated that there may be two or more Ss in a paragraph. In the paragraph below, provided by Becker, only the first S is given.

> *(P)How obsolete is Hearn's judgment? (S₁) (T) On the surface the five gentlemen of Japan do not by themselves seem to be throttled by this rigid society of their ancestors. (R) Their world is in fact far looser in its demands upon them than it once was. (I) Industrialisation and the influence of the West have progressively softened the texture of the web...*[22]

Becker (1965) wrote of possible variations in these two paragraph types: deletion (most commonly R in the TRI slot); reordering (e.g. inversion TRI to IRT), which Young and Becker (1965: 465) believed to be common in opening or closing discourse; addition (e.g. a repetition of T at the end of the paragraph as would be the case in T_1RIT_1); and combination (two "paragraphs"[23] combined perhaps because of contrast or semantic parallelism). After discussing these functions, Becker (1965: 240) went on to detail the formal signals of paragraph tagmemes, arguing that they are complex, "usually redundant combinations of graphic, lexical, grammatical and phonological signals." Each of these is described, in turn, below.

The first signal, the graphic signal, is the decision to indent and related to all of the other signals, though Becker noted that constraints on paragraphing are not as rigid as other punctuation marks. He suggested that this flexibility enables the writer to create an interesting interplay between the additional signals elaborated on below (i.e. lexical, grammatical, and phonological signals).

Becker (1965: 241) divided lexical markers into two types: equivalence classes[24] and lexical transitions. Regarding the former, he commented on the lexical head of the TRI paragraph noted above, that is, "*English Constitution,*" and how it "designates an equivalence class" (p. 241) throughout the paragraph with *indescribable entity* and *it*. He elsewhere termed this a "dominant equivalence chain" (Becker, 1966: 72), that is, one which extends across the whole paragraph. However, he also observed that equivalence classes may only occur within a specific tagmeme slot, terming the resulting connection a "subordinate equivalence chain" (*ibid.*). Turning to the second type of lexical marker, Becker

(1965: 241) defined "lexical transitions" as "words and phrases which mark the semantic concord of the paragraph," examples of such words being *but* and *then*. He suggested that certain words or phrases tended to occur in *particular* slots – in slot I he believed that *for example* is a common lexical transition item, and *in other words* a common phrase in signaling the beginning of R.

Turning to the grammatical signals of the tagmemic structure, Becker (1965) argued that there was a relationship between lexical equivalence classes and sentence grammar within the paragraph. As a result, he believed that "major changes in the grammatical roles of equivalence classes, especially the head classes, signal either new slots or new paragraphs" (Becker, 1965: 241). An example of this can be seen in the paragraph extract provided above in which the *English constitution* moves from subject slot in T to object slot in I. Becker (1965: 242) also believed that verb form changes often indicate transition to a new slot, particularly "expanded verb forms" (e.g. perfect and continuous aspect), and that tense changes could do the same, noting that the I slot in the TRI (*English constitution*) paragraph above is signaled by a shift to the past tense.[25] The reasons for these shifts (in equivalence chains or grammar) may be due to changes in location, time, viewpoint, or topic (Becker, 1966: 72). Young, Becker, and Pike (1970: 348) believed that choice in sentence structure in expressing a proposition is affected by the writer's focus within the text.

Regarding the final factor – phonological markers – Becker (1965: 242) commented that when paragraphs are read aloud, tagmemes are indicated by changes in "pitch register, tempo and volume."

Becker appealed to (consistently similar) reader partitioning of non-paragraphed text to support his theory, that is, he argued that conventional patterns and cues could be recognized in such experiments, and as a result a reader could identify where the indentations originally occurred in a deparagraphed text, and he believed that "most paragraphs are conventional units" (1966: 69). However, as will be discussed in more detail in Chapter 7, human paragraph segmentation research has not always supported Becker's view, which is somewhat idealistic.

Becker (1966: 69) argued that his theory acknowledged, more than others' theories, that paragraphs are "multi-systemic," that is, that grammar, phonology, lexis, rhetoric, and punctuation all work together within the paragraph. Regarding the contrary belief that paragraphs in segmentation studies are only recognized as such because of semantic cues (rather than lexical and grammatical cues), he argued that this view is inadequate, as it fails to account for people's agreement on paragraph indentation in experimentally altered paragraphs in which lexical items have been replaced by nonsense words and grammatical items and markers have been left unchanged.[26] He did not agree with Christensen's argument that his theory was just the description of the structure of the paragraph because, unlike previous descriptive work, he described the formal relations between the parts in his model.[27]

In his symposium piece, Becker (1966) suggested that the essential difference between his theory and Christensen's and Rodgers' was its orientation. Becker believed that they described paragraphs from the writer's point of view, whereas his model sought to explain how readers recognize paragraphs (and consistently paragraph de-paragraphed text). Young et al. (1970: 319) suggested that the "discernible pattern[s]" of discourse are what makes text comprehensible for a reader. A secondary spin-off of Becker's focus, was, he argued, the concomitant help that an instructor can give to students in identifying the formal features of paragraphs which can then help them to develop their writing accordingly,[28] or at least edit written work on principled grounds through the use of plot cues, focus, and managing "overloaded" sentences (Young et al., 1970: 51).

Critique

The 9-cell tagmemic matrix concept was challenged by Charles Kneupper (Kneupper, 1980)[29] because of its perceived abstractness and redundancy (i.e. repetition of information within the cells).

Further, the idea that completing cells necessarily helped in matters such as composing (rather than editing) was challenged by James Kinney (Kinney, 1978); see also Lee Odell's response to Kinney (Odell, 1978). The importance of the paragraph in editing rather than composing is evident in Young et al. (1970).

Christensen (1966: 62) argued that while tagmemic theory was valid when considering sentences, it was less so when discussing the paragraph: "We do not learn paragraph patterns, either the slots or the slot fillers, in the same way [as with sentence grammar]." He suggested that Becker's theory was incomplete in this regard; however, in fairness to Becker, he did not talk about learning paragraphing so much as the reader's awareness of, and recognition of patterns within the paragraph. Rodgers (1966b: 75) argued that the units T, R, I, P, and S in Becker's theory were stadia, or parts of stadia, but that writers do not consciously follow certain patterns. Again, though, it should be remembered that Becker's focus in his theorizing was the reader, not the writer. Pattern, Rodgers (1966) believed, was a discourse phenomenon, not a paragraph attribute. Starting with the paragraph unit, as Becker did, could only result in failure from Rodgers' discourse-oriented perspective, and his point is essentially sound – Becker's work was somewhat idealized. Rodgers (1966b) was also critical of vagueness and imprecision in Becker's theory. He suggested that "R" (i.e. restriction) as explained by Becker was multi-purposeful: narrowing the assertion, defining it, restating it (and therefore changing it slightly), or expanding it. He argued that the term "restriction" was, accordingly, inappropriate and noted the presence of too many "fuzzy terms" (Rodgers, 1966b: 77) in Becker's work, including vagueness about what was meant by the topic statement. Further, Rodgers (1966b) suggested, as Christensen (1966) had, and as Kinney (1978) was to argue later on, that Becker's work was not far removed from Bain's (with the main idea being developed by following proofs, applications or other means of developing the thought). Rodgers also provided a paragraph which did not seem to fit into any possible variation of

Becker's TRI or PS models. Rodgers' points about vagueness in terminology within Becker's model seem largely valid.

Impact

W. Ross Winterowd endorsed the value of Becker's work in an educational context (Winterowd, 1973), and Victor Vitanza suggested that it had potential to be extended to the whole composition (Vitanza, 1979). However, Stewart (1978: 172) observed that tagmemic theory did not seem to be have been "widely understood or adopted." The key student text, *Rhetoric: Discovery and Change* (Becker and Pike, 1970) did not have a significant impact on practice, and Stewart (1978) noted that of 34 books he reviewed (containing handbooks, rhetorics, and readers), only seven of them showed any influence from a number of influential writers *including* Becker and Pike's own text. Mark Branson (1988), cited in Duncan (2007), similarly noted minimal impact of paragraph tagmemics – only five of 32 texts reviewed followed Becker's theory in any way, and Duncan (2007: 491) suggested that this may have been because of the complexity of the tagmemic model.

Hoey's (2005) work on textual colligation (discussed in detail in Chapter 7) acknowledged and built on Young and Becker's (1966) study, particularly with regard to grammatical parallelism and lexical equivalence chains, and how shifts within these may indicate shifts between paragraphs. Hoey developed Becker's work with the use of corpus linguistic tools and also tested his hypotheses through the use of segmentation experiments. Hoey, however, was not interested in understanding the paragraph from a theoretical tagmemic perspective, or in developing tagmemic theory, though his interest in the reader's interaction with the paragraph (specifically, in lexical priming, see Chapter 7 for more on this) strongly resonates with Becker's (1965, 1966) stated focus. Some computational work (discussed in detail in Chapter 6) can also be seen to follow on from and develop Becker's work, including research into identifying the functional parts of textual units, such as that of Douglas Biber, Eniko Csomay, James K. Jones and Casey Keck (Biber et al., 2007), and inter-paragraph lexical transitional phrases, such as that of Caroline Sporleder and Mirella Lapata (Sporlder and Lapata, 2006).

Conclusion

The 1960s was something of a watershed in the study of the paragraph. Some of the traditional orientations to its study were maintained: sentence-based theories, a pedagogical orientation (though a much greater emphasis on the process *how* than the product *what*), and a number of deductive, normative pronouncements. However, there was also much that was new: greater recognition of non-formal factors affecting paragraphing (Rodgers); deeper and more subtle studies of the internal structuring of the paragraph (Lord, Becker, and Christensen); and a greater awareness of the place of the paragraph within the wider discourse and to other suprasentential semantic, syntactic, or functional units within text – indeed, this growing awareness began to work against, and even overtake, the sentence as a reference point for paragraph theorizing.

Regarding pedagogy, Christensen, more than any other theorist before him, provided practical advice on *how* to develop good writing and his approach was, understandably, appreciated by many in the teaching community. In tying together form and style, and in seeking to take the mystery out of paragraph writing, his contribution was a significant shift away from the work of the 19th century academics. However, his legacy has, with hindsight, perhaps not been as important as Becker's, whose theory was the first to specifically relate lexis and grammar to functional relations within the paragraph. Although Becker's work was tentative in a number of ways, some of his observations have been broadly confirmed or developed by recent corpus and computational linguistic research (as discussed in Chapter 6), though not from a theoretical tagmemic approach. It should also be mentioned that it was Becker who was the first to raise awareness of the reader's expectations in encountering paragraphs in the 1960s (though note also the work of Scott and Denney, 1895, as discussed in Chapter 3). The idea of reader anticipation or expectation in reading is an issue that has more recently been taken up by George Gopen (2004), and is discussed further in Chapter 7.

Regarding normative statements about the paragraph, Becker seemed to be particularly aware of a possible descent into chaos if educators were to embrace Rodgers' descriptive theory, arguing, quite rationally, that from an educational point of view simplified models are of value. Christensen, likewise, argued the need for prescriptivism in education. However, educators, were not, by and large, convinced by Becker's or Christensen's models and, somewhat ironically, it is Bain's approach which is still dominant in many student textbooks today.

Rodgers was the first to consider the paragraph, in any detail, from a wider discourse – and writer – perspective. It would be fair to say that the notion of stadium of discourse, alongside Pitkin's discourse bloc, knocked the paragraph off its 19th century pedestal (or at least should have done so). The paragraph, post-Rodgers and post-Pitkin, needs to be viewed in a different way. Rodgers and particularly Pitkin attempted with some success to put the paragraph in its place, and not to assume its role or function. This is not to say that the paragraph became less worthy as a unit of study, as research in Chapters 5 to 8 make clear. However, while still viewed as a unit after the 1960s, it has often been viewed as a unit in a different way, part of a bigger unit, or even a combination of smaller (non-sentence) units, and unit-like only in a very simple way – as a block of text, but not functionally, or formally. The term "unity," prolific in the work of 19th century theorists in discussing the paragraph, fell into disuse during this era, in part, I believe, because of this new awareness.

In sum, the academic atmosphere of the 1960s and the work of Lord, Christensen, Becker, and Rodgers injected new life into an area of academic inquiry which had, in many ways, become rather staid, abstract, and wooden. Rodgers' work, though significant, failed to connect with educators' needs, and the educational implications of a descriptivist approach to paragraphing were not worked out, or readily apparent. With the benefit of hindsight, and largely because of the more recent work of corpus linguists and computational linguists, I suggest that Becker's scholarship is the most valuable work from this era for educators, in that it considered predictable functional patterns, and how lexis, grammar, and phonology signal these patterns. Becker attempted to document (albeit in a rather vague way) how these signals interact and govern paragraph organization (both formally and functionally). Although I am not convinced by Becker's arguments for the psychological reality of the paragraph (see Chapter 7) or for the necessary relationship between a paragraph's form and its function, I believe Becker's work could usefully be reconsidered by educators today, in the light of new data on discourse patterns uncovered by corpus and computational linguistic researchers (to be discussed in Chapters 5 and 6). Learner-writers may well benefit from being made aware of recurring functional patterns within paragraphs and how these are typically signaled.

Notes

1   In 2016 there were just four references to his work on Google Scholar.
2   Rodgers (1966a) was clearly aware of the work, as he cites from it. However, neither Christensen nor Becker referred to it in their writings on the paragraph.
3   It should be mentioned that, like Bain (1890), Lord (1964) differentiated good from bad paragraphs.
4   Though he does not use the word "coordinate," Lord (1964) clearly has this relation in mind in the example he provides.
5   In addition, an important article by Karrfalt (1966) was included in this symposium, along with a short piece by Josephine Miles (Miles, 1966).
6   Richard Graves characterized Christensen's style as "the participialized style – the use of elements such as participial phrases, absolutes, and appositives to give sentences more vigor" (Graves, 1981: 417).

7   Christensen and his wife, Bonniejean, used the original sentence from Lewis in their *Notes Toward a New Rhetoric: 9 Essays for Teachers* (Christensen and Christensen, 2007 / 1963: 26).

8   From Dorothy Thompson, *The Education of the Heart* (as cited in Christensen, 1965: 146).

9   From Jacob Bronowski, *The Common Sense of Science* (Bronowski, 1960: 111).

10   See also Becker (1966: 70), who argued that coordination, subordination, and mixed sequence (in Christensen's model) are not enough, in and of themselves, to explain reader competence in recognizing paragraphs.

11   Bonniejean Christensen responded to this point by arguing (B. Christensen, 1970) that Francis Christensen, in his generative model, was trying to redress an unhealthy dependence on the subordinate clause in writing; that the value of the subordinate clause was never in question – only its dominance; and that his model provided a rounder, more comprehensive way of looking at subordination.

12   Larson (1967) went further and described in more detail different relational roles that sentences have to one another in a paragraph (e.g. *conceding, concluding,* and others, in addition to *combining*).

13   Note that Michael Grady argued that a *cause–effect* sequence is brought about through subordinate structures (Grady, 1972: 873).

14   He includes subordinate clauses in this classification, and Margaret Ashida has criticized this inclusion and the terminology used by Christensen (Ashida, 1968).

15   Rodgers (1967: 185) stated, "If an indentation obscures structural relationships, it obstructs comprehension...."

16   He argued that the key to understanding structural relationships within text lies "...in the psychology of literary intention" (Rodgers, 1967: 179).

17   In a significant footnote in his symposium piece, Rodgers (1966b: 73) stated: "Most stadia, perhaps all stadia, correspond to divisions in structure (i.e. to identifiable stages in argument)."

18   Thus, Rodgers (1996a: 11) remarked: "I have been concerned mainly to demonstrate that the paragraph is just one of several kinds of stadia...."

19   One could of course argue that Christensen started with the sentence.

20   It should be mentioned that Young and Becker (1965) also provided a *Question / Answer* type of paragraph, in which the Answer has a TRI pattern – which they termed a "compound" paragraph structure.

21   From Lytton Strachey, *Queen Victoria* (Strachey, 1924: 192).

22 From Frank Gibney, *Five Gentlemen of Japan* (cited in Becker, 1965: 239–240).

23 The use of the term "paragraph" here was pounced on by Rodgers, who criticized its use, as, in his words, "it is obviously not paragraphs that are combined in the sample passage" (Rodgers, 1966b: 73).

24 He noted his indebtedness to Zellig Harris (Harris, 1963) for this term.

25 Christensen (1966: 63), though generally critical of Becker's work called this grammatical observation "most perceptive."

26 This comment, made on the basis of the results from a particular experiment, is discussed in much greater detail in Chapter 7, which considers reader psychology and the paragraph.

27 This criticism was also leveled against him by Kinney (1978: 143). Young and Becker (1965: 453) made reference to the Ciceronian rhetoric "slot" system, namely: "the exordium; the narrative…exposition…; the proposition; the demonstration, the refutation of alternative propositions; and the peroration." They also mentioned that the patterns of arrangement could be modified in various ways. While the slot system is common to Cicero and tagmemic theory, crucially, Becker (1966: 70) argued he not only provided a *structure* of the paragraph, but also described the *formal* relations existing within it.

28 Pike (1981: 64) commented that tagmemics is not, primarily, concerned with helping students write, but may do so incidentally.

29 Kneupper (1980) developed a revised 6-cell matrix to address the redundancy which he believed existed in traditional tagmemic work.

5 The Paragraph Break and other Discourse-Managing Tools

Introduction

In this chapter, I focus on what is known about the language choices that are made at the paragraph juncture, specifically when beginning and (to a lesser extent) closing a paragraph, and how these choices influence what the paragraph unit is and does. As will be made clear, the decision to indent is not a solitary decision – a point hinted at by Becker (1965), and as mentioned in the previous chapter. In your own writing you probably know, intuitively, that you cannot just insert a break in a text when you return to a paragraph that seems too long: there are textual repercussions of such an action, and various changes to the text may need to be made. I believe that most writers are at best only vaguely aware of paragraph-initial and paragraph-closing lexis and grammar (at least when considered in an abstract, decontextualized way), and how these choices may actually influence the effect of the paragraph break for the reader. Therefore, in this chapter I consider the relationship between indentation and other discourse signaling tools, and what these interactions mean for understanding the paragraph and paragraphing.

In Chapter 2 I reported on research indicating that in a particular Koiné Greek text paragraphing was associated with the use of certain paragraph opening linguistic elements – particularly conjunctions in Gospel narrative. As discussed in Chapter 3, most of the 19th century theorists commented on the use of connective words between sentences and sometimes between paragraphs, in their discussions on the paragraph. In addition, in Chapter 4, "bloc signals" associated with Pitkin's (1969) "discourse bloc" theory were mentioned (e.g. *it follows*) as were Becker's (1966) "lexical transitions" (e.g. *but, for example, in other words*) in his tagmemic theory of the paragraph. However, comments from educational rhetoricians in the 19th century, and scholars in the 1960s were, generally speaking, rather vague, ad hoc in nature, and often lacking a solid research base. Further, the idea of a dynamic relationship existing between language choice and paragraphing was rarely considered, and the idea that language choice at the paragraph juncture may actually affect the role of the paragraph break in any particular instance, not considered at all.

Since the 1970s, discourse analysts, corpus linguists, and, to a lesser extent, computational linguists (whose work is considered in more detail in Chapter 6) have researched language choice in relation to the paragraph, focusing primarily on paragraph-opening language. Of this work, Hoey's (2005) textual colligation and lexical priming theory is probably the most well-known. Hoey's work is considered in more detail in Chapter 7 as it is not only a theory of language, but also a theory related to the psychology of reading. Less comprehensive in scope, yet more focused in terms of the language items studied, is the work of various scholars who have researched or made reference to language choice elements in relation to the paragraph in recent years. In this chapter I focus on this research.

Goutsos' Taxonomy of Text Organizing Tools

To help provide structure to this chapter, I borrow from Goutsos' (1997) work on sequential relations in text, and utilize a taxonomy he developed in relation to topic continuity and shift in text. However, unlike Goutsos, I utilize his taxonomy for a particular goal, namely, investigating six[1] of the seven tools he discussed, and their presence in paragraph opening and closing position. My goal is to consider why these shift and continuity signaling devices are used at the paragraph juncture, and how their use impacts the role of the paragraph break.

Goutsos (1997: 49) suggested that there are three techniques to manage topic shift (framing, introduction, and closure) in addition to a (single) topic continuity technique which writers can use to manage text. In his analysis of how these techniques were realized by a writer, Goutsos (1997: 73) provided a taxonomy of seven "tools" which manage the shift and continuation functions. These tools are listed below in Table 5.1. in the first column. The second

Table 5.1. Discourse managing tools and functions (adapted from Goutsos 1997: 73, 82)

Tool	Shift / Continuation Function	Examples
Orthographic markers	the paragraph break (indicating topic framing and closure), and parentheses (indicating continuation of topic)	( )
Metadiscourse markers	explicitly indicating topic framing, closure	*At this point* *To sum up*
Prediction pairs	Predictive (framing), predicted member (signal of topic introduction)	Question Answer
Discourse markers	conjunctions and adjuncts having a discourse function (framing, closing, or continuing)	*but* *therefore* *of course*
Cohesive devices	both local (signaling continuation) and long range (signaling topic frame and closure)	Encapsulation
Time framing	tense shift (introducing topic intro-duction) or tense continuity (indicating topic continuation[2])	*spend / spent* *spend / spend*
Sentence structure	sentence-initial adjuncts (topic framing) and *light-thematic* structures (indicating topic introduction)	*For the ecological movement...* *Although the way ahead now seems clear...*

column details the particular function associated with the tools, and the third provides examples.

Goutsos (1997) believed that the tools are what writers have at their disposal to indicate topical continuity and shift in expository discourse, and he went on to state that the signaling strength of each tool varies. Goutsos argued that in expository text, the top-most item in the table above (i.e. orthographic markers) is a stronger topic structuring item than the second one, and so on down to the last item. On the basis of his analysis of three corpora of expository texts, Goutsos (1997: 82) came to the conclusion that:

> … paragraph breaks, metadiscourse items, and prediction pairs usually are sufficient indicators of a specific technique [of topic shift / continuity]. Discourse markers and cohesive devices, on the other hand, are not always unequivocal in the identification of a sequential technique and need corroborating evidence from other signals. The role of these markers crucially depends on determining their scope.... [T]ime framing and sentence-structure arrangements are indirect signals of sequential strategies, because their main function is to establish time deixis and articulate the function of sentential constituents respectively.

Goutsos stated that the taxonomic hierarchy given above is valid in explaining expository text sequencing but not shift and continuity in other genres or text types. For example, he commented that narrative tends to use certain devices (e.g. time framing and initial adjuncts) more than other text types to help manage textual development, and he believed that in some types of journalistic discourse[3] (specifically, news discourse) the paragraph marker is not used in the same way as in expository text paragraphing (i.e. the paragraph is not so important in indicating topic framing or closure and so moves down the hierarchy in terms of its signaling significance).

The key observation made by Goutsos that I wish to build on in this chapter is that the above-noted signals can work together cumulatively and / or collectively. That is, though a single tool may (technically) be all that a writer needs to effect topic framing, introduction, continuation, or closure, a writer may choose to employ two or more signals to reinforce shift or continuity. Accordingly, in some cases there may appear to be an element of textual redundancy when a paragraph break co-occurs with a(nother) relatively strong signal of framing (e.g. the use of a metadiscourse marker). However, as will be discussed in Chapter 7, the fact that the paragraph break is a visuo-spatial typographic or orthographic cue, rather than a lexical or grammatical one, means that the paragraph break has psychological effects on readers, and as such the notion of redundancy may be weakened.

However, it is not just reinforcement that needs to be considered when signals co-occur. A simple redundancy view of multi-signaling fails to take into account cases in which the signals are actually different, rather than being cumulative, reinforcing or supporting. For example, a shift signal may be placed alongside a continuity signal. As an illustration of this, we can consider cases where pronominal anaphora occurs in paragraph-initial position. In such a case, framing for a new topic (i.e. the paragraph break) co-occurs with a signal of local textual continuity (e.g. *he* referring to *Lincoln* mentioned in the previous paragraph). The complex interaction between these various tools has, I believe, profound implications for our understanding of the role of the paragraph break in text.

Returning to the reinforcement idea of co-occurring signals, Goutsos (1997) suggested that the tools towards the middle and bottom of the table need further support from elements higher up in the table to send an unequivocal topic development signal to the reader. The paragraph break being the strongest indicator of framing and closure does not need such support; however, Goutsos (1997: 84) observed that a new paragraph commonly co-occurs with another signal, and in his corpus-based analyses he observed that of 274 paragraph breaks studied, 44.52% occurred with a definite subject (including clauses as subjects and shell nouns, i.e. nouns which are dependent on co-text for their complete meaning, described in more detail below), 24.45% began with adjuncts (adverbials and bound, i.e. dependent clauses), and 13.14% began with conjunctions.[4] My own work (McGee, 2014) examining paragraphing patterns in argumentative text broadly supports Goutsos' observation that multi-signaling is the norm when one encounters the paragraph break; that is, an additional tool indicating shift, or indeed continuity, often co-occurs with the paragraph break.

In what follows, I review research which has looked at examples of the last six topic-organizing indicators provided in Goutsos' taxonomy, and their co-occurrence with and relationship to the paragraph break (the first organizing tool in the taxonomy). Of specific interest is how and why writers use these signals together with the paragraph break, and what can be learned about the paragraph and paragraphing from examining multi-signaling practices.

While advocating the use of Goutsos' taxonomy for this enquiry, it should be mentioned that his classification is somewhat problematic on both theoretical and pragmatic grounds. The theoretical problem is in the characterization and the discreteness or non-discreteness of the classes. Specifically, discourse markers are often considered to be a subset of metadiscourse markers, as in the work of Ken Hyland (Hyland, 2005), though Goutsos (1997: 50, 51) differentiated the two, on the grounds that discourse markers are a closed class and have little referential meaning.[5] Further, some scholars have attributed discourse marker status to the paragraph break (Marcu, 2000a,b) and to tense change (Taboada, 2006: 584), both of which Goutsos has as separate discourse-organizing devices – the latter in the category of "time framing." A related problem is that a particular indicator of framing, introduction, continuation, or closure could be classified in more than one way. For example, what is categorized as an "advance label" (see below) might be considered part of a prediction pair, a cohesive device, or a metadiscourse marker. Similarly, topic foregrounding (see below) can be classified as an example of a prediction pair or a cohesion marker, and *so* and *because* could be thought of as both cohesive markers and discourse markers. However, despite these problems, I utilize the taxonomy, given its overall usefulness.

Metadiscourse Markers

Academics do not always agree about what metadiscourse means. Indeed, Hyland (2005) bewailed the vagueness and fuzziness surrounding the term, criticizing simplistic notions that metadiscourse is simply text about text (p. 16), arguing that metadiscourse must be considered from rhetorical and pragmatic perspectives (p. 25). Hyland (2004: 134) defined metadiscourse as "the linguistic devices writers employ to shape their arguments to the needs and expectations of their target readers." Hyland and Polly Tse (Hyland and Tse, 2004: 159) sought to build their own model of metadiscourse on three principles, which I comment on below.

1. The Non-Propositional Meaning of Metadiscourse

While acknowledging the challenges inherent in differentiating propositional (i.e. content, broadly speaking) from non-propositional (i.e. non-content, namely, text-managing) material, Hyland and Tse (2004: 161) argued that metadiscourse is related to the "internal argument and its readers," rather than to the message of the text itself. However, they were keen not to draw so sharp a distinction as others have done between propositional and non-propositional material. An example of a sharp distinction can be found in Susanne Hempel and Liesbeth Degand, who believed that metadiscourse signals can be removed and the essential message of the text remain (Hempel and Degand, 2008: 679).

2. The Reader-Writer Interactive Focus of Metadiscourse

Hyland and Tse (2004) questioned the textual (i.e. organizational) versus interactional (i.e. reader-oriented) classification of metadiscourse markers – as propounded, for example, by William Vande Kopple (Vande Kopple, 1985) and Avon Crismore, Raija Markkanen, and Margaret Steffensen (Crismore et al., 1993). Hyland and Tse (2004: 161) argued that *all* metadiscourse has some kind of interpersonal function as it is reader-oriented. For example, Hyland (2004: 137) believed that an interpersonal function is clearly present in language elements typically considered to be only textual (e.g. concessives acting as conjunctions). According to Hyland and Tse (2004), a reader-focused (interpersonal) orientation is considered to be essential in all metadiscourse, whether indicating to the reader how the text is organized or indicating to the reader what the writer thinks or feels about the subject matter.

3. The Internal Textual Relations Indicated by Metadiscourse

For Hyland and Tse (2004: 167), it is only within a textual context (i.e. when considered in relation to co-text) that language can function as metadiscourse. Accordingly, metadiscourse markers are only metadiscourse markers in a text (and hence cannot be labeled as discrete items, or simply listed). Further, they insisted that all metadiscourse markers be text-related, rather than world-related (i.e. referring to extra-textual material – knowledge of how the world works, for example).

A Taxonomy of Metadiscourse Markers

In rejecting some of the typically held distinctions and classifications of metadiscourse markers, Hyland and Tse (2004) advocated an alternative functional classification of "interactive" versus "interactional" markers. The former describes how the writer orients the reader through the text; in the latter, the writer comments on the text, involving the reader and showing solidarity with him / her. Hyland and Tse (2004: 169) provided a taxonomy of metadiscourse markers in academic texts for these two functions, which I provide below, with an example of each.

Interactive
- Transitions (e.g. *in addition*)
- Frame markers (e.g. *finally*)
- Endophoric markers (e.g. *noted above*)
- Evidentials (e.g. *according to X*)
- Code glosses (e.g. *in other words*)

Interactional
- Hedges (e.g. *might*)
- Boosters (e.g. *in fact*)
- Attitude markers (e.g. *surprisingly*)
- Engagement markers (e.g. *note that*)
- Self-mentions (e.g. *I*)

Hyland and Tse's taxonomy is well-respected, and some researchers have further adapted and subclassified elements of it – for example, Hempel and Degand (2008: 681), and more recently, Feng Cao and Guangwei Hu (Cao and Hu, 2014: 18). Hyland (2005) provided a list of 300 language items that had the potential to act as metadiscourse markers in an appendix to his book on metadiscourse, and the items listed include words belonging to most word classes: verbs (e.g. *show, prove*), nouns (e.g. *focus, goal*), adjectives (e.g. *certain, appropriate*), adverbs (e.g. *surprisingly, unclearly*), conjunctions (e.g. *and, but*), pronouns (e.g. *I, we*), and punctuation marks (e.g. *( ) , ?*).Various multi-word prepositional phrases are also listed (e.g. *in this section, for the moment*) and one clause (*I mean*). It is enlightening to note the preponderance of certain grammatical classes having specific functions in Hyland's taxonomy. For example, attitude markers seem to be typically adjectives and adverbs, and engagement markers tend to be verbs. Hyland believed that metadiscourse is an "open category" (2005: 27), as opposed to discourse markers, all of which can be listed.

Both the prevalence and genre-specific distribution of metadiscourse markers have been noted by a number of scholars. Hyland (2004: 140) observed that a metadiscourse marker occurred, on average, every 21 words in his postgraduate writing corpus (the most frequent subcategory being hedges). Having said this, the distribution of metadiscourse markers has been observed to vary in different genres. For example, Cao and Hu (2014) found that psychology research articles used more exemplifiers (a type of code gloss in their taxonomy) such as *for example* than education research articles, and Hempel and Degand (2008: 690) observed that fiction used fewer sequencers (a subset of frame markers in their taxonomy) such as *first* or *next,* as compared to academic writing. Hyland documented that self-mention was more common in Ph.D. theses than in Masters dissertations (Hyland, 2004: 143), and that fewer hedges and boosters were used in popular science than in academic writing (Hyland 2005: 99). Annelie Ädel found fewer question marks were used in the essay writing of British as compared to American university students (Ädel, 2006).

Metadiscourse and the Paragraph

Surprisingly little research has been conducted into metadiscourse usage and paragraph position (either paragraph number or sentence placement within a specific paragraph), as noted by Ädel (2006: 125). Hyland (2005), in his comprehensive text on metadiscourse, not once referred to the paragraph positioning of metadiscourse items, although a number of the examples from the taxonomy provided above would, intuitively, seem to be suitable candidates to open a paragraph. One might expect, for example, that frame markers (such as *finally*) would typically be paragraph-initial in a text (see Cao and Hu 2014: 19), and it would seem reasonable to assume that some engagement markers (e.g. *I, Note that*) would find particular potency in paragraph-initial position, and further that other metadiscourse markers would not be well-suited to being used in such a position (e.g. code glosses, such as *in other words* which, one might assume, would be more suited to signaling continuation in text). However, I am not aware of any research focusing on metadiscourse usage and paragraph position. A plausible explanation for this neglect, and the rather large gap in the literature resulting, is that corpus software has only recently begun to allow researchers to flag the paragraph location of sentences within a corpus. In essence, the software has dictated – and up until recently seriously limited – the types of enquiries which researchers have been able to conduct into the specific textual placement of metadiscourse markers.

A rather unique study which did set out to investigate the textual location of metadiscourse markers is found in Ädel (2006). Ädel's goal was to research the distribution of personal metadiscourse markers (i.e. *I*, *we*, and *you*) and impersonal markers (specifically, the words *essay* and *question*) within three student writing corpora representing different varieties of English (American, British, and Swedish). While commenting that her ideal objective would have been to observe which specific paragraphs the markers occurred in, she stated that the paragraphing of the sentences within her corpus was not clearly marked in the text files; as a consequence, she chose to simply split the texts up into equally sized segments and identify metadiscourse distribution within the segments. She found, inter alia, that the beginnings and endings of the student texts contained more personal metadiscourse markers than other parts of the text, and that the impersonal metadiscourse markers *essay* and *question* references were most common in the beginning of the texts.

Other than this quite focused research, references to metadiscourse marker paragraph location are few and far between. Anna Mauranen suggested that "[t]he orienting aspect of metatext is particularly important in initial positions, such as introductions" (Mauranen, 1993: 11); however, as noted earlier, it is probably only some kinds of metatext that would be suitable candidates to be in such a position. Heather Adams and Elena Quintana-Toledo found that epistemic stance markers (e.g. *of course, perhaps, probably*) were more common in conclusions than introductions in research articles (Adams and Quintana-Toledo, 2013), and Hempel and Degand (2008: 688) observed numerical sequencing (*firstly*, etc.) across paragraphs, though noted that they were more typically inter-sentential rather than inter-paragraph items in their corpus. Finally, Henna Makkonen-Craig, in her analysis of an aspect of Finnish newspaper metadiscourse (transitional elements such as the Finnish versions of *let's move on* or *let us assume that*), observed that such forms are common in paragraph-final or paragraph-initial position, and that their basic function is to guide the reader through the text (Makkonen-Craig, 2011).

Focused research into the presence of certain classes (or specific instances) of metadiscourse markers within paragraphs is generally lacking and is clearly needed. Not only will such studies help refine genre-based distinctions of text patterns, findings will probably be of considerable help to teachers. Hyland (2004: 135) characterized current approaches to the teaching of metadiscourse markers as largely "piecemeal." Teachers clearly need more accurate and specific information about metadiscourse usage in relation to paragraphing which they can then pass on to their students.

Prediction Pairs

As John Sinclair observed, a writer may "prospect" (Sinclair, 2004: 88) to the reader what is to follow, that is, provide a signal about the direction that the discourse will take, in either general or specific terms. Sinclair elaborated on three such types of prospection in his analysis of a magazine article: namely, attribution, advance labeling,[6] and the introduction of a new topic. Concerning the first, attribution, Sinclair (2004: 98) commented on how the author of the extract below used the phrase *his message* to close a paragraph, before giving the content of the message in the following paragraph:

> *...Last week he addressed British industrialists and his message was typically forthright:*
>   *'In two years' time, the United Kingdom will find itself...*

The second class of prospection observed by Sinclair, which he termed "advance labelling," concerned an author's use of the paragraph-initial expression *the implications are daunting*, with the details of the daunting implications (i.e. the advance label) following this comment. Sinclair's third class of prospection was when a new topic is introduced which the reader expects to be developed. This last class seems to be very similar to what Rachel Giora (1983a,b, 1985, 1990) had in mind in her discussion surrounding topic foregrounding, a subject discussed in more detail later in this section.

Goutsos' (1997) corpus-based work on prospection added three other kinds of predictive pairs (in addition to examples of the advance labeling class noted by Sinclair). These are:

- Enumeration (*three...advantages*, followed by *first, second, and third*);
- Hypothetical pair (*Take one, newish problem*);
- Question–Answer pairs (*What is the advantage...?* followed in a later sentence by *...answer...*).

It should be noted that of the above, only one type of predictive pair (enumeration) prospected across paragraph boundaries in Goutsos' data. In my own analyses of paragraphs in argumentative text (McGee, 2014), another two predictive pairs were observed, both occurring in paragraph closing and opening position:

- Apothegm (a popular saying) followed by its justification
  Specifically, the writer closed a paragraph with *It's not that simple*, and the following paragraph explained why gun control is more complicated than gun advocates might argue.
- Illocutionary invitation
  In this case, the author closed a paragraph with *let us take a closer look*, the next paragraph explaining how, exactly, western culture is in decay (note also the reference made in the Metadiscourse section to the observation by Makkonen-Craig, 2011, on the Finnish equivalent of such language occurring in a similar textual position).

There are probably other types of predictive pairs which operate at the paragraph break or across paragraph breaks, and further research into this area should reveal interesting patterns. In terms of more detailed research on the above-mentioned predictive pairs operating across the paragraph break, two types (both of which were observed by Sinclair) have been examined in more detail: advance labeling and topic foregrounding. I leave discussion on advance labeling to the section on cohesion (specifically, shell nouns) below, and here focus on Giora's work on topic foregrounding.

Giora (1983a,b, 1985, 1990) suggested that if a new topic or subtopic is mentioned towards the end of a paragraph, it prospects the to-be-developed topic of the next paragraph. Below I provide an example from Giora to illustrate this point.

> *Wherever you go in the world, be it New York or Nairobi, and whatever you do, business or pleasure, be sure to take Thomas Cook Euro Travellers Cheques.*
>
> *Thomas Cook Euro Travellers Cheques are sold in 153 countries, and are welcomed throughout the world.* (Giora, 1990: 27)

In her research, Giora (1983a,b, 1990) found that paragraphs from a considerable number of the text types which she studied exhibited discourse topic foregrounding (such as seen in the extract above): 26% of her data exhibited this feature (Giora, 1990: 26). Further, in her own manipulation of texts, she found that readers seemed to expect and be quite comfortable with such foregrounding in their reading: it did not confuse them, and neither did it seem strange or awkward.

The traditional view of the paragraph has equated the orthographic paragraph with a semantic or functional unit; that is, a particular paragraph treated a particular subject, or functional relation, and the next paragraph treated the next subject or relation, and so on. Such a situation does, of course, happen – and frequently, as Giora (1990) herself acknowledged. Giora (1985) believed that the discourse topic proposition within such paragraphs will typically be paragraph-initial for the simple reason that from this position it can govern or control the readers' comprehension of what follows. If it is left to the end of the paragraph, the reader does not have this orienting and controlling assistance, and reading speeds have been shown to be slower as a result (Giora, 1985: 129, see also Chapter 7 of this book). In paragraphing of this kind Giora (1990: 26) argued that some other paragraph-initial signal which links the new topic to the previous paragraph is typically required after the paragraph break, such as a conjunction (e.g. *yet*), to signal how the new discourse topic (and paragraph) is related to the preceding one.

Discourse topic foregrounding (i.e. when the new discourse topic is given at the end of the paragraph, preceding its actual development in the following paragraph) clearly does not sit comfortably with the traditional view of the paragraph, for obvious reasons, since the new topic mentioned at the end of the paragraph is only loosely linked to that paragraph, and much more in focus and actually developed in the following paragraph. The key to understanding such a phenomenon, Giora argued, lies not only in the need for inter-paragraph cohesion, but also textual position and informativeness. Giora (1983a: 179) saw her work as developing František Daneš' theme and rheme work on the sentence (Daneš, 1974) and extending it to larger discourse units. Giora echoed Daneš' view that rheme position tends to be informationally high. She suggested that when a reader comes across a new point or topic at the end of the paragraph (i.e. one not covered by the discourse topic of the paragraph) which has the potential to be developed further, the reader will understand, if a paragraph break follows, that this topic is to become the next discourse topic. In Giora's (1983a: 155) words, rheme positioning of the next topic in such a context "endows...foreground status" on the to-be-developed discourse topic. When this occurs there is a natural flow between the paragraphs.

In Giora's view, topic foregrounding can be considered to be a particularly smooth cohesive, informationally motivated, inter-paragraph device. It should be mentioned here that the fact of topic foregrounding challenges the view that lexical cohesive links reflect, or indeed determine the formal unit of the paragraph; that is, the idea that lexical cohesive links are distinctly intra-paragraph phenomena, rather than inter-paragraph phenomena – a subject considered in more detail in Chapter 6.

So, why would a writer choose to mention a new topic and then segment the text, rather than simply leave the new topic to be introduced in the new paragraph? I have already mentioned the idea of cohesion, and information signaling, as possible reasons for this. In addition to these (or perhaps more accurately in relation to them), Giora (1990: 33) suggested that topic foregrounding is a cognitive aid to the reader (and writer): "Material in the final position is immediately available [i.e. mentally, in terms of information processing] for readers and writers to retain for further discussion in the following segment." Giora (1983b: 177) suggested a bimodal view of memory storage as a possible reason for, or advantage associated with, topic foregrounding; that is, material positioned in rheme-final position benefits from a "recency" effect being stored in short-term memory, and the topic sentence position of the new discourse topic (in the new paragraph) benefits from a "primacy" effect and is stored in long-term memory. Giora suggested that the combined recency and primacy effects help readers' comprehension and management of topic continuity and shift.

Giora's work on topic foregrounding touched on a key issue, and one which paragraph theorists had not previously considered in any detail before her work, namely, discourse-topic inter-paragraph cohesion, and the potentially prospecting relation between the end of one paragraph and the beginning of the next. As will be discussed in Chapter 6, computational linguists have focused on cohesion within the paragraph unit and their insights have been important. However, a complete understanding of paragraphing must also consider how paragraphs relate to each other, and Giora's efforts to understand this particular type of relationship between paragraphs broke new ground.

Discourse Markers

As mentioned earlier in this chapter, discourse markers are sometimes considered to be a subset of metadiscourse markers; thus, for example, Cao and Hu (2014) list many conjunctions in their "transitions" category, which is a subset of "interactive metadiscourse" in their taxonomy. In this section, I provide a brief overview of discourse markers, before considering some research into how they might indicate text structure and their use at the paragraph juncture.

Discourse markers (DMs) have been variously classified. A well-known and respected taxonomy is that provided by Bruce Fraser (Fraser, 1999). According to Fraser (1999: 938), DMs "impose a relationship between some aspect of the discourse segment they are a part of, call it S2, and some aspect of a prior discourse segment, call it S1." For Fraser, the meaning of a DM is "procedural not conceptual" (p. 931), in the sense that DMs do not have a set of semantic features, but rather interpret the relation between two text segments, though he stated that DMs do have a core meaning (p. 945) which co-text makes clear. Key to Fraser's understanding was the idea that the DM imposes certain possible interpretations on S2, in the context of S1.

Given the above characterization of DMs, many segment-initial expressions are excluded from consideration as discourse markers, as they do not play an inter-discourse role. For example, Fraser (1999: 942) noted that *frankly* as used in the following example is only related to S2, and therefore disqualified as being a DM:

Harry is old enough to drink. ***Frankly****, I don't think he should.*

Fraser (p. 943) believed there to be four grammatical classes of DMs:

- conjunctions (e.g. *and, but*)
- adverbs (e.g. *consequently, conversely*)
- prepositional phrases (e.g. *as a consequence, in particular*)
- idioms (e.g. *all things considered*)

Fraser (1999) classified all DMs into two broad classes: relating messages and relating topics. He subclassified the former into four categories:

- contrastive (e.g. *but*)
- elaborative (e.g. *and*)
- inferential (e.g. *so*)
- miscellaneous-explanatory (e.g. *after all*)

Fraser's second broad class related to topics (e.g. *incidentally*). Although not all theorists will agree with Fraser's requirements and taxonomy, as Degand (2009: 174) commented there is general agreement that a discourse marker relates two parts of discourse, is optional (in the sense that the item can be removed with no syntactic change needed), and is non-propositional.

Discourse Markers, Text, and the Paragraph

Some research has considered the presence (and absence) of certain DMs in paragraph-initial position. It seems that some DMs are not particularly good candidates to open a new paragraph in English, with *and* and *but*, in particular, singled out and proscribed in sentence-initial and paragraph-initial position in some composition manuals, as remarked by David Bell (Bell, 2007). As mentioned in Chapter 2, the translational equivalents of certain conjunctions not typically associated with paragraph-initial position in English do occur frequently in early Greek text (e.g. *and, but*), and the common sentence- and paragraph-initial use of *and* in modern-day Arabic is well attested (see the treatment by Abdulkhaliq AlAzzawie; AlAzzawie, 2014). Although *and* and *but* may not be common paragraph-initial markers in English, they do occur in these positions, as observed by Colleen Cotter, who found that they are used to connect short paragraphs, in particular, and believed that such usage may be for the purpose of creating a more reader-oriented text than would be the case otherwise (Cotter, 2003). Bell (2007) also provided examples in which paragraph-initial *but* was used to add the final part of a list, and to indicate topic shift, in academic writing.

Other DMs have also been noted by their absence or rarity in paragraph-initial position. Goutsos (1997: 65, 66) observed the almost total absence of *also* and *too* in paragraph-initial position and the lack of adversative conditionals (*yet, however, meanwhile, but, of course*) in the same position in his exposition corpora. These findings suggest that certain kinds of relationship are not typically signaled across the paragraph break – or perhaps, more specifically, certain lexical or grammatical items which signal certain relations do not do so across the paragraph break. This is an area where more research would certainly help develop a better understanding of which relations are or are not signaled across paragraphs.

Rhetorical Structure and the Paragraph

Perhaps the most interesting work in relation to discourse markers and text structure is Marcu's (2000a,b) computational work, which was based on William Mann and Sandra Thompson's Rhetorical Structure Theory (RST; Mann and Thompson, 1988). RST provides a means of analyzing a text's coherence in terms of its non-overlapping coordinate and subordinate relations, documenting the rhetorical relations (e.g. background, elaboration, justification, condition, etc.) between the parts of text in order to build tree structures (see example below).

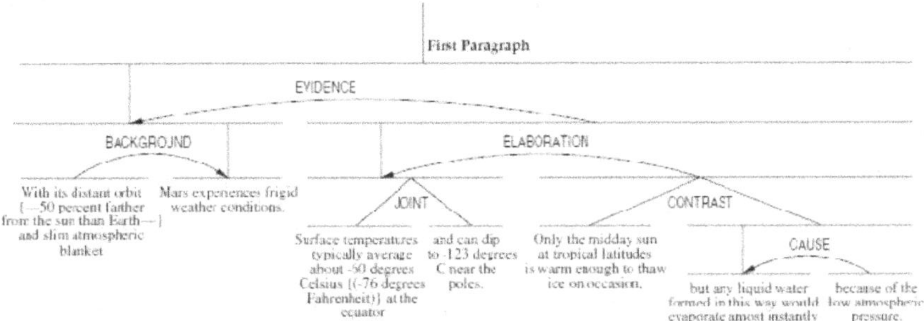

Figure 5.1. Textual Rhetorical Relations in a Paragraph [From *The Theory and Practice of Discourse Parsing and Summarization* Figure 1.3 (Marcu, 2000b, p. 4). © 2000 Massachusetts Institute of Technology. Used by permission of The MIT Press.]

In the above figure it can be observed that *but* is used to signal contrast towards the latter part of the paragraph, and *because* introduces the reason for a particular phenomenon in the final clause. Marcu's (2000a,b) work focused on how discourse markers such as those in the figure provided are used by writers to signal the various rhetorical relations between elements of a text. Below I provide a very brief summary of this work.

Although Marcu's research was computational in orientation (i.e. his goal was to create software which could parse a text), I do not focus on this aspect of his work, but rather how he utilized the presence of discourse markers in text to help identify its rhetorical structure, and how the paragraph break fits into his work. Marcu was interested in finding out whether the rhetorical structures of text could be identified (computationally) simply due to the presence of discourse markers present within a text, which signal the structural relations. The feasibility of such an endeavor, Marcu (2000a: 399) argued, lay partly in the ubiquity of such markers in text – one for every two clauses, according to Gisela Redeker (Redeker, 1990) – and partly in previous work which had explored the discourse organizing roles of such markers. Marcu recognized the serious obstacles facing any attempt to exploit the presence of these markers to identify text structure or rhetorical structure. The first of these problems is that DMs can play various roles, and unless these roles can be differentiated computationally, one cannot utilize the markers to identify the text structure. Secondly, there is the issue of span. Some markers may have a more local text span, and others a wider span, and it is not necessarily the case that a new DM "cancels" the span or effect of a previous DM. Finally, there is the issue of multiple relations being signaled by a single marker: *but*, for example, can signal antithesis or concession, but computationally it would be difficult to identify the function at any one time.[7]

The problems documented by Marcu seem quite insurmountable (particularly when considered together), but he argued that they could be overcome. Regarding the problem of differentiating sentential and discourse functions, Marcu pointed to work by Hirschberg with Diane Litman (Hirschberg and Litman, 1993) which suggested that punctuation marks could help in differentiating about 80% of ambiguous cases, and he developed a corpus (containing cue phrases) to construct an algorithm to further improve this percentage. Regarding the scope of a cue, Marcu (2000a: 400) argued that all of the possible spans of a particular marker (e.g. *in contrast*) can be documented and an "exclusively disjunctive hypothesis" can be formulated, that is, only one valid structure of several possible hypothesized relations actually holds in any particular case. For example, if *in contrast* occurs between sentences 2 and 3, in a four-sentence paragraph, although it could relate sentences 1 and 3, 2 and 3, 1 and 2 with 3, etc., it will actually relate to only one set of all the possible sets. Thirdly, with regard to rhetorical function ambiguity, he believed that an exclusive-disjunction hypothesis could also resolve this problem, that is, assuming that only one valid rhetorical function actually holds in a given case. In addition, Marcu (2000a: 401) noted that in his analyses he had not come across a case in which a discourse marker signaled more than one relation at a time.[8] Marcu's work was significant in that the identification of the rhetorical structure relations within various text types (*Scientific American*, *Time*, and narrative) by human analysts was comparable to computer analysis by means of his algorithm, this being solely dependent on the presence of discourse markers.

Concerning the paragraph break, Marcu believed it should be considered a type of discourse marker. Part of the reason for making this assumption was pragmatic, as Marcu (2000b: 112) candidly acknowledged: it helped to limit the numerous RST hypothetical options for the algorithm to deal with, and so the paragraph break was considered just one of many potential discourse markers. Spelling out the relationship between RST and paragraphing (along with other punctuation marks), he commented:

> The algorithm presented…assumes that the rhetorical structure of
> a text correlates with the orthographic layout of that text. That is,
> it assumes that sentences, paragraphs, and sections correspond to
> hierarchical spans in the rhetorical representation of the text that
> they subsume. (Marcu, 2000a: 410)

This assumption is, of course, contentious, and the idea that the function of the paragraph is to map the rhetorical representation of the text was challenged by both Rodgers (1965, 1966a,b) and Pitkin (1969, 1977), as documented in Chapter 4. However, Marcu's assumption would appear to be valid, at least in some kinds of expository texts, given the satisfactory performance of his algorithm in identifying rhetorical structure.

Marcu (2000a,b) observed that markers which link two paragraphs may occur either at the end of one paragraph or the beginning of the following paragraph. In addition, he observed that rhetorical spans can cross a paragraph, that is, a group of paragraphs may be joined together to function as a single rhetorical structure span (Marcu, 2000b: 93). He believed that his algorithm worked well with certain relations (e.g. contrast, concession, and cause) but not others (e.g. elaboration and evidence). The reason for this difference he suggested, is that paragraphs which use few markers tend to elaborate on the first sentence (containing the most important information) but that other more complex relations within a paragraph generally utilize discourse markers to indicate these relations (hence the positive effect on the performance of his algorithm with contrast, concession and cause relations). Maite Taboada's work (Taboada, 2006: 579) confirmed Marcu's observations with regard to the presence of DMs connecting certain text relations (specifically, concession, circumstance, and result) and their absence, or reduced usage, in signaling others (e.g. background, elaboration, and summary).

Marcu was not particularly interested in looking at whether certain DMs had a statistical tendency to occur in paragraph-initial position, and neither was he interested in investigating whether particular markers typically span several following clauses or sentences, or indeed the whole of the paragraph. This was because his focus was on identifying rhetorical structure textual relations within a text, rather than on analyzing paragraph structure per se. However, his work is helpful to our present enquiry in showing that a paragraph break may indicate the beginning of a rhetorical span (see also further comments on the relationship between RST and paragraphing below), and be considered a type of discourse marker (in the sense that it has the potential to indicate a relationship between two text segments), although the nature of that relationship may not be specified without the presence of some additional signal.

Cohesion

Textual cohesion is typically discussed in relation to the internal patterning within the paragraph, rather than in terms of the links made across paragraphs, as mentioned earlier. A break in cohesion has often been considered to be indicative of a paragraph break, as will be discussed in more detail in Chapter 6. However, as the observant reader may have noted in the section on prediction pairs, the particular example of topic foregrounding given (the Thomas Cook travellers cheques example) involved lexical repetition functioning as a cohesive link across the paragraph break. In what follows, I focus on what has been said about textual cohesion links (both lexical and grammatical) across paragraphs.

Anaphora in Text

Does pronominal anaphora occur across the paragraph break, and should it? For example, if a paragraph is about Abraham Lincoln, and the next paragraph continues to talk about Lincoln, will the paragraph begin with *He* or *Lincoln*, if the writer wishes to begin the paragraph by referring to the same actor? If both are possible, why is one or the other used in any particular instance? A related phenomenon to be considered is anaphoric encapsulation, that is, the use of a general noun (e.g. *this tragedy*) in paragraph-opening position to refer to a previously mentioned state of affairs or event(s) in the preceding paragraph, and when and why this can occur.

Anaphora has been extensively studied from multiple perspectives, including linguistic, psychological, and philosophical, as noted by Jeanette Gundel, Nancy Hedberg and Ron Zacharski (Gundel et al., 1993) as well as pragmatic, the perspective taken by Yan Huang (Huang, 2000). In this section, I provide a very brief overview of some of the key work in this area, to contextualize the focus within this section on the use of full noun-phrases (e.g. *Lincoln*), pronominal anaphora (e.g. *he* to refer to *Lincoln*), and anaphoric shell nouns (e.g. *this tragedy*), and their cohesive linking functions across the paragraph break.

Huang (2000), in his overview of discourse perspectives on anaphora, differentiated three approaches: topic continuity, hierarchical, and cognitive. He then presented his own pragmatic model (in relation to conversation paragraphs[9]). Below I consider each of these approaches in turn, although it should be made clear that these different approaches cannot be neatly differentiated, a fact which Huang openly acknowledged when discussing the relationship between the second and third perspectives.

In the first perspective, that of topic continuity, epitomized in the work of Talmy Givón (e.g. Givón, 1983), three factors affect the choice of which reference form to use. These are the textual proximity to the referred to item(s), the effect of potentially confusing alternative elements, and the theme under discussion. For example, we might expect to see zero anaphora or pronominalization (i.e. semantically "light" referencing) when the antecedent is textually close to the reference to it, when no other elements within the text could be confused with the referent, and / or when the theme is continuous. However, when there is greater distance between antecedent and the referring form, competing referents are present in the co-text, and theme switch occurs, a fuller and semantically richer reference may be considered necessary to help the reader follow the writer's meaning. This might be through repetition or the use of a subordinate or superordinate term.

The second (hierarchical) perspective is driven by the discourse structure, rather than by the surface text. Because the paragraph is generally considered to be a type of discourse structure, this perspective is the one most relevant to my focus in this book (and hence elaborated on in more detail later in this section). Briefly, we can say that hierarchical perspectives on anaphora (see Hinds, 1979; Hofmann, 1989; Longacre, 1979) suggest that when a new segment or section of text begins, one will expect to see full NPs. Within the same section, on the other hand, pronominal reference will tend to occur (when such will not confuse the reader) and when a new section starts, one will expect to observe fuller semantic referencing (in all likelihood this being related to some shift in the discourse topic). Barbara Fox differentiated two different roles of anaphora: one in which "context determines use," that is, when the existing discourse structure determines the anaphoric reference to be used and one in which "use accomplishes context," that is, when the form of reference signals a shift in the hierarchical structure, rather than simply fitting in with the existing one (Fox, 1993: 16, 93). The first case is a kind of unmarked reference usage, in which the writer signals to the reader a continuation / elaboration by the use of a pronoun. However, when a NP rather than a pronoun is used by the writer this may be an attempt to indicate to the reader a shift to a new rhetorical structure. The idea that the relationship between indentation and reference form is dynamic is elaborated on further below.

The third approach to anaphora (the cognitive approach) is primarily concerned with reader (and, to a lesser extent, writer) cognition. Important considerations within this perspective include the ideas of *activation* and *attention*. The basic premise of cognitive approaches to anaphora is that if the antecedent is not activated in the reader's mind, a fuller anaphoric reference is required to refer to it, compared with cases where the referent is already activated (in which case zero anaphora or pronominalization would be more expected). Gundel et al. (1993) provided a cline of cognitive states (six in all), ranging from the referent being "in focus" (in which case only light referencing is needed) to "type identifiable" (in which case the fullest referencing is required – i.e. an NP). Gundel et al. posited that a particular type or level of reference will be more or less appropriate, given the reader's cognitive state at a certain point in time. Huang (2000: 162) believed that a strong relationship existed between the cognitive state perspective and the hierarchy perspective, viewing the latter as, in some ways, subordinate to cognitive constraints, in that episodes in text are directly related to memory limitations:

> ... alternation between full and reduced NPs inside and outside an episode is **merely** a function of the limitations imposed on the limited capacity of short-term working memory, which is manifested in the discourse artefact mainly through its episodic structure (emphasis added).

Huang (2000) summarized the shortcomings and the problems he observed in the above-mentioned perspectives before putting forward his own pragmatic theory, in which anaphor choices are governed by well-known Gricean maxims specifically adapted to anaphor: not giving more anaphoric reference than required, not giving less, and not using a marked form without reason. Huang's pragmatic explanation of anaphor choice is one of a number of pragmatically based perspectives (see e.g. Bolinger, 1979). The main attraction of such approaches to understanding anaphora is their ability to deal with problem cases and exceptions – an ability which the other perspectives struggle to cope with.

Below I focus on the hierarchical perspective on anaphora, and discuss, in some detail, whether the orthographic paragraph can be characterized as a unit beginning with a semantically rich reference, in which later referential tracking is achieved through semantically weak anaphoric reference (where possible), switching to full NP structures in beginning a new paragraph.

Pronominal Reference and the Paragraph

Thomas Hofmann believed the orthographic paragraph break to be a barrier to anaphora: "a pronoun cannot find an antecedent embedded in a previous paragraph" (Hofmann, 1989: 239). He used a blackboard metaphor to explain why he believed this to be the case, suggesting that ending a paragraph is like wiping the blackboard clean in a lecture hall. Just as the lecturer cannot point to erased text on the board, so the writer cannot ask the reader to refer back to the previous paragraph to find the antecedent of a pronominal anaphor. Hofmann is not alone in making a connection between hierarchical structure and memory: Giora (1996: 430), for example, used similar language when discussing the paragraph break and memory:

> Beginnings of episodes and paragraphs are where new discourse-topics are introduced. Introduction of a new discourse-topic involves shifting...and triggers suppression of previous information. Previous information, therefore, is less accessible in segment-initial position, which explains why anaphors are expected to be more explicit at the beginning of a paragraph or a new episode.[10]

Great care must be taken when considering Hofmann's blackboard metaphor. Hofmann himself acknowledged that some kind of mental saving operation occurs in the mind of a reader when completing a paragraph. Although the board may be wiped clean, it would be a dangerous analogy indeed to suggest that memory is similarly "wiped." Giora's comments (noted above in the long quotation), on the other hand, are more considered and careful, in acknowledging that anaphoric reference *can* cross the paragraph, while at the same time suggesting that the paragraph break may well have some kind of cognitive limiting effect on the type of referencing so allowed.

Perhaps surprisingly, given the rather wide-sweeping and unqualified scope of his paragraph barrier pronouncement, Hofmann went on to provide an exception to his rule, specifically in relation to narrative. Hofmann (1989: 245) stated that pronominal references occurring in the first or second sentence of a paragraph without the presence of another antecedent within the same paragraph, could refer to "something like the topics of their preceding paragraphs." What he meant by this is not entirely clear (discourse topic? last mentioned subject?). Hofmann believed that such anaphoric use de-emphasizes the paragraph break, in essence uniting the paragraphs into a larger unit. This was a critical observation, as it suggests that what might be considered to be the default role of the paragraph can be undone by the presence / absence of a particular word or expression in paragraph-initial position. Hofmann referred to paragraphs in the latter part of D.H. Lawrence's *The Prussian Officer* to support his argument. Although Hofmann did not provide actual examples from this text, below I note the opening words of five consecutive paragraphs from it, in which *he* refers to the servant, or the orderly, of the Prussian Officer:

> *He came to with a start...*
> *When he opened his eyes again...*
> *He lay down again exhausted...*
> *He came to with a further ache of exhaustion...*
> *He sat up...*

As can be seen in the above sentences each of the paragraphs refers to the subject (the orderly) only as *he*. I would suggest, however, that the name of the orderly not being mentioned in the story may be behind this interesting usage, hence lessening its significance as an example of unusual pronominal referencing across the paragraph juncture.

Gotthold Lessing (the German writer, playwright, and poet) was known for his use of paragraph-initial pronominal anaphora, as mentioned by Sergei Gindin (Gindin, 1978). However, it is not just in narrative that such referencing occurs. Pronominal anaphora across the paragraph juncture in newspaper articles has been observed and commented on by Francis Cornish, who found that in an article containing 10 paragraphs, two contained anaphoric *it* with antecedents in preceding paragraphs (Cornish, 2003). Fox

(1993) also noted such usage in expository text, as did Mira Ariel (Ariel, 1988).

The data mentioned in the previous paragraph challenge Hoffman's barrier view. However, there is also plenty of evidence to support his belief. Goutsos (1997: 49), for example, observed that in a mixed (expository) corpus (including academic, journalistic, and editorial texts), only three of 274 paragraphs analyzed began with anaphoric pronominalization. In addition, Ariel (1988: 72) found the reintroduction of the semantically full noun phrase to be extremely common in opening a paragraph, though not strictly necessary, in the sense that pronominal anaphora would not have been ambiguous, the referent being in close proximity.

Further support for the barrier view of anaphora across paragraphs comes from human segmentation tasks, such as Heather Stark's (Stark, 1988) and Hoey's (2005) research, in which participants are faced with de-paragraphed text and are required to reparagraph the text. It has been observed that the presence of a full NP rather than a pronominalized form affects people's segmentation decisions, suggesting that the full NP may function as a discourse (specifically, paragraph) organizing clue to the reader in completing such a task. In Hoey's (2005: 140) words, "...names are primed to start paragraphs and pronouns are not." While there does seem to be some counter-evidence to Hofmann's broad barrier claim, there appears to be more support for it than evidence against it – with genre convention differences perhaps responsible for the variable data.

An easy way to resolve some (perhaps all) of the various findings concerning pronominal anaphoric usage across the paragraph juncture is to appeal to the structural and orthographic paragraph distinction noted in the opening chapter of the book, the idea that there are suprasentential structural or functional units in text which are not orthographic units (alternative terms for such units being "stadia" or "blocs," as mentioned in Chapter 4). Simply put, it may be that when the orthographic paragraph maps onto the structural paragraph, one can expect there to be a full noun phrase at the "peak sentence" (Stark, 1988: 291) within the segment, introducing the to-be-defined topic. However, when the orthographic paragraph is not so aligned, anaphoric pronominal reference may be employed by the writer in orthographic-paragraph-initial position, indicating both continuation within a larger structural / functional unit, together with some kind of "mini" shift or movement being indicated (hence the paragraph break). Cornish (2003) explained paragraph-initial pronominal referencing in newspaper articles by employing such an argument, and Fox (1993: 113), in discussing the relation between the paragraph and anaphora in the context of Rhetorical Structure Theory (RST, see previous section), proposed a similar explanation to deal with instances of paragraph-initial pronominal anaphora that cross the paragraph juncture:

> Although rhetorical breaks are often signalled in expository prose by paragraph breaks, it would not be accurate to say simply that in expository prose all paragraphs begin with full NPs...while paragraphs are rhetorical units of a sort, they are not the major units which influence anaphora....

Such explanations may indeed solve many of the problems inherent in an orthographic paragraph hierarchical perspective of pronominal anaphora. No doubt, however, problematic cases remain, solvable only with the help of what one might term the pragmatic "silver bullet." Bolinger (1979: 290), an advocate of a pragmatic understanding of anaphora, suggested that an important question to ask was why at a particular time a speaker may choose to use a reference word lighter or fuller in semantic content than another option. While the hierarchical perspective can, I suggest, shed considerable light on anaphoric reference across the paragraph juncture, there will be times when specific usage is difficult to explain, and as such, the hierarchical view of anaphora can never be watertight, and it would be wrong to expect it to be so, given arguments over the presence of other textual units within text mentioned in Chapters 1 and 4.

If the preceding argument covering the orthographic and structural paragraph distinction is sound, it would follow that a detailed study of paragraph-initial pronominal anaphora may help us better understand which genres allow a more casual relationship between orthographic and structural paragraphs, and which tend to have the two units more closely aligned and contiguous. In addition, deeper analyses of such data may also give us some clue as to why some genres may adopt mapping and others not.

Before leaving this section, I want to comment a little more on the idea noted earlier that anaphora (and anaphoric choice) not only tracks a referent, in a purely cohesive sense, but also indicates (weak view) or organizes (strong view) discourse structure. These views have been advanced by several scholars. Lesley Stirling, for example, in surveying a number of languages, suggested that there is clear evidence of a discourse-boundary indicating role related to anaphoric choice (Stirling, 2001: 7). Such a role is usually delimited to the phenomenon of "over-referencing," that is, using a fuller referencing form than strictly required according to the four perspectives on anaphoric use discussed above. In a similar vein to Stirling (2001), Wietske Vonk, Lettica Hustinx, and Wim Simons suggested a discourse-structure indicative role when the anaphor is semantically richer than strictly required:

> ...if...anaphoric expressions are more specific than necessary for their identificational function, they not only relate the current information to the intended referent, but also contribute to the expression of the thematic structure of the discourse and to the comprehension of the thematic structure. (Vonk et al., 1992: 301)

What this means, in practice, is that the function of the paragraph break can only be interpreted or understood, alongside the choice of the reference device used: the use of pronominal anaphora at the paragraph juncture would tend to indicate that the shift function of the break is reduced, and the use of a full NP would seem to give full shift status to the break.

While scholars will not always agree on what constitutes over-referencing (due largely to the complexities of pragmatic considerations), the above explanations do, I suggest, help to better understand the relationship between pronominal anaphora and the paragraph, and why full NPs are typically considered to occur more commonly in paragraph-initial position than pronominal anaphora in expository text.

Shell Nouns and the Paragraph

Shell nouns, variously termed (see below), have occasionally been discussed in relation to paragraphing, although it would be fair to say that this interest is a fairly peripheral one in some of the literature. For example, Miguel-Angel Benitez-Castro (2015) in his recent overview of work on shell nouns only mentioned the paragraph once, in referring to another researcher's work. In what follows, I seek to provide a brief overview of work on shell nouns, before considering their presence and functions within paragraphs, and how their study may help us better understand an aspect of paragraphing and the organization of the paragraph.

Shell nouns and their functions

A number of terms have been used to classify a set of nouns whose meanings are largely dependent on co-text (Rahime Nur Aktas and Vivianna Cortes provide a summary of these terms and their definitions; Aktas and Cortes, 2008: 5). Halliday and Hasan (1976: 274–277) used the term "general nouns" to refer to a set of nouns (e.g. *the man* or *the thing*) which can function to refer to more specific nouns in context. They termed these nouns "borderline" in the sense that co-text (or context) is required by the listener or reader to know exactly what a general noun means in any given instance. As such, they operate between open set (lexical) and closed system (grammatical) items. Many other terms have been used for such kinds of noun: Gill Francis has called them variously "anaphoric nouns" (Francis, 1986), "labelling nouns"

(Francis, 1994), and, in his work with Susan Hunston, "shell nouns" (Hunston and Francis, 2000), a term also used by Hans-Jörg Schmid (Schmid, 2000). Roz Ivanič used the term "carrier nouns" (Ivanič, 1991), while John Flowerdew referred to this class as "signalling nouns" (Flowerdew, 2009). I use the term "shell noun" within this chapter because of its wide acceptance and usage in the applied linguistics community.

It is important to note that there has been some hesitancy to label (definitively) a noun as a shell noun. Schmid (2000) preferred to talk of the *potential* for a noun to function as a shell noun, rather than a word being a shell noun in a definitive sense, context being critical in indicating such a function. Regardless of the terminological differences noted above, the above-noted scholars appear to have in mind a similar set of nouns and functions, though, as noted below, Halliday and Hasan's perspective on the textual reference of general nouns is rather different from other scholars' views.

According to Schmid, shell nouns have three functions: semantic, cognitive, and textual. In what follows, I utilize Schmid's classification to guide the discussion, and interact with his views and other scholars' views on these functions.

Concerning the semantic function referred to above, Schmid (2000: 14) described the shell noun as "characterizing and perspectivizing complex chunks of information which are expressed in clauses or even longer stretches of text." Regarding characterization, he believed that shell nouns fall between full content nouns and pronouns (see also the reference to Halliday and Hasan's general noun comments above). Shell nouns are always considered to depend on their co-texts, to a greater or lesser extent, for a reader to understand their full semantic import. In Benitez-Castro's (2015: 191) words, a noun is not a shell noun if it is "semantically bounded." Nouns such as *problem, situation,* and *result* can be differentiated from other nouns (even abstract nouns, such as *love* or *friendliness*) because they are typically considered to have both a constant meaning (e.g. a *problem* is a difficulty), and also a variable meaning, which is totally co-text dependent (see Ivanič,

1991: 109)[11] when they function in a bound way, anaphorically or cataphorically. Drawing on Eugene Winter's terminology (Winter, 1977), Hunston and Francis (2000: 185) stated that all shell nouns share a need for lexicalization (i.e. they cannot be used "without some kind of expansion in the surrounding text)."

Turning to the idea of "perspectivization" within the semantic function, Benitez-Castro (2015) spoke of the *interpretational* function, and Halliday and Hasan (1976) and later Francis (1994: 90) spoke of the *interpersonal* potential of shell nouns to carry authorial perspective. As Benitez-Castro (2015) pointed out, a demonstrative, like a shell noun, can refer to and encapsulate prior information; but what shell noun usage facilitates which demonstrative or pronoun usage does not is writer evaluation, either retrospectively or prospectively: compare the use of *this*, which simply refers, with *this achievement*, which can both refer and categorize in a positive way. Francis (1994: 96) discussed the possibilities for modification of shell nouns and the further options for adding interpersonal (and ideational) meaning that such modification afforded (e.g. a writer choosing to use *this hotly-debated question* rather than *this question*).

With regard to the stretch of text to which the shell noun refers, scholars have typically excluded a synonym-style referencing role (see Benitez-Castro, 2015: 183–185; Francis, 1994: 85; Hunston and Francis, 2000: 188). A notable exception to this view can be found in Halliday and Hasan (1976: 274, 275), whose contextualized examples of general nouns included such synonym (more exactly superordinate) NP referencing (e.g. *the man* referring to *the minister*, and *the stuff* referring to *this crockery*). Shell nouns are typically considered to refer (either anaphorically or cataphorically) to larger stretches of texts – clauses, sentences, and paragraphs. Of these, it is larger text referencing which is considered more common: "the encapsulation of long discourse segments appears to be the norm for shell-noun use" (Benitez-Castro, 2015: 184).

Concerning the second, cognitive, function, Schmid (2000: 14) believed that shell nouns facilitate "temporary concept formation."

What Schmid (2000: 118) meant by this was the discourse-processing cognitive aid which could result from large-scale encapsulation: "often pieces of information that are too complex to be rendered by single clauses occur as shell nouns...." For example, the use of *the fact* before a long *that*-clause may enable the reader to more easily process (and package) the complex clause because of the prospective encapsulating function of *the fact*. Schmid also believed that shell nouns were good *reifiers*, i.e. particularly good at concretizing / hypostatizing information. In sum, the concomitant cognitive-easing effect of temporary concept formation by means of use of a shell noun was viewed by Schmid (2000: 123) as providing "the necessary relief for short-term memory" required to facilitate reader comprehension.

With regard to the third, textual, function, Schmid considered the cohesive link created by the shell noun and its referent, and how this signaled to the reader how the text is organized and how it is to be interpreted. The signaling function of shell nouns has been discussed by a number of authors. Goutsos (1997: 53), for example, observed that shell nouns function as topic framing signals. However, it is not just the retrospective encapsulating function that was noted by Goutsos. He observed that a noun may not only encapsulate anaphorically, but also play a cataphoric role at the same time: for example, *the problem* in theme or initial position may both encapsulate preceding discourse and also predict or indicate what is to follow (p. 54). A similar signaling function was suggested by Francis (1994: 86), who described the role of discourse labels, or labeling nouns, to "signal that the writer is moving on to the next stage of his / her argument, having disposed of the preceding stage by encapsulating or packaging it into a single nominalization." The above mentioned linking-shifting function of shell nouns has been of particular interest to scholars when considering the location of shell nouns in paragraph-initial position, as discussed in more detail later in this section.

Shell nouns occur in a variety of different grammatical patterns. Some researchers have focused on just one pattern: Hunston and

Francis (2000), for instance, focused on prospective *-that* clause shell nouns. Schmid (2000: 36) proposed two basic patterns each for anaphoric and cataphoric uses of shell nouns, and Aktas and Cortes (2008) extended these four general patterns to seven on the basis of their corpus-based work. Although it might be assumed that these nouns will require a modifying demonstrative or definite article (see Halliday and Hasan 1976: 275), this need not be the case. As Benitez-Castro (2015: 187) stated, indefinite nouns can also function as shell nouns, providing the example of how *a joke* (rather than *the joke*), was used to refer to a prior incident in discourse. Aktas and Cortes (2008) included *a(n) N* among their seven types of grammatical patterns within which shell nouns typically occur, along with another indefinite pattern: *a(n) + N + of* (e.g. *a process of*). I am not aware of much research which has sought to investigate which of these patterns are most commonly seen in paragraph-initial position. However, Hoey and O'Donnell (2008) found that for the shell noun *move, a move* was strongly preferred in text-initial sentences, whereas *the move* occurred more typically in paragraph-initial position – particularly, the first part of the sentence. Their corpus data further indicated that *in a move* was more typically present in the second part of a text-initial sentence, but in the first part of a sentence in paragraph-initial position.

Shell nouns have been classified in various ways. Hunston and Francis (2000) divided those occurring in *that*-clauses as: discourse referring (e.g. *accusation*), mental (e.g. *belief*), and miscellaneous (e.g. *fact*). Schmid (2000: 4) classified shell nouns into six broad classes: factual (e.g. *fact, reason*), linguistic (e.g. *question, report*), mental (e.g. *issue, decision*), modal (e.g. *possibility, truth*), eventive (e.g. *act, reaction*), and circumstantial (e.g. *situation, way*). Further analysis of the paragraph positioning of specific nouns, or certain classes of nouns, such as eventive nouns (e.g. *measure*) or linguistic shell nouns (e.g. *report*) in particular genre types would help teachers give principled advice to learners on what types of nouns are used in paragraph-initial position.

Paragraphing and shell nouns

Goutsos (1997) observed the presence of shell nouns in paragraph-initial position in his corpora analyses, and I have noted their fairly common use (12 instances in 47 paragraphs examined) in the same position in an analysis of popular argumentative texts (McGee, 2014). The reason why they occur in this particular location is no doubt related to the semantic, cognitive and textual functions mentioned above, as I discuss further below.

With regard to the linking-shifting textual function of some shell nouns, mentioned earlier, Francis (1994: 86, 87) suggested how this is supported by the paragraph break: "This signaling function is reinforced by an orthographic division: clauses containing retrospective labels are usually paragraph-initial." Schmid (2000: 351) observed the use of shell nouns by journalists in paragraph-initial position in a second or last paragraph of a newspaper piece and he explained such positioning in the following way: "It preserves (discourse) topic continuity, by relating the new paragraph to the previous ones, and it marks the topic change, by serving as a starting-point for new information." Michaela Mahlberg, in a detailed study of the shell noun *move* in the phrase *move follow** (the asterisk represents various endings: *s / ed / ing*) in business articles and news articles, found three textual features associated with the phrase in her study corpus (Mahlberg, 2009a: 276). The first was that the phrase generally occurred at the beginning of a paragraph. The second was that it tended to occur in a specific paragraph in an article – namely, the second paragraph (note the earlier Schmid reference on this). The third was that it referred to the main idea nucleus present within the text (not peripheral detail).

Little research has focused on the cataphoric (i.e. prospection only) use of shell nouns in paragraph-initial position, or considered why writers might use such devices in a prospective way in this position (though note the earlier comments by Schmid regarding a possible aid to cognition). Different shell nouns, in various grammatical structures, may well have distinct functions in paragraph positions and different genres (e.g. *fact* may be found to be exclusively prospective, and *move* be observed solely in journalistic discourse in the ways described above), and further exploration of these patterns would clearly be of value to teachers and learners.

Before leaving the subject of cohesion, it is important to refer back to Hoffman's blackboard metaphor, and briefly consider shell noun anaphoric referencing across a paragraph break (typically considered a barrier to anaphora). Clearly, shell nouns have such a referring capacity, and they seem to be used as inter-paragraph linkers far more often than pronominals. I suggest that the two key reasons for the difference between pronominal anaphora and shell noun usage in referring across the paragraph break lies in the specificity of the antecedent referred to, and the link and shift function. Regarding the first reason, as mentioned earlier in this section, shell nouns are not typically understood to refer to other NPs, but rather to clausal, sentential, and suprasentential material. On moving from one paragraph to the next, it seems reasonable to assume that readers need to carry with them the gist of the text (though not specific surface-level textual detail) to a new paragraph. Shell nouns are ideally suited to performing this gist-carrying function; a pronominal reference, on the other hand, having a highly specific antecedent noun phrase, is not. The fact that a shell noun's textual antecedent can be rather fuzzy and indistinct, as noted by Varada Kolhatkar, Heike Zinsmeister, and Graeme Hirst (Kolhatkar et al., 2013) does not appear to pose a comprehension problem for the reader, and it seems that writers themselves are not averse to rather general packaging and signaling, either. Psychologically and cognitively speaking, such inter-paragraph gist referencing seems to correspond well with the idea (to be discussed in more detail in Chapter 7), that readers may well consider the paragraph juncture (not just the break, but also the first sentence of a new paragraph) as a point within text to chunk together information, and move it to long-term memory, before proceeding (see also endnote 10 in this chapter). I suggest that this is a reasonable explanation for the use of an anaphoric shell noun but not a pronominal anaphor in paragraph-initial position in text.

Concerning the second point (the link and shift function), an anaphoric shell noun is a continuity marker, and at the same time it occurs together with the paragraph break – a shifting technique: superficially, such signaling might be considered to be illogical, but in reality, these signals complement one another, rather than sending ambiguous signals to the reader. The function of some shell nouns to both encapsulate, and prospect, makes them rather special discourse management tools, ideally suited to paragraph-initial position: they can help overcome the potentially abrupt beginning of a new paragraph, and aid the writer and reader manage both discontinuity and continuity in text. Having said this, given the arguments in Chapters 1 and 4 concerning the presence of non-orthographic structural, functional, and semantic units in text, it would be wrong to assume that these nouns are always used in paragraph-initial position: they are not. However, their presence and use may well help us discern the larger functional or structural units operating within text.

Time Framing

As Goutsos (1997) stated (see earlier reference towards the beginning of this chapter), time frame changes are not typically considered to be discourse-managing tools, but may contribute to discourse management when linked to some other corroborating signal. This might be the paragraph break alone, or together with another kind of signal or signals.

I am not aware of any focused research investigating the phenomenon of tense change across the paragraph break. In a previous study (McGee, 2014), I observed that this does occur (in conjunction with other signals in Goutsos' taxonomy) in argumentative text. Here are two examples of this:

Example 1 (Tense change alongside temporal adverb, adapted from McGee 2014: 60)

....There is no reason to think that different guns cannot fall on different sides of the line.

Today, as has been the case for a long time, if the U.S. government seriously wanted to impose its will on the people through force, all the assault rifles in the world would be of no use.

As can be seen in this example, along with the presence of the opening adverbial, and the paragraph break, there is a switch from the present simple to the present perfect across the paragraph break.

Example 2 (Tense change with change of subject NP, adapted from McGee 2014: 60)

.... Israel on the other hand has fewer fighter jets at its disposal and therefore has a shorter window to prevent Iran from bomb-making capabilities.

Obama has discouraged Israel from unilaterally bombing Iran and instead has asked for time to further pursue sanctions and diplomacy.

This example illustrates change of subject occurring at the paragraph break together with a switch from the present simple to the present perfect tense.

Tense change can, of course, occur within the same paragraph, and as discussed in Chapter 4, Becker (1966) suggested that within a paragraph tense change could indicate the move from one tagmeme to the next. Tense change across paragraphs and within a paragraph are clearly areas of study which would benefit from more research. Perhaps all that can be said at the current time is that tense change is a possible indicator of textual shift when accompanied by other discourse-managing cues, one of which is the paragraph break.

Sentence Structure

Sentence structure, the final class of discourse-managing signalers provided by Goutsos (1997), has been studied by a number of scholars. The idea that discourse cues (specifically, temporal adverbs) might help in understanding textual structure was suggested by Brown and Yule (1983: 99). In their analysis of a text, they believed that writers might use certain adverbs (e.g. *at first, then, generally*) and adverbial expressions (e.g. *by the end of the week*) in paragraph-initial position to indicate or precede topic shift, and hypothesized that certain genre types might use specific topic shifting devices in particular ways. If such were found to be the case, they argued, discourse analysts might then be able to make generalizations about generic structural organization. More recent work into paragraphing has suggested that such generalizations can indeed be made. Below I provide a brief overview of some of the key research in this area.

Firstly, and most generally, the presence of various adjuncts in paragraph-initial position has been noted. For example, Gary Prideaux and John Hogan observed that preposed subordinate clauses of time tended to occur in a statistically significant way at the beginning of a discourse unit, suggesting that these units played an important discourse flow management function (Prideaux and Hogan, 1993). Similarly, Yves Bestgen and Vonk found that temporal adverbials were often placed in paragraph-initial position in narrative and were, accordingly, good segmentation markers (Bestgen and Vonk, 2000). In addition, Shaojun Ji observed that episode- and paragraph-initial preposed phrases and clauses were common in narrative and believed that such positioning indicated "major temporal, spatial discontinuities or thematic reorientation" (Ji, 2002: 1262). Ji (2002) believed that the marked preposed position of such language has the potential to both connect to previous discourse and further develop the discourse (in a rather similar way to shell nouns, discussed earlier). The orienting role of sentence-initial adverbials has been observed and commented on by Lydia-Mai Ho-Dac and Marie-Paule Péry-Woodley (Ho-Dac and Péry-Woodley, 2009).

More in-depth research has investigated the scope and structuring power of sentence-initial adverbials. Ho-Dac and Péry-Woodley (2009) defined *scope* as "the semantic continuity of the reference expressed by the adverbial" (p. 3), and *structuring power* as "the capacity of initial adverbials to divide information into blocks..." (p. 4). They identified nearly 1500 temporal adverbials (collected roughly equally from their three different corpora: social geography texts, international relations argumentative text, and descriptive biographies), and in their analyses found that temporal adverbials were more likely to occur in a start-of-section position, followed by paragraph-initial position, followed by intra-paragraph position, across all three of their corpora. They stated that this finding could not be generalized to space adverbials. They went on to ask a critical question of relevance to understanding the paragraph, namely: "are these expressions intrinsically good discontinuity markers, or do they simply 'ride' on the segmentation potential of the paragraph break?" (Ho-Dac and Péry-Woodley, 2009: 9). They found that the answer to this question was that by themselves – that is, not in conjunction with a paragraph break – temporal adverbials were not markers of discourse discontinuity, and neither did they exert structural power, findings which concur with Goutsos' (1997) previously noted observations regarding the relative weakness of these signals to indicate topic framing and topic introduction, as mentioned at the beginning of this chapter.

Ho-Dac and Péry-Woodley (2009) found that a paragraph-initial adverbial tends to have influence across the paragraph unless or until a contrary signal occurs within the same paragraph. They explained Peter Crompton's contrary findings that initial adverbials did not have greater supra-sentential scope than non-initial adverbials (Crompton, 2006) by suggesting that was because he studied only very short texts. Crompton believed that it is not adverbial clauses but rather non-clausal adverbials (specifically, adverbial prepositional phrases) that tend to have supra-sentential scope, noting in passing that *in conclusion* often has influence over an entire paragraph.

When talking about the possible structuring power of different grammatical class units, it is necessary to make differentiations within particular classes in terms of their cue signaling roles. Michel Charolles, for example, commented (Charolles, 2005: 16) that while spatial and temporal adverbials are commonly used as frame builders, other adverbials are not: evaluative adverbs (he gave the example of *heureusement* "fortunately") and adverbials which are (necessarily) more closely linked to the sentence in which they occur (e.g. *Quand il est arrivé...* "When he arrives").

In contrast to Goutsos (1997), Ho-Dac and Péry-Woodley (2009) did not believe that the paragraph break, in and of itself, is a significant discourse framer, but they did believe that paragraph-initial temporal adverbials can have the effect of elevating the paragraph break to discourse-framing status. According to Charolles (2005: 16), preposed adverbials in paragraph-initial position not only contribute to the content of a text, but organize the discourse and affect the resulting interpretation of the text by a reader.

When considered together with the comments made earlier about the potential discourse organizing function of over-referencing, the observations of Ho-Dac and Péry-Woodley (2009) and Charolles (2005) challenge Goutsos' hierarchical taxonomy, in which the paragraph break is assumed to be a default topic frame opener or closer. Indeed, Charolles' comment suggests the need for a far more dynamic (rather than hierarchical) understanding of the relation-ships and interactions between the different signals discussed in this chapter. In the words of Ho-Dac (2010: 83), "discourse organization is signalled by configurations of cues rather than by single markers." Accordingly, initial adverbials, being one potential signal, cannot be studied, or understood, in isolation; and neither, one might add, can any of the signals mentioned in this chapter, the paragraph break included. The different signals discussed in this chapter do not organize discourse independently. As a result, one must question the value of most of the traditional theorizing on the paragraph, in which it was considered in isolation, and its function was largely predetermined.

Conclusion

It follows from the discussion within this chapter that if the paragraph break is just another discourse organizing technique, even a particularly powerful one at times, it should be viewed very differently to how it was considered by 19th century rhetorical theorists and 1960s education scholars. Neither group considered paragraph opening and closing as options among many discourse management techniques which interact in complex ways. Rather than being compared with discourse markers or prediction pairs (to name but two of the management tools considered here) or being considered alongside and together with these tools, the paragraph was more commonly compared with the sentence as a (smaller) unit of discourse and indentation with the full stop as a (lesser) marker of completion.

As I noted in passing earlier in this chapter, Goutsos believed that the paragraph break may be more or less significant in terms of its discourse-managing role in different text types, when considered alongside the other techniques discussed above (making specific reference to journalistic discourse as a genre type in which the paragraph had a less significant structuring role). Earlier attempts to understand the paragraph in the late 19th century and some of the work in the 1960s gave the paragraph break a rather unique discourse-management or organizing role – one which it does not really merit. A logical consequence of a multi-signaling perspective on discourse management is that a focus on any one technique at any one time is inadequate. All of the discourse-managing techniques, and the complex interactions between them, must be considered if we wish to understand the paragraph and paragraphing. The idea that other techniques (e.g. adjuncts, over-referencing, shell nouns, anaphora) interact dynamically with the paragraph break, indeed may actually elevate the paragraph break to playing a significant discourse-organizing role, or, indeed play down such a function, is a new way of considering paragraphing. Rather than the role of the paragraph break being assumed, such a viewpoint challenges us as educators to engage in a fundamental rethink of paragraphing and how we approach it in class.

It is evident that writers can manipulate the seven discourse management techniques discussed in this chapter for their own purposes. For example, a writer may soften the potential topic-shift framing impact of the paragraph break by the use of a continuity signal such as an anaphoric pronoun, shell noun or adverbial; prospect at the end of one paragraph what the following paragraph will deal with, and hence provide a particularly smooth inter-paragraph transition through foregrounding; send a clear signal at the beginning of the paragraph, through the use of a preposed adjunct, that things have moved on (significantly) since the last paragraph; or clearly guide a reader, who might otherwise be unnecessarily challenged by the complex material to follow, through the use of reader-oriented metadiscourse in the form of a forward-looking, cataphoric reference in paragraph-initial position. While the potential interactions between the different signals are many, I believe that future research may well indicate the presence of general patterns within particular genres, although at the current time we must acknowledge that we do not know what those patterns are.

In terms of classroom study, paragraph closing and opening should be considered and analyzed alongside the other discourse management signals discussed in this chapter, and we can draw students' attention to the multi-signaling phenomena detailed here. Questions that can be asked of any text, and which might result in potentially fruitful discussion might include:

- Why does the author start this paragraph with this phrase?
- Why is encapsulation used here, and what does it signify?

- Why are there no particularly obvious co-signals functioning alongside the paragraph break here?
- How does the use of many signals (together) help the writer, and how does it affect the reader?
- How is the role of the paragraph break influenced by its co-occurrence with other signals?
- How is continuity (and / or shift) being achieved within this paragraph transition? Which movement is stronger?

Rather than a particular role of the paragraph break being assumed, a multi-signaling approach to discourse management will consider, in any particular case, the related issues of why the break occurs where it does, its co-occurrence with discourse-organizing signals, the resulting impact on the reader, and how the writer is managing the discourse within the genre constraints and conventions.

In terms of writing instruction, I suggest that dealing with the paragraph break, and paragraph textual block alone or in isolation, should be considered of limited value. Just as the study of discourse markers alone or adverbial phrases alone is of questionable value, the paragraph and paragraphing clearly need to be considered in relation to their wider discourse context and to the use of other discourse-management techniques.

As this chapter has made clear, only partial progress has been made by scholars in their attempts to better understand how discourse is organized by the various discourse management techniques identified and discussed in this chapter. We need to know more about paragraph-initial language in different genres, the use of prospection, tense change across the paragraph break, and many other phenomena related to discourse organization. It is to be hoped that researchers will engage in an ever-expanding agenda of studies examining such issues, and that these data might result in a clearer understanding of discourse organization. If this happens teachers will then be able to consider how to make pedagogical use of this material, in the guidelines they give to learner-writers.

I suggest that a rethink of the discourse management significance of the paragraph break will be highly beneficial for educators and students alike. Indeed, a rethink may help us deal with many of the struggles and problems associated with understanding the paragraph documented in Chapters 3 and 4. What the paragraph break means can only be understood contextually – that is, in terms of the break's interactions with other discourse-organizing tools described in this chapter, and the writer's intention in using these tools.

Notes

1 Six, not seven, as the seventh is the paragraph break itself.
2 Maite Taboada also believed (Taboada, 2006: 584) that tense change can be a discourse signal in Rhetorical Structure Theory (see below).
3 I return to this point when considering Hoey's work in Chapter 7.
4 The remainder (17.89%) were a mix of dummy elements (i.e. subject *there* or *it*), indefinites, metadiscourse markers, and *wh*-items.
5 The examples provided by Goutsos suggest that he viewed metadiscourse specifically as text about the text, a view criticized by Hyland (2005), as noted in this chapter.
6 This term was also used by Gill Francis to refer to the function of a nominal group labelling a part of a text cataphorically (Francis, 1994: 83).
7 See also Yves Bestgen (1998: 761), who suggested that there are two opposite functions of *and* – discourse continuity or discontinuity .
8 Redeker (2000) suggested that this is not so, and that a single marker may signal more than one relation at a particular time.
9 On the idea of oral or spoken paragraphs, see Chapter 1.
10 See also Joost Schilperoord on anaphora across the paragraph break: "Apparently, memory scope is crucially related to paragraph units. Closing signals for paragraphs result in the release of information from Working Memory, thus necessitating the reintroduction of already established referents" (Schilperoord, 2001: 317).
11 Of course, one might wish to argue that this is true of all words, in the sense that context must always disambiguate word meaning, as argued, for example, by Adam Kilgarriff (Kilgarriff, 1997).

6   Cohesion and the Paragraph

Introduction

The idea of paragraph unity was discussed and critiqued in Chapter 3. As noted there, the concept of unity in relation to the paragraph is rather difficult to get a handle on, and while unity was a popular subject of discussion in relation to paragraphs by rhetoricians and education scholars in the 19th century, it moved into the shadows in 1960s' discussions, for the reasons documented in Chapters 3 and 4.

The question I seek to answer in this chapter is whether the paragraph can be considered to be a unit, not just visibly, but semantically, that is, as a kind of topical unit. For such an enquiry to be addressed scientifically the topicality of a paragraph needs to be measured in some way. What can be measured, and indeed has been measured (through the use of a variety of techniques, as described and discussed in this chapter) are the cohesive links within a text and within a paragraph. If these links are in some way specific to a paragraph rather than just randomly occurring across a whole text, we would have a warrant to speak of an objective textual semantic unity in relation to the paragraph (rather than unity being considered to exist in the realm of reader response, a somewhat subjective notion as discussed in Chapter 3).

While there is a kind of superficial commonsensical attraction in the idea of paragraph textual semantic unity, it is far more complex when one considers the issue in detail. Specifically, for a relationship between cohesion and a paragraph unit to be established, not only would cohesive links need to shape a particular paragraph in some way, the links would need to be sufficiently distinct to differentiate one paragraph's cohesive unity from its neighbor's. Simply tracking repetition (one kind of lexical cohesive link) would not seem to help in this enquiry, as a word may be repeated within the same paragraph, across two adjacent paragraphs, or indeed may occur in different paragraphs throughout the whole text. How then can repeated lexis (admittedly just one type of cohesive link) be said to map the paragraph unit?

In this chapter, my main goal is to review and comment on research which has attempted to utilize a text's cohesive links (in addition to other textual features) to identify where the original paragraphs began and ended, in a de-paragraphed text. Do the results from this research provide a warrant to use the term "unity" in a very specific and objective way in relation to paragraphs? Specifically, can we speak of the semantic cohesive unity of the paragraph?

There has been considerable research interest shown by the computational linguistic community into paragraph identification within deparagraphed text over the last 40 years, but this is not an area of research about which language educators or writing instructors are typically aware. In what follows, I seek to provide a simplified overview of some of this work, and in so doing seek to answer three key questions:

- On what textual features do attempts to identify paragraphs depend?
- How successful (or how unsuccessful) are such attempts, and why?
- What can we learn about the paragraph and paragraphing from such studies?

Finally, I consider what educators can take away from this body of research, and the possible pedagogical applications of the various findings.

Computer Algorithm Segmentation of De-paragraphed Text: The Basics

How can computer software or algorithms be developed to identify where the paragraph breaks occurred in a de-paragraphed text? As computer software does not and cannot read as humans do, and therefore cannot be sensitive to the relationship between general meaning (i.e. coherence between ideas) and paragraphing, computational linguists can only exploit the textual features of a text in trying to map paragraph units. An example of a related research project was mentioned in the previous chapter. As discussed there, Marcu (2000a,b) sought to utilize the presence of discourse markers to help identify rhetorical text structure (though not paragraph structure, per se). Unlike Marcu's research approach, however, most computational linguists have focused on the presence of textual cohesive links within text when trying to identify paragraphs, rather than utilizing the presence of discourse markers, or some other textual element(s) to aid in such an enterprise. Having said this, as will be mentioned towards the end of this chapter, some of the more recent computational approaches to paragraph identification have considered the role of both cohesive relations and phraseological textual colligation data (i.e. the presence of certain lexical or grammatical items, typically occurring in paragraph-initial position) when attempting to segment de-paragraphed text, to approximate its original paragraphing.

Computer applications are much better than humans when it comes to crunching data and making calculations, and it is these capabilities that have been exploited by computational researchers in their quest to develop accurate text segmenters. The assumption behind much of this research is that when there is a break in textual cohesion (however measured, see below), it is at this point that a paragraph break occurs within the text; that is, there is a belief that textual cohesive links and breaks map paragraphs and paragraph junctures, respectively, within text.

The idea that cohesive links are somehow connected to paragraph identity has been criticized – even by some computational linguists, and there are a number of problems associated with this relationship as will be made clear throughout this chapter. One problem has already been mentioned in Chapter 5, namely, that of topic foregrounding. As mentioned in that chapter, foregrounding will typically result in some sort of inter-paragraph cohesive linking, and as such it does not sit comfortably with the idea that a break in textual cohesion indicates a paragraph ending – indeed suggests the very opposite. Not only this, the fact of inter-paragraph (rather than intra-paragraph) cohesion was noticed and flagged in the very earliest work on textual cohesion. For example, although Halliday and Hasan (1976) argued that cohesive links are normally related to the paragraph unit (as mentioned in Chapter 1, and commented on further below), they stated that this was not always the case, noting that there may be loose cohesion within a paragraph, in addition to many cohesive ties between paragraphs. They suggested that such dissociation is fairly typical of what communicators do with language: we manipulate associated variables for a particular semantic or rhetorical effect.

While it is clear that the key underpinning premise of most of the computational work into paragraphing is not watertight, the fact remains, as the research reported below makes clear, that textual cohesion relations do seem to be related to the paragraph structure in some or even many paragraphs. Before considering the key computational work in this area, in the section that follows I step back a little from computational applications in order to consider in general linguistic terms the concept of textual cohesion and its relation to the paragraph.

Cohesion and Coherence

Much has been written about cohesion and coherence and the relationship between these two concepts (see Patricia Carrell, 1982, and later work citing this study and my own brief comments in Chapter 3). It is not my intention here to add to this debate, although it is important to state that neither cohesion nor coherence occur in a vacuum: a reader must know how texts typically hang together to appreciate cohesive links, and must also have some background knowledge of the subject matter and the world in general to be able to interpret the message of a text as coherent. Despite different views about what the terms mean, and their relationship, what is clear is that surface-level textual cohesion alone cannot account for coherence and reader comprehension and in this sense cohesive links are not always necessary in the development of a paragraph, or required for reader comprehension. In support of this comment, consider the paragraph below from Nils Enkvist:

> *The net bulged with the lightning shot. The referee blew his whistle and signaled. Smith had been offside. The two captains both muttered something. The goalkeeper sighed for relief.* (Enkvist, 1990: 12)

As can be observed, the paragraph contains no inter-sentential cohesive links (although there are some semantic field word connections), and yet it should be perfectly comprehensible to any reader familiar with the game of English football (soccer).

The paragraph is, admittedly, unusual in its total absence of inter-sentential grammatical or lexical cohesive links,[1] but as stated above, I believe it is coherent to anyone familiar with the rules of soccer. However, for those unfamiliar with the game, it may be only vaguely understandable even if the individual field-specific words are known (including *net, shot, referee, whistle, offside, captain* and *goalkeeper*). The text may appear to be about a game, although the reader may have no idea who any of the people involved are, including the named *Smith,* or what event is being described. However, for those who have some familiarity with the rules of the game, the text describes a disallowed goal, and the relationship between one sentence and the next is clear, although nowhere explicitly signaled. For example, *Smith* will be interpreted as being a person either directly involved in the action (and the offense), or who may have actually scored the goal. For a reader who does not have this kind of specific knowledge, the paragraph may be read more as a group of sentences, which are assumed to be related in some way, but the cause-and-effect relations existing from one sentence to the next may well be missed. John Sinclair (2004: 94) suggested readers expect relevance between sentences even if there are no cohesive links, and that they will actively look for such relations. This expectation of relevance appears to be governed by ideas about what the text is about, which a reader will try to work out, even though the topic or function may not be stated explicitly. Based on the fact that cohesive links are not essential to creating this topicality, as is clear in the above example, Giora (1983b: 155) maintained that paragraphs display pragmatic unity, rather than being semantically cohesive units. In her own words, "….'being about' a certain topic does not require that the various sentences predicating something about that topic be cohesive with it."

The example paragraph given above is a rather unusual case, but it does prove a point: cohesive links are not necessary to maintain coherence, and a paragraph may make sense, and be coherent without exhibiting such links. However, it must also be said that it is more commonly the case that cohesive links occur both within and between sentences in a text (and not only in adjacent sentences). Depending on one's viewpoint, this cohesion may or may not be considered to contribute to the overall coherence of the text.

Halliday and Hasan (1976: 299) defined cohesion in the following way: "Cohesion expresses the continuity that exists between one part of the text and another." The idea of textual continuity is critical in discourse analysis, and Halliday and Hasan believed there to be two ways in which cohesion is achieved: grammatical (reference, substitution, ellipsis, and conjunction) and lexical, which can be further divided into reiteration (repetition, near synonym, super-ordination, and general items) and collocation.[2] Halliday and Hasan's seminal work on cohesion remains an important reference today, though there are issues with their taxonomy. One of these, commented on by Mahlberg (2009b: 106), expresses reservations about equating cohesion with grammatical and lexical features alone. Mahlberg maintained that these two features constitute only part of the cohesiveness of text:

> Connectedness in text is not only reflected by the choice of vocabulary words or grammatical linking words; the choice of tense and aspect also contributes to textual relations.... [W]e can include parallelism and adjacency pairs in lists of cohesive devices.... [T]he flow of information, that often progresses from given to new, plays a role in the transition from single sentences to connected text...and eventually genre conventions have an impact on the links between parts of a text. (Mahlberg, 2009b: 106)

Whether we embrace a narrower or broader perspective on textual cohesion, it is clear that the types of cohesion in a text vary according to genre and text type. As Ulla Connor pointed out, grammatical substitution and ellipsis are less common in writing than in conversation (Connor, 1984: 302), and as Greg Myers observed, superordinate cohesive links are less common in scientific articles than in popular science texts, which tend to use lexical repetition as the primary way of creating textual cohesion (Myers, 1991: 13).

Paragraphs and Cohesion

As discussed in Chapter 3, early theorists of the paragraph believed unity to be one of its defining characteristics. More recently, when ideas about paragraph unity have been put forward, these have often been framed with specific reference to textual cohesion. For example, Halliday and Hasan (1976: 296, 297) considered the sentences within a paragraph (with the exception of the first) to typically exhibit (anaphoric) cohesion and considered that a break in cohesiveness indicated the existence of a textual boundary: "in principle, we shall expect to find a greater degree of cohesion within a paragraph than between paragraphs." Likewise, Quirk et al. (1985: 1445) believed that "…a paragraph has on the one hand a relatively strong sense of internal coherence[3] and on the other a relatively loose linkage with the textual material before and after it." Finally, David Crystal suggested the following: "The function of a paragraph is to show the reader that the sentences in a particular set are more closely related to each other than to the sentences in adjacent text" (Crystal, 2001: 249). It is this assumed cohesion and closeness of relationship between the sentences within a paragraph that is the foundation of much of the computational work into paragraphing.

Early Corpus Linguistic and Computational Interest in Lexical Cohesion, Text Structure, and Paragraphing

It was a number of years before Halliday and Hasan's work on cohesion was taken up and considered by computational and corpus linguists in research into the paragraph. Jane Morris working with Hirst in an early computational study (commented on in more detail below), termed sequences of lexical cohesive links within a text "lexical chains" (Morris and Hirst, 1991: 23). They believed that these lexical chains were significant in helping understand the overall discourse and that they "provide a clue for the determination of coherence and discourse structure" (*ibid.*). This observation echoes Becker's (1965, 1966) discussion of equivalence classes within tagmemes, as mentioned in Chapter 4. The idea that discourse structure (including the paragraph structure) is somehow related to cohesive links, and particularly cohesive links of a lexical kind, was also considered by Hoey (1991) in the same year as Morris and Hirst's paper was published.

Hoey (1991) was interested in understanding the role of the lexical links present between words in different sentences within a text, noting the dominance of lexically cohesive ties, as opposed to the lesser amount of grammatical cohesion that occurred. He classified lexical cohesion into two types: "lexical repetition" and "paraphrasing" (the latter category including synonymy and super-ordination). In Hoey's view the two classes of lexical cohesion are significant in creating discourse in that, unlike grammatical cohesion, lexical items can form many links within a text (rather than more local relations effected by grammatical cohesion). Consequently, Hoey (1991: 10) argued that lexical cohesion is more important than grammatical cohesion in creating text structure, that is, *texture*, in discourse.

Hoey (1991) differentiated between what he termed "central" and "marginal" sentences within a text, and he believed that such a distinction has value for effective text summary. According to Hoey, the central sentences within a text are those which are significantly linked to other sentences. He deemed significant linkage to occur when there are three or more lexical links to or from a particular sentence to other sentences within the text. In Hoey's theory, these central sentences form bonds, and combinations of bonds form nets within the text. For example, if a sentence in a text has no lexical cohesive links to previous sentences, but bonds to three sentences coming after it (not necessarily the next three sentences, but any three sentences within the rest of the text), the coordinates of "zero" and "3," can be given to that particular sentence, signified by Hoey as (– ; 3). In relation to paragraphing, Hoey believed that a high number in the second set of coordinates, that is, links to following sentences, might be a typical profile of a topic sentence, since the lexical items present in the topic sentence are those most likely to be recalled or developed in the following sentences. Sentences having a high number of bonds in the first set of coordinates (i.e. showing backward, or anaphoric, referencing) could indicate the presence of a summarizing or concluding sentence. Krisztina Károly's work – a development of Hoey's – suggested that this was indeed the case in a number of the texts she examined, as she found that "many of the bonds... are located at paragraph boundaries" (Károly, 2002: 138).

Hoey's work on lexical cohesion was taken up and developed by Anthony Berber-Sardinha from a computational linguistic perspective (Berber-Sardinha, 1997, 2001, 2002), as discussed in more detail below. Berber-Sardinha's work, in effect, turned Hoey's on its head in focusing on the breaks in cohesion within a text, rather than on its cohesive links, which was Hoey's main interest and focus.

Computational Work into Paragraph Identification: An Overview

Broadly speaking, there have been two rather distinct areas of research within computational linguistics of relevance to my focus in this book. The first, and dominant, interest has been in the automated segmentation of de-paragraphed text, in which different types of textual information or textual relations have been incorporated in the construction of segmentation algorithms, or the training and then testing of segmentation systems. A secondary, and much less researched area, has been the automated classification of paragraphs according to their position in a text, that is, the development of a measure which can predict where a particular paragraph occurred in a text – whether it is an opening paragraph, a closing paragraph, or a paragraph in the main body of the text. In the overview that follows, most of the discussion relates to the dominant interest in textual segmentation (the former of these concerns), and I leave comments on the latter, less developed area of research, to the end of the chapter.

Computational Research, Linguistic Theories, and Corpus-Linguistic Research

Some computational linguistics researchers have made connections between their work and text-structure linguistic theories. For example, Morris and Hirst (1991) connected their work to that of Barbara Grosz and Candace Sidner (Grosz and Sidner, 1986), and Berber-Sardinha's (2001, 2002) work built on Hoey's (1991). As noted in the previous chapter, Marcu's research (2000a,b) on discourse markers utilized Mann and Thompson's (1988) important work on RST, and the significant research of Marti Hearst (Hearst, 1994a,b, 1997), noted below, was related to Eduard Skorochod'ko 's text structure type analyses (Skorochod'ko, 1972). However, much of the computational work has no prior theoretical connection or foundation (as noted by Berber-Sardinha, 2001, 2002), and the reason for this is probably to be found in the practical and applied nature of the computational focus. Key interests have included how to segment text for use in information search, or how to automatically summarize a text. Corpus linguists have sometimes based their research on theories developed by other corpus linguists, such as Mahlberg's (2009a) reference in her work on textual colligation to Sinclair's (1991) idiom principle and Hunston and Francis' (2000) pattern grammar; or, like some computational linguists, they have worked with no theoretical underpinning.

The paragraph-based research of corpus linguists is quite different from that of computational linguists. Corpus linguists have, generally speaking, conducted focused textual analyses. For example, research has considered the presence of a particular lexical item, phrase, or concgram (i.e. two word variable combinations) within a specific genre subtype in paragraph-initial position. An example would be Mahlberg's (2009a) research into *move*, discussed in the previous chapter. Computational work, on the other hand, typically has a strong mathematical basis, deals with large amounts of data, and is often concerned with the development and testing of algorithms, or measures to accurately segment text.

Writing at the turn of the millennium, Hirst (2002) commented that there had been very little open recognition of the work of corpus linguists by computational linguists, and vice versa, even though, at times, research goals had overlapped. For example, Hirst commented on the similarities between Morris and Hirst's (1991) research and that conducted by Hoey (1991), referred to above. Whether this lack of awareness or absence of a multi-disciplinary outlook can be explained with reference to the different levels of generality / specificity at which the two groups work, their different theoretical or atheoretical underpinnings, or simply the different questions that they have addressed, is not clear.

However, since Hirst made the above comments, there has been some very important borrowing between the two disciplines. Several of the more recent computational studies (discussed later in the chapter) have picked up on the work mentioned in Chapter 5 and taken into account some of the discourse management tools typically co-occurring with the paragraph break, in developing their methodology for determining where paragraph breaks occurred in text. That is, the "traditional" focus of computational linguists on the textual cohesiveness of the paragraph unit (measured in different ways, and discussed in more detail below) has more recently been complemented by a recognition of the value of considering the language which typically occurs (or does not occur) in paragraph-initial position, in helping identify paragraph breaks in deparagraphed text. I suggest that this relatively recent development in computational studies should be considered a milestone in our understanding of the paragraph and paragraphing, as it objectively and scientifically endorses the notion that some paragraphs are not just internally cohesive units, but also combining units, in the sense that paragraph-initial language often links two paragraphs (e.g. through the use of a discourse marker, or prediction pair, or any of the discourse-managing tools mentioned in Chapter 5).

Computational Linguistics and Automatic Text Segmentation

In considering feasible ways of automatically segmenting (de-paragraphed) text into paragraphs, computational linguistics researchers have identified a number of textual features of potential value, though, as Jeffrey Reynar (Reynar, 1998: 49, 50) noted, lexical repetition was (and indeed still is) the most important feature utilized. Other forms of reiteration (e.g. synonymy), as well as collocation and other linguistic features such as syntactic patterns, have also been incorporated into algorithms, often cumulatively (i.e. in addition to lexical repetition), rather than individually. In this section, I seek to provide an overview of some of the key research.[4]

Paragraph Segmentation Based on Lexical Chains

Morris and Hirst's (1991) work, alluded to earlier, is important in its own right but also in that it paved the way for Hearst's (1994a,b, 1997) TextTiling algorithm (see below), which has, arguably, become the most well-known and respected paragraph-segmentation algorithm. Morris and Hirst, as mentioned earlier, termed lexical cohesive links operating within a text *lexical chains*, and they suggested that the identification of lexical chains within a text makes it possible to identify a topic or subtopic within a text. Their most significant theoretical contribution to work on paragraph segmentation, was to suggest that lexical chains correspond to the intentional structure of text as characterized in Grosz and Sidner's (1986)[5] theory – in other words, that surface level lexical links (linguistic structure) correspond to the purpose of the discourse. Morris and Hirst (1991) noted that, computationally, implicit or deep coherence cannot be uncovered in a text, but that lexical cohesion, being computationally traceable, can assist in identifying text structure and hence coherence. In their research, Morris and Hirst examined five texts from general interest magazines, and after taking out closed class and high frequency words, they formed lexical chains from the remaining words within the texts. This was done manually with reference to thesaurus-based semantic relations. Critically important to their work was that they allowed only one transitive link in each lexical chain (*a* linked to *c*, e.g. *cow-sheep-wool*), rather than documenting larger lexical chain relations, as they discovered that to do so would be to end up with chains in which the individual items within them were not, intuitively, related.[6] Morris and Hirst found that these (reduced) lexical chains might occur within a sentence or between sentences. Those occurring across a large number of sentences, rather than being in closer proximity, were termed *chain returns*, and they suggested that these may signal a return to a previously introduced topic, which might occur after a digression, or indicate a high-level intention spanning across text.

Morris and Hirst (1991) found that a 2- or 3-sentence range was a typical span within which these lexical chains operated within the texts they studied, though suggesting that different text types may have different typical span lengths. They compared the reduced lexical chains they identified (i.e. the start and end points of the chains) with the intentional structure of the text from which they were taken and found that the identification of the chains provided "a good clue for the determination of the intentional structure" (1991: 39) of the text – at times exactly so, but not always. Morris and Hirst suggested that the significance of their work lay, partially at least, in its focus on the reduced lexical chain and its value in identifying subtext structure, noting that Halliday and Hasan's (1976) simple identification of lexical cohesion links (i.e. listing lexical items in a chain), was not helpful in identifying linguistic text structure as such (see also comments made earlier on this point, and Figure 6.1 below).

TextTiling and Repetition-focused Segmentation

The goal of Hearst's (1994a,b, 1997) work on text segmentation was to develop an algorithm able to automatically segment expository texts[7] which had been de-paragraphed, according to the subtopics (and paragraphs) of the text. The idea that a subtopic can be equated with a paragraph is inherent in Hearst's work, and this relationship has been criticized, as commented on later. The algorithm which Hearst developed, and which she found to have reasonably good agreement with human-rater segmentation, is probably the most widely known and respected text segmentation algorithm, and her work has spawned numerous adaptations. Drawing on Skorochod'ko's (1972) text type differentiation, Hearst (1994a) suggested that textual topic structure might be deduced from lexical cohesion: there were problems with a focus on discourse cues and their role in segmenting text,[8] and, computationally, measuring lexical cohesion was not difficult. However, unlike Morris and Hirst (1991), Hearst's own algorithm was based on a narrower perspective of lexical cohesion – repetition alone,[9] and her methodology was more complex. The crux of Hearst's work was the identification of significant lexical changes in a text evidenced through repetition and non-repetition of lexical items: breaks in repetition patterns were considered indicative of a change in topic, which indicated a probable paragraph break. Hearst acknowledged her debt to Morris and Hirst (1991) as reviewed above, in helping formulate her own algorithm, though she differentiated her research from theirs in a number of ways. The first of the differences (as noted above) is that the TextTiling algorithm incorporated only lexical repetition links, and not other types of reiteration relations. Secondly, it made no claim to referencing to the hierarchical structure of text. Thirdly, Hearst (1994a: 20) saw a problem in Morris and Hirst's methodology, namely, that some chains overlapped, that is, they are not paragraph specific.

Hearst (1994a) provided a text (a popular science text on astronomy), and showed that simply looking at the number of times a word occurred within it, and where it reoccurred, did not help in determining the location of paragraph breaks. Figure 6.1 lists a number of words recurring in the text, along with the sentence numbers (given across the top and bottom of the figure in terms of their order in the text) where they occur and the number of occurrences (listed vertically at the left edge of the figure). The 1's, 2's and 3's in the figure indicate the number of occurrences per sentence.

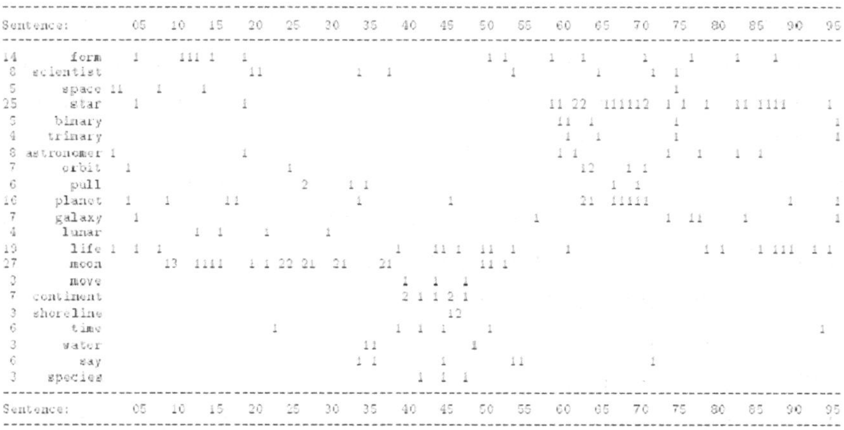

```
Sentence:        05   10   15   20   25   30   35   40   45   50   55   60   65   70   75   80   85   90   95
----------------------------------------------------------------------------------------------------------
14     form   1      111 1    1                            1 1      1    1      1      1      1    1
 8  scientist              11             1    1           1         1       1    1
 5     space 11    1      1                                                    1
25      star  1              1                         11 22  111112 1 1  1     11 1111       1
 5    binary                                              11 1           1                        1
 4    trinary                                              1    1        1                        1
 8 astronomer 1              1                            1 1         1    1    1 1
 7     orbit  1                       1                          12     1 1
 6      pull                      2       1 1                          1 1
16    planet  1    1         11             1           1             21 11111              1    1
 7    galaxy  1                                    1               1 11      1              1
 4     lunar          1 1      1         1
19      life 1 1  1                  1     11 1  11 1       1              1 1   1 111 1 1
27      moon     13  1111   1 1 22 21  21    21            11 1
 3      move                                 1    1   1
 7  continent                              2 1 1 2 1
 3  shoreline                                   12
 6      time                  1           1 1 1    1                                          1
 3     water                        11          1
 6       say                        1 1     1      11           1
 3    species                            1 1 1
----------------------------------------------------------------------------------------------------------
Sentence:        05   10   15   20   25   30   35   40   45   50   55   60   65   70   75   80   85   90   95
```

Figure 6.1. Distribution of Key Words across a Text [From *Context and Structure in Automated Full–text Information Access* (Hearst, 1994a: 22). Reproduced by permission of the author.]

As Figure 6.1 indicates, there are some very specific repetition clusters in the text analyzed by Hearst. For example, the word *species* occurs in only three sentences, which are very close to each other (note also *shoreline*). At the same time, a quick examination of some of the other cases of repetition suggests that locating the distributional patterns of specific lexical items will not be very useful to researchers interested in identifying the paragraphs within a text (as already recognized by Morris and Hirst, 1991). For example, the word *planet,* occurring 16 times, is quite widespread in its distribution (as is *life)* and as such these repetition links do not correspond to paragraph structure. Hearst (1997: 48) suggested that words co-occurring throughout the whole text may indicate the main topic, and that clusters are more important in determining "sub-topic structure." However, even while there might be hints at a specific subtopic developing or ending (as she noted with regard to the clustering around lines 35–50 in the text), it is clear that a simple analysis of vocabulary clustering is not sufficiently sensitive, in and of itself, to indicate where, exactly, paragraphs begin and end in text.

Despite these less than encouraging beginnings, Hearst persisted in focusing on the role of repetition in indicating paragraph structure, and she developed an algorithm with lexical repetition and distribution at its heart. Three steps were taken in the procedure she adopted to develop the algorithm: tokenization of lexical items, lexical score identification of tokens, and boundary identification.[10] Since these steps are fairly common in computational work attempting automatic text-segmentation by algorithm, I will describe them here. The first step, tokenization of lexical items, divides the text into individual (root) lexical units, after which high frequency words are excluded, as they are considered to have little value for assisting in text segmentation. The text is then divided into pseudo-sentences all of a predefined size (Hearst found that 20 tokens provided the best performance for her algorithm), these sequences termed *token sequences*. These token sequences are then grouped together to form blocks (Hearst found a block of six token sequences to be best in her research), and the adjacent blocks are then compared for similar lexis, specifically, repetition between the blocks. For example, a block containing words 1–120, is compared to a block containing words 121–240 (and, of course, the block size can be adjusted). A similarity value for the lexical repetitions between blocks is obtained, and after calculating a score between any two sets of blocks, a moving window across the vectors calculates a new score (e.g. block 2–121 can then be compared with 122–241, after completing the comparison between the blocks 1–120 and 121–140). A change in the similarity value between blocks (0 = no similarity, 1 equals perfect similarity in lexis) can be plotted, and depth scores can be calculated indicating how sharp the changes between blocks are, the bigger the depth score the more likely that a paragraph boundary occurs at that point.

Hearst compared the results from her algorithm with segmentation data from human judges who were asked to mark the paragraph boundaries of the de-paragraphed text according to topic change.[11] Figure 6.2 shows the paragraph segmentation of seven readers for the text, and Figure 6.3 gives the results of the algorithm for the same text.

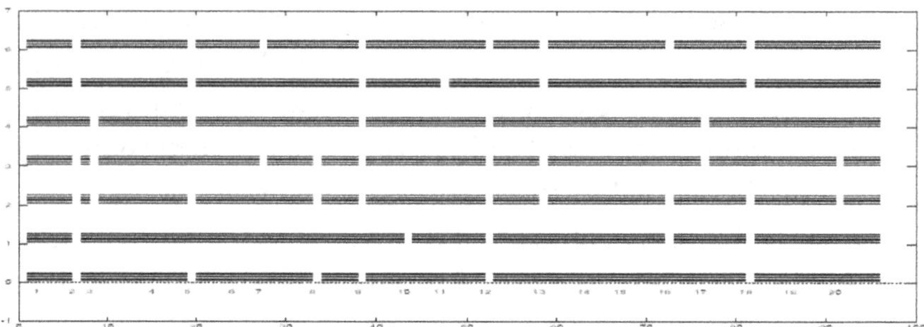

Figure 6.2. Human Segmentation of the Text (x-axis = token sequence gap number; y-axis = judge number; a gap in the horizontal line indicates human judge segmentation) [From *Context and Structure in Automated Full-text Information Access* (Hearst, 1994a: 31). Reproduced by permission of the author.]

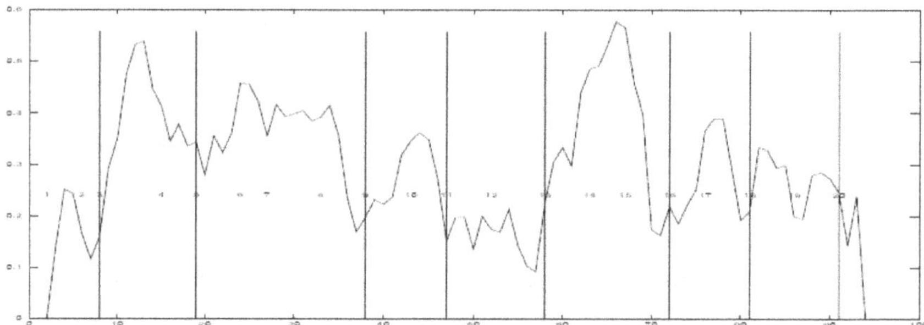

Figure 6.3. Algorithm Performance on the Text (vertical lines = segmentation boundaries chosen by the algorithm) [From *Context and Structure in Automated Full-text Information Access* (Hearst, 1994a: 31). Reproduced by permission of the author.]

If we look at Figure 6.2, we can see that of the seven judges, six believed a paragraph break occurred between sentences 2 and 3. If we look at Figure 6.3, we can see a sharp drop in the repetition links, as calculated by the algorithm, as peaks indicate greater repetition similarity, and troughs repetition dissimilarity. Accordingly, the human segmentation and algorithm segmentation are comparable in this case. A similar pattern of agreement between readers and the algorithm performance can be observed for sentence 9. However, it can also readily be seen that there are times when there is less agreement. For example, although five judges believed there to be a paragraph break after sentence 5, the algorithm did not indicate a sharp change in lexical repetition at this point; hence a paragraph break was not considered likely to occur there. However, on the whole, Hearst observed that strong agreement between the raters was reflected in the similarity scores between the raters and the TextTiling results, and she provided some reasons for the weak agreement between the algorithm's performance and the judges' segmentation decisions when there was a disparity, such as the role of an introductory discourse framing phrase influencing the judges' decisions, but not affecting the performance of the algorithm.[12]

Although Hearst depended solely on repetition in developing her algorithm, finding that the incorporation of additional semantic (thesaural) relations resulted in a deterioration of its performance,[13] she left the door open to the potential value of incorporating additional types of lexically cohesive relations into a paragraph-segmentation algorithm generally, and specifically with respect to narrative text (Hearst, 1997: 48). While algorithms based on repetition do seem to be particularly powerful indicators of text structure, as noted by Stefan Kaufmann (Kaufmann, 1999; see below), later work has generally supported Hearst's reservation regarding an exclusive focus on repetition for segmentation purposes, and algorithms developed after her work have successfully incorporated other cohesive relations, as noted in the studies reviewed below.

Incorporating Collocation Information

Kaufmann (1999)[14] developed the VecTile segmentation system to incorporate collocation-style cohesion found in texts, following the same basic three-step process described above used by Hearst. In addition to incorporating repetition data, collocation relations were also tracked if items within adjacent blocks were linked collocationally. Collocation relations were established on the basis of their presence in other related texts, which were used to train the algorithm. Collocation identification was considered to contribute positively to the performance of the algorithm, and the VecTile system achieved slightly improved results over TextTile in segmenting five popular science magazine texts. In noting the only small increase in accuracy performance due to the incorporation of this additional textual cohesive element,[15] Kaufmann (1999: 594) stressed the particularly powerful role of repetition as an indicator of similarity or dissimilarity between text sections. Olivier Ferret's work developing the TOPICOLL system also incorporated collocation relations in addition to repetition when investigating text segmentation (Ferret, 2002), and his algorithm also produced better results than those achieved through repetition-alone algorithms, including TextTiling.

Segmentation Sensitivity

Igor Bolshakov and Alexander Gelbukh, working on Spanish texts, suggested that for low-level text segmentation – specifically, paragraph segmentation – not only semantic links but also syntactic (namely, collocational) links and pseudo-syntactic links[16] (e.g. the relationship between *chief* and *demanded* in *She insulted her **chief**. He **demanded** an apology*) should be considered (Bolshakov and Gelbukh, 2001). They sought to detect cohesive pairs (semantic, syntactic, and pseudo-syntactic) between adjacent sentences in their research, and compared the performance of their algorithm with human raters analyzing a Mexican newspaper article. The results were generally comparable in that, in the words of the researchers, "…the algorithm restores the paragraph boundaries not worse than educated native speakers of Spanish" (p. 164).

Alexandre Labadié and Violaine Prince argued that systems of text segmentation which are based solely on lexical cohesion are more effective in identifying where concatenated texts (i.e. a number of texts grouped together one after the other) begin and end than in identifying more sensitive or subtle cohesive shifts (i.e. those associated with paragraphs) within a particular text (Labadié and Prince, 2008). They suggested that the inclusion of syntactic information in algorithmic calculations, such as whether a noun is the object or subject of the verb, together with synonym relations and stylistic considerations, could make an algorithm more sensitive to smaller text-internal changes, and hence the identification of paragraph breaks. In support of their claims, Labadié and Prince compared the performance of an algorithm which did not include such elements – Freddy Choi's c99 algorithm (Choi, 2000) – with their own algorithm (Transeg) for two tasks: the computer segmentation of 22 (French) concatenated (political) texts, and paragraph identification within these same texts. They found that their own algorithm was not as good as c99 in segmenting the concatenated texts, and they believed that this was due to its hyper-sensitivity to such a task – c99 being more effective in detecting more marked vocabulary shifts within the texts. In the second analysis, the intra-text segmentation task (i.e. a task requiring a more fine-grained sensitivity – specifically, paragraph segmentation within the texts), they found that Transeg equaled or outperformed c99 in 16 of the 22 texts, in terms of paragraph identification. This study is an important one as it suggests that paragraph identification benefits from a consideration of multiplicity of textual data, not just lexical repetition.

Vocabulary-based Discourse Units

Biber and colleagues coined the term *vocabulary-based discourse units* (VBDUs) to refer to "a block of discourse defined by its reliance on a particular set of words" (Biber et al., 2007: 156). Their work used the same methodology of Hearst, and they suggested that VBDU analysis could help in identifying within-segment shifts, not just between segment shifts. For example, they believed changes in vocabulary could identify the two distinct parts of an introduction to a research article. They showed that syntactic information (e.g. the presence of passive form verbs) and semantic information (e.g. the presence of modal verbs) were different in different sections of a text, and they believed that once such patterns within particular genres or subgenres were identified, this would open the possibility for making generalizable statements about how discourse develops in specific text types, and the role of specific vocabulary or grammatical forms in indicating this development. Their key contribution, I believe, was to show qualitative interest in segmentation data, and consider the role of individual words signaling shifts within a text. Following on from discussion in previous chapters, it is clear that the paragraph unit is not the only significant unit within text, and VBDU work hinted at the possibility of tracking detailed rhetorical shifts within text. Biber et al. found good agreement between human raters and their algorithm, when the human raters tended to agree with each other about particular text segmentation.

Text Effects

It is possible, of course, that part of the explanation for the varying degrees of agreement between the performance of an algorithm and that of human segmenters, and / or the original segmentation is due, in part, to different text types containing different kinds of lexical cohesion relations (as noted earlier in the chapter). This possibility was specifically considered by Elke Teich and Peter Fankhauser, who found that there were longer cohesive chains in learned (i.e. scholarly), governmental, and religious texts than in journalistic texts and fiction, with more repetition in learned texts than in fiction (Teich and Fankhauser, 2005). They believed that this last point could be explained by the need to avoid ambiguity in scholarly text. Such differences will affect how an algorithm performs, although parameters (i.e. block sizes of text for comparison) can be changed to try to cope with these differences.

Alternative Computational Approaches to Segmentation

There are several notable exceptions to the approach to text segmentation typified by the TextTiling algorithm, and other research which has built on that work. Three of the more well-known of these are discussed below.

Cohesion relations between contiguous sentences

Berber-Sardinha (1997, 2001, 2002) based his text segmentation algorithm (Link Set Median procedure) on Hoey's (1991) work on lexical patterns in text, mentioned earlier. He argued that it was more linguistically robust than Hearst's work and Berber-Sardinha (2002: 276) criticized Hearst's work on a number of grounds, including its use of pseudo-sentences as opposed to real ones and the effect of this on the last step in the procedure, where adjustments to boundary segmentation are made. Hearst's work, Berber-Sardinha argued, did not consider *how* sentences and clauses relate to each other (lexically), and he sought to redress this perceived deficiency in his own computational procedure.

Berber-Sardinha (2001: 216) commented that Hoey's (1991) research into text structure was based on the view that "… lexical cohesion forms clusters among sentences." As mentioned earlier, Hoey used the term "link" to refer to a lexical semantic cohesive relation between two different sentences, and Berber-Sardinha used the same term in his LSM procedure. At the heart of the measure was the comparison of the link similarity or dissimilarity between two contiguous sentences, rather than two blocks within a text (Hearst's methodology). Berber-Sardinha observed that there may be no lexical links between contiguous sentences, and yet they do cohere and are treated as a segment by the reader (see the earlier discussion on coherence and cohesion). The way to deal with this (computationally) problematic situation, he argued, is to examine "…similarity between all the sentences with which each adjacent sentence shares lexical items" (Berber-Sardinha, 2001: 219). To do this, a link set must be formed; for example, if sentence 1 has two links (i.e. two shared lexical items) with sentence 4 and three links with sentence 6, the link set can be represented as {4,4,6,6,6}. After discussing problems with possible approaches to measuring similarity based on shared links, Berber-Sardinha suggested that the best way of doing this was to compare the mid-points (specifically, medians) of the link sets of adjacent sentences. For example, the median of the link set for sentence 1 above would be 6, as this is the middle number within the set. If the next sentence (sentence 2) in the text had the following links: {4,6,8}, the link set median would also be 6. Berber-Sardinha argued that the medians obtained from the link sets of two adjacent sentences give a general idea about how the links of these sentences are spread. For example, in the scenario provided above, even though it is clear that sentences 1 and 2 have no links between them (i.e. sentence 1 has no cohesive links to 2, and vice versa), they have the same link set median (i.e. 6). As such, Berber-Sardinha argued, they would very likely be connected, and as a consequence be located within the same paragraph. He maintained that the closer (numerically) the medians of the link sets of two contiguous sentences, the more likely they were closely related. To determine what is or is not "close," he recommended comparing the median difference between two adjacent sentences and then comparing this to the average median difference between all of the sentences in the text. For example, if the average median difference between all of the sentences in a text is 2, and the median between two specific contiguous sentences is 4, this would tend to indicate that the two sentences are not linked, as this number is higher than the average. However, if the difference between the two sentence median scores is less than two – for example, 0 (as in the example above, where the medians of both sentences are 6), then there is evidence for lexical continuity between the two sentences.

To test his algorithm, Berber-Sardinha (2001) conducted analyses on 300 texts (100 each for academic, business, and encyclopedia texts). Berber-Sardinha found the LSM to perform better than chance and some other algorithmic tools, but it was not as accurate as results obtained by using the TextTile algorithm. Berber-Sardinha suggested that the LSM procedure could perhaps be improved through using alternatives measures to the median as the basis for the calculation, by lemmatizing lexical items (i.e. considering all forms of a word), or considering additional linguistic features or types of reiteration in the link sets. By including derivational affixation links (e.g. *develop-development*) in addition to inflectional affixation links (e.g. *develop-develops*) I found a marginal increase in the performance of the LSM when used on a set of 10 argumentative texts (McGee, 2014), although the small set of data do not warrant generalization of that finding. Berber-Sardinha also noted that the procedure may not work very well on literary texts because of the different types of cohesive links involved in such writing, citing Hoey (1994) as support for this reservation.

Analysis of the Introduction of New Vocabulary

Gilbert Youmans' initial work into vocabulary use and distribution in text (simply) plotted word tokens (the total number of words in a text) by types (the number of different words in a text) for various literary texts (Youmans, 1990). He observed that a type–token curve for a text rises rapidly at first (as new words are introduced), but then begins to flatten over the duration of the text, as fewer new words are introduced into the text, and as more repetition occurs. He found that over the first 4000 tokens in four different texts, there were different degrees of curve flattening, which was indicative of different writers' lexical style and range of vocabulary usage (i.e. some writers continue to introduce new lexis as their writing proceeds, for others there is more repetition).

Youmans (1991) later went on to develop his initial work by considering whether the introduction of new words in a text might be indicative of the commencement of a new topic or episode within the text, and whether this could be computed. Looking at type-token curves, Youmans commented, would not help in this enquiry as they are not sensitive enough to flag this kind of topic- or episode-change information. However, Youmans believed that a more sensitive procedure could be used, namely, tracing the introduction of new vocabulary over a particular number of words within the text. That is, he considered type-token rate of change over a range of words within a text, finding that a 35-word segment produced the most interesting data.[17] He called the resulting data a Vocabulary Management Profile (VMP). Figure 6.4 (data from an extract from "The Dead" by James Joyce), provides the ratio of the number of new types divided by the number of new tokens over a period of 35 words, across the first 2000 words of the text. Accordingly, the valleys in the figure indicate fewer new tokens within a 35-word range of text being introduced, and the peaks indicate more new tokens being introduced (in which 1 = all new tokens are new types, and 0 = all new tokens are existing types within the 35 word segment). Youmans believed that the valleys, indicating a lower type-token ratio, were indicative of episode change in text. It is readily apparent that these occur in a fairly rhythmical fashion throughout the text as can be seen in the figure, with slightly more repetition evident over the whole of the text extract, evident in the gradual left to right decline.

The key question which Youmans went on to consider is whether the patterns evident from such analyses are somehow indicative of episode change with the text. Youmans conducted a very detailed comparison of VMP data with what he termed the "entry-hall episode" of the Joyce text (comprising the first 1189

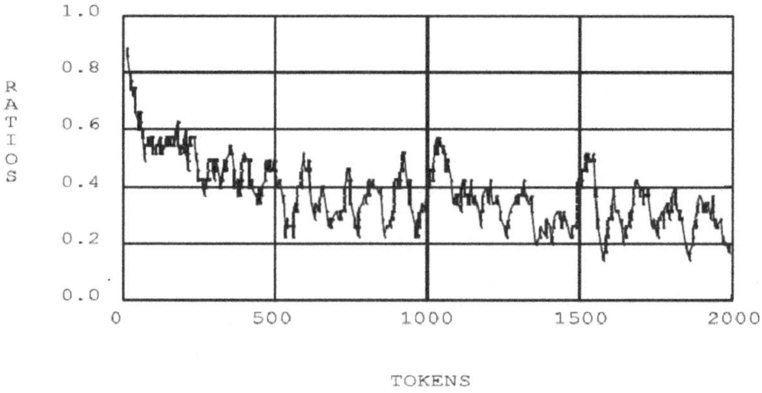

Figure 6.4. The Ratios Δy / Δx for the Text "The Dead" by James Joyce (Δx=35) [From *A New Tool for Discourse Analysis: The Vocabulary-Management Profile* (Youmans (n.d.: 14). Reproduced by permission of the author.]

words). Youmans found that the VMP profile correctly identified the shift between the three opening monologic paragraphs and the beginning of the fourth starting with dialogue. He also showed how it successfully identified the breaks between the first three opening paragraphs, in addition to signaling episode change within a paragraph in which there was a character shift (from Lily to Katy and Julia within the first paragraph). Where the match between the VMP and actual indentation was not perfect, Youmans provided possible reasons why this was not so, including what he termed the presence of "head-tail" relations (i.e. topic foregrounding, see Chapter 5) as negatively affecting the prediction of the beginning of a new paragraph by a sentence or two. Youmans believed that the VMP concept could be a valuable tool in discourse analysis, though he limited his observations to professional writing. Youmans' work was highly original, and the VMP concept was also used by Michael Stubbs (Stubbs, 2002).

Entropy Rate

Dmitriy Genzel and Eugene Charniak's work examined the entropy rate, representing informativeness, of various sentences in a paragraph (Genzel and Charniak, 2003). As they commented, the first sentence of a text is context-less, and the 10th is more informative and more difficult to process since it contains reference to entities noted in previous sentences. It therefore has a higher entropy rate, meaning higher informativeness. They found that sentence entropy increased according to the sentence number in a text. For example, sentence 5 in a text has a higher entropy rate than sentence 1. However, Genzel and Charniak (2003: 66) observed that this increasing entropy rate is likely to stop at a paragraph break: "If there is a topic shift at the boundary, the context probably provides more information to the preceding sentence, than it does to the new one." That is, a paragraph-initial sentence may be similar to a text-beginning sentence, at least in terms of its informativeness. In their research, based on an analysis of *Wall Street Journal* articles and three different language versions of Tolstoy's *War and Peace* (English, Spanish, and Russian), they found that paragraph-initial sentences did indeed tend to have lower entropy rates than other sentences within the same paragraphs. They also observed that correlations between entropy rate and sentence number were higher in information-high (i.e. informationally dense) genres (e.g. academic writing) as compared to information-low genres (including popular magazines and tabloid newspapers), in which information is more gradually introduced to the reader. They noted, however, that paragraphs do not necessarily represent shifts in topic, and that this fact weakens the underlying assumption of their model. Commenting about journalistic literature, Genzel and Charniak observed that the articles tend to stay on one topic across multiple paragraphs, hence the weakening of the relationship of a paragraph break to the introduction of a new topic, whereas fiction appeared to maintain the relationship between paragraphs and topics to a greater extent. Because the topic = paragraph equation is contentious, they argued that it is unrealistic to expect the entropy measure to always accurately identify paragraph beginnings.

Incorporating Discourse Management Techniques into Algorithms

In Chapter 5, the concept of multi-signaling in relation to discourse management was discussed. Some of the most recent computational work, summarized below, has built on the concept of multi-signaling, in particular utilizing paragraph-initial phraseology to help in identifying the presence of a paragraph break in deparagraphed text. As such, this is an important area of cross-over between computational and discourse / corpus linguistic research.

As mentioned earlier, Hearst was skeptical regarding the usefulness of discourse markers with regard to the aid they could provide in the computational signaling of discourse relations. She referred to their ambiguity, citing Brown and Yule (1983) and their comments on this in support of her claim. However, the presence of discourse-managing tools (discussed in the previous chapter) signaling continuity or transition (and at times including discourse markers) have been considered to be significant aids to paragraph identification in some computational work.

Sporleder and Lapata (2004, 2006) argued for the incorporation of cue phrases (i.e. phrases in specific paragraph positions) into automatic paragraph segmentation measures. They noted that much of the earlier computational work on text segmentation was not actually specifically paragraph-oriented but topic-oriented, thereby, in effect, conflating topic and paragraph – an important observation. While in some texts this relationship may be a reasonable assumption, it is not a clear relation, as Genzel and Charniak (2003) had noted earlier. In their own research, Sporleder and Lapata used BoosTexter, originally developed by Robert Shapire and Yoram Singer (Shapire and Singer, 2000) as a machine learning system,[18] on three register domains (fiction, news, and parliamentary proceedings) and in three different languages (English, German, and Greek). The system considered and incorporated many textual features from the texts, including various surface features (e.g. paragraph-initial language), language modeling features (i.e. information and entropy rate), and syntactic features (including discourse markers). The rationale for the inclusion of the paragraph-initial word position information in the training of BoosTexter was given as follows: "Although paragraph breaks are not necessarily correlated with topic and consequently vocabulary change, there are certain words that may occur frequently at the start of a paragraph..." (Sporleder and Lapata, 2006: 9). In terms of the performance of their system on paragraph identification, they found word position features to be particularly important for identifying paragraph breaks in news domains and in parliamentary proceedings, but less so in fiction. Below I provide the cue words which they found to be common in paragraph-initial position in the English news corpus.

In New York
For the nine
In composite trading
In early trading
In addition to
At the same
One of the
The White House
In addition the
In an interview   (Sporleder and Lapata, 2006: 18)

Sporleder and Lapata observed domain-specific differences in the performance of their system, and suggested that machine learning systems would have to be trained on and for specific domains to be sensitive to the cue-phrase clues typically used in paragraph-initial position within them. They then went on to compare performance of their system with a non-training (topic-segmentation) algorithm, that of Masao Utiyama and Hitoshi Isahara (Utiyama and Isahara, 2001), and found their own system to be superior across the different corpus domains and languages in terms of its paragraph segmentation performance. They concluded that non-trained (generic) algorithms were not sensitive enough for automatic paragraph segmentation tasks. In addition, they found that their system approximated well to human rater segmentation.

Katya Filippova and Michael Strube (Filippova and Strube, 2006), like Sporleder and Lapata (2004, 2006), were careful to differentiate topic and paragraph segmentation, noting that while a topic boundary is typically signaled by a paragraph boundary, the opposite is not the case, as a group of paragraphs may constitute a single topic (as others had previously observed). They also commented that topic segmentation algorithms have, typically, depended on relations of lexical cohesion, but that when the paragraph unit is considered stylistically as opposed to topically, it is possible that functional words (i.e. grammatical words, specifically, pronominalization) may be as important for paragraph segmentation as the tracking of lexical items (see comments on this issue in Chapter 5). Filippova and Strube collected 970 biographies of scientists from the German Wikipedia site, comprising over 5 million paragraphs. After annotating the corpus, they used 95% of the material in training and developing their system, and the remaining 5% to test the system. They compared the performance of their algorithm against a random insertion method, a topic boundary algorithm, and the strongest features of Sporleder and Lapata's (2006) work noted above. Their own algorithm was designed on the assumption that paragraph segmentation occurs at points of weak cohesion, and so their algorithm incorporated lexical cohesion in addition to pronominalization, discourse cues, and information structure.

After training the algorithm, Filippova and Strube (2006) discovered that discourse cues weakened performance (contrary to their expectations), and suggested that this may have been because of an insufficiency of data rather than a real effect and that by increasing the data (in future research), they might find more reliable indicators of the correlation of discourse markers and paragraph-initial position. The best results for their algorithm occurred when both surface features (e.g. word position clues) and textual cohesion cues were considered together, and they also noted the importance of pronominalization cues (not utilized by Sporleder and Lapata, 2004, 2006) in positively affecting the performance of their measure. Their algorithm outperformed Sporleder and Lapata's (2006) algorithm in some respects, and they stressed in their conclusion the importance of both content and style for identifying paragraph boundaries.

The Computationally Measurable Characteristics of Paragraph Types

As mentioned earlier in this chapter, computational linguists have researched two issues of relevance to my focus in this book. The second of these interests, which I consider in this section, is research into the particular characteristics of certain paragraphs within a text. Crossley et al.'s (2011) research is of particular significance in this respect. Crossley et al. investigated whether the linguistic features of a paragraph differ according to the paragraph position (initial, medial or final) in an essay, in a corpus of freshman argumentative essays. Crossley et al. used a measure developed by Arthur Graesser and colleagues McNamara, Max Louwerse, and Zhiqiang Cai (Graesser et al., 2004) – the Coh-metrix system – to investigate whether paragraphs could be identified by their position in an essay. The system incorporated a large number of textual features in its training: lexical coreference (including content word links between sentences), semantic coreference (e.g. semantic relations – cat and mouse); word frequency; word-information (i.e. familiarity, concreteness, imagability, meaningfulness, age of acquisition, based on psycholinguistic database data); hypernymy and polysemy (i.e. ambiguity and specificity); causality (i.e. the ratio of causal verbs, e.g. *throw* to causal particles e.g. *because*); syntactic intricacy; connective density; and text length. They trained the Coh-metrix system by analyzing similarities and differences in these areas for the different paragraphs, and then ran their system on new texts, not used in training it, and compared its precision (correct identifications divided by correct and incorrect identifications) and recall (correct identifications divided by correct identifications and false positives) with the actual positions of the paragraphs, and also with human raters. The human raters achieved a combined precision and recall score of .66 in identifying paragraphs as introductory, supporting, or concluding, and the Coh-metrix system achieved a score of .65 on the same measures. Below I summarize their key findings and how they interpreted them.

Initial Paragraphs

Crossley et al. (2011) found that initial paragraphs tend to be shorter than final paragraphs, which they believed to be because of the generality of initial as contrasted with final paragraphs. There was also less co-referencing (i.e. lexical cohesive links) within these paragraphs than the others, as points were not elaborated on, and they were also found to contain fewer connectives (e.g. *and, but, also*). In addition, initial paragraphs tended to have a greater number of more meaningful words[19] in them, also containing more imageable words than final paragraphs. Not surprisingly, they contained less in the way of given as opposed to new information.

Middle Paragraphs

Middle paragraphs were seen to be longer than initial and final paragraphs, and they contained more given information and word overlap (i.e. lexical cohesion) than initial paragraphs, which Crossley et al. suggested was due to the grouping of ideas and expansion of points only noted (but not developed on) in introductory paragraphs.

Final Paragraphs

Crossley et al. found that final paragraphs were less specific in terms of vocabulary (with regard to hypernymy) than initial and middle paragraphs and they contained more familiar words than the other two paragraph types, which they suggested to be consistent with the summarizing function. They also documented the presence of many connectives and sentence modifiers in final paragraphs.

The results obtained by Crossley et al. (2011) demonstrated that features of syntactical complexity, word frequency, and causal cohesion were not as useful as the other features noted above in terms of their value in differentiating the paragraph types. Interestingly, final paragraphs were less accurately identified by human raters than the other paragraphs. Crossley et al. suggested that this may have been due to confusion over whether the summarizing element within this type of paragraph was considered to be introductory or concluding. Their system, on the other hand, tended to err in classifying conclusion paragraphs as supporting (i.e. middle paragraphs) because of the similar linguistic features (e.g. presence of connectives) between the two types. Crossley et al. also noted that raters had greater success in classifying longer paragraphs than shorter ones, and higher quality paragraphs than ones of lower quality, as judged by expert raters.

Crossley et al. (2011: 135) believed that the ability of their measure to identify rhetorical paragraph types suggested that paragraphs are "… recognizable units of linguistic structure." They further suggested that their findings contradicted Stern's (1976) argument that the paragraph was not a logical unit: if it were not a logical unit exhibiting rhetorical functions, then the Coh-metrix measure would not have been as successful as it was. Crossley et al. (2011) were careful to delimit the generalizability of their observations to American student argumentative essays. They also suggested that there were possible pedagogical implications of their findings, which I note at the end of the chapter.

Commentary

Research by computational linguists that has had some kind of bearing on our understanding of the paragraph has been both rich and varied. From the early work of Morris and Hirst (1991) to the more recent work of Filippova and Strube (2006), and Crossley et al. (2011) a wide variety of textual features (lexical, grammatical, and informational) have been investigated in relation to their value in helping automatically segment text, or identify paragraphs according to their lexis or grammar. As such, paragraph segmentation has become quite a well-researched area, although much less work has been conducted into paragraph identification.

The focus of interest of the older computational research was generally quite different from the linguistic interest in the paragraph considered in the previous chapter. Computational linguists have generally, though not exclusively, focused on textual cohesion: Goutsos (1997), on the other hand, focused on the tools used to signal shift or continuity between these cohesive units. The two foci seem to be very different: using a metaphor, one set of scholars has considered the train cars and the other the couplings between the cars, in considering paragraphs within text.

As discussed above, results from some of the more recent computational work indicate the value of considering the paragraph both as a semantic unit, that is, a unit exhibiting distinct internal text cohesive links, and also as a unit which may exhibit distinct phrasing in paragraph-initial position (whether that be primarily lexical or grammatical). As such, it seems clear that we need to consider these two types of data (broadly speaking, cohesion and discourse-managing) together to understand the textuality of paragraphs. Following on from Sporleder and Lapata's (2004, 2006) research, and their comments on the need for corpus-trained systems, one can expect to see more genre-specific computational research in future work on paragraph segmentation, and it may be that computational work such as that conducted by Crossley et al. (2011), together with VBDU work (Biber et al., 2007), will help develop new genre-specific formal models of the paragraph.

While it is important to consider both cohesion and discourse-managing tools when studying paragraphs, it should be recognized that the relative significance of one or other of these two textual features in defining the boundaries of the paragraph may well vary for different genres (and even different paragraphs within these genres). In expository text, for example, the topicality of the paragraph unit seems to be more established than it is in journalistic writing, where paragraphing may be less a matter of topicality and instead reflect stylistic or visual concerns. As such, paragraph-initial frames or lexis may be more important (relative to the case with expository text) to keep the discourse flowing, and in managing the text in journalism genres. It is also clear that cohesion appears to be more important in middle, as opposed to initial paragraphs, within the same genre (according to the findings of Crossley et al. 2011).

However, I suggest that these two foci (cohesion identification and textual management) may not be as distinct or unrelated as considered at first sight. As I have noted elsewhere (McGee, 2014), computational linguists have not, generally speaking, been interested in exploring why an algorithm is successful in any particular instance in identifying a particular paragraph within a particular text, but not another break within the same text. The reason for this lack of interest, as noted earlier, is because of the quantitative as opposed to qualitative focus of this work, and also, I believe, a rather simplistic assumption that topic shift is the key variable affecting the performance of a procedure. That is, there appears to be an assumption that new clusters of words, indicative of a new topic being developed, are responsible for the success of an algorithm or system. On occasion, this may well be the case. However, I believe such an assumption can, at times, be challenged on the grounds that it may be the introduction to a new topic (i.e. the presence of some kind of management tool), rather than the introduction of the new topic itself, which positively affects the performance of a segmentation tool. I explain this in more detail with an example below.

In using a slightly adapted form of the LSM procedure, I found (McGee, 2014) that quotations, sayings, and rhetorical questions occurring in paragraph-initial position of paragraphs in argumentative texts were, at times, totally disconnected (in terms of their lexical repetition links) from the topic that had just closed, or was to be developed. As such, the LSM procedure correctly identified these paragraph-initial sentences as being at the paragraph juncture, but, critically, this was not because of topic shift per se, but rather because the discourse-managing transitional devices were very different from the preceding and the following text, in terms of their lexical links. In the two examples below, from McGee (2014) an adapted form of the LSM procedure correctly identified the presence of the paragraph break (signaled by a pilcrow ¶) between the two sentences. It is clear, however, that it is not the introduction of a new topical subject that positively affected the performance of the procedure in identifying the paragraph break, but rather the presence of a discourse-managing tool (specifically, the first element of a prediction pair; see Chapter 5, in both cases) with a very different LSM profile than that of the preceding or following sentence. In Example 1, the new paragraph opens in asking a question, and there are no lexical links between the words in this sentence, and the rest of the text. In contrast, the sentence closing the paragraph preceding this question has many links. This difference was (successfully) identified as indicative of a break by the LSM measure. Similarly, in Example 2, the personal emotional response of the expression "The justifications only get worse" in paragraph-opening position contrasts with the paragraph-closing sentence preceding it, in having no lexical links within the text, resulting in a significant difference in the link set medians of the two sentences.

Example 1
(*closing sentence of a paragraph*)
The social science is clear: Marriage provides better conditions than any other form of relationship for couples' well being. *(multiple repetition links within the text)*
¶---
Where does this advantage come from? *(no links within the text)*

Example 2
(*closing sentence of a paragraph*)
Banning religious clothing because of a blind appeal to laïcité is as mind-bogglingly asinine as supporting McCarthyism with *The Communist Manifesto. (multiple repetition links within the text)*
¶---
The justifications only get worse. *(no links within the text)*
(Adapted from McGee, 2014: 63)

Discourse-managing tools may not have many (or indeed any) cohesive links within the text. Whether this may actually contribute to their role in managing text is an intriguing possibility, but this is a subject of enquiry outside of my focus here. What is clear, however, is that it may be overly simple to believe that people move from one textually cohesive unit to the next as they write and read, but rather at least some (and perhaps many) breaks in cohesion, as identified by segmentation algorithms, result from the presence of discourse-managing tools within the text, rather than being due to the juxtaposition of clusters of different topic-related vocabulary. That is, the language co-occurring with – or, more accurately, immediately preceding, – topic change, may have a positive effect on the performance of a particular cohesion-break tracking segmentation measure. As such, it may be discourse management, rather than topic shift, which triggers successful computational paragraph identification, at least at times. The only way to investigate this subject further would be to subject successful paragraph identification data to qualitative analyses.

Before ending this section, I would like to make one further observation concerning some of the computational approaches to paragraph segmentation, in relation to the types of words included in text segmentation algorithms and measures. In Chapter 3, educational interest in the functionality and topicality of the paragraph was mentioned (in relation to discussions of unity in the 19th century). It was suggested that a focus on topic without regard to function is, in many ways, an inadequate or incomplete conceptualization of the paragraph: for example, if a writer is writing about a car (i.e. the topic), we want to know why (i.e. the function or reason in writing). In terms of algorithm cohesion tracking, it is not only topicality (narrowly defined) that has been calculated, i.e. words relating to the topic. By virtue of their non-discriminatory vocabulary tracking, some measures have incorporated not only semantic lexical cohesive links or chains (e.g. *car...car...vehicle)* but also captured something of the purpose of the text, in tracking purpose language too. For example, if a text is trying to persuade the reader to buy the car being described, then links such as {*bargain... bargain...deal}* may also form lexical cohesive chains within the text. These two different types of vocabulary are not differentiated by algorithms, and neither have their individual roles in the success or failure of various segmentation procedures been considered. For an example of what I am trying to argue here, the reader is referred, again, to Figure 6.1. As can be seen, recurrence of the word *say* is evident between sentences 33–55, with one additional mention later in the text. This word is very different from the more obviously content-oriented vocabulary (e.g. *orbit, planet*) within the text about astronomy. It may be (and this is pure hypothesis) that the cluster is associated with claims that have been made (e.g. *X says this, Y says that*) or an issue of debate, and as such may indicate the presence of a particular functional unit within the text, as opposed to (or possibly in addition to) being a section devoted to a specific subtopic in astronomy. Only qualitative analyses of data will be able to show the role of different types of vocabulary in affecting the performance of algorithms, indeed, may show some interesting differences between genres, with regard to the presence and lexical link patterns of what may be termed for want of better terms *topical vocabulary*, and *textual function vocabulary*.

Educational Applications

On the basis of their data findings reported above, Crossley et al. (2011) suggested that teachers could draw the attention of students, particularly weaker students, to the specific linguistic features of different paragraph types (initial, medial, and final), as a way to help such learner-writers better organize and develop their writing. Helping learners to notice how paragraphs develop, or the kinds of links, or types of words used within them clearly makes sense. Below I make further comments on the teaching of cohesion. It should be made clear that these points are only loosely related to the research findings given above, more accurately following on from them.

Lexical cohesion is an area which needs to be revisited in our classrooms and in our thinking about paragraphing. As I have noted elsewhere (McGee, 2009), this subject is more complex and challenging than one might think, and this, together with an overemphasis on grammatical correctness and a focus on logical development in writing classes (rather than language crafting), may be responsible for its neglect. Problems facing weaker students in this area are many, as I mention below.

Repetition, more common in speech than writing, may not be considered problematic by students when writing, particularly so if they are not made aware of different tolerance levels of this aspect of cohesion in different genres. It is clear from the research reported in this chapter that repetition is common in expository text: but what types of repetition are acceptable, and what types make a text feel heavy and dry is a complex matter. Simplistic advice to avoid repetition is clearly wrong, but how, exactly, to identify inelegant or repetitious repetition, is far more difficult, as there may be an element of subjectivity affecting views concerning what is acceptable. There may also be the issue of local repetition versus longer-range. Is only the former flagged by writing instructors, as it is considered more grating? Encouraging students to consider complex repetition (i.e. changing word form, such as using *development* rather than repeating the form *develop*) can also cause problems, because learners (especially L2 learners) may not be aware of the appropriate associated collocational or colligational forms to use complex repetition correctly (see McGee, 2009).

Simplistic advice to increase the use of synonyms, rather than depending on repetition is also problematic, essentially because pure synonymy does not exist. For example, if a *policeman* is referred to as a *cop* in the same text, repetition has been avoided, but the level of formality has shifted, and this may not have been the intention of the learner-writer. Another example in which simplistic pedagogical advice might be unhelpful is the encouragement to vary the use of different reporting verbs in writing (in the case of the overuse of just one or two types). There are, however, different denotational (and connotational) nuances involved in the use of various reporting verbs (which pedagogical materials may, unfortunately, group together under the 'reporting verbs' heading). Such differences may not be fully appreciated by learners, who may consider *argue* to be a synonym for *show*, and as such, misrepresent the basis for a claim made by a researcher (*argue* more typically related to the interpretation of data, *show* related to the less subjective matter of reporting research results).

Encouraging the use of superordination and subordination links appears to be less of a problem in terms of usage (e.g. a *gun* is always a *weapon*, and can be referred to as such without concerns about formality, denotative or connotative shifts in meaning). However, even here the order of linking needs to be considered. For example, definitions typically (though not always) move from the more specific to the more general (e.g. *a gun is a weapon*....) whereas exemplification typically goes the other way (e.g. *...some weapons, for example, guns...*), but one may wish to manipulate readers in certain ways, by changing typical patterns (for example, by being deliberately vague in initial reference, to create reader suspense, or imagination). The uses of definite or indefinite forms when using superordinate and subordinate forms can also be a challenge for students. Specifically, while *the / a* appropriacy may not often be a problem for comprehension in learner writing, it can be problematic in this area. For example, consider the sentence pair *The Titanic left Southampton. A ship [rather than **the ship**] hit an iceberg*. Such misuse can result in quite catastrophic comprehension confusion (in addition, of course, to damage to a rather indeterminate ship!).

Students can be encouraged to trace reiteration links in their own writing, and redraft their texts after considering the reiteration (and collocation) links within them. Raphael Salkie's textbook, with its unique focus on exploring lexical cohesion in text (Salkie, 1995), is a valuable resource in this regard, which I believe can help teachers effectively explore reiteration and collocation with their students.

Another area of related pedagogical engagement is the development of students' discourse sensitivities to cohesion patterns and phraseology. The research referred to in this chapter indicates that cohesive patterns and paragraph-initial phraseology are not the same in different texts and genres, and students can be encouraged to notice these differences. Coherence may or may not be achieved by cohesive links, and learners can be challenged to think about the effect of different paragraphing patterns for the reader. Paragraphs with few cohesive links would, I suspect, result in a paragraph feeling more *choppy* for the reader. Finally, if learners are aware that cohesion may be achieved both by intra- and inter-paragraph links, this should ensure that paragraph units are not isolated, but integrated within the wider text.

Conclusion

In closing this chapter it is worthwhile considering, briefly, how the research mentioned above relates to, further refines, or challenges ideas about the paragraph discussed in previous chapters.

The idea of the paragraph being a topical unit is a longstanding one, and it was central to discussion of paragraph theorizing in the late 19th century. However, the role of lexical cohesion (and in particular lexical repetition) in defining or helping understand topicality and the paragraph was never really considered. In the 1960s Lord (1964) and Becker (1965, 1966) discussed the presence of lexical cohesive links within paragraphs, and Becker, in particular suggested that lexical chains (what he called lexical equivalence chains) might help in identifying tagmemes within paragraphs, and indeed differentiate paragraph units (see Chapter 4). After Becker, discourse linguists – most notably, Halliday and Hasan (1976) – drew attention to lexical cohesion and its relation to discourse structure. Computational linguists went on to explore the value of these links, and their research has shown that many paragraphs can be considered to be cohesive units, though this cohesion is not simple, rather, requires the creation of algorithms and training of computational measures to track it. Over time, other textual elements (as discussed above) have been incorporated into attempts to segment text, and many of the discourse-managing tools discussed in Chapter 5, perhaps with the exception of shell nouns, as commented upon by Kolhatkar et al. (2013), have been considered to be of value by computational linguists, in helping map paragraph units.

When cohesive links and paragraph-initial discourse-managing links are considered together, computer measures more accurately identify paragraphs within deparagraphed text, than measures solely developed on the basis of tracing cohesion, and cohesive breaks. It has been suggested that one of the reasons for this increased accuracy is that topicality (related to cohesion) may be considered to be more or less a characteristic of the paragraph unit. A consideration of stylistic considerations, when incorporated into computational linguistic work, has helped us appreciate the more subtle factors affecting the shape of paragraphs.

Notes

1   How unusual a case this is, is a subject for further research. See the Crossley et al. (2011) reference below, which suggests that there is less cohesion between sentences in introduction paragraphs than in body paragraphs.

2   It should be mentioned that Halliday and Hasan's (1976) view of collocation is not considered mainstream in applied linguistics today.

3   Although using the word *coherence* here, Quirk et al. (1985) seem to be referring to cohesion as suggested towards the end of the quotation, by the use of the word *linkage*.

4   Rather than attempting to provide an overview of all of the work in text segmentation (which is vast), I focus here on just a few key studies, and do so (largely) in chronological order.

5   This theory differentiated and considered interaction between the linguistic structure, that is, "the structure of the sequence of utterances that comprise a discourse" (Grosz and Sidner, 1986: 177), intentional structure (i.e. purpose or purposes), and attentional state (i.e. focus of attention within the discourse) of a text.

6   For example, if the chain noted here continued to include *scarf, boots, hat,* and *snow*, the relation between *cow* and *snow*, is obviously less salient than *cow* and *wool*, and as such the chain is less likely to be related to the same textual purpose, or be within the same textual segment.

7   Hearst (1994a: 8) limited the scope of TextTiling to "expository text that is not heavily stylized or structured." The reference to style in this quotation is important, and elaborated on further, later in this chapter.

8   Hearst (1994b: 10) specifically referred to Brown and Yule (1983) in support of this argument. However, Marcu's (2000a,b) work challenged its validity, though he was less interested in paragraph identification, rather rhetorical structure.

9   And, as a consequence, Hearst (1994a) noted that her algorithm is more coarse-grained than some other text segmentation algorithms, because of this simplicity of approach.

10   In what follows, procedures are more or less simplified for the sake of the non-specialist reader.

11   In passing, Hearst (1994b: 14) noted a key problem in evaluating an algorithm's performance, namely, that judges do not always concur on segmentation decisions, an important point discussed in more detail in Chapter 7.

12   Hearst (1997: 56) observed how the phrase "For the last two centuries, astronomers have studied" was picked up by the readers as a topic-shifting cue but not by the computer algorithm (which was not developed to take into account the discourse signaling function of such a phrase). This observation is very important, given the discussion on the presence of discourse signaling tools in Chapter 5 and the more recent work in computational linguistics which has incorporated such paragraph-initial language into the development of segmentation algorithms, reported later in this chapter. What Hearst noted in passing was, in fact, a highly significant observation.

13   She suggested that this was so due to ambiguous links being formed (Hearst, 1997: 46); however, she also mentioned that she used a different thesaurus to that used by Morris and Hirst, and that this may have affected the results accordingly.

14   It should be noted that Kaufmann was not interested in paragraph segmentation per se, but topic segmentation.

15   Kaufmann (1999: 594) suggested that a key reason for the only marginally positive effect might have been because of "the co-occurrence of uncommon words not in the training corpus (personal names, rare terminology etc.) that ties text together."

16   They defined these as "links that are similar to syntactic ones but hold between words of different sentences" (Bolshakov and Gelbukh, 2001: 159).

17 After working with various spans, Youmans (1991) found a segment of 35 words to be the most interesting or valuable.

18 That is, calculations of where paragraph breaks occur depend on the training of BoosTexter on previous texts of the same genre.

19 According to the MRC Psycholinguistic Database compiled by Max Coltheart (Coltheart, 1981).

7 The Psychological Effect of Paragraphs and Paragraph Organization on Readers

Introduction

In Chapter 5, I discussed and elaborated on the proposition (put forward by Goutsos, 1997) that the decision to indent is one among several discourse management tools available for use by a writer to signal textual development. The paragraph break is, however, quite unlike the other devices discussed in that chapter, for the simple reason that it is not a grammatical or lexical tool but a paralinguistic one and a typographical entity. It is that uniqueness that I wish to focus on in this chapter, and I do so from the perspective of how readers experience paragraphs. The key questions which I seek to engage with are:

- What do readers do at the beginning and ending of paragraphs?
- What are the effects of manipulating paragraph structure on readers' comprehension, memory, and learning?
- Can readers segment a de-segmented text into paragraphs so that it approximates the original text?

These three questions, addressed in three different sections below, cover the main research interests in reader psychology and paragraphs, although the last question has also been researched from a textual-interest perspective, namely, what can be learned about the nature of the paragraph from reader segmentation studies (rather than what can be learned about readers). In the overview that follows, I attempt to answer these questions, and then go on to consider the possible implications of the various research findings for educators and writing instructors.

What Readers Do at the Beginning and Ending of Paragraphs

In this section I consider research data relating to eye-tracking research and reading, different ways in which the data have been interpreted and consider what the research and explanations mean for our understanding of the paragraph, from the reader's perspective.

Eye Tracking and Reading

One of the ways that reading behavior has been investigated is through eye-tracking technology, typically involving video and computer applications. Eye-tracking devices (whether attached to the eyes,[1] head, or remote) record how people's eyes move as they are reading. This methodology is attractive for two main reasons: it is non-invasive, and it enables researchers to study and record natural reading behavior, in the sense that it simply tracks what the eyes are doing when reading, as noted by Keith Rayner and Alexander Pollatsek (Rayner and Pollatsek, 2006: 613). However, even though the resulting data from such research are free from many of the problems inherent in observation or experimentation methodologies, there are a number of complicating variables to overcome when considering the data. These include task effects (i.e. what the reader is supposed to do while or after reading), reader interest (i.e. interest in the subject matter of the text) and different reading styles (i.e. the particular way that a reader normally processes text, see below). Issues surrounding interpretation of the data are also problematic, as will be discussed.

Background to eye-movement research

As we read, our eyes fixate on the words on the line being read, one by one.[2] The amount of time spent on these fixations, occurring between saccades (i.e. the eye jumps between words), can be measured by eye-tracking devices, the fixations being timed in milliseconds (ms = 1 / 1000th of a second). The focus of a fixation is captured by what is termed foveal vision (i.e. central, perfectly clear vision); the words ahead of the word in focus at any one time are in the parafoveal vision range (5 degrees of visual angle); and peripheral vision is understood to be everything beyond parafoveal vision, and typically considered to be of little value in the reading process (Rayner and Pollatsek, 2006: 615).

Kuperman et al. (2010), in their review of the literature on eye movements in relation to reading text, observed that the findings have not been consistent. Some research has indicated that fixation time increases across a sentence (i.e. that there is a slow-down effect), and other research has indicated that eye fixation time decreases (i.e. reading speeds up), and it is not clear why this is so, although they suggested a number of feasible reasons including the effect of the word itself (including word predictability, frequency and length) the length of the text to be read, and effects due to the different methodologies and analytical tools employed by researchers. Despite differences, there is an admittedly oversimplified belief that words at the beginning and ending of a line, a sentence, or a paragraph receive greater fixation time than other words, as some of the research referred to below indicates.

Reading behavior at certain points within text

Kuperman et al. (2010) found that word fixation at the beginning of a single line of text and also at the beginning of a paragraph was longer than for a word in medial sentence position. Marcel Just, Patricia Carpenter, and Jacqueline Woolley observed the first key paragraph topic word to be fixated on 342 ms longer than average, with a smaller increase (94 ms) than average fixation time for the first content word in a paragraph (Just et al., 1982: 231). Particular phrases in sentence-initial position have been shown to result in greater reading fixation time than other words in a sentence – *to summarize* is an example remarked on by Robert Lorch and Elizabeth Lorch (Lorch and Lorch, 1986) – and sentence connectives in text have been observed to facilitate faster processing of upcoming information, as pointed out by Gerdineke van Silfhout, Jacqueline Evers-Vermeul, and Ted Sanders (van Silfhout et al., 2015). It has been found that readers fixate longer on words that introduce new topics than on words which continue with the same topic (Just et al., 1982: 229), and Jukka Hyönä found that readers spent more time reading sentences signaling a shift in the discourse than sentences within the same topical segment, what he termed "the topic-shift effect" (Hyönä, 1994: 77).

Concerning ending effects, Just and Carpenter (1980: 330) observed that words at ends of sentences were fixated on for longer than average. Just et al. (1982: 234, 235) observed extra fixation on the last word of a sentence (an extra 403 ms), and an even longer fixation on the last word of a paragraph (719 ms). They also found that a new topic introduced at the end of a sentence resulted in extra fixation time than average.

Some of the research referred to above has considered how people read a sentence, and focused solely on "first-pass" reading, that is, the fixation patterns from word to word on initial reading. Other research has considered how people process larger textual units, in particular paragraphs. In one such study, Hyönä working with Robert Lorch and Johanna Kaakinen considered not just reader fixation from one word to the next in the first reading (termed "forward fixations"), but also reinspection of words in a sentence, and "look-backs" to and from a previously read sentence (Hyönä et al., 2002). On the basis of the patterns of reading recorded in their experiment, Hyönä et al. (2002) differentiated four types of reader:

- slow linear (no look-back, but more time on forward fixations);
- fast linear (no look-back, with less time spent on forward fixation);
- topic structure (frequent look-back, especially to main points); and
- non-selective reviewers (frequent look-back, non-discriminatory).

In their experiment, Hyönä et al. tracked readers' eye movements when reading two sequential, related paragraphs, in which the topic sentences of both paragraphs clearly signaled the import of the main idea of each paragraph. The first sentence of the first paragraph also indicated the general subject matter of both paragraphs, and a heading signaled the subject matter of the two paragraphs. The readers were required to write a summary of the text after completing the reading (with no time limits imposed).

The researchers found that for first-look reading (i.e. forward fixation), all of the different readers had similar fixation profiles, with the heading of the paragraph receiving the most fixation time (with topic structure readers, in particular, spending more time on this). Hyönä et al. (2002) believed that the attention given to this textual feature could have been because of its location on the page, or due to the extra processing involved in managing new information (see below for further elaboration on this idea). No significant difference between the four classes of reader was found regarding the time spent on reading the other types of sentences within the text (topic sentences, paragraph-medial sentences and paragraph-final sentences).

In terms of their general profiles, slow linear readers had the same kind of profile as fast linear, but simply differed in the speed of first-pass reading. Hyönä et al. suggested that their slow reading behavior may have been because of their smaller working memory as compared to the other readers. Like the slow linear readers, the fast linear readers were involved in very little reprocessing, reinspection, and look-back, but exhibited a shorter fixation time on words as compared to the slow linear readers. Topic structure readers performed many look-backs to the heading, and spent more first-pass forward fixation time on the heading as compared to the other readers. They were also involved in more reinspection of final sentences. The best summaries of the paragraphs were provided by this group of readers. The non-selective reading group was a very small group of readers – indeed, a type not found in a later replication of this experiment conducted by Hyönä and Anna-Mari Nurminen (Hyönä and Nurminen, 2006). These readers were involved in many look-backs, for quite a long period of time. However, the look-backs did not appear to be related to key discourse structuring sentences or features of the text. In terms of the relationship between reading style and language proficiency, the researchers found that fast linear and topic structure readers had better first language grades in school.

Which of these reader types is more typical? Hyönä et al. (2002: 53) found that slow linear readers constituted 25% of their participants, the fast linear readers constituted 48%, topic structure 20%, and non-selective readers, 7%. Hyönä and Nurminen (2006), in a replication of the above study, found a reversal in the relative percentages of fast and slow linear readers, with the percentage of readers belonging to the slow linear readers being the largest category, though the percentage of topic structure readers was similar to the 2002 data. As mentioned earlier, there were no non-selective readers found in this replication. Hyönä and Nurminen (2006) also found that readers were reasonably aware of their behaviors, according to data gathered from a questionnaire.

The results from Hyönä et al. (2002) and Hyönä and Nurminen (2006) are of interest for three main reasons. Firstly, it is clearly the case that readers are not a homogenous group, and our thinking about the paragraph should take this into account. Secondly, only around 1 / 5th of readers seem to be sensitive to, and be particularly affected by paragraph structure in their reading habits. Thirdly, the fact that topic sentences were not given special attention by any group of readers is a finding which might be seen to balance some of the research findings reported in section 2 below, indicating the importance of topic sentences to many readers. In the next section I look at various attempts to explain why slow-down and speed-up occur when reading a text.

Explanations for Speed-up and Slow-down Times in Reading

One influential and respected psychological explanation for the increased fixation time spent on certain words within a text, or certain positions within a text, is Morton Gernsbacher's (1991) Structure Building Framework (SBF). This theory proposes that comprehension necessitates the building of mental structures. The building of structures develops in three stages: (1) the laying of the foundation; (2) the development of the structure in which related and coherent information is mapped onto that foundation; and (3) the abandonment of the structure, and the shifting to the building of a new structure, when the new incoming information does not seem to fit with the existing structure. Following on from abandonment, a new foundation is laid for a new structure, if the discourse continues. Gernsbacher appealed to data from some of the studies referred to above as support for her theory. Concerning the start-up effect, the laying of the foundation, Gernsbacher (1997a: 267) argued that increased sentence-initial eye fixation time is indicative of the laying down of the structural foundation: "comprehenders slow down when they are presumably laying mental foundations for their mental structures." Concerning the processing and mapping of incoming information, she suggested that coherence clues facilitate this, these being referential, temporal, locational, or causal in nature (p. 269). For example, a sentence within a story which continues the story in an expected way is read faster (as it is assumed to contribute to the building of a particular structure), when compared with a sentence within a story containing unexpected consequences. The slower reading associated in such a case is suggestive of the reader being unsure of its place in the ongoing story. In SBF when new information does not easily fit into an existing structure, and a shift to a new mental structure occurs, a byproduct of this is for information in the previous structure to become less accessible to the reader. Gernsbacher (1997a: 292) suggested that her theory may help explain why less skilled readers fail to comprehend text: a lack of skill in suppressing irrelevant or inappropriate information (i.e. a failure to read new clues) may result in the continued building of a structure, when a shift to a new cognitive structure should have taken place.

Specifically in relation to the paragraph, Gernsbacher (1997b) stated that whether or not the first sentence of a paragraph functions as a topic sentence, it is read more slowly than later sentences. She interpreted this phenomenon as being structural rather than content-related. Concerning the increased attention given to first position in a paragraph, Gernsbacher pointed out that readers tend to recall the initial sentence of a paragraph as being the main idea of a paragraph, even when it does not contain the main idea (see the second section in this chapter for more on this issue). Further, she believed that the effect of a paragraph break is to weaken the relation between new text and the information present in the last sentence of the previous paragraph: "…if you put a paragraph indentation, people are worse at remembering the sentence that they just read than if you don't have a paragraph indentation there" (p. 3).

Although Gernsbacher did not say much about the paragraph break and its role in her theory, she seemed to suggest that indentation is a cue for the abandonment of a structure and the building of a new one. It is reasonable to assume that the presence of an upcoming paragraph break within peripheral vision, while reading, might indicate this, because as Bruce Britton argued, the paragraph is one of many paralinguistic devices which can help make clear the intended structure of the text (Britton, 1994: 652). However, Giora (1996) argued that the paragraph break should not be considered a signal to abandon a structure in Gernsbacher's theory, because of the nature of actual paragraphing in some texts. As discussed in Chapter 5, the paragraph break, at times, occurs *after* a subject shift, not prior to the shift, in cases of topic foregrounding. In such situations, to view the paragraph break as a cue to abandon an existing structure and build a new one seems to be at odds with what is happening textually. Giora's (1996: 426) solution to this problem was to challenge the idea that the paragraph break has this default role in texts where topic foregrounding occurs:

> By placing the next discourse-topic at the end of a given paragraph, writers allow for the next paragraph to be mapped onto the previously developed substructure. Such concatenation of new discourse-topics must facilitate processing: It does not require the activation of new memory cells for the foundation of a new mental structure [as Gernsbacher had suggested].

In texts where the previous paragraph ends with the to-be-developed topic, Giora argued that the paragraph break is not a radical shift indicator, certainly not as radical as that required for structure abandonment and a signal to begin a new structure. Like Giora, Hyönä and Lorch (2004), did not commit themselves to a necessary connection between the paragraph break and a signal to abandon a mental structure and to begin the building of a new one. However, the reasons they stated for this were rather different from those given by Giora. Hyönä and Lorch (2004: 133) argued that wrap-up of a topic at a paragraph break is dependent on the reader identifying a new paragraph topic starting in the next paragraph:

> Paragraph formatting suggests the possibility of a major topic shift at the start of the new paragraph, although paragraph formatting alone is ambiguous as to the magnitude of the shift. Thus, readers will need to process the entire first sentence [of a new paragraph] in order to determine that a new topic...has, indeed, been introduced. When the new topic is identified, readers will need to wrap up processing of the preceding topic and clearly distinguish it from the new topic so that subsequent information in the new paragraph is not mistakenly connected to a topic that is no longer relevant.

One piece of evidence in support of the idea that it is not the paragraph break per se, that influences reading speed, but rather a more sensitive interaction between text and the paragraph break together is provided by Hyönä and Lorch (2004: 133) who observed that the type of textual material opening a new paragraph affects reading speed. They reported on research which indicated that the degree of slowdown in reading paragraph-initial sentences is related to the degree of topic shift present between paragraphs. That is, when the new topic is less obviously related to the previous topic, slowdown is greater, and when it is more closely related, reading is faster. This finding suggests that readers adjust their reading according to the textual material present at the paragraph break, not just in response to the presence of the paragraph break.

Rather than assuming that the default response to a paragraph break is for a reader to abandon a particular mental representation and lay a new foundation for another (using SBF terminology), it would seem wiser to allow for various mental processes to take place at the paragraph juncture, all of which could be associated with increased fixation time. As Ruth Wodak commented, part of a reader's formal schematic knowledge includes knowing what to expect in a text, and where to expect it; and readers may well have genre-specific expectations concerning how one paragraph will end, and another begin (Wodak, 1992: 504, 505); Karl Haberlandt has also discussed this (Haberlandt, 1982: 246–247). For example, a reader expectation at a particular time might be that a paragraph-initial sentence will be a topic sentence, or, alternatively, will develop a topic-foregrounded subject mentioned at the end of the previous paragraph. A reader may expect a new paragraph within text to signal a significant shift in the developing discourse and this might be confirmed through the use of a metadiscourse marker or adverbial of some kind, in paragraph-initial position. In other cases, the reader may expect only the slightest of discontinuity shifts from one paragraph to the next, this being confirmed through the presence of certain paragraph-initial continuity discourse markers, adverbials, etc. In such instances the reader response to the paragraph break may be indistinguishable from the response to the sentence break, and such paragraphing may well be common in some journalistic discourse. Accordingly, it would seem safer to speak of the potential of the paragraph break to signal structure abandonment, this potential realized by the nature and / or content of the incoming information. Of course, writers can challenge the expectations that a reader may have by manipulating the discourse at the paragraph juncture, and breaking with convention. This possibility may also be part of the reason why readers need to take special care on moving from one paragraph to the next.

In closing discussion of SBF, it is important to point out that some of the existing eye-tracking data could be interpreted as supporting the idea that SBF structural development shifts can occur mid-paragraph as well as at the beginning or ending of a paragraph. For example, research indicates longer eye-fixation (i.e. reading slowdown) for certain words which can occur anywhere within a paragraph, such as *then* or *next* (Gernsbacher, 1991: 237) and on reading words not obviously related to the main topic under discussion (Just et al., 1982: 229). Accordingly, these data indicate that paragraph-initial and -final position should not be considered the only places in text where SBF abandonment and foundation laying may take place.

A number of alternative explanations to the SBF theory for the slow-down effects of eye-fixation data have been suggested. The first of these, and the best known of the alternatives, explains increased fixation time at the end of a paragraph due to limits placed upon working memory during reading. The need to chunk information into manageable units, and the limited capability of short-term memory to manage such units was argued by Teun van Dijk and Walter Kintsch (van Dijk and Kintsch, 1983: 349). From such a viewpoint, it can be argued that increased eye fixation time is a consequence of memory constraints, rather than because of structure building, although one may wish to argue that the two can be related. I mention some of the research and views in support of this idea below.

Just et al. (1982: 235) argued that not all comprehension processes can occur immediately, but that the presence of a constituent boundary might be the cue to end postponement of incomplete processes – one of the boundaries mentioned being the paragraph break. Hyönä and Lorch together with Mike Rinck similarly believed the paragraph break to be a particularly appropriate place where "global text processing" might occur, that is, a key point in a text where integration of information from the wider text (not just the adjacent sentence) occurs – this additional processing taking time, as reflected in greater eye-fixation time (Hyönä et al., 2003: 313). Hofmann (1989: 243) suggested that the paragraph break was a signal to the reader to unitize or wrap up information, resulting in the freeing up of working memory and a "memory freeing" argument was also put forward by Wallace Chafe in his discussion of the role of paragraphing (Chafe, 1994: 119). Chafe spoke of the cognitive constraints surrounding paragraphing, and how writers paragraph differently because of their assumptions about readers' cognitive capacities. One writer might paragraph on the assumption that the readers of the text have limited cognitive capacities, and another write long paragraphs because of the assumed "enormous capacity" of the working memory of the readers.[3] The cognitive-easing function of shell nouns when occurring in paragraph-initial position and the discussion on this in Chapter 5 can also be recalled here. To re-iterate, the argument given by Schmid (2000: 123) for the particularly valuable aid afforded to a reader by the use of a shell noun in paragraph-initial position was that it enabled the reader both to consolidate previous text, and move the discourse forward, thus freeing up overloaded short-term memory.

Two additional explanations for increased fixation time of some words in text have been suggested, in addition to SBF and working memory arguments documented above. The first of these is the effect of punctuation marks on the reader, which Kuperman et al. (2010: 1839) suggested could "give rise to a low-level hesitation response of the oculomotor system." That is, increased fixation time could be explained solely by reference to the presence of punctuation marks, rather than more meaningful cognitive processing. The final explanation for increased fixation time at the end of a sentence or paragraph is related to textual prosody (as suggested by Kuperman et al., 2010), an interesting explanation with strong links to the Aristotelian perspective of paragraphing documented in Chapter 2. According to this argument, prosodic considerations coincide with a boundary. As such, increased fixation time may be due to prosodic rhythm effects in the mind of the reader, rather than SBF structure abandonment, memory-freeing, or a physical response to the presence of punctuation marks on text.

The research reviewed in the first part of this section suggests that indentation may affect the reading process, and in the second part of this section various explanations for why slow-down and speed-up occur have been considered. The data mentioned in the first section are, at times, contradictory. For example, Gernsbacher (1997b) suggested that the response to a paragraph initial sentence is to automatically slow down, whereas Hyönä et al. (2002: 53) found that this was not the case in their data. It is possible that the presence of the textual heading affected the reading patterns of their participants, who may have treated it like a major topic sentence (see Popken 1987, referred to in chapter 3), the topic sentences being perhaps rather redundant in such a case. It is important to remember that it is not only indentation that affects a reader's attention. Certain words, the position of certain words, topic shift, and other textual features affect how our eyes move when we read. Although some of the data are contradictory, and explanations for reading patterns vary, it is clear that indentation and the position of material in paragraph-initial and paragraph-final position may well attract reader attention, as evidenced in some of the research summarized above. However, it is also clear that different readers may have different patterns of attention in their reading. As such it is difficult to make generalizable comments regarding how learners experience paragraphs, an issue to which I return in the conclusion.

To summarize, we can fairly safely hypothesize that readers expect paragraph-final and paragraph-initial positions of text to be important discourse management locations within text, with the result that reading is often more careful, and hence may be slower (to a greater or lesser degree) at these points within a text. At the same time, readers are aware that material present anywhere in a text may need to be given special attention.

The Effects of Manipulating Paragraph Structure on Readers' Comprehension, Memory, and Learning

Various experiments have been conducted by educators, psychologists, and psycholinguists of relevance to our interest in how readers read paragraphs and how changes to a paragraph affect their comprehension, retention of textual information, and learning. Below I make four summary statements concerning paragraph structure manipulation effects on readers and provide an overview of some of the key studies supporting these claims.

Statement 1: An Initial Topic Sentence Facilitates Reading

> *The location of a topic sentence within a paragraph affects readers' speed of reading and their notions about what the main idea of a paragraph is.*

In a well-known study, David Kieras investigated the effects on readers of re-ordering a series of sentences constituting a paragraph (Kieras, 1978). He observed that information processing can proceed top-down or bottom-up,[4] and that participants in his experiment were affected by the order of the presentation of the sentences when they were required to choose which sentence was the best title sentence for the passage. That is, when the topic sentence of the passage was presented first, it was chosen as the passage title more often than when it was given in final position. Further, Kieras found that when the topic sentence was the last sentence in the passage, the text took longer to read than when it was in paragraph-initial position. Kieras interpreted his results as suggestive of the facilitating, framework-creating role of the topic sentence in paragraph-initial position, with sentences following such a "true" topic sentence being more easily integrated with it. As a consequence, the cognitive processing load is lighter for the reader, and hence such texts are read more quickly, as compared to cases in which the topic sentence is at the end of the paragraph.

In an fMRI study investigating how the different position of a topic sentence in a text affected brain activity, Lêda Tomitch and Sharlene Newman together with Carpenter and Just found that when the topic sentence was in final rather than initial position of a short paragraph, the left temporal region of the brain indicated greater activity (Tomich et al., 2008). Tomitch et al. suggested that the left and right hemispheres work together in reading comprehension, but it is clear that different patterns of mental activity result from different organization patterns in text.

Statement 2: A Topic Sentence in Text, or one Generated by the Reader Aids Recall

In the absence of a topic sentence, if one is generated by the reader at the time of reading this facilitates later recall.

Connie Bridge, Susan Belmore, Susan Moskow, Sheila Cohen, and Patricia Matthews considered the effect of the presence or absence (simple omission) of a topic sentence on various comprehension and memory tasks related to the main idea of a paragraph (Bridge et al., 1984). Before completing the tasks given to them, their participants were tested and classified as "good" or "poor" readers (though all were university students, and so the terms *good* and *poor* should be considered relative to the population). In the first experiment, the participants read paragraphs (in a timed condition) with or without topic sentences, and they created a summary sentence for each paragraph on completion of their reading. Then, after reading all of the paragraphs, the participants were given a memory test (either immediate or delayed) for the main ideas.

Bridge et al. (1984) hypothesized that comprehension of paragraphs without the topic sentences might be poorer than those with topic sentences; however, they also argued that the absence of a topic sentence could result in deeper processing of the text, and so not negatively affect comprehension, though weaker readers might benefit from the presence of the topic sentence. Regarding later recall, they noted two possible results: better recall for those passages with a topic sentence (because of its assumed facilitating effect) or better recall for non-topic sentence paragraphs because of the deeper processing involved to comprehend them.

Bridge et al. (1984) found that in the timed condition the good readers created significantly better summary titles than the weaker readers, but that recognition of the main idea was similar for both groups. For both immediate and delayed recognition of the main ideas, topicalized paragraphs (i.e. those with an explicitly topic sentence) facilitated more accurate recognition. For both groups the titles produced for passages with a topic sentence were significantly better than those created for the paragraphs without topic sentences.

In their second (non-timed) experiment, the participants engaged in one of three post-reading tasks. It was found that there was no effect of text type for comprehensibility or recall of the main ideas, though it was found that having to produce a main idea at the end of the task did facilitate better later memory of the main idea of the paragraphs. Bridge et al. maintained that the requirement to provide a main idea sentence at the time of reading might have helped readers to comprehend paragraphs which did not have topic sentences – indeed that the absence of a topic sentence in a reading actually stimulated more active or deeper mental processing for some readers, hence facilitating better performance in a memory task. Accordingly, they proposed that the deeper processing resulted in better recall of the content of what was read.

Statement 3: Proper Indentation Affects Readers' Processing of Text; Manipulated Indentation Does Not

Original indentation affect readers' decisions about what sentences are important in text, but misparagraphed indentation does not.

Stark (1988) investigated how three different textual conditions (original paragraphing, misparagraphed text, and non-paragraphed text) affected reading rate and the ease of reading of three texts written by Orwell, Russell, and Didion. She found that altering the paragraphing of the original text did not affect reading speed but did affect which sentences were identified by the participants as being of particular importance in the text. Stark found that paragraph-initial sentences were marked as important in 46% of instances in the original versions of the texts, but that these same sentences were marked as important only 27% of the time in the unparagraphed versions (a statistically significant difference). At the same time, Stark found that simply reparagraphing, by changing which sentence was in paragraph-initial position, did not automatically elevate the importance of that sentence – with only 21% of such sentences being signaled as important by the participants. Stark (1988: 299) interpreted her findings as follows:

> If the paragraph break occurs at an arbitrary place in the text, then the break doesn't make the initial sentence more important…. [T]he effect of a paragraph cue is an interaction between the cue and the content of what is being cued…. [P]lausible paragraph marking has an effect on importance, and bad paragraphing does not.

The results of this study suggest reader discernment of sentence importance, a finding at odds with other research (including some referred to earlier in this chapter – e.g. by Gernsbacher) which has emphasized the powerful role of the first sentence of a paragraph in affecting students' identification of the main idea of a text. How can these differences be explained? A possible reason may be the research participants. Danhua Wang found that over a fifth of her sample of university students incorrectly identified the main idea of a paragraph as the first sentence of paragraphs given to them (Wang, 2009). Wang suggested that such a response was due to inflexible and ingrained ideas about the location of the main idea in text. Accordingly, it would seem plausible to suggest that readers' educational backgrounds and possible training effects may be responsible for some of the different findings.

Statement 4: The Effect of Paragraph Structure Interacts with Background Knowledge

> *The influence of paragraph structure (including paragraph-initial topic sentences) interacts with readers' background knowledge, such that structure may be more or less helpful for comprehension, memory, or learning.*

A number of researchers have been interested in considering the effects of manipulating micro- and macro-level cohesion within text and considering the effects of this in relation to readers' background knowledge; notable among these are Baumann (1986); Cathy Roller (Roller, 1990); Susan Goldman, Elizabeth Saul, and Nathalie Coté (Goldman et al. 1995); McNamara and colleagues Eileen Kintsch, Nancy Songer, and Walter Kintsch (McNamara et al., 1996); and Alexandra Gasparinatou and Maria Grigoriadou (Gasparinatou and Grigoriadou, 2013).

In a commentary article, Roller (1990) sought to make sense of various conflicting research findings in relation to the role of reader background knowledge and text structure (her understanding of this being topic sentences and DMs, i.e. textual material which helps indicate the cohesion of the text) on comprehension. After reviewing research investigating various manipulations of text (specifically, rearranging the order of information, omitting structural support material, and changing the superordinate to subordinate ordering), and the relationship with readers' background, Roller (1990: 84) observed that some research has suggested that the two variables of text structure and reader background knowledge, or world knowledge, impact each other such that "the text structure variables function differently at different levels of world knowledge." Roller sought to reconcile differences between research findings indicating that superordinate information is processed quickly (in some research) or slowly (in other research) by appealing to the role of background knowledge: if a reader has some background knowledge of the subject matter, then s/he can go over text-structuring material quickly due its redundancy, but when a reader has only partial or limited knowledge, such textual support can be helpful. Further, when the text is very difficult for the reader to understand, structural support, such as the presence of a topic sentence, does not help, as the concepts are not understood; clear structure cannot compensate for significant semantic challenges.

Gasparinatou and Grigoriadou (2013) manipulated a text to maximize its local cohesion by replacing pronouns with nouns when the referent was possibly ambiguous, and also by providing elaboration and inserting sentence connectives. They found that high-knowledge students performed better in some post-reading tasks after they had read the non-manipulated, low-coherence texts than when they had read the "cohesively improved" texts, whereas low-knowledge readers performed better when they read the manipulated texts. The researchers explained their findings as due, on the one hand, to the positive effects of the more active processing which the more knowledgeable readers were able to apply to the less explicit text and, on the other hand, to the facilitating effect of the cohesion cues for the less knowledgeable readers.

Of more relevance to our focus on the facilitating function of macro-textual rather than micro-textual text-structuring elements is McNamara et al.'s (1996) provocatively entitled article: "Are good texts always better? Interactions of text coherence, background knowledge, and levels of understanding in learning from text." McNamara et al. considered the effects of manipulating not only local, micro-level cohesive textual elements but also global, macro-textual elements, through the provision of macrosignals which explicitly indicated the macrostructure of the text (e.g. paragraph initial statements indicating the place of the paragraph and its subject matter within the overall text). McNamara et al. hypothesized that recall would be easier for all readers when the text is more coherent both locally and globally but that when the post-reading tasks involved the testing of deeper understanding of the text (i.e. sorting tasks, inferencing questions, and problem-solving questions), successful completion of such tasks would be better when readers with strong background knowledge read the cohesion-weak texts. In such cases, they believed readers would apply deeper active processing to the texts, integrating textual material into their long-term memory, since they would need to provide more of the coherence themselves. McNamara et al. found better recall by participating readers who read the global cohesion enhanced versions, but those with stronger background knowledge actually performed better on questions involving deeper under-standing when the text did not provide micro- and macro-cohesive support than when it did. What is interesting about this study is the suggestion that structural clarity may be positive, neutral, or even have negative effects on certain aspects of readers' textual processing, depending on both readers' background knowledge and the type of task they are asked to perform after their reading.

Baumann (1986) termed school textbook passages which did not signal main ideas explicitly "inconsiderate" passages, and he investigated the effects on readers of modifying these passages by placing clear main idea sentences in paragraph-initial position. After reading the "inconsiderate" and modified ("considerate") versions, his research participants, school students, were required to perform several tasks. The students were also required to compare their reading experiences of the two texts, indicating: which passage they liked better and why; which was easier to read and why; and for which passage identification of the main idea was easier. Baumann found mixed results for a task requiring the writing down of the main idea for a whole passage of text (one group performed better on the modified version, one did not), significant improvement in writing the main idea of each paragraph in the text for both groups on the modified version, and no difference in performance on main idea identification for either group. Baumann suggested a number of possible explanations for the difference in findings between recall and recognition tasks, namely, the format of the question may have helped, or may have tapped a different, more tacit, kind of knowledge (rather than more conscious knowledge required to actually write). Concerning their experiences, interestingly, the students did not seem to be influenced by the original or modified versions in their judgments of ease of reading and preference.

Baumann suggested that textbook writers reconsider their writing styles in terms of how they might make their texts more accessible to readers on the basis of some of his data. The idea that texts be adapted with different readers in mind was also suggested by McNamara et al. (1996). Although Baumann's (1986) conclusions concerning the value of an increased amount of signaling of textual structure are superficially logical, if textbook writers were to adapt their practices to follow Baumann's recommendations, it is possible they might actually disadvantage their readers from developing deeper text processing skills that would enable them to deal with real-world writing, much of which would presumably be termed "inconsiderate" writing by Baumann.

A study of relevance here is that of Peter Johnston and Peter Afflerbach, who used a think-aloud procedure (see Chapter 8 on some possible problems with this research method) to try to discover how readers who were given a text with no clear topic sentence and who were unfamiliar with the subject matter arrived at a main idea (Johnston and Afflerbach, 1985: 220). The research participants – termed "expert readers" (p. 210) – were required to generate a summary sentence for each paragraph read, in addition to a summary sentence for the complete text segment. The researchers found that in the absence of a topic sentence the readers were creative in trying to provide one, and used a variety of strategies to create a main idea for each of the paragraphs. They differentiated four approaches: hypothesis testing (i.e. proposing a possible main idea, and then verifying or rejecting it), drafting and revising (a more responsive approach involved in determining the topic, and then commenting on it), a goodness of fit approach (very similar to drafting and revising, but involving more risk-taking) and listing (i.e. identifying key words and trying to build up the topic from them). If text is always considerate, we might suppose these strategies to remain under- or undeveloped, a state of affairs probably detrimental to the long-term benefit of readers.

Goldman et al. (1995) investigated the ability of readers (university students) to summarize the main ideas of two differently paragraphed texts. The two text conditions were original paragraphing and changed paragraphing. For the original paragraphing, the indentation coincided with the main points of the text (i.e. topic sentences). In the changed paragraphing condition, indentation was placed at a sentence which was not so central to the main ideas of the text. The participants had to summarize from memory the main points of the text, and were told in advance that this would be required of them after reading the texts. In addition, the participants were required to indicate their familiarity or unfamiliarity with the subject matter of the texts. It was found that the "conflicting" paragraphing condition did not have a significant (negative) effect on those readers' summarizing abilities who were familiar with the subject matter, but it did have such an effect when the subject matter was less familiar to other readers. Thus, it would seem that "coincident" paragraphing (i.e. main idea statement being present in paragraph-initial position) is of particular help to readers unfamiliar with the subject matter of a text, but not those who have a better background of the textual material. Goldman et al. (1995: 297) therefore concluded:

> The results…challenge the algorithmic hypothesis that being the first sentence of a paragraph automatically gives a sentence an advantage, with readers believing it is the main idea. Rather, readers treated paragraph-initial status heuristically and in interaction with the semantics of the text and their own prior knowledge to determine the main ideas for these passages.

Goldman et al. (1995: 300) interpreted their results, in conjunction with those from previous research (Goldman and Saul 1990), as demonstrating that semantic cues are more powerful than structural clues in helping readers identify the main ideas of text, part of the reason for this advantage being the multiplicity of semantic cues present in text.

In summary, the four statements provided above indicate the value of structural support for comprehension, but some also challenge the value of such support in certain contexts, largely dependent on the reader and the task to be performed. What is clear is that the research findings challenge overly-simplistic notions concerning how paragraphs should be structured, and how they are read by readers.

Readers' Ability to Paragraph a De-segmented Text Like the Original Text

The Textual Segmentation Studies

Segmenting a de-segmented text, or portion of a complete text, according to what one believes to have been the original paragraphing of the text is clearly not a normal reading activity; and attempts to document and understand the mental processes involved in text segmentation through tools such as think-aloud protocols, while commendable, should be interpreted with great care.[5] Care should also be taken in drawing conclusions about the linguistic status of the paragraph on the basis of the results of such studies. It is not entirely clear what segmentation abilities / non-abilities indicate, although some attempts have been made to explain the data, as I document below. Of the various studies discussed in this section, only one had an overt interest in paragraph psychology (Hoey, 2005), the majority of the others being more interested in what reader segmentation indicated about the nature of the paragraph, rather than what it showed about readers. However, for the sake of completeness I mention the key segmentation studies here, as they all have a bearing on reader psychology.

The first of the segmentation studies was published in 1966, and two of the important later studies examined the segmentation of the same text extract. When what amounts to half (i.e. 3) of the (significant) studies have examined the segmentation of just one piece of text, there are clearly issues surrounding the generalizability of the findings. Rather than provide a chronological summary of the important studies, I group together those which have been motivated by similar objectives, to the extent this is possible. I suggest that there have been three distinct hypotheses underpinning these studies: support for the idea that the paragraph is a formal unit; that reader segmentation skills are dependent on background; and that segmentation skills support Hoey's (2005) lexical priming theory. I consider each, in turn, below.

Hypothesis 1: Segmentation studies indicate that the paragraph is a formal unit, not a semantic unit.

Advocates of a semantic unit understanding of the paragraph question that the paragraph is a formal unit, and argue that the paragraph does not have "an identifiable structure independent of meaning" (Bond and Hayes, 1984: 148). In such a view, the paragraph is not like a sentence (which does have such a structure), and if it is not, then the paragraph is best considered to be a semantic unit rather than a structural one (e.g. see Halliday and Hasan, 1976: 7). Those who view the paragraph as a formal grammatical unit (and foremost among this group, historically, were tagmemicists, notably, Pike), believe that, like the sentence, the paragraph has a discernible form: "beyond the sentence lie grammatical structures available to linguistic analysis, describable by technical procedures" (Pike, 1964: 129). Although the particular view expressed by Pike in this quotation may not be considered especially contentious, the belief that the orthographic paragraph constitutes one such unit definitely is. Indeed, as mentioned in Chapter 1, some tagmemicists (e.g. Longacre) specifically limited their paragraph theorizing to the structural, rather than the orthographic paragraph, due to concerns about the idea that the formal unit actually mapped onto the typographical one.

Richard Young and Becker (Young and Becker, 1966), Frank Koen working with Young and Becker (Koen et al., 1969), and later Bond and Hayes (1984) all sought to investigate whether data from segmentation studies could provide support for a formal theory of the orthographic paragraph, a view which they all espoused. The way they went about this, methodologically, was to have some participants segment an unmodified (though de-paragraphed text), and others segment a nonsense version of the same de-paragraphed text. The original text used in two of the above studies begins:

> *Grant was, judged by modern standards, the greatest general of the Civil War. He was head and shoulders above any general....*

The nonsense version ran thus:

> *Blog was, moked by grol nards, the wilest nerg of the Liver Molk. He was dreed and bams above any nerg...*

It should be noted that in the nonsense text, the original sentence structure, punctuation, and function words are retained as are grammaticality markers (e.g. *moked* – signifying past tense), whereas nonsense words are substituted for all content words and the same nonsense word (e.g. *nerg*) is repeated according to its sense-version equivalent. The underlying rationale of such research is that if segmentation decisions are similar in the two conditions (original and nonsense versions), then semantic clues (present in the original text but not in the nonsense text), can be discounted from playing a role in paragraph identification abilities, hence lending support to the formal view of the paragraph – or so the researchers argued.

Young and Becker (1966: 1) provided the text extract to 12 participants (freshman students[6]), six of whom received the original extract (de-paragraphed), the other six receiving the de-paragraphed nonsense version. They found that the nonsense text segmentation decisions were very similar to the original text responses. The orthographic paragraph breaks were (successfully) identified by the majority of the participants, though most of those (5 / 6) who segmented the original text also (wrongly) believed that there was a paragraph break at a sentence beginning *In war*.... Young and Becker did not remark on this decision, but I comment on it later in this section. With regard to the human segmenters' stated reasons for their decisions, Young and Becker documented topic change as being the prevalent reason given, followed by move to a new rhetorical pattern (e.g. comparison) and then the presence of certain words (e.g. *fundamentally,* or its nonsense equivalent *dantially*). In interpreting their data, they suggested that lexical cues were of limited value in aiding text segmentation: "helpful but not essential" (p. 5), and they argued that the relationship between grammatical (e.g. subject) and situational roles (e.g. agent), together with grammatical parallelism were the important elements affecting segmentation decisions. Based on their results, they believed that "paragraphs are not arbitrary units" (p. 5).

Stark (1988: 281) argued that reference and co-reference (even of nonsense words) can be considered to be "a semantic notion," and that when dealing with nonsense texts, readers may well make use of such semantic clues in their segmentation decisions. Some later research (specifically, Bond and Hayes, 1984) recognized this, and adapted methodological approaches accordingly.

Koen et al. (1969) pursued a very similar methodological approach to that of Young and Becker (1966) though with a larger range of texts, and with a larger variety and number of participants. Their participants were elementary, junior high, and high school students. The research participants were required to segment 11 texts of various types (including exposition, description and narration), for both original and nonsense versions (though a particular participant was not required to segment an original and nonsense version of the same text). The number of students reading any particular text ranged from 9–32. In contrast to the Young and Becker (1966) study, Koen et al. provided correlational data for the agreement between the participants when segmenting each text by providing a Kuder-Richardson Formula 20 (K-R 20) score for each text version. They also, occasionally, gave some indication of the paragraph segmentation accuracy, although no reasons were given by the authors for their focus on inter-rater agreement, or why the original orthographic paragraphs did not function as a benchmark against which the segmentation decisions were measured, a subject which I discuss later in this section. Koen et al. recorded high inter-judge consistency for the students' segmentations of the original versions of the texts, K-R 20 scores ranging from 0.75 to 0.98. Scores for the nonsense texts were somewhat lower, ranging from 0.53 to 0.92. However, they believed consistency within the nonsense version decisions supported the idea that "the paragraph is a psychologically real unit" (p. 51). Pearson product-moment correlations between conditions 1 and 2 for the same text ranged from 0.42 to 0.95, with a median correlation of 0.71. With the exception of one of the texts, the degree of agreement among the subjects was higher for the original texts, compared with the nonsense versions. Unlike the earlier study by Young and Becker (1966), Koen et al. (1969) did not find segmentation in the nonsense texts to be comparable to that of the original text versions, admitting that for a number of the texts, the only way to explain the difference in agreement between the two conditions were the "semantic cues" (p. 51) provided in condition 1, not present in condition 2. However, when K-R 20 scores were very similar between original and nonsense conditions (as was the case for three of the 11 texts) they believed such similarity to be supportive of the argument that the most important cues in aiding segmenters were the formal ones (p. 52).

Bond and Hayes (1984) were sympathetic to the work of Young and Becker (1966) and Koen et al. (1969), and considered their own research as building on these earlier studies. Their specific goal was to further explore the role of semantic and formal cues in affecting segmentation of text, and to identify which was of greater importance to participants required to segmented de-paragraphed text. They used the same text as was used in the Young and Becker (1966) study but recruited a much larger number (118) of university students. Semantic cues were considered to be meaning related, and formal cues were considered to be the physical properties of the word (e.g. its form, position, and whether it was repeated or not), the use of a pronoun or full noun, and the length of the paragraph within the text. The researchers replicated the first two conditions used in the previously mentioned studies (i.e. normal and nonsense versions, conditions 1 and 2), while adding three more conditions. The reason given for these additional conditions was that like Koen et al. (see also the Stark, 1988: 281 reference above), Bond and Hayes recognized that nonsense words could still be providing clues related to meaning (through repetition and the presence of lexical equivalence chains); hence they augmented the methodologies of the previous two studies by introducing three new conditions:

> Condition 3: content words replaced with XXs
> Condition 4: content words and pronouns replaced with XXs
> Condition 5: X marks beginning of sentence, squiggly lines the sentence (same length retained)

In essence, Bond and Hayes were attempting to remove, incrementally, every clue which might be considered to be providing semantic support and which might be helping the participants successfully guess where the segmentations occurred. For conditions 1 and 2, Bond and Hayes (1984) stated that their findings were "very similar to" (p. 151) and "strongly paralleled" (p. 152) the Young and Becker (1966) data, though they did not provide a similarity statistic. They noted a Pearson product-moment correlation of $p = 0.83$ between conditions 1 and 2 in their data.

Bond and Hayes (1984) found increased variation among participants in their segmentation decisions for condition 3, suggesting that this was because the nonsense words in condition 2 actually gave the participants clues to segmentation (e.g. through repetition). The correlation between this condition and condition 1 was $r = 0.48$. For condition 4, rater consistency was similar to condition 3, but the correlation between this condition and condition 1 was only r = 0.17. They interpreted the lower correlation to have been due to the important role of pronouns in helping participants decide where to indent the text in condition 3. Despite the lower correlation, they believed that condition 4 still gave (formal) clues to the participants, as inter-rater agreement was significantly higher in this condition than in random text trial runs. Condition 5 (where no words were retained) resulted in a great degree of variation in segmentation decisions among the participants, and a correlation of r = 0.23 to condition 1 results. Bond and Hayes (1984: 156, 157) suggested that spatial (locational) factors and the number of sentences were still important aids to paragraphing, and that the segmentation decisions even in condition 5 were more consistent than could be expected by chance. They believed content repetition, the use of pronouns and spatial considerations to be the main cues used by participants in their segmentation decisions (p. 157).

In their second study, Bond and Hayes (1984) used think-aloud protocols from four university teachers who segmented the original text (i.e. in condition 1) to try to found out what was influencing their decisions. Two strategies were noted. The first was the response to the occurrence of clear topic change (sentence-initial, with a lexical equivalence chain break or break in subject continuity). The second was when the amount of text was getting longer, and the text was re-read to look for "secondary cues" to indentation (e.g. the presence of a sentence initial adverb). Bond and Hayes (1984: 166) concluded their paper by stating that formal cues (according to their understanding of this term as including the length of a word, its position in text, its grammatical form, and its repetition / non repetition) were more important than semantic cues in affecting segmentation decisions. However, they did not go so far as to claim a formal status for the paragraph, recognizing the role of semantic cues in aiding the segmentation decisions of the human judges.

I suggest that the three studies discussed above arrived at their conclusions of the paragraph's psychological reality rather too easily. While there is no doubt that formal cues may be important in influencing segmentation decisions (see Hoey discussion below), this does not mean that orthographic paragraphs are formal units for the following reasons.

First, as pointed out by Stark (1988) and mentioned earlier, the nonsense condition texts in the studies reported above may well have been providing semantic cues, and it seems that this possibility was not given enough attention by the researchers. In reviewing the Bond and Hayes (1984) study, Stark (1988) re-considered the actual correlations provided for conditions 4 and 5 and noted that neither was significant. Accordingly, she argued that claims concerning the importance of formal cues (compared with the semantic cues) were at variance with the data, the last two conditions from this experiment being the only distinctively "formal" conditions tested, if one classifies co-repetition as being semantic, as mentioned earlier. As discussed in the second section of this chapter, there is good reason to believe that semantic relations in a text have a significant impact on readers' reading processes and their notions about main and secondary points (see especially Goldman et al., 1995). Further, according to the discussion in Chapter 6, it is reasonable to state that there is often a semantic, topical unity surrounding the paragraph's entity, on the basis of computational research data.

An additional issue is the generalization of findings on the basis of one key text used in the first and third study reported above. Hoey (2005) found considerable variation in the segmentation responses of students to the same text used by Young and Becker (1966) and Bond and Hayes (1984), and he commented that this finding did not sit comfortably alongside earlier interpretations of the data: "the lack of unanimity casts doubt upon claims for the structural status of the paragraph" (Hoey, 2005: 138). Other researchers have been similarly skeptical about the formal status claim based on other human segmentation data from different texts. For example, Stern (1976: 257) expressed his reservations about the paragraph being "a logical unit" in observing that just five out of a hundred English teachers segmented a 500-word expository text as the original author had, and Stark (1988) observed that only one of 21 students correctly identified a particular paragraph break in a Bertrand Russell text. Ji (2008), in commenting on the different paragraphing decisions of research participants asked to read and segment deparagraphed versions of *Readers Digest* articles, stated that there was more agreement among the participants for paragraph breaks signaling discontinuities through significant shifts (temporal, locational, participant, or topical) than for those indicating "local thematic discontinuities" (p. 1727). Ji (2008: 1728) observed that readers were not so able to identify paragraph breaks signaled by these minor discontinuities in the *Readers Digest* stories: "Most of the subjects in the experiments simply do not regard the local thematic discontinuities marked by these paragraph divisions as a sufficient basis for an independent textual unit." It should be noted that in the Stern, Stark, and Ji studies mentioned here, all focused on participant agreement with the actual text type segmentation, rather than inter-rater agreement – a point I discuss further at the end of this section.

Concerning the relationship between segmentation agreement, non-agreement, and text type, Stark (1988) put forward three possible reasons for why readers' segmentation decisions may differ from the original orthographic paragraphing. The first possible reason is that a text can sometimes be legitimately paragraphed in different ways (see also the comments by Scott and Denney, 1895, on this issue, as mentioned in Chapter 3). The second is that the structure of a text may be ambiguous in some way. The third possibility is that a text may be "inherently unparagraphable" (p. 300) for the human segmenter, in the sense that it contains "…a multitude of networks rather than linear or hierarchical relations" (*ibid*). This last comment strikes at the very heart of the claim that the orthographic paragraph is "psychologically real," and a formal unit: some may be considered to be so, but certainly not all.

I would argue that segmentation tasks test reader sensitivity to textual continuity and discontinuity, patterns of textual development, and to awareness of discourse management tools commonly occurring at the paragraph break. If the paragraph break occurs *alone*, that is, if the writer decides to indent leaving no trace (semantic or formal) within the text indicative of or working alongside indentation, then readers will not be able to guess where the break occurred if it is removed. Indeed, the methodologies adopted by the second and third studies mentioned above, in which statistical analyses centered on inter-rater agreement, rather than agreement between the participants' indentation decisions and the indentation present in the actual text, indicates the drift away from interest in the orthographic paragraph, in this research.

It would seem reasonable to posit that there is a range of organizational redundancy present in texts: at one end of the spectrum there is a clear paragraph signal, perhaps the presence of one of the discontinuity tools mentioned in Chapter 5, together with significant topic switch. At the other end of the spectrum is the largely unpredictable paragraph break, which the author utilizes for particular effect and which the segmenter cannot hope to retrieve in a de-paragraphed version of the text. As Stark (1988: 299) stated, the importance of paragraph breaks lies (partially at least) in the fact that they cannot always be predicted. I suggest that this important observation has been largely overlooked by segmentation study researchers, whether computational, textual, or psychological. This unpredictability may be the bane of those who struggle to align orthographic units and functional or formal ones, but it is an essential part of the paragraph's multifunctionality.

One final issue to be discussed here is what one does with data that show high inter-rater segmentation agreement by participants in experimental studies that is not however in agreement with the original author's segmentation. Young and Becker (1966) chose not to elaborate on the fact that five out of six of their study participants incorrectly "identified" a paragraph break in the original text provided to them, and Koen et al. (1969) largely discounted the original authorial segmentation decisions in their analyses. The Young and Becker data are interesting, as are other internally consistent human segmentation decisions which do not agree with the actual orthographic paragraph, such as those in the research of Stark (1988) and also of Sara Garnes (Garnes, 1987), since they suggest that participants (as a group) in paragraphing studies do occasionally see something in the text representing a suprasentential textual unit or text segment, though not the original orthographic paragraph. One might argue that such identifications are perceptions of structural paragraphs or other textual units (blocs, stadia, etc.); however, it must be stressed that the researchers mentioned above made claims about the orthographic paragraph, not other suprasentential units in their work, and yet their analyses, at times, excluded reference to the very units which they were attempting to characterize.

Hypothesis 2: Segmentation abilities are related to age, experience, and text familiarity.

The main focus of Garnes' (1987) research was a comparison of the paragraph segmentation results of different sets of readers, an issue also touched upon by Koen et al. (1969), who found greater consistency in segmentation judgments among high school students as compared to junior high students, and among junior high school students as compared to elementary students. Garnes compared the paragraph segmentation decisions of 241 participants grouped into seven different categories. Each group contained at least 30 participants; the first four groups comprised undergraduates at an American university at different stages of their studies, and the latter three groups comprised post-graduate students, teachers, and university faculty. All of the participants were native speakers of English. The text Garnes used was a 50-sentence essay on death by Lewis Thomas containing three distinct sections and 11 paragraphs.

Garnes' (1987) data indicated increasing uniformity in the segmentation decision patterns as the level of education increased, with the undergraduate students showing less agreement with each other than the graduates. The most highly educated group (university faculty), whom we would expect to be the most discourse-sensitive, responded (in their segmentation decisions) in a more uniform way to the text than the teachers, new graduates, and undergraduates. This would seem to indicate that they were more aware of the norms of paragraphing present in such texts, when compared to the other groups (although at times they agreed consistently with each other, but not with the actual text segmentation). Garnes found that clear topic shift within the texts was identified by the majority of participants at all educational levels (i.e. there seemed to be broad universal organizational sensitivity; see also Ji, 2008, referred to above) but that more subtle paragraph choices were not so well identified by the participants.

Josep Guzman and Eva Alcón investigated the paragraph segmentation decisions of three groups of non-native speakers of English (for whom the first language was Spanish or Catalan), studying different subjects at university (Guzman and Alcón, 1997). The data indicated substantial variety in the segmentation decisions. This finding does not appear to be particularly surprising, if we consider segmentation abilities to be related to sensitivities to text norms. As the authors commented, "L2 learners may not feel as confident as native speakers and consider any signal they can recognize as a paragraph boundary" (p. 19). The fact that Abbass Rasekh and Bahareh Toluei found no significant difference in the paragraph identification decisions of two groups of non-native speakers of English (31 intermediate-level and 30 advanced-level) on three texts (Rasekh and Toluei, 2009: 32) underscores the same point.

It is unfortunate that the Garnes' (1987) study has not received more attention. I suggest that the most valuable element to take from it is the need to remember that readers are not a homogeneous group, and to differentiate research participants according to their familiarization with a particular text type when conducting segmentation tasks. I make further reference to this study in the next section in relation to reader-specific priming.

Hypothesis 3: Segmentation abilities support an aspect of lexical priming theory.

Hoey's (2005) work on paragraphing and his co-authored work with O'Donnell (Hoey and O'Donnell, 2007, 2008a, 2008b) has, I believe, made a significant contribution to our understanding of the paragraph. I consider this work in some detail below.

Hoey's (2005) lexical priming theory encompassed three claims, the third of which is relevant to the discussion in this chapter:

> Claim 3: Every lexical item (or combination of lexical items) is capable of being primed (positively or negatively) to occur at the beginning or end of an independently recognized "chunk" of text (p. 129).

Hoey termed this phenomenon "textual colligation." Hoey adopted a two-pronged approach to establishing the above claim: through an examination of corpus linguistic data (some of which was referred to in Chapters 5 and 6) and by appealing to the results of paragraph segmentation studies (in the light of corpus data). It is this latter area of research which is of interest to us in this section.

Hoey (2005) asked 67 first-year university students to segment the same text as used in the Young and Becker (1966) and Bond and Hayes (1984) studies. Although his results were similar to those from the previous studies, they were not uniform, as mentioned earlier. Hoey was not particularly interested in the formal or semantic identity debate surrounding paragraphs; like Stark (1988), he was far more interested in the text and how the students responded to it. Specifically, Hoey focused on the organizational features of the paragraph and the paragraph-initial lexical characteristics, and how data from his segmentation experiment could be explained by his lexical priming and textual colligation theory. After recording the segmentation responses to the text, he referred to corpus data information (from *Guardian* newspapers 1991–1994) on word or phrase position of certain items within the investigated text to try to understand the variation in segmentation decisions, whether these were in agreement or not with the original paragraphing. Hoey (2005) made a number of text-based observations in this study, which are summarized in the paragraphs that follow.

Sentence-initial surnames were 50% of the time paragraph-initial in his corpus. He suggested that this explained both agreement with the original text (i.e. segmentation success) and disagreement with it (i.e. putting in a paragraph break where one did not occur in the original text, due to the presence of a name).

Concerning pronouns, he found that the pronoun *he* was negatively primed to occur in paragraph-initial position (i.e. that it was very unlikely to occur in this position in his corpus).[7] He also found that anticipatory *it* was weakly positively primed to occur in paragraph-initial position (occurring in 24 out of 65 instances) and as such could explain several paragraph segmentation decisions by raters.

In relation to frames, he observed that of the 17 instances of *As a [job] / [work role]* (e.g. *As a politician*) in his corpus, eight of them were paragraph-initial, and half of his judges placed a break at such a frame in the text (a sentence beginning *As a theatre strategist*), where there was no break in the original text. Similarly, the prepositional phrase *in war* was found to be primed to begin a sentence or paragraph, and a number of subjects believed it to be paragraph-initial in the segmentation task (wrongly in this particular instance, as it was not paragraph-initial, note also the reference to this phrase in the Young and Becker, 1966, study referred to earlier). Half of the instances of *Had [surname] been* in Hoey's (2005) corpus were paragraph-initial and typically occurred in a short paragraph. Hoey suggested that this fact could explain why some raters incorrectly inserted a paragraph break when this phrase occurred in the text given to his research participants.

With regard to individual lexical items, Hoey (2005) noted that *fundamentally* occurred in paragraph-initial position 50 times more frequently than expected in random distribution in his corpus, and that *illustrate* was 1½ times more likely to be in the first sentence of a paragraph than in a later sentence. Again, Hoey suggested that these frequency data could explain some of the incorrect paragraph segmentation decisions in his investigation: his participants were sensitive to the placement of certain lexical items or frames in text, and were acting on this sensitivity in making their decisions (whether these were in accord with the original segmentation or not).

Hoey suggested that there were principled organizational and / or textual colligational priming reasons which could explain the segmentation (or non-segmentation) decisions within the investigated text. Hoey found that on all five occasions when organizational considerations and colligational priming factors co-occurred and pointed to the need to segment, participants did indeed segment the text at that point (though the percentage actually segmenting ranged from 20% to 94%, the former figure being one which Hoey rather downplayed). He suggested that at times organizational reasons and colligational priming reasons tug at one another, hence the variety and non-uniformity of the decisions. Although Stark (1988) hinted at such tensions, I believe that this was the first attempt to systematically explain variant segmentation decisions. Further, by manipulating colligational priming data, Hoey (2005) was able to fairly accurately predict how an altered de-paragraphed text would be segmented by his student participants. For example, by adapting the text to make organizational and colligational grounds both positive at a certain point within the text, Hoey was able to quite successfully predict increased segmentation decisions at that point in the text, and likewise, by making both negative, he could predict a reduction in the number of segmentations at a particular point within the text. Specifically, changing one of the pronouns to a proper name resulted in more than double the number of paragraph breaks being inserted by a group of student research participants, as compared to the number of paragraph breaks which a different group of students inserted at the same point in the text when it contained a pronoun. Removing a surname and replacing it with a pronoun also had the opposite, yet predicted, effect of reducing the number of breaks.

Reader psychology in Hoey's (2005) lexical priming theory is in no way secondary to his ideas, as lexical priming and textual colligation priming are in essence psychological phenomena: it is not so much that words are primed to occur in certain positions (though Hoey did say this), but rather that readers are primed to see certain words in certain positions. Writers, being readers themselves and following certain discourse community norms, are, similarly, primed to put them there. Human segmenters will, therefore, act on their primings in segmentation testing, that is, they will respond to the presence (or absence) of what Hoey termed "paragraph triggers" (p.138) in deciding where to insert breaks.

Unlike some of the more questionable generalized claims made by the researchers under Hypothesis 1 (above) within this section, Hoey (2005: 131) was more cautious about his findings, calling the evidence he provided "suggestive rather than conclusive." Nonetheless, a further study (Hoey and O'Donnell, 2007) investigating textual colligation in a *Guardian* news article with corpus data and human raters confirmed the hypotheses of the earlier work. Changing pronouns to nouns and re-ordering word or phrase position in sentences or paragraphs did indeed affect the segmentation decisions of the human raters. Hoey and O'Donnell (2007) went on to argue that such results challenge the idea that paragraphs are topical, content-based units: if small changes to a text can affect segmentation decisions, then paragraphing cannot be explained by reference to content shifts per se. They went on to suggest that paragraphing is better understood as a process, and its function is similar to other textual emphasizing techniques, including underlining and using bold font.

I suggest that Hoey's work, with its connections to the material considered in Chapters 5 and 6 and its basis in reader psychology, should be considered a significant milestone in attempts to understand and explain human paragraph segmentation abilities. While in broad agreement with Hoey's views, I suggest that further thought may be needed when considering three aspects of the theory: readers' primings, the orthographic paragraph unit as the base suprasentential unit against which to understand textual colligation, and the nature of the paragraph triggers in the theory. I elaborate on each of these issues in turn below.

Concerning primings, Hoey and O'Donnell (2008a) assumed that the readers of their article would detect paragraph amendment of a *Guardian* news article. However, logically, one can only make this assumption if the readers of the article were *Guardian* readers. If people's lexical primings are genre-specific, then one should test people who have been *appropriately* primed and who can detect similarities to and deviations from the norm. One of the problems in comparing language intuitions with corpus data is to ensure that the (textual colligation) intuitions have been formed by the right kind of data and can therefore be compared (legitimately) with a sample from this pool; otherwise, the researcher will be comparing apples with oranges. As the discussion in Chapter 5 indicated, it is clear that in different text types different discourse organizing elements co-occur with the paragraph break: generalizations in this area are as unjustified as are comments about language use in general.

The kind of testing which would give more convincing support to Hoey's theory would be a more controlled test: if the text is from the *Guardian*, then the participants should be *Guardian* readers. Even here, however, is it not possible that other primings will interfere in the decisions that readers make? I am not aware of any instance in which Hoey and O'Donnell suggested that errant segmentation is due to cross-genre priming conflict,[8] but a particular example from their 2008a article can be used to illustrate this point. Hoey and O'Donnell (2008a) argued that *Yesterday it was announced that* is an untypical paragraph opener in a *Guardian* article. However, some news items do begin with this clause,[9] and it is quite possible that readers of the article may have been familiar with such instances and that exposure to these would have affected their views about whether a *Guardian* news article (rather than another text type) beginning with this clause was typical or not. Just as it is unreasonable to expect an individual to be familiar with multiple subgenre text types[10] and to be sensitive to textual colligation differences within these, so too is it unreasonable to expect the same individual to be able to seal off exposure to non-relevant or misleading textual colligation experiences in a particular segmentation experiment. Hoey and O'Donnell (2008b: 191) acknowledged that lexical priming is "a personal matter" and that our primings are all different because of our different language experiences. However, they nowhere proved, but only assumed that "there is a considerable overlap in the resultant primings…" (*ibid.*).

If lexical priming were as clear-cut as Hoey and O'Donnell suggest in the above quote, one still has to address the problem of significant variation in human segmentation decisions. As described above, Hoey's (2005) way of dealing with these differences was to appeal to places within the text where organizational and textual colligation clues tugged at one another, thereby confusing readers. Another way to explain variation is to appeal to the results of the Garnes' (1987) study mentioned earlier, which indicated that certain readers may be more or less aware of the paragraphing conventions in a particular text type. In addition, it should be remembered that readers vary in their reading styles (as referred to earlier in this chapter). Hoey (2005) and Hoey and O'Donnell (2007, 2008a) collected data from research participants with mixed reading styles and different knowledge backgrounds. I suggest that the uncontrolled variables present in such research muddy the waters. More controlled tests may provide further support for the lexical priming theory, and if they do not, they may help in tweaking it.

Another key issue which might be further considered in the lexical priming theory is the choice of the orthographic paragraph as the base suprasentential unit against which textual colligation phenomena are observed. As mentioned throughout the preceding chapters, there is good reason to believe that there are other kinds of suprasentential units (grammatical or functional) other than the paragraph unit present within text. These units have been variously termed and variously understood. Some of those mentioned in previous chapters include: structural paragraphs, tagmemes, moves, episodes, discourse blocs, and stadia of discourse. In focusing on the orthographic paragraph, Hoey (2005: 129) has considered the most obvious "independently recognized 'chunk' of text" that is larger than the sentence, and sought to understand textual colligation by reference to it. However, as some of the data from reader segmentation studies have indicated, there do seem to be suprasentential chunks that do not correspond with or map to the orthographic paragraphs existing within text, but whose independent existence is recognized by readers. One can argue that support for the existence of such suprasentential chunks comes from some of the research noted earlier in this section, such as that of Young and Becker (1966), in which the majority of research participants incorrectly inserted a segmentation break in a de-paragraphed text at a location where none existed in the original text. While this could be interpreted as being a false response to a trigger (i.e. the phrase or word is often paragraph-initial, and readers respond to it as a paragraph trigger), one can also explain it with regard to the discussion in Chapters 1 and 4, that is, due to structural units present within text, not aligned to the orthographic paragraph. Lexical priming theory might benefit from further thought about the existence of other units within text (e.g. moves in genre theory, blocs, etc.), and how reader priming is related to them. Hoey's "paragraph triggers" may actually be better understood as discourse bloc (or some other suprasentential entity) triggers, rather than signaling the beginning of paragraphs, per se.

Finally, I suggest that a consideration of the strength of the different triggers in Hoey's lexical priming theory would be of value. Hoey did not grade his triggers (cf. Goutsos' 1997 strength of discourse signaling argument in Chapter 5), but it would seem reasonable to argue, following on from the data provided in Chapter 5, that certain types of trigger (e.g. adverbials and questions) may be more or less powerful, may typically work (or not work) together with other triggers, and may vary in their shift- or continuity-indicating strength in different text types. Research into these areas could, I suggest, help further refine the lexical priming theory.

Hoey's (2005) and Hoey and O'Donnell's (2007; 2008a,b) work on reader segmentation of text should be considered a significant contribution to paragraph studies and to our understanding of an aspect of reader psychology. At the same time, it should be acknowledged that there is still much that we do not yet understand about the relationship between paragraphing, other textual units, and textual colligation in reader segmentation decisions. In what follows, I suggest that part of the reason for this is that the experience of the paragraph for the reader is more complicated than often considered, and needs to be viewed as a mediated phenomenon.

Commentary on the Paragraph and the Reader

In Chapters 5 and 6, the paragraph and paragraphing were examined from two different textual perspectives. It was suggested that paragraphs can be better understood when they are considered in relation to their co-occurrence with other discourse-managing tools (Chapter 5) and in terms of their textual cohesion (governed by writer-specific goals, as discussed in Chapter 6).

In this chapter, we have seen, inter alia, that human segmentation of de-paragraphed text can, at times, be explained by appealing to the presence of content shifts, and formal aspects of the text, including the presence of paragraph-initial formulaic expressions. That is, we can explain and predict paragraph segmentation decisions in some or many instances on the basis of the textual features of paragraphs, both formal and semantic. It is thus evident that both humans (this chapter) and computers (Chapter 6) can, at times, identify where paragraph breaks occur in a text. In some ways, therefore, it seems that the paragraph break may, on occasion, be considered to be redundant – a kind of over-signaling that might not be strictly necessary for the reader. At the same time, the non-predictability of the paragraph break (on other occasions) must also be acknowledged.

Even if a paragraph break can be predicted when readers are given de-paragraphed text, the overview provided in the first two sections of this chapter strongly suggests that the actual instance of indentation or white space between lines of text in normal reading affects readers in certain ways. In this sense, the paragraph break is not redundant, even if it can be predicted: it affects readers, perhaps automatically, perhaps due to previous experience, or perhaps due to training effects. Biologically, cognitively, and psychologically, things seem to happen to the reader on encountering a paragraph break, and on reading the first and last sentences within the paragraph. However, what actually happens in the mind of a reader in any particular instance of encountering a paragraph break is complex and difficult to understand. SBF can probably account for some psychological processes in relation to how readers experience paragraphs, but not all instances: the significant role of incoming information in paragraph-initial position seems to be critical in affecting how readers read, and how the function of the paragraph break is interpreted.

As is clear from the overview provided in all three sections within this chapter, research into paragraph reader psychology can be contradictory. It therefore seems wise to avoid making simplified statements about what paragraphing actually does to or for readers. I suggest that a logical way of resolving many of the different research findings noted above is to insist on the reality of the mediated effect of the paragraph break on the reader, or its joint effect alongside other reader-specific factors. That is, the effect of the paragraph break and the organization of the paragraph on the reader is dependent on, or co-occurs with, one or more of six reader variables, each one of which may well interact with one or more additional variable. In light of the research reported above, I suggest that these variables are:

- The reading style of the reader;
- The background knowledge of the reader (in relation to the subject matter of the text);
- Reader rhetorical and formal textual awareness and expectations;

- The time given to the reader to read the text;
- The reason for reading (and task following the reading, if any); and
- Wider semantic considerations within the text (and whether the reader appreciates these or not).

If these variables mediate the effect of the paragraph break or organization, or if the reader's response to the break and organization occurs in conjunction with one or more of these factors, the effects of paragraphing will vary from one reader to the next – a key finding from a number of studies reported in this chapter. For example, a paragraph break highlighting a distinct element of the rhetorical structure of a text (perhaps together with the use of a topic sentence) might assist a particular reader in understanding what a paragraph (and the text) is about (i.e. it has a facilitating effect on comprehension). At the same time, it may not help another reader, indeed it may be of only marginal value, even a hindrance to deep learning as some of the research reported above makes clear.

It is often believed that paragraphing is primarily for the benefit of readers, that is, the writer considers the reader as the text is written (see comments on this in Chapter 3, especially the discussion concerning the work of Scott and Denney, 1895). In light of the research reviewed in this chapter, it seems that a writer cannot know with any certainty how his / her paragraphing decisions or organization will affect readers: there are too many unknown variables at work, whose effects the writer cannot hope to account for. In summarizing some of the challenges that a writer must overcome in successfully paragraphing for the reader, Heurley (1997: 184) questions whether "the average person" can adequately cope with such problems when writing. If these problems are so challenging, one might question whether writers really do paragraph for the sake of the reader, and in the next chapter I engage with Heurley (1997) and others who have suggested that paragraphing is primarily (though not exclusively) a writer-driven rather than a reader-driven phenomenon, and consider the various reasons advanced in support of this position.

In questioning the efficacy of the writer–reader relationship as I have above, I do not mean to say that writers ignore their readers in their paragraphing practice: it seems clear that many writers do consider their readers when indenting and organizing their texts, as will be discussed in Chapter 8. What I am suggesting is that there is no guarantee that writers' considerations of their readers' engagement with text will be correct, if, as I have argued above, the reader encounters the paragraph's organizational elements via or alongside one or more of the six above-listed variables. If the reader's experience of the paragraph break is mediated, or co-mediated, then writer considerations of their readers' mental state on encountering the paragraph break must, of necessity, be speculative. I suggest that a major oversight in the work of the scholars reviewed in Chapters 3 and 4 was the failure to consider this issue of the interaction between the reader and his / her mental state (knowledge, processing patterns, purpose in reading, etc.) and the paragraph break. Just as the paragraph break does not occur alone in terms of its discourse-organizing role (as reviewed in Chapter 5) so too the effect of the paragraph break cannot be stated in absolute terms – it depends on reader mental state and awareness. We have recognized for many years the fact of readers' interactivity with text; however, I believe we have, for too long, spoken in unjustifiably absolute terms about paragraph organization and its effects, or about why writers should paragraph in a particular way or ways, and how doing so will help the reader.

Pedagogical Issues

Structural simplification, or the provision of macrostructural assistance to a reader, through certain types of paragraphing, may be appreciated by certain readers, in specific contexts. However, as we have seen above, such support may only occur at the more superficial level (i.e. recall) and at times primarily be of assistance for only some (poor) readers.[11] We might argue, therefore, that there is a kind of irony surrounding some tightly prescriptivist approaches to paragraphing in certain educational settings, in which students write primarily for their teachers, who are (in effect) treated by their students as weak readers needing maximum textual structural support. The possibility that students might see through the possible absurdity of such pedagogies should also be considered: students might recognize that, in some contexts, as writing scholar Lil Brannon and colleagues maintained, they are "being groomed to be good little automatons" (Brannon et al., 2008: 19); a similar point is made by Jennifer Gray (Gray, 2014). As a consequence, these learner-writers may begin to resent pedagogy which revolves around highly predictable and possibly redundantly transparent textual organization. I suggest that some teachers may well groan at the impeccably structured paragraphs of their students, and yet mark this writing as good, and yet recognize it as poor because of the (taught) structural constraints within which the writer composes. If, on the other hand, students were being taught to write for school children, or for readers who have difficulty in managing text, this is an entirely different matter, and the emphasis on structural clarity would seem, in such cases, to be justified.

Some approaches to paragraphing which focus on the formal entity of the paragraph and insist on its tight organization may have an unfortunate, unforeseen side-effect in drawing student writers' attention away from working through the semantic dimensions and richness of their writing – the actual content and the message to be conveyed. As Goldman et al.'s (1995) research has made clear, it is the semantic aspects, rather than the organizational aspects of text, that are paramount in affecting reader comprehension: only in certain contexts is an emphasis on structural predictability and transparency justifiable, and students need to be encouraged to think about when such would indeed be the case and the relationship between writing task, textual organization and readership.

In discussing problems with the five-paragraph essay, as taught in certain contexts in U.S. high schools, Jeanette Miller (2010: 99) observed, "The five paragraph essay relieves students of responsibility to make decisions about form and organization." Some of the research reviewed above provides sound empirical reasons to bring decisions about form and organization back into the decision-making realm of the writer, as a template might not be appropriate for a particular writing task. As McNamara and Kintsch (1996: 249) stated, "Placing obstacles into the path of the reader prevents the reader from assuming a superficial mode of processing and forces a deeper level of processing," and this might be just what a writer wants to do on occasion.

In many educational settings today, we educators encourage learning which is more interactive, and more learner- or learning-centered. We recognize that the presentation of material may negatively or indeed positively affect its reception or consumption, whether that be a lecture, a series of PowerPoints, or a wiki activity. We appreciate the need to involve the learner. However, it seems that we rarely consider paragraphing conventions in terms of encouraging mental activity and reader engagement. According to the review provided above, we should allow for the writer to require more of the reader than being a passive passenger in the reading process, both in what is said (which I believe we do consider), and also its organization (which I believe is too often considered a given). After all, when was the last time you told students to take out the discourse markers and topic sentences of their texts, and to consider the possible value of such features for their readers?

Conclusion

Bainian paragraphing is of value in certain contexts, but according to some of the research reported above, there will be (or at least should be) times when a writer chooses to depart from the Bainian norms of paragraphing: the writer may wish to consider both text-structuring material, as well as the textual material itself, in order to more effectively engage the reader. Writers were doing this pre-Bain (see Chapter 2), and other writers have continued to do so since. While such writing might be termed inconsiderate, and indeed could be difficult for some readers, it may nonetheless be the kind of text that other readers need to help them develop their understanding or appreciation of a particular subject. The challenge is to get our learner-writers to think about the when, where, and how of these different possibilities.

Notes

1   This might be in the form of contact lenses.
2   Occasionally, words are skipped – most commonly functional or small words (Just and Carpenter, 1980).
3   It should be noted, however, that Chafe (1994) recognized cognitive constraints as only one aspect influencing paragraphing – the other being the manipulation of the reader in various ways.
4   I do not elaborate here on the breadth and depth processing dimensions noted by Kieras (1978) as they are not directly relevant to the focus of this chapter.
5   Johnston and Afflerbach (1985) sounded a note of caution concerning the use of such tools (though using them in their own research), and Graesser, Keith Millis, and Rolf Zwaan maintained that "… the protocols do not reliably tap unconscious comprehension processes" (Graesser et al., 1997: 166).
6   The texts were actually given to 37 students, but the segmentation decisions of 25 of those students were excluded from the resulting data, as these participants were taught by the researchers, and there were concerns that teaching effects had played a role in affecting the decisions.
7   See also Goutsos (1997: 49), who found that only three out of 274 paragraph-initial sentences utilized anaphoric pronominalization.
8   Note, however, that Hoey (2005: 133) maintains lexical priming is "domain and genre specific."

9   For example, "Yesterday it was announced that Apple and HTC had settled its patent dispute with a 10 year license agreement." (http://www.neowin.net /news/htc-may-pay-apple-6---8-per-device-in-patent-settlement). An interesting hypothesis might be that this is a typical text opening sentence when the focus of the text is specifically about, and indeed limited to, discussion of the announcement.

10 Note also the following comment by Sporleder and Lapata (2006: 14) on human segmentation of de-segmented *Wall Street Journal* articles: "Determining paragraph boundaries in such texts may be difficult for non-experts, i.e. people unfamiliar with that particular writing style."

11 I say *some*, not *all* here, as reader-supportive paragraphing may not help a poor reader at all if the subject matter is not understood.

8   The Process of Writing Paragraphs

Introduction

In this chapter, I review research on how paragraphing fits into writing behavior. Most of the scholars of the 19th century believed paragraphs to be units of planning (i.e. they believed, or at least encouraged, writers to think and plan in paragraphs), and some pedagogical materials in wide use today – such as Reid's (1994) book and those of Gayle Feng-Checkett and Lawrence Checkett (Checkett and Checkett, 2006) and Andy Gillett, Angela Hammond, and Mary Martala (Gillett et al., 2009: xxiv) – still advocate this idea. However, as noted in Chapter 4, Rodgers (1966a) challenged this commonly held assumption when he argued that his own paragraphing belonged to the revision, rather than the prevision[1] stage of his writing, and Lindemann (1995: 144) also noted the reality of revisional paragraphing in her pedagogical volume.

The idea that one might make decisions which affect the paragraphs of the text, including indentation decisions, in a later draft of writing, or when reviewing previously written text, is at variance with some prescriptive pedagogy and clearly at odds with Christensen's (1965, 1966) generative rhetoric theory (described in Chapter 4). However, it is not too contentious to state that neither Rodgers' nor Christensen's view is able to adequately describe how writers paragraph. The commonly held idea that writing proceeds through simple linear steps (planning, followed by writing, followed by revising) is now largely discredited. As a consequence, unless paragraphing decisions are radically different from other planning and revising ones (and there is no reason to think that this is the case), neither simple previsional nor simple revisional perspectives on paragraphing can account for the reality of people's writing practices.

It is clearly important for writing instructors to understand how paragraphing decisions fit into the overall planning, drafting or composing, and revising aspects of writing, and to consider the possible implications of research findings for how paragraphing should fit within writing pedagogy – hence the focus on this subject here. I close the chapter by engaging with Heurley's (1997) views on the paragraph and paragraphing, and I consider whether paragraphing may be better understood as a writer-facilitating tool, which only at times has the reader in mind, rather than being understood primarily as a tool employed by the writer for the benefit of the reader.

The questions I seek to address throughout this chapter are:

1. What do we know about the writing process, and how do paragraphing decisions fit within it?
2. How is pausing in the writing process related to paragraphing?
3. What are the key variables that affect paragraphing within the overall writing process?
4. Is paragraphing primarily a writer-facilitating tool, rather than a reader-oriented one?

Development of a Process Writing Model

It is only relatively recently that researchers have considered and investigated the writing process. Historically, more interest was shown in understanding language products, rather than how people speak or write. Nancy Sommers suggested that classical (oral) rhetoric models influenced the development of early linear writing process models (Sommers, 1980). While there are similarities between how messages are developed within the two modes of communication,[2] there are also many differences. Because of the differences, Sommers questioned the ability of models which mirrored the speaking process – such as the *conception, incubation,* and *production* model of James Britton, Tony Burgess, Nancy Martin, Alex McLeod and Harold Rosen (Britton et al., 1975) – to adequately account for the writing process. Simply adding revision to these three steps and labeling such an adaptation a model of writing, Sommers (1980: 379) argued, would be inadequate, creating "a parody of writing." Over time, more sophisticated models of writing have been developed in an attempt to mirror, or more adequately represent, the writing process, and these will be discussed later in this section.

In her historical overview of revision in writing, Jill Fitzgerald maintained that up until the 1970s, the linear process view of writing was dominant (Fitzgerald, 1987), and she suggested that Donald Murray (Murray, 1978) was the first to challenge it.[3] Murray's study was an important, and a rather iconoclastic, one. He differentiated "internal revision" (the writer discovering what s/he has to say, an ongoing process in writing) and "external revision" (the audience-oriented aspects of revision traditionally considered to be the last step in the writing process). Murray was struck by his discovery of the importance of the first (and under-appreciated) type of revision, and he put forward cogent arguments, including numerous statements from well-known writers, to support the distinction he drew between these two types of revision. Obviously, this wider view of revision does not sit comfortably with the traditional view of it as being the last step in the writing process. Carol Berkenkotter working together with Murray expounded in some detail their skepticism regarding the value of a linear process view of writing, while highlighting the role and importance of internal revision in the writing process:

> In the act of composing, writers move back and forth between planning, translating (putting thoughts into words) and reviewing their work. And as they do, they frequently "discover" major rhetorical goals. (Berkenkotter and Murray, 1983: 163)

Along with Murray (1978), Ann Humes, in her review of research into the writing process (Humes, 1983), indicated problems with the idea that writing proceeded in clearly identifiable discrete sequential steps. She suggested that a linear model of writing be replaced with a dynamic hierarchical one involving the four processes of planning, translating, reviewing and revising, in which revision could happen at any time in the composing process. The idea that composing is an iterative or recursive process in which planning, drafting / composing, and revision constantly interact within the writing process is now widely accepted.

Writing Pedagogy and the Paragraph

If current models of writing accurately describe the writing process as nonlinear, it is natural to ask what should be done with simple sequential, step-by-step writing pedagogies. These are often presented to learners and students in teaching materials, and are also present in state / government policies in some educational contexts; Bonnie Warne has discussed the relevant policy in the U.S. state of Idaho (Warne, 2008: 23), and Myhill and Susan Jones have described the Department for Education 1999 *plan–draft–revise–proofread–present* process of writing in U.K. schools (Myhill and Jones, 2007: 339). As mentioned earlier, in linear models paragraphing decisions are typically considered to belong to the planning stage of writing; however, such a view would seem to be at odds with current writing models, in which planning (like revising) is considered to be an ongoing process when writing. There are various possible responses to this apparently contradictory state of affairs.

Firstly, some educators might want to keep the current linear-step pedagogies on the grounds that there is evidence that some recursive models of writing do not adequately describe the writing process. Research indicates that certain writers may consciously control aspects of their writing in quite principled ways, as observed by Myhill and Jones (2007: 333). One might argue that because of the multiple demands made on the writer's cognitive processing capacity, a writer may make *conscious* decisions to separate the different processes, that is, to follow particular patterns of focus and attention at different times in the writing process (rather than the less ordered or preplanned interactions between processes one might consider to be typical in recursive writing models).

Indirect support for this position is found in the work of N. Ann Chenoweth and John Hayes, who discovered that revision carried out as a distinct activity *after* composing (rather than co-occurring with it) enabled second language writers to more successfully manage the writing process; in other words, separating the processes seemed to help the students (Chenoweth and Hayes, 2001). A case study by Jack Selzer indicated that some writers do proceed with the writing task in clearly identifiable steps (Selzer, 1983). Selzer described in some detail an engineer's writing practices based on an examination of drafts, prespective and retrospective accounts, and interview data. He found that the writing process of the engineer (Nelson) comprised quite distinct steps: "planning, arranging, writing and revising activities" (p. 179). In addition, he noted that consideration of audience was an early (rather than a late) consideration, and that there were fairly minimal revision activities. Selzer observed that Nelson wrote traditional topic sentences, and explained that he wrote short paragraphs for the sake of his readers. Further evidence of linear-step writing comes from Stephanie Dix, who referred to research indicating that young children revised only when their drafts were completed – not throughout the writing process (Dix, 2006: 9). Kellogg (1988) indicated that some writers had a distinct pre-writing stage in their approach to writing, and Vivian Zamel documented that a skilled ESL writer adopted a principled procedural approach in which revision was a distinct (and final) step in the writing process, described by the student as: "[T]he first draft is for getting the ideas down. The second is for finding the way to say it the way I want..." (Zamel, 1983: 178). All of the above data suggest that "simplistic" pedagogical advice on how writing should proceed is (at least for some writers) not that far removed from actual writing behavior.

Secondly, some academics advocate a step-by-step pedagogy, even though they recognize that this may not match the cognitive processes involved in writing. Humes (1983), as noted earlier, challenged the ability of a linear model to adequately capture the writing process. However, she still believed that the presentation of a linear model of the writing process to learners was justifiable because "the activities of each sub-process are more easily presented in separate stages" (Humes, 1983: 205). Such a view seems to be rooted in a learning-centered pedagogy, in which ease of explanation and simplification strategies are considered more important or perhaps more effective than pedagogical efforts to match complex writing patterns and processes.

In spite of the two points made above, I believe there are two challenges to traditional linear step views of writing pedagogy. Firstly, there is evidence of the stultifying effects of such approaches. Sommers (1980: 382–383), in her analysis of 20 freshmen students' writing and their revisions, noted a problem which students faced:

> Since they write their introductions and their thesis statements even before they have really discovered what they want to say, their early close attention to the thesis statement, and more generally the linear model, function to restrict and circumscribe not only the development of their ideas, but also their ability to change the direction of these ideas.

Mike Rose contrasted the difficulties faced by writers working within a linear-step approach to writing with other writers who considered composition in a fluid and flexible way (Rose, 1980).

He observed that the latter group of writers were likely to face fewer difficulties or problems in their writing because of the way in which they viewed the writing task.

The second challenge to pedagogical linear step models is evidence that for some writers composing is indeed a recursive process – quite unlike that documented for Selzer's engineer. Zamel (1983) found that she could not actually analyze ESL writers' behavior according to simple linear pedagogies, because their writing patterns did not correspond to the steps in sequential step processes. In a similar vein, Warne (2008) discussed in some detail how she responded to two students who did not write following the series of steps she taught in writing. Likewise, Brian Monahan commented on the writing processes of a student named Anne, and how her writing patterns were clearly recursive (Monahan, 1984; see later for more details). In terms of professional writers' activities, Umberto Eco spoke of moving his already written paragraphs around and editing them (Eco, 2007: 175) – quite unlike Nelson's practice.

The above-noted differences no doubt stem in part from variety in writing tasks and individual writers' practices, together with other variables which will be discussed later in this chapter. It is fair to say that the bulk of research suggests that the processes by which the writing product come into being are highly complex, and more adequately explained by recursive models of the writing process, rather than traditional simple sequential perspectives. Having said this, the consequences of such an understanding of writing for pedagogical engagement with paragraphing are not altogether clear.

Writing Models and the Place of the Paragraph within Them

Writing has been described by Olive (2015: 32) as "one of the most complex cognitive activities that Human Beings [sic] accomplish during their life." This statement hints at the challenges that have faced scholars who have proposed and refined various models over the years to describe the writing process, including Kellogg (1996), Linda Flower and John Hayes (Flower and Hayes, 1981a); Hayes (1996), and Marlene Scardamalia and Carl Bereiter (Scardamalia and Bereiter, 1983, 1986). Probably the most well-known models of writing are the Flower and Hayes (1981a) and Hayes (1996) models, and so I engage with these here. It is not my intention to examine these models in any detail, but rather to very briefly trace their development, with a specific focus on paragraphing.

Flower and Hayes' (1981a) model comprised three parts:

- long-term memory of the writer (comprising audience, topic, and genre knowledge);
- task environment (the assignment and the progress in task production); and
- cognitive processes (planning, translating, and reviewing controlled by a monitor, discussed in more detail below).

In this model, information passes to and from long-term memory to the cognitive processes, and between the cognitive processes and the task environment (and vice versa). Flower and Hayes (1981a) believed that the three cognitive processes worked interactively, possibly simultaneously, and not in a linear fashion. In Hayes' (1996) revision of the model, there are just two connected components:

1. The task environment (incorporating the social environment and the physical environment); and
2. The individual (incorporating motivation / affect, working memory, cognitive processes, and long-term memory).

In the revised model, interesting new elements in the task environment are the physical environment, including the medium of composing (e.g. computer versus pen and paper) and also the text produced so far. Working memory was understood by Hayes

(1996) as comprising three elements: phonological memory, the visual / spatial sketchpad (which I discuss in more detail below), and semantic memory. In the new model, the cognitive processes have been renamed – "planning" becomes "reflection," "translation" becomes "text production," and "revision" becomes "text interpretation." Hayes (1996: 5) called the newer model "an individual–environmental model."

Where do paragraphing decisions fit in these models? Paragraphing practice is affected by genre and audience (which were mentioned in the 1981a model), although paragraphing was not specifically referred to as being affected by these considerations. There were just two specific mentions of the paragraph in the authors' discussions of their models. The first was in the discussion of the earlier model (Flower and Hayes, 1981a), where, in a description of goals and planning, the authors indicated that paragraphing considerations were part of the planning process. This is a widely held traditional view of the place of paragraphing in the writing process. The second mention of the paragraph is in the Hayes' (1996) model, in discussion of the visual / spatial sketchpad in working memory. The idea of the visual / spatial sketchpad originated with Alan Baddeley and Graham Hitch (Baddeley and Hitch, 1974), and Hayes (1990: 249) explained it in terms of the writer maintaining some kind of awareness of the text not only as a linguistic product, but also as a product that occupies space (on paper or screen). Hayes (1996) referred to the study he conducted with Bond (Bond and Hayes, 1984; see Chapter 7), specifically to the finding that paragraphing decisions of a de-segmented text seemed to be influenced by spatial considerations, as part of the support for the inclusion of the visual / spatial sketchpad as a working memory component in the writing process. Annie Piolat working with Jean-Yves Roussey and Olivier Thunin found that a writer's planning is affected by the look of the page (Piolat et al., 1997), and Olive and Passerault (2012) discussed research suggesting that writers build a visuospatial mental image of the texts they are producing and hypothesized that different modes of writing and canvas size are likely to influence visuospatial considerations. In an earlier study, Christina Haas and John Hayes reported that hard copy (i.e. paper) documents facilitated writers' "high level" revision (i.e. more global revision) rather than revision done from a computer screen, which typically contains less text than is encountered on a page of paper (Haas and Hayes, 1986). This finding is also suggestive of the role of spatial awareness and visual considerations in such decisions. The effects of visual / spatial considerations on the writing process are attracting increased research (e.g. Olive et al., 2008; Olive and Passerault, 2012), and results from such studies may well help us better understand the vexing issue of aesthetic considerations and paragraphing, an issue mentioned in Chapter 1, but still little understood.

Researching the Writing Process: The Methods and Tools

Before considering research into planning and revising and how paragraphing fits in with these activities, I provide a brief overview of the various methods and tools that have been used by researchers in investigating aspects of the writing process. It is necessary to emphasize that concerns related to the value or validity of the data generated by these methods and tools can be raised with most of the research findings reported below. The most common methods / tools used in process writing research are: retrospective accounts, think-aloud protocols, keystroke logging, and eye tracking and keystroke logging combined.

Concerning retrospective accounts, there is the danger that these may simply reflect what a writer believes s/he should have been doing when writing, or what s/he has been taught, rather than accurately documenting what a writer was actually doing when writing. A good example of this problem was documented by Myhill and Jones (2007), who found that many writers believed their revision processes were the final part of their writing, whereas the empirical data indicated considerable online (i.e. in-process) revision. Regarding this finding, they commented, "It is likely that common pedagogical practices have had an impact on shaping writers' perspectives on revision..." (p. 339). Another type of disparity was noted by C. Michael Levy and Sarah Ransdell, who, on comparing writers' self-reported and actual practices, discovered that writers tended to underestimate the time they spent in planning before generating text, and to overestimate the time they spent in reviewing and revising previously generated text (Levy and Ransdell, 1995: 775).

Turning to the think-aloud technique (mentioned briefly in the previous chapter), a common criticism of this research method is that such a procedure might disrupt the writing process, as Sondra Perl maintained (Perl, 1980). Kristyan Spelman Miller suggested that when writers are forced to provide a running commentary on what they are doing (a very unnatural activity), they might provide additional comments, irrelevant to the writing process (Spelman Miller, 2000: 124–125). In addition, the need to comment adds an extra burden on the writer, and this may materially affect how scarce cognitive resources are allocated while writing (Kellogg, 1994: 51). There are also some doubts concerning whether think-aloud protocols can tap all of the cognitive processes involved in writing, particularly processes which are generally considered to operate at a subconscious level (see Humes, 1983: 213).

With regard to keystroke logging, the automatic recording of a writer's keyboard activity, the key problem is that one must interpret what the pauses or bursts of writing activity indicate, as a pause may signal any one of a number of cognitive processes, or indeed be unrelated to cognitive processing. This shortcoming is being addressed by combining keystroke-logging and eye-tracking tools and techniques, as in the research of Sven Strömqvist, Kenneth Holmqvist, Victoria Johansson, Henrik Karlsson, and Åsa Wengelin (Strömqvist et al., 2006) and that of Åsa Wengelin, Mark Torrance, Kenneth Holmqvist, Sol Simpson, David Galbraith, Victoria Johansson, and Roger Johansson (Wengelin et al.,

2009). A combined keystroke-logging and eye-tracking research methodology seems to offer some potential for better understanding writing, since knowing what writers' eyes are doing when they pause in their typing or as they write will tend to limit the number of interpretations for why the pause occurs – though even here there are problems, as noted below.

Some researchers, aware of the possible limitations of the research techniques mentioned above, have, at times, combined tools, including Levy and Ransdell (1995) and later Rosa Manchón and Julio de Larios (Manchón and de Larios, 2007). In what follows I briefly comment on ideas about how planning and revising are managed, before summarizing some of the research on planning and revising in the writing process. I then turn to a consideration of the place of paragraphing within these processes.

Managing the Writing Process

Since the Flower and Hayes' (1981a) model was developed, there has been considerable interest shown in the three basic cognitive processes of writing (planning, composing, and revising), variously termed. As noted earlier, Flower and Hayes (1981a) hypothesized that these processes are managed by a monitor and Kellogg (1996) adopted the term "central executive" to describe a similar cognitive managing mechanism in his model of writing. Because the writing process is demanding and complex, and because a writer cannot do everything at once, the theory is that the monitor or central executive blocks off certain processes, and facilitates attention on others at any one time.

On the basis of research into cognitive effort and different composing sub-processes, Olive and collaborators Rui Alves and São Castro found that translating (i.e. putting ideas into words), was less effortful than planning and revising (Olive et al., 2009: 769, 780), and that when participants were actually writing (transcribing), translating also went on, along with lesser amounts of planning and revising (p. 773). They provided evidence to show various levels of activation of the sub-processes during any one time in composition.

Research on Planning and Revision

Even if it is the case that there is a dynamic, multi-directional interaction between the three main processes involved in writing, intuitively one might expect there to be more planning at the beginning stages of writing and more revision at the end. Below I consider some of the research findings in relation to this issue, before focusing on matters of paragraphing.

Planning

A number of taxonomies of planning have been proposed (see Haas, 1989, for a review of some of these). On the basis of an examination of think-aloud protocol data, texts produced, and (post-task) questionnaire data, Manchón and de Larios (2007) subdivided planning activities into four types:

- Position planning (i.e. writer stance);
- Textual organization (i.e. textual framing, including paragraphing);
- Ideational content (i.e. what the writer wants to communicate); and
- Procedural aspects (i.e. advance think-aloud comments on what the writer will do next).

According to their data, Manchón and de Larios (2007) found that higher proficiency students planned more throughout their writing and produced outlines more often than less proficient writers. They also discovered that planning, whether writing in a first or second language, was more prevalent during the first third of a writing task. They believed that these findings challenge, to a certain extent, the implicit idea within recursive models that the relationship between the processes is simply interactive, rather than sensitive to where the writer is in the writing task (Manchón and de Larios, 2007: 578–579). Kellogg (1987, 1988) and Kellogg together with Suzanne Mueller (Kellogg and Mueller, 1993) also reported that, according to their writers' own judgments of what they were doing in their writing, the amount of time spent on planning declined over time during the writing process, being replaced by more reviewing activities. The amount of time spent on planning has been reported to account for between 30–65% (see Levy and Ransdell, 1995: 771), and even from 65–85% (see Humes, 1983: 207) of time spent in the writing task.

Revising

Why do writers revise? Various models or reasons for revision have been proposed. Hayes (2004: 11) believed that writers revise for the most part not to edit mistakes, but to improve what is being written because they find a way of saying something that is more satisfying, or indeed something more worthwhile to say. Scardamalia and Bereiter (1983, 1986) developed the Compare, Diagnose, Operate (CDO) model of revision, in which the writer compares the text with his / her intention. If there is a mismatch the problem is diagnosed, and mentally corrected before actual changes are made to the text.

Revision as a writing activity has been classified in various ways. Lester Faigley together with Witte developed a highly respected (and much used) taxonomy of revision with two main categories (Faigley and Witte, 1981). Under the first, labeled "surface changes," are formal and meaning-preserving adjustments. Under the second, labeled "text base changes," are changes to the microstructure and macrostructure of the text (i.e. content changes). Witte (1987: 397), on the basis of protocol data, wrote of the possibility of the revision of what he termed "pre-text," which he defined as "mental construction of text prior to transcription." Accordingly, he argued that the term *revision* should not be limited to actually changing text already transcribed. Fitzgerald (1988: 124) likewise suggested that revision could occur before the generation of text, and Scardamalia and Bereiter (1986: 790) had the same belief, though coining the term "reprocessing" for mental revision and preferring to limit the use of the term "revision" for an actual instance of textual change: "revision is a special case of reprocessing, applied to actual text." More recently, Linda Allal and Lucile Chanquoy, in their review of revision (Allal and Chanquoy, 2004: 2–3), and referring to Witte (1985), distinguished "pretextual revision" (associated with planning), "online revision" (while writing), and "deferred revision" (after writing is finished). They also distinguished "editing" (for errors) and "rewriting" (changing the text by adding, deleting, reordering, etc.).

There is general support for the view that revision (as a text changing activity) is an ongoing activity within the writing process. Zamel (1983: 172), for example, noted that the ESL students she studied "rewrote as they wrote." She also observed that revision while writing was often of a global nature – to the extent that initial plans were at times totally abandoned. Levy and Ransdell (1995: 777), in their examination of the writing behaviors of American undergraduate students, found that reviewing and revising occurred throughout the whole of the writing process, not just at the end, and constituted between 5% and 10% of the time spent on the writing task. They also observed a clear relationship between revision which took place later in the writing process and the overall quality of writing, and further commented that "Our analysis reveals that revision takes less total time than other sub-processes, but that it disproportionately determines writing success" (Levy and Ransdell, 1995: 778).

It is generally understood that when reading to revise written text, the writer treats the existing text in a specific way. Flower and Hayes, working with Linda Carey, Karen Schriver, and James Stratman (Flower et al., 1986: 23) suggested that when revising, a writer "imposes additional goals or criteria on the text," and Hayes (1996: 14, 15) maintained that the change in focus is governed by sensitivity to the following issues: "bad diction, wordiness, and poor organization" – the latter issue presumably including paragraphing considerations. Robert de Beaugrande believed that the change in a writer's focus during revision was related to putting oneself in the place of the future reader of the text (de Beaugrande, 1979), and Richard Beach suggested that writers, when revising, consider their textual product from the position of a reader who is sensitive to Grice's maxims of communication (Beach, 1982: 75). Gerhard Augst termed this new role (the writer transforming him/herself into the anticipated reader of the text) that of "implicit reader" (Augst, 1992: 71). Sommers (1980: 385) also observed how awareness of the reader seemed to affect the revision process, and Monahan (1984) suggested that a key difference between the competent and less able writers in his study was a consideration of the reader when revising.

Some of the above findings concerning revision processes differ from Nelson's practice (Selzer 1983), noted earlier, in which reader considerations seemed to affect planning rather than revision. Research findings occupying the middle ground between Selzer's (initial, planning-oriented audience awareness) and Monahan's (later, revision-oriented audience awareness) data are those provided by Gesa Kirsch, who investigated the writing processes of five experienced writers when writing for an audience of either first-year students or faculty (Kirsch, 1991). In addition to documenting different drafting processes when aiming for the two audiences, she observed that the writers seemed to have their audience in mind at different stages of the writing process, both at the beginning of the process, and later on (Kirsch, 1991: 48).

In which part of the writing process is audience focus more effective? It is probably not possible to answer this question with any degree of certainty. However, it is interesting to note that Duane Roen and R. J. Willey, in their study of the writing of 60 first-year university students (Roen and Willey, 1988), found that writers who revised with the audience in mind wrote better quality compositions than writers who considered their audience only in the planning stages of writing.

Planning, revising, and paragraphing

Turning specifically to paragraphing, research indicates that writers consider paragraphs as both units of planning and units of revision.

Regarding planning, Haas (1989: 194) differentiated conceptual planning (ideas and their organization) and sequential planning ("lexical or syntactic arrangement, or the textual expression of meaning"). She included paragraph considerations within both. For example, she provided think-aloud protocol comments such as, "… I need to tie all this together in a concluding paragraph" (*ibid.*) as an example of conceptual planning, and "I'll make this two paragraphs" (p. 195) as an example of sequential planning. Russel Durst provided a similar think-aloud comment from one of his participants, concerning planning and the paragraph: "This next paragraph is going to be on Hoover's policies" (Durst, 1987: 352); and Berkenkotter (Berkenkotter and Murray, 1983: 164), based on her analysis of Murray's think-aloud protocol data, observed that Murray planned in paragraphs, in particular, what information would go into which paragraph. These research findings suggest that some writers think in paragraphs, rather than in more global planning terms or units, a practice which has been observed for other writers as documented by Charles Stallard (Stallard, 1974: 217).

Turning to revision, Zamel (1983: 174), in studying the revision processes of advanced ESL students, noted how writers were quite willing to move around paragraphs or parts of paragraphs, to create new ones, or to cut paragraphs in revising their work. She provided the example of one writer who, in a think-aloud protocol, commented on finding a paragraph in the middle of the text and decided that it would be more suitable as an introduction. Monahan (1984), in a think-aloud protocol study of 12th grade writers, observed that one of the students (Anne) made 29 revisions to a first draft, two of these being insertions of new paragraphs. The reason Anne gave for making the changes was that that they would make the material clearer for the reader. Gail Hawisher recorded the following pre-revision comment of a student, again indicative of paragraph considerations in relation to revision:

"Right now my essay is just a bunch of ideas. I need to write separate
paragraphs describing male stereotypes and pull these together in
my conclusion." (Hawisher, 1987: 150)

Stallard (1974) observed that a feature of revision which distinguished 30 good writers from a random selection of 30 other writers
in a senior high school was attention to paragraphing in the revision
stage of writing. While the random selection group made only one
change to paragraphing (i.e. changes to the number of paragraphs
in the text), the good writers made five (a statistically significant
difference between the two groups). Lillian Bridwell (1980: 204)
developed a seven-level classification of revision with "multi-
sentence level" being one category, this class including indention
and de-indention. This broad category of revision constituted
11.80% (p. 207) of the total number of revision changes for 12th
grade writers. However, Bridwell gave no specific details about
the number of instances of indention and reindention within this
category in her data analysis.

Summing up, it appears that different writers consider their
paragraphs when planning and / or when revising, and at different
stages of the writing process. Explanations for why paragraphing
considerations vary may well lie in writer differences, the text type
being written, familiarity with the text type and the mode of writing,
and I consider each of these variables in more detail later in this
section. However, before I do so, I focus on a specific subarea of
writing research in which paragraphs are often mentioned – that
of writers' pausing behavior and its relation to planning, revising
and paragraphing.

Pausing and Paragraphs

The study of pauses in writing is an area of research with potential
for helping understand the writing process, though as noted
earlier, matters of interpretation can be problematic. Technological
innovations – in particular, the development of keystroke logging –
have facilitated the study of the periods of writing activity (whether

initial drafting or various types of revision) and the pauses that punctuate them.

Pausing is very common when writing; Alves et al. (2008) pointed to research indicating that half of writing time constitutes pauses of more than two seconds. There is fairly consistent evidence that the juncture between paragraphs is a significant place of pausing for writers. Marianne Phinney and Sandra Khouri, in their research with second language writers (Phinney and Khouri, 1993), observed that longer pauses occurred at the larger junctures within a text (including the paragraph), and Luuk Van Waes and Peter Schellens established that writers' pauses at paragraph boundaries were approximately two and a half times longer than their pauses at sentence boundaries (Van Waes and Schellens, 2003: 849). Deborah McCutchen found that syntactic unit boundaries seemed to be related to pauses and the length of pause in turn related to the size of the syntactic unit, the paragraph being the largest of these in her view (McCutcheon, 2011: 57). Spelman Miller (2006b: 150), on the basis of her own analyses of writers' pausing behavior, stated that, "… the data point to consistent patterns of increased pausing and decreased productivity associated with paragraph transitions."

Yet the picture is not quite so simple as to warrant the conclusion that long pauses occur only at a paragraph break, or indeed, necessarily occur between paragraphs. Using a think-aloud protocol as their research procedure, Flower and Hayes (1981b) considered pausing behavior in relation to sentence-level linguistic planning, and higher-level rhetorical planning. In their think-aloud research with four writers (three expert and one novice), they interpreted long pauses as indicative of composing episodes, with boundaries between these possibly being signaled by signal words such as "all right" (p. 237), which were often related to shifts in focus, and which independent judges were able to identify as "meaningful episodes in the process of the writer's thought" (p. 238), when given the protocol data. Flower and Hayes (1981b) observed that the composing episodes were not the same as the paragraph breaks in the text, in that the episodes were goal oriented (possibly indicated by goal setting language used at these points in text), rather than being topic oriented (which they believed to be more typically characteristic of the paragraph). While new paragraphs were generally connected with such episodes (and hence were locations of pauses), only 12% of the episode boundaries (identified by the judges) occurred at actual paragraph breaks of the text, there being more episode boundaries than paragraph boundaries. Accordingly, Flower and Hayes (1981b: 242) concluded that "[t]he composing process has an episodic pattern of its own which is not dictated by the patterns of the text." This is an important finding, as it suggests that extended planning is not necessarily or specifically related to paragraphing decisions, which also suggests that the place or role of the paragraph break in planning may need to be reconsidered.

The idea that pausing may be related to something other than syntactic structure (which some writers have considered to extend to the paragraph unit) was also advanced by Sanders together with Daniël Janssen, Els van der Pool, Joost Schilperoord, and Carel van Wijk (Sanders et al., 1996). They suggested that RST might shed light on pausing behavior. As noted in Chapter 5, the linguistic hierarchical structure of a text does not necessarily map onto or match the syntactic units of the text (e.g. sentence, paragraph), and the idea that rhetorical structure may be related to pausing and planning activities is probably worth further investigation.

Spelman Miller's work (Spelman Miller, 2000, 2002a,b, 2006a,b), including with co-authors Eva Lindgren and Kirk Sullivan (Spelman Miller et al., 2008), has moved pausological studies forward through developing a more sophisticated approach to understanding pausing. Spelman Miller (2002b) hypothesized that pausing might be related to positions in text where framing devices occur, these being linked to framing decisions within the text. She defined a framing device as:

> ...an element or structure (single word, phrase or clause) which serves to establish the starting point of the message at the clause / sentence level. This may be in one of a number of ways, either

in constituting the topic itself, or in preparing the scene for the introduction of the topic (Spelman Miller, 2002b: 130).

The five types of framing device that Spelman Miller (2002a: 263) identified were: theme (e.g. *This*), adjunct or complement theme (e.g. *Around puberty*), non-experiential theme (e.g. *In addition*), empty theme (e.g. *There are*), and thematized structure (e.g. *Since I was a child*). As can be seen, these bear some similarity to Goutsos' (1997) discourse-managing tools discussed in Chapter 5, though Spelman Miller (2006b: 136) noted that Goutsos' work was published after her initial work on framing.

In her research, Spelman Miller (2002a: 265) found what she termed "an interesting coincidence" between the presence of framing devices and pauses (as recorded by keystroke logging):[4] approximately a third of the framing devices present in the keystroke logged texts were at locations of significant pausing while writing. Further, the position of one type of thematic device, the subject theme, involving the "establishing and management of topic" (Spelman Miller, 2006b: 132), was a common place for pausing among all of the logs of the writers she studied, despite the otherwise considerable variation among them (p. 144).

In one of the few studies to examine in detail the pausing behaviors of particular writers in relation to paragraphs, Spelman Miller (2000: 138), using the keystroke logging procedure, documented how one writer's longest pauses occurred both between paragraphs and also within them. Concerning a pause within a paragraph she observed the writer had produced a paragraph-initial general introductory clause, and then paused (for a long period of time) before the specific topic of the paragraph was written. Spelman-Miller also found a strong relationship between the occurrence of a framing device within a new clause and a pause in writing at this point. Further support for Spelman Miller's framing device – pause nexus has come from a study examining textual revision. Lindgren and Sullivan (2006: 167) conducted research into the English writing revision behavior of 13–15 year-old Swedish children's writing.

The researchers developed a revision taxonomy based on their analysis of keystroke logging data from their participants, and they focused in their analyses on "pre-contextual revision" (p. 166), which is revision when writing is being executed, or has just finished. The researchers stated how this kind of revision, when associated with topic maintenance or development of the topic, and when accompanied by a pause, fitted into Spelman Miller's ideas about framing devices being important pause locations in text. In the example sentence below, from their data, the student writer deleted the subject of the sentence (*Sweden*) after a pause, replacing it with *summer holidays in Sweden*, which became the revised subject of the following clause.

> Student sentence
> *I want you to come to Sweden therefor Sweden (pause and deletion of Sweden) the summer holidays in Sweden (pause) are really great*
> (adapted from p. 162)

Lindgren and Sullivan (2006) suggested that the relationship between the pause, deletion and replacement of the subject was supportive of the idea that the topic framing location (in this particular case subject theme in Spelman Miller's taxonomy, see above) could be a significant pause (and also revising) location in text.

Interpreting Pausing in the Writing Process

Although it seems fairly well established that a significant pause in writing often occurs at a paragraph break (i.e. after one paragraph has been completed and another has not yet been started), around the locations of framing devices, and at the beginning of composing episodes, why pausing occurs within the writing process and how writers' pausing behavior can be interpreted are nonetheless problematic.

Firstly, we can address the question of why pausing occurs during acts of writing. A number of researchers (e.g. Alves et al., 2008; McCutchen, 2011: 57; Spelman Miller et al., 2008) have connected the pausing phenomenon primarily to the demands being made on working memory, and the challenges a writer faces in managing the complexity of the writing task. However, other scholars believe cognitive overload to be just one of the reasons for pausing. Schilperoord (2002: 75) for example, added socio-psychological (e.g. anxiety), and physical (e.g. tiredness) factors as possible causes for pausing, in addition to cognitive overload pressures.

Scholars seem to be fairly evenly split over whether a pause at the paragraph juncture is primarily for planning text to come or for reviewing text already written, as the following overview makes clear.

Firstly, there are those who consider the pause to be primarily related to planning. Flower and Hayes (1981b) believed pausing to be related to thinking about what to write and global rhetorical considerations. Schilperoord (2002: 77) interpreted the longer pause before the paragraph as compared to that between sentences as being related to planning needs, and believed that the difference in length of pause between paragraphs and between sentences could be easily explained: "planning paragraphs is more effortful than planning sentences." Schilperoord went on to elaborate this point by arguing that paragraph planning includes planning of smaller units, too. Thus, paragraph-level pauses include smaller level pauses – for example, how to start off the paragraph, which decision in turn includes how to begin the clause and the sentence. Spelman Miller (2006b: 147) argued essentially the same point:

> …[P]auses during hesitant phases may generally be associated with forward planning for content, but this is not the complete picture. The more complex reality is that major constituent boundaries act as loci not only for major conceptual macroplanning, but also for local, microplanning activity.

Van Waes and Schellens (2003: 849) believed the increased pause time before the paragraph to be "…largely conceptual and rhetorical in nature," and Ann Matsuhashi, in her study of four skilled high school writers (Matsuhashi, 1981), interpreted long pause times of paragraph-initial t-units to be related to planning. In her view, "…planning for paragraphs is an important moment of decision-making throughout all discourse" (p. 130).

However, other researchers have suggested the possibility of reviewing being a key reason for pausing at the paragraph break. Wengelin et al. (2009: 338), in their review of previous studies on pausing suggested five possible reasons for pausing and looking back to the text already produced when writing. These were: looking for ideas, managing cohesion, correcting errors, comparing text with intention, and revising. In their own experiment combining eye tracking and keystroke logging, they found that extended pause times at paragraph breaks were related to a particular kind of eye movement – reading back in the text (pp. 347, 349). While noting that the interpretation of this activity is probably complex, the observation, at the very least, serves to balance the notion that pausing is exclusively related to planning.[5] Schilperoord (2002: 71) included revision as a possible reason for pausing, differentiating three kinds of pause: retrieval of information from memory, monitoring what has already been written (i.e. reviewing), and repairing text which has already been written down (i.e. revision).

Other scholars have related pausing to both planning and revising. Spelman Miller (2006b: 152) was keen to stress that the pause must not automatically be equated with planning, and Matsuhashi (1981: 130) related the pre-paragraph pause not only to planning, but also to the reviewing of text up to that point: "[Planning for paragraphs] provides the writer time to review what has already been written as well as time to plan ahead for the next section of the text." Olive et al. (2009), on the basis of their analyses, maintained that pauses were indicative of planning, translating (i.e. putting ideas into words), and revising.

Those who study the writing process can only make at best educated guesses as to what cognitive processes are engaged during a particular pause, given the current state of knowledge within this field of study; and it is not easy to see how more light can be shed on this subject if we cannot fully trust writer retrospection or think-aloud data to help understand complex and possibly subconscious processes. While paragraphing and pauses are related (in the sense that paragraph juncture and framing position at paragraph-initial position may well be places in text where writers pause), the pause–paragraph relationship is not a universally reciprocal one: there are other places in text where a writer may pause when composing, and at times the paragraph break is not a place for a significant pause in writing.

Key Variables Affecting the Paragraphing Process

It is evident from the overview provided above that paragraphing practice is a complex and challenging area of writing to understand. In this section, I seek to draw out and discuss some of the factors that researchers believe affect the writing process. With one or two exceptions noted below, I am not aware of researchers making specific comments about how these variables affect paragraphing, though the assumption that paragraphing practice is affected by these variables seems reasonable. Research has not, to date, controlled these variables in ways to help us learn more about paragraphing behavior.

Writing and the Individual

Research findings indicate that writers manage the challenges of producing text in different ways. For example, Manchón and Larios (2007: 578) differentiated what they termed "advanced planners" (those who plan ahead from the beginning) from "emergent planners," those who plan as they write. Van Waes and Schellens (2003), on the basis of their analyses of the writing practices of both computer and paper and pen writers (40 university faculty and graduate students) proposed that there are five different types of writer:

- Initial planner – pausing for a long time before beginning, making few revisions;
- Average writer – pausing, planning, revising behavior in the average range of the data (no distinctive behaviors);
- Fragmentary stage 1 writer – revising most at stage 1 (first draft) and not planning much at the beginning, pausing for short periods during their writing;
- Stage 2 writer – revising most at stage 2 (i.e. after the first draft is completed), with higher-level revision and initial planning time, and with infrequent though long pauses;
- Non-stop writer – not initial planners, pausing less often than writers in the other categories above, and finishing more quickly.

Writers have also been categorized according to their ability to escape their egocentric tendencies, a developmental process taking many years. Kellogg (2008) differentiated knowledge-telling writers (author-oriented); knowledge-transforming writers (author- and text-oriented), and knowledge-crafting writers (author-, text-, and reader-oriented).

The above classifications are helpful, and it seems reasonable to assume that these differences will result in different approaches to paragraphing, but currently we do not have data to make specific claims.

Writing and Text Type

Some research suggests that writing certain genres is cognitively more demanding than writing others. If this is the case, it would seem to follow that different types of writing behavior would result, and writers might approach paragraphing differently. Kellogg (2001) believed that writing narrative is easier than writing a persuasive text, because of the assistance afforded to the writer of long-term memory schema in writing a story. A consequence of this, he argued, would be a reduction in planning demands. Using an auditory probe (occurring at approximately every 30 seconds during the writing process), the writers in Kellogg's experiment stated what they were doing at the particular point in time of the noise. Through this methodology, Kellogg found that cognitive capacity was freed up in the narrative (low–planning) writing task, with the consequence that the writer was able to redistribute the freed-up cognitive capacity. Matsuhashi (1981), in a study of the writing of four high school students, found that there was less pausing in the writing of reporting texts as compared to persuading and generalizing texts for the same group of writers. A case study which clearly indicated the effect of text type on writing behavior is that of Berkenkotter and Murray (1983). In this detailed study on Murray's varied writing processes and practices, Berkenkotter, drawing on a considerable amount of data (including drafts and think-aloud data), found that the planning, evaluating, revising, and editing times for Murray's writing varied (considerably) in the three articles he was writing. The fact that there was so much variation present in the writing processes of the same author suggests that text type, audience, and purpose exert a profound effect on the way people write, and presumably the way individuals approach paragraphing.

Writing and Language Proficiency or Familiarity with Text Type

Writers feel different pressures during the writing process according to their proficiency. A six-year-old child's cognitive resources may be largely consumed with the process of holding his / her pencil correctly, and the execution of the tricky curve in the letter *e* when writing. As a result, the child may actually forget the word being transcribed. Monik Favart and Pierre Coirier commented on the cognitive challenges facing beginning writers, and the need for writers to automate transcription to develop their writing skills (Favart and Coirier, 2006). That weaker writers allocate most cognitive resources to low-level writing activities has also been noted by Myhill and Jones (2007: 326).

Expert writers, on the other hand, face far fewer challenges in balancing the various demands placed on them when writing (Flower, 1981: 67). It would seem logical to argue that an important factor playing a role in how writers proceed in the writing process is the familiarity and proficiency with the particular text type or genre being written, rather than just linguistic proficiency per se. McCutchen (2011: 58) suggested that access to long-term memory schema (which includes familiarity with the text type) not only assists in planning and revising, but also lessens demands on working memory when writing. Faigley and Witte (1981) also observed that poorer writers were predominantly surface-level revisers.

Several researchers have compared writing behavior in a first or second language. Manchón and de Larios (2007) investigated how linguistic proficiency affected planning processes, analyzing think-aloud and retrospective accounts data obtained from first-language and second-language writers. They differentiated two types of planning: that involving the writer's position (i.e. stance), and that involving textual organization (the latter category included paragraphing, in addition to ideational and procedural aspects of planning). They found that time spent on planning and L2 proficiency level in the language were positively related (p. 570). In particular, the researchers noted increased planning awareness in relation to the latter type of planning (textual organization) as proficiency increased (p. 574). Turning to revision and proficiency level, Elizabeth New documented that lower-level writers did not revise as extensively as higher-level students in her research, and that revising took more time in a second language than in the mother tongue (New, 1999).

With regard to pausing behavior, Van Waes and Mariëlle Leijten (2015) found that pausing time was related to the language of composing, with significantly more pausing when writing in a second as compared to when writing in the first language (an average increase of 10–15%). In terms of the location of pauses, Spelman Miller (2006b: 145) noted some interesting differences between first- and second-language writers, with a tendency for the latter to pause for longer than the first-language writers at locations where they inserted a full noun subject theme.

Writing with Pen and Paper or Computer

How are writing processes affected by typing on a keyboard, facing a computer screen, and making use of a computer's automated word processing tools and storage capacity, as compared to writing using pen and paper? A number of studies have considered this question from different perspectives. In terms of the general cognitive effects of working with different modes, Colette Daiute in documenting more editing and the addition of more text by students using a computer as compared to those writing with a paper and pen (Daiute, 1986), maintained that word processing helps writers overcome various constraints present in the writing process. A number of specific findings have been recorded by researchers who have studied planning and revision differences between the two modes of writing (for a detailed review of studies, see Pennington, 1996).

A general finding of comparative research on writing using word processing versus traditional tools is that writers plan more when writing with pen and paper and less when writing with computers, as noted, for example, by Jean Lutz (Lutz, 1987). Van Waes and Schellens (2003: 849) suggested that the inviting nature of the flashing cursor influences writers to forego planning and quickly move on to production when working on a computer. Haas (1989: 202) believed that the reason was related to the ease of making changes when using a computer keyboard, suggesting that this mode of writing encourages "fiddling."

Much has been written about writers' revision practices with pen and paper versus a word processor. Clara Lam found that writers using computers made more revisions to their texts than pen and paper writers, and observed that the patterns of revision were more recursive when writing on the electronic machine (Lam, 1991).

New (1999: 81) reviewed previous research indicating that students view computer keyboard writing as "more malleable and fluid," and also referred to studies showing that word processing seems to encourage revision of form, though, importantly, she noted hardly any paragraph format changes among the French writers who participated in the research she conducted. She commented: "The participants made a far greater proportion of local changes than global ones, despite their view, expressed via postwriting questionnaires, that ideas were important" (New, 1999: 91). Confirming this finding, Van Waes and Schellens (2003: 829) noted more high-level revision in pen-and-paper mode than when writing on a computer, and Olive et al. (2009) concurred about the tendency for computer-facilitated revision to be focused at the local level of text.

Lutz (1987: 403, 404), in her study of four professional writers and three experienced academic writers (Ph.D. students working on writing theory), and their writing in the two different modes identified three major categories of revision (both for peer-revision and own text revision). These were classified as:

- Meta-operations: making items smaller, or larger (e.g. changing a phrase to word, or vice versa) or substituting units of the same size (e.g. removing a phrase and replacing it by another phrase);
- Operations changes (adding to or removing from text, and changing the order of textual items);
- Levels changes (including changes to punctuation, paragraph, and introducing idea changes).

Lutz (1987: 410) found that writers using computers revised more at the lower linguistic levels (punctuation, word, sentence), whereas higher-level changes (including paragraph-level) were more commonly made by pen-and-paper writers.

In a contrasting set of findings, Amie Goldberg, Michael Russell, and Abigail Cook, in a meta-analysis of research on K-12 students writing with computers and with pen and paper, determined that students made more revisions when writing with computers (Goldberg et al., 2003: 18). They also found that when students used computers, "the process of producing and revising text was more integrated" (*ibid.*), in the sense that revision began earlier, was ongoing, and included more idea revision, as compared to patterns of pen-and-paper revision.

In terms of pausing patterns, Van Waes and Schellens (2003: 838, 839) determined that computer keyboard writers paused more often, with more frequent in-sentence pausing, than pen-and-paper writers. They also discovered that when pen-and-paper writers paused, they did so for a longer period of time than computer users, and that the paragraph boundary constituted 45% of their pausing time – whereas computer writers paused at the paragraph break only 20% of the time (p. 840). They suggested that this indicated not only more planning, but also more evaluation and advance revision before production when working with pen and paper to compose.

Before leaving this subject it is important to mention research by Van Waes and Schellens (2003: 846, 847) which found that writers generally changed in their behavior according to the writing tool (handwriting versus using a keyboard) with which they were working – rather than having a distinct signature, immune to the effects of writing in the different modes. Although paragraphing was not specifically mentioned in this study, one might assume that it is also affected, so that the same writer might paragraph differently according to the mode of writing.

All of the above findings seem to point to a fairly consistent pattern – using computers to write affects writing behavior. How much it affects paragraphing is not clear, however. Concerning planning, it would seem possible to argue that there may be more attention to paragraphing when writing with a pen and paper – for the reasons noted above. A fairly consistent finding reported is the tendency for revision on computers to be more locally focused, rather than globally, which suggests that paragraphs may be less of a focus in revision when writing with computers. It is important to remember, however, that the type of research, and the type of writers studied, may well be behind this finding. That is, studies of professional writing behavior using computers in which the writing manuscript evolves over days, weeks, months and even years is seriously under-represented in currently reported research. High-level revision may now be the norm for professional writers when using computers, but I am not aware of research which has actually set out to investigate this issue.

Paragraphing as Facilitative for the Writer or the Reader

As documented in the previous chapter, paragraphing is commonly understood to assist or affect the reader in various ways. For example, it has been considered to be an aid to text processing (see e.g. Ji, 2008: 1719) and an opportunity afforded to the writer to manipulate the reader in some way (Eden and Mitchell, 1986). Indentation can also be considered, in some circumstances, to provide a certain amount of helpful redundancy in a text (see Chapter 5), redundancy being a key element of readable writing according to Alice Horning (Horning, 1993).[6] Nystrand (1983: 60) pointed out that part of the contract between the writer and reader includes an understanding that the writer will mark textual boundaries and break the text into units to help the reader comprehend the message. If readers are primed to expect certain paragraphing patterns in different text types (see Haberlandt, 1982: 246, 247), then it might be considered the duty of the writer to fulfil these reader expectations, an argument that Gopen (2004) has made in his work on the paragraph. Some of the research reported in this chapter supports such a view of paragraphing, particularly references by writers (in think-aloud or retrospective accounts) to audience considerations in relation to their paragraphing decisions.

But how do such views fit in with actual writing practice? How significant are reader considerations in affecting paragraphing decisions, in the light of our current knowledge concerning the cognitive constraints under which writers compose, and which seem to materially affect the writing process? Might it not be the case that paragraphing conventions are primarily to assist the writer in managing the writing process, rather than a means to help readers comprehend a message?

Of course, one may choose not to adopt an either / or (reader- or writer-oriented) position with regard to the reasons for paragraphing. A psychological perspective which holds the two perspectives together is SBF. Gernsbacher (1997a), as noted in the previous chapter, suggested that data on how readers actually read paragraphs are consistent with SBF (i.e. comprehension proceeds according to the theory she developed). Gernsbacher (1997a: 294) also argued that SBF could explain discourse production data too, that is, the writer's behavior. Pausing patterns in the production of text might also be explained by this theory, being affected by the laying of foundations and the shifting and abandoning of structures.

However, a scholar who has questioned the reader-facilitating perspective of paragraphing is Heurley (1997). Heurley, as noted in passing in the previous chapter, did not believe that a writer could know enough about his / her audience to make paragraphing decisions which would be interpreted as intended. In challenging the reader-oriented view, he pointed to reader non-agreement in segmentation decisions (see Chapter 7), and the fact that paragraphs as visual units do not necessarily map onto structural units (see Chapters 1 and 4).

While Heurley (1997) did acknowledge that paragraphing could be an aid for both reader and writer, he believed indentation to always be a trace of the writing process, that is, the fundamental fact of indentation is as a trace of the writing process. Heurley provided a snow footprints metaphor to help convey his argument. Heurley noted that prints in snow – like paragraph indents – may or may not be signals for someone to follow, but they are always a trace of where the writer has been. In the same way, Heurley argued that we should not always believe the writer to have the reader in mind when paragraphing: a particular indentation may be deliberate and a guide, but at other times, it may simply be a trace of the writing process, although he believed that the two often coincide.

Heurley (1997) advanced four arguments in support of his view that the reader is not at the forefront of the writer's mind when writing. The first was that the organization of writing may simply reflect the type of information being communicated, organization being related to text type, rather than reader considerations. A process, for example, will be written in a linear manner, because this matches the essential elements of what a process is: it is not written in such a way for the sake of the reader. Secondly, he maintained that organization was strongly influenced by background knowledge – or schema. If such is the case, writing behavior is affected by the existing schema of the writer (rather than reader considerations per se). Thirdly, he argued that both long and short-term memory influence textual organization – a contention finding support in some of the data referred to above connecting cognitive constraints and paragraphing, and models of writing. The fourth argument proposed by Heurley was in relation to planning. He argued that planning is topic-oriented, and cohesion may come about incidentally while writing, rather than being planned. Heurley argued that none of these considerations are reader-oriented. Though he commented that textual organization cannot be limited to paragraph considerations per se, it seems reasonable to include paragraphing decisions within these four considerations.

Heurley (1997) developed the concept of the information block, which he differentiated from the orthographic paragraph. In his view, the orthographic paragraph may be considered to be a signaling device primarily for the reader (though is not so always), whereas information blocks – which may or may not coincide with orthographic paragraphs – are the products of the writer's encoding processes. This view sits well alongside research reported above – particularly regarding pausing at episode boundaries and at the locations of framing devices, not just at paragraph breaks. Specifically, it can be argued that the orthographic paragraph is not the only planning unit within text nor the only unit within which revision occurs.

Heurley's view is a rather interesting one, and his skepticism of an exclusively reader-oriented view of paragraphing does seem justified to an extent. However, I suggest that two issues need further consideration within his argument. Firstly, Matsuhashi (1981) noted that different types of text tend to have different audience orientations. Although Heurley believed that textual organization might mirror the nature of the thing being discussed (e.g. a linear process is reported in a linear way, the first of his four points noted above), he did not go on to consider how the nature of the communication may be more or less audience-oriented by its very nature. Matsuhashi (1981: 116) suggested that expressing feelings or opinions is primarily a writer-oriented activity ("The writing remains close to the self"), whereas reporting and generalizing are information-oriented, and persuading is reader-oriented. Accordingly, in writing a persuasive argument, it would seem reasonable to argue that writers may be more reader-oriented as they write (this orientation possibly affecting textual signaling and considerations of paragraphing).

Secondly, Heurley's work does not take into account some of the research noted within this chapter, particularly findings which suggest that paragraphing may, initially, be writer-oriented and then shift to become reader-oriented over time, through the revision process. Heurley (1997: 195) did mention revision in his work, but only from the writer perspective (i.e. not according to reader considerations):

> When revising a draft before writing the definite version of a text, one can add, delete or modify some parts of an existing information block. In this case, the resulting information block must be considered as the trace of two or more encoding episodes.

It is important to state that paragraphing decisions may change, and paragraphs may appear and disappear. Heurley's snow print metaphor is essentially linear, and in this regard it does not take into account the walker turning back, covering his / her tracks and making new ones. There is always the possibility that the final (probably more reader-oriented) textual product is quite different from the initial writer-trace product, because of revision. What I am suggesting here is that actual writing processes are perhaps more fluid and multi-layered than Heurley's metaphor suggests.

Conclusion

To date, not much attention has been focused on how writers paragraph their texts, and it is clear from the attempt made above to better understand this process that detail and solid findings are rather thin in many important areas of investigation. The fact that a considerable number of variables seem to affect how people write would suggest that paragraphing decisions are complex, making it difficult to provide generalized statements or propose universal rules to be followed. However, given this caveat, below I attempt to categorize and summarize the key issues which have arisen in this chapter.

Firstly, paragraphing does not seem to be a unique or wholly independent activity in the writing process. Some writers may plan in ideas, rather than in paragraphs, and even though pen and paper writers may plan more than computer users, this does not necessarily mean that they spend more time on considerations of paragraphing. Pausing phenomena, often considered to be indicative of planning decisions, are not tied to paragraph breaks. That is, writers exhibit extended pausing patterns throughout text, both within and between paragraphs. While the paragraph may be a unit of planning and revision, it is not so exclusively: long pauses also occur within paragraphs, are associated with episodes and framing decisions, and may possibly mirror the rhetorical structure of the text. Although writers' pause patterns do not necessarily map onto their paragraph patterns, the fact that paragraphs are places for pausing in the writing process suggests the writer's use of the paragraph break as a place to consider progress so far, or for planning, with such considerations being more or less reader-oriented. However, the fact that extended pausing is not limited to the paragraph break challenges 19th century views of the paragraph as the main higher-level unit of planning.

Secondly, paragraphing revision happens, though it is unclear how often. Writers who revise their texts may make paragraphing changes at any time throughout their writing process. Low-level revision seems to be more frequent when using a computer, whereas high-level revision is more associated with pen-and-paper writing, but as mentioned earlier the research data supporting these claims may be a product of the kind of research conducted. There are various factors which impact our revision processes. These differences may be related to visual / spatial considerations. The writer's level of proficiency also plays a role in how writing is managed. It also seems reasonable to argue that "knowledge crafting" writers (Kellogg, 2008) may well think about indentation more than writers who are more focused on simply transcribing their ideas. I suggest that the paragraph unit as a trace of the writing process may well be a reality in writing performed at a lower level, with a greater degree of mapping of indentation decisions to reader considerations in writing performed at an advanced level. Further, we should allow for an advanced level writer to proceed in a similar way through drafts of writing, with initial writer-trace indentations changed to reader-focused indentations when reviewing and revising.

Thirdly, paragraphing pedagogy such as that advocated by Christensen (1965, 1966) does not seem to match typical writing patterns. Neither, on the other hand, do views which suggest that paragraphing is accomplished largely within editing or revision processes (e.g. Rodgers 1965; 1966a,b). The variables which affect writing processes are many, and it is not unreasonable to suppose that these affect aspects of paragraphing. Accordingly, I suggest a more flexible view of the place of the paragraph in the writing process be developed. In Chapter 9, I put forward seven principles to be considered when paragraphing, and suggest that different writers may usefully consider these principles before writing, while writing, or after writing. At the same time, I note that there may be specific principles which are valuable for the majority of writers to consider at particular points in the composing process.

Notes

1   I borrow the term "prevision" here from Murray (1978: 86)
2   These were summarized by Manchón and de Larios (2007: 550) as conceptualization of the message and access to syntactic representation leading to the production of sentences and lexical items.
3   It should be noted, however, that Janet Emig's often-cited study (Emig, 1971) was a significant challenge to the linear process idea of writing and that her article, though it did not focusing exclusively on revision, was written before Murray's.
4   Spelman Miller (2002a: 259) classified pause locations as sentence completion point, clause completion point, intermediate constituent point, word completion point, and character completion point. The long pauses she was interested in were at clause and sentence completion points (Spelman Miller, 2000: 133).
5   Admittedly, this looking back in text could be related solely to looking for ideas, in which case it would be related to planning.
6   Horning's (1993) work focused primarily on psycholinguistic redundancy and cohesion in text, and how these aid the reader. In making the comment above about indentation in relation to textual redundancy, I extend the notion of redundancy beyond Horning's focus on cohesion.

9   Wrapping up the Paragraph

Introduction

In Chapter 1, I outlined various possible understandings of what the paragraph break and the paragraph unit are and do from both product (i.e. text) and process (i.e. reader and writer) perspectives. In addition, I provided a brief overview of issues surrounding paragraphing pedagogy. Throughout Chapters 2 to 8, numerous research findings, ideas, theories, and pedagogies relevant to our goal of understanding the paragraph and paragraphing have been presented, discussed, and critiqued as necessary.

In this chapter, I seek to wrap up this study by returning to the issues introduced in Chapter 1, in addition to briefly considering contrastive studies of the paragraph in languages other than English. The outline of the chapter is as follows. Firstly, I reconsider each of the perspectives on the paragraph and paragraphing mentioned in the first chapter in the light of the material discussed in the remainder of the book and evaluate the usefulness of each one in turn. Secondly, I (re)define the paragraph from three perspectives: text, reader, and writer. Three new definitions of the paragraph appear to be necessary, as existing definitions have tended to blur issues through attempting to combine different foci. Thirdly, I address the issue of pedagogy, mentioned in various chapters throughout the book (particularly, in Chapters 3 and 4), and do this by advancing a descriptivist pedagogy of paragraphing, an alternative approach to current prescriptivist and laissez faire approaches. Fourthly, I provide a brief overview of some contrastive work on the paragraph in other languages, and do this to heighten awareness of the relationship between culture, thought, discipline, and language. Finally, I close the chapter, and the book as a whole, by suggesting a number of areas where future research may help further our knowledge and understanding of the paragraph and paragraphing.

Reconsidering Perspectives on the Paragraph

The paragraph is a block of text, and the break or paragraph juncture is part of what defines that block, separating one textual unit from another. As mentioned in Chapter 1, the block and juncture need to be understood together, although different perspectives on the paragraph have tended to focus on one or other entity. I reconsider the perspectives discussed in Chapter 1 here (divided into two broad camps) in the light of the overviews provided over the last seven chapters.

The Paragraph Break

The paragraph break: A big period

In terms of readers' reading behavior, there is some truth to the big period view of a paragraph break, in the sense that like the "little period" it represents a break point at the end of an orthographic unit, the difference between the two being the size of the unit marked off. It is evident that readers often pause for a longer period of time after a paragraph-closing sentence as compared to their pause time after a sentence within a paragraph. Writers also tend to pause for longer after they finish writing a paragraph than after they finish writing a sentence. The reasons for these pauses, as discussed in Chapters 7 and 8, may be linked to cognitive easing and cognitive wrap-up (i.e. a juncture being a good place to complete incomplete mental processing), prosody (i.e. closing the rhythm of the text), and structure building. However, there are problems with the "big period" view of the paragraph break.

Firstly, extended pausing is not a phenomenon limited to paragraph junctures in either reading or writing. Pausing for writers can also be related to instances of framing within paragraphs or to shifts in episode or rhetorical structure which do not co-occur with the orthographic paragraph, and for the reader, pausing may occur on encountering certain words within any part of a text. Secondly, the "big period" perspective cannot adequately account for the fact that a paragraph break, may, at times, be indistinguishable from the sentence break, in terms of its management of textual flow and the semantics of the text. While the paragraph break does have the potential to signal a radical shift to a new topic – such potential possibly being confirmed by an adverbial clause, introduction of a new subject, or other topic-signaling device – at other times the shift from one paragraph to another seems to be indistinguishable from semantic shifts between sentences within the same paragraph. This may be especially true for certain types of writing other than expository type. As Goutsos (1997) indicated, one should not consider the paragraph break in journalistic news to be like that in expository text: while in the latter the semantic shift between paragraphs might be considered comparable to a "big period" in the sense that the paragraph break signals a break-point between a group of sentences, this may not be so in the former, where the movement from one paragraph to the next might, to all intents and purposes, be indistinguishable from shifts between sentences. In sum, there may be some truth in the "big period" analogy for some genre types, but this is an inadequate and incomplete view of the paragraph and paragraphing.

The paragraph break: A discourse-managing technique

For the writer, the paragraph break is one of many tools that may be used to manage the text by framing and closing topics. However, a problem with the discourse-managing view of the paragraph break is that this function is dependent on other factors: the paragraph break does not manage alone. It would be more accurate to argue that the paragraph break has the *potential* to manage the discourse when working alongside other management tools, but it may well need some kind of supportive co-signaling textual cue to confirm and / or elaborate on the detail of the shift function. If such a cue is not given, the framing and closing potential of the paragraph break may not actually be realized. Continuity relations across the paragraph break (e.g. pronominal anaphora) are difficult to explain if one gives the paragraph break a default shifting function.

For example, when the paragraph break comes just before the introduction of a new subject or before an adverbial time clause indicating a shift in time from the previous paragraph, then one can safely say that the paragraph break is framing a topic or episode shift. However, when the first sentence of a new paragraph starts with the same subject as in the previous paragraph, especially if it contains some kind of inter-paragraph linking device (e.g. anaphoric pronominal reference), and continues with the same point, then it can hardly be argued that the paragraph break is framing a new topic: the potential closing or framing function is not actually activated in such a case. In terms of the reader's engagement with text, s/he cannot know in advance what exactly a paragraph break is doing or signaling, unless the text being read is from a genre type which treats paragraph units and breaks in a very rigid and predictable way. Although such rigid and predictable signaling through paragraph breaks does occur at times, on other occasions the specific discourse-managing function of a paragraph break can only be realized when certain kinds of co-textual support are present – that is, if the text immediately preceding the break, or more commonly following the break, activates the functional potential. Accordingly, it would seem better to describe the paragraph break as a tool that has the potential for managing discourse, and for doing so in different ways, rather than being considered to be a default text managing tool.

The paragraph break: A highlighting technique

Research clearly indicates that the paragraph break affects readers: the presence of blank space or indentation within continuous text is often associated with slowing down in readers' reading patterns. Whether this behavior develops through being taught to focus on the first or last sentence in a paragraph, or through reading experience, and whether it is dependent on text type, or is largely an automatic response is a matter for further research. Given the reality of longer eye fixation for some readers at the beginning and end of paragraphs, and the rereading patterns of some readers who pay special attention to first and last sentences within a text, the highlighting device perspective of the paragraph break seems reasonable, particularly when considered alongside various plausible psychological reasons for increased attention (for both reader and writer) at those textual break-points. Further, this view implicitly combines considerations of both text and break, rather than just considering the physical paragraph break, as the break cues the textual highlighting. The highlighting function of indentation has been argued historically and also more recently (e.g. Hoey and O'Donnell, 2007; Gopen, 2004).

The problem with this view is that if the paragraph break is a default highlighting tool, then key information would always be placed in paragraph-initial and paragraph-final position by writers – but it is not: the main point (if there is one) within a paragraph is not bound to be placed in one or the other of these positions. It would, accordingly, be safer to argue that the paragraph break is a potential highlighting tool, if a writer chooses to place key information in paragraph-initial and / or paragraph-final position. How conscious are writers of this potential paralinguistic supporting role of paragraph-initial and final position? Contemporary textbook writers often emphasize these positions for the placement of key information (see e.g. Wallwork, 2011: 141), and late 19th century writers did the same. If we can assume that writers are aware of this possibility, why is such awareness not translated into a default pattern of highlighting information at paragraph breaks?

I offer a tentative and rather simple suggestion as to why such a practice is only sometimes exploited. If the relationship between information importance and paragraph position were always exploited by writers, readers would probably change their reading behavior. If the highlighting of information in paragraph-initial and paragraph-final position were the standard practice, then reading would probably evolve (in perhaps a rather negative way), such that skimming which focused only on information at the beginnings and endings of paragraphs would become the new norm of reading. This might well militate against the writer's purpose to engage a reader with the complete text and to ensure that the reader does not treat it superficially. Rather than adopting a view that such highlighting is the default for paragraphing practice, I believe writers choose to punctuate their texts with occasionally significant material in such positions as required, but do so selectively, not by default, although it may be that writers have distinctive practices in this regard. Currently we do not know which genres exploit this highlighting function – though, journalistic news writing may stand out in this respect (and does seem to allow for the kind of skimming for key information that I would predict for this mode of paragraphing) – and more research would be helpful to explore this possibility in detail. As a way of understanding paragraphs, the highlighting potential view is of value, though incomplete, as it fails to account for other kinds of paragraphing decisions.

The paragraph break: An aesthetic device

As mentioned in Chapter 1, there is no school of thought that suggests that paragraphing is governed by purely aesthetic or page look considerations. However, the idea that paragraphing on the page should look right, and be aesthetically pleasing is as relevant a concern for writers today, noted, for instance, by John Foster (Foster, 2008: 43–44), as it was in the 19th century (see Chapter 3). The aesthetics of the page are normally considered from the reader's perspective, and typically related to possible reader response to that page. For example, an unbroken page of text or very long paragraphs have been described by Foster (2008: 43) as "unreadable," by David Hogstette (Hogsette, 2009: 78) as "quite uninviting," and by Carol Roberts as "overwhelming" for the reader (Roberts, 2004: 182).

As documented in Chapter 8, Hayes (1996), building on data from Bond and Hayes' (1984) research into reader segmentation of de-paragraphed text, suggested that visual / spatial factors affected readers' ideas of where paragraph breaks should exist in text. Extrapolating this finding, Hayes believed that writers carry around with them, in their short-term memories an awareness of the physical spatial layout of text, this knowledge interacting with other cognitive processes, long-term memory and the task environment and thereby affecting indentation decisions. As Bodle (2015) has noted, paragraphing practice seems to be adapting to the challenges in reading e-text, and the size of the reading artifact and writers are writing shorter paragraphs in some e-texts accordingly. As mentioned in Chapter 8, the influence of physical factors in influencing text production is a growing research area. The decision to indent is influenced by the aesthetics of the page, but how exactly, is poorly understood.

The Paragraph Unit

The paragraph: A formal grammatical unit (a big sentence, or a little essay)

The various attempts to theorize the orthographic paragraph as a formal unit, discussed in Chapters 4 and 7, have, I suggest, failed to establish their cases. Indeed, one can interpret early redefinitions of paragraphs as structural units as an admission that the orthographic unit cannot be so theorized. Yet some recent research does seem to indicate that specific texts within certain genres may contain paragraphs which could be considered formal units, though perhaps not as traditionally understood.

It is the case that some paragraphs have a set form related to their role within a larger structure of text. Thus, some paragraphs are made up of a topic sentence, supporting sentences, and a concluding sentence, although the prevalence of such formally defined, topically organized paragraph units outside of some educational contexts is open to question. Further, some paragraphs comprise Problem–Solution patterns or Topic Restriction Illustration patterns, as Becker (1965) argued. However, one cannot generalize these findings and argue that (all) expository paragraphs are formal units as Becker and others tried to do on the basis of data from segmentation studies and some of the questionable methodologies employed in that research (see Chapter 7). What is needed is a more genre-sensitive and empirically based approach to the formal unit concept of the paragraph, as I suggested in Chapter 4.

Since the 1970s, data from computational linguistic and corpus linguistic research suggest that specific paragraphs within certain genres may well contain predictable functional units signaled lexically or grammatically (as Becker suggested). The opening sentence or sentences of a specific paragraph within a particular genre type may be considered to perform a particular function, this being signaled through the use of a grammatical frame (e.g. full NP in subject theme position), and / or rhetorical or lexical elements (e.g. adverbials or discourse markers), or even the absence of certain elements (e.g. pronominal anaphora) in such positions. Although Rodgers may well have been right to argue that Becker's TRI and PS tagmeme patterns were discourse, rather than paragraph, patterns, one need not give up on the paragraph being a formal unit, at times. It may well be that particular functions in text are paragraph-position specific, and the work of Hoey has been important in highlighting the lexical and grammatical colligational properties of paragraphs, i.e. the signals of textual development. Computational work has also recognized the formulaic ways in which paragraphs may begin and end, and hinted, at times, at signals of internal paragraph development, although this work has not been conducted from full-blown functional perspectives.

Unfortunately, outside of some computational and corpus linguistic work, the paragraph is rarely mentioned in mainstream genre analysis research. I suggest that the only way to address Brown and Yule's (1983) largely forgotten plea to locate paragraph theorizing firmly within the discipline of genre analysis and discourse analysis is for genre-focused studies to put more focus on formatting and textual design issues (specifically, paragraphing) in discussing macrolinguistic functions, rather than focusing on moves alone. If this were to happen, we might well get closer to a position where the formal status of certain paragraphs in texts from particular genres could be established. Recent computational work has hinted at this possibility, but it is up to genre analysts or cross-disciplinary researchers to investigate this issue further. In sum, at the present time, the orthographic paragraph is not best considered a formal unit in the way that Becker (1965, 1966) and Christensen (1965, 1966) suggested. However, work such as that conducted by Crossley et al. (2011; see Chapter 6), has, I believe, shown a way forward for a formal view of paragraphing to be developed, within specific genres.

The paragraph: An aid to text structuring

The "considerately paragraphed"' text, in some ways analogous to embossing the outline of a picture, is one in which the textual linguistic divisions (e.g. rhetorical structure shifts) are marked as such by the use of paragraph breaks, perhaps alongside clear paragraph-initial signals of developmental intent, function, or content. The five-paragraph essay can possibly be viewed as the considerately paragraphed text par excellence, with a division between paragraphs clearly signaling and mapping rhetorical, functional, and / or thematic shift. There are sound reasons behind such paragraphing decisions, as there appear to be clear benefits resulting for some readers, especially weaker readers, in mapping such texts in this way, as mentioned in Chapter 7. Such paragraphing decisions can be considered to guide the reader to make the connections and shifts within the ongoing discourse, indentation being a paralinguistic attempt to manage the reader's behavior by exploiting known reading behavior (i.e. focus and attention) at paragraph-initial and paragraph-final position to serve the writer's purpose and the intended message of the text.

However, as has been noted throughout this book, the paragraph break cannot be reduced to playing this function – it refuses to be so straitjacketed. Why is this? There are a number of reasons. The first, I believe, is related to the potential highlighting function of the paragraph break discussed earlier. Simply put, a writer might decide to highlight *any* element of the text: to indicate a point as being of particular importance, little understood, or often forgotten, for example. This function is unlike the text-structuring perspective being discussed here because highlighting is not predictable, whereas textual mapping is relatively predictable. When a writer maps the textual shifts with paragraph breaks, the writer guides the reader. However, when a writer chooses to indent a particular part of the text which would not normally or necessarily be considered a unit, the writer is able to manipulate the reader (in the sense of affecting the reader's attention and focus regarding the significance of the material so indented), rather than just guiding the reader.

Secondly, this rather simple view of paragraphing does not take into account the problematic issue of managing real text and the delivery of a message. When writing a five-paragraph essay, the quantity of material that can be managed is affected by the format: format determines content. In a five-paragraph essay, the writer cannot have 42 points in support of a position contained within a paragraph and three points against it in another paragraph. The issue is that the decided-upon format constrains the quantity of material included and its treatment. Other genres, however, may well give a writer the opportunity to develop the 42 points – but the formatting (i.e. paragraphing) will be affected accordingly. Thus, the content often determines the paragraphing rather than the other way around. It was noted in Chapter 3 that several paragraphs may group together, and this grouping may be signaled and managed by a major topic sentence in the first paragraph. Paragraphing is not solely governed by the subject matter, but also its management, whether management is considered in relation to the reader (who may not appreciate long paragraphs) or in relation to the writer (who may find it easier to manage shorter paragraphs, given the cognitive constraints affecting the writer process).

Thirdly, as mentioned in Chapter 7, there is the argument that a less "considerate" text (and within this category we may wish to include indentation decisions that do not necessarily map a shift in RST, or a move in genre analysis, etc.) might actually be a better text from the point of view of its potential to result in deeper comprehension or learning for some readers. As mentioned in Chapter 7, providing all of the scaffolding structures within the text (including formulaic paragraph introductions, and close mapping of orthographic structures and textual functions) may result in a more superficial and less attentive engagement with the text by the reader. Anyone who has read 19th century (or earlier) commentaries or essays, in which writers make scant use of such scaffolding structures, knows that a lot is being asked of the reader, who faces long detailed paragraphs. Mentally, readers adjust their concentration and cognitive engagement in such situations. A writer may at times, and for many reasons, want the textual product to be more reader-responsible than writer-responsible – although the latter is typically considered to be the norm in writing in the English language today, as discussed later in this chapter. However, there is probably a cline in this regard. Writers may consider it their duty to avoid any possibility of ambiguity, and make the reading experience as comfortable as possible for the reader on one polar position on the cline. On the other side, a writer may choose to make the reading experience less (narrowly logically) mapped, not because of insensitivity to reader needs, but rather as a means to fully engage the reader. Different genres may be more or less "reader-friendly" (in a possibly superficial sense) in terms of their paragraphing patterns mapping discrete textual semantic or functional units, and this is an area of study requiring more research.

In sum, I believe that writers may choose to map developments in rhetorical structure, topics or moves with paragraph indentation. However, this is just a role that the paragraph break has, and paragraphing will not be limited to playing this role alone: writers refuse to be bound by such a limited view of what paragraphing does; and readers also know, and indeed expect, paragraphing to be more varied than this, as the research reviewed in Chapter 7 indicated.

The paragraph: A cohesive unit

As discussed in Chapter 3, the idea of paragraph unity is problematic. The possibility that the concept of cohesion may help concretize or objectivize unity was discussed in Chapter 6. As documented there computational linguists have been quite successful in utilizing the presence of various cohesive devices (predominantly lexical) in text to help identify the paragraphs within a text. However, the measures employed to track and calculate cohesivity have typically involved complex algorithms or computer system training. As observed in Chapter 6, the automatic identification of a paragraph unit or break by computational algorithms is not at all related to an eyeball test of textual cohesive ties (see Figure 6.1): only complex algorithms can help identify paragraphs or paragraph breaks. As Berber-Sardinha (1997) documented, some of these measures disregard aspects of the actual text in their procedures of operation, thereby losing connection with the original text (e.g. discounting the actual sentences in the text, as is the case in TextTiling). As mentioned in Chapter 6, there may be no cohesive devices present between adjacent sentences within the same paragraph, but the relationship between them is evident to the reader, and there may or may not be strong cohesive links between paragraphs. For example, some instances of inter-paragraph topic foregrounding will result in strong cohesive links being present across the paragraph break. Another problem with the cohesive identity view of the paragraph unit is that the cohesion may extend beyond the paragraph to a clearly identifiable larger textual unit – in which case a particular paragraph is not, by itself, a cohesive unit, but is rather an incomplete part of a larger cohesive unit (e.g. in the case in which three paragraphs constitute an identifiable part of the text). A final argument against the value of a cohesive unit understanding of the paragraph is that the reader and writer are, arguably, more focused on the larger issue of textual coherence, and the contribution of a particular paragraph or group of paragraphs to that, rather than intra-paragraph cohesion per se. I believe that all of these issues are problematic in terms of considering the paragraph as a cohesive unit.

I suggest that the most useful thing that can be said about paragraph cohesion is in relation to the kinds of cohesive links that exist between and within paragraphs: namely, these patterns within the same text may well be different. For example, pronominal anaphora may be less common across some paragraph breaks than between sentences within paragraphs in the same genre. Some discourse markers may be less commonly used to connect sentences across the paragraph juncture than to connect sentences within the same paragraph (e.g. *but*). Patterns of cohesive relations within and between paragraphs have not been studied in any great deal; all we can say with confidence is that cohesive patterns seem to be affected by the paragraph break. The reason for possibly different patterns of cohesion within and between paragraphs may be related to reader psychology, but when, how, and why cohesive links do, or do not, cross the paragraph juncture is not a particularly well-researched, or well-understood area at the current time (perhaps with the exception of pronominal anaphora studies). This being so, the view that the paragraph is a unit defined by its cohesion, though interesting, does not seem to be a very useful or meaningful perspective of paragraphing for educators.

The Paragraph Break and Unit: A Cognitive-easing Device (for Writer and Reader)

The processing of paragraphs, whether how they are read or how they are written, is a necessary consideration in trying to understand paragraphs and paragraphing, as the final written product is constrained by factors influencing the writing process, and the effect of indentation on the reading process. Historical treatments of the paragraph did not, generally speaking, incorporate such a perspective into their theorizing of the paragraph, but newer research tools (e.g. eye-tracking technology and keystroke logging) have facilitated research into paragraph processing.

Research on the writing of paragraphs is still in its infancy, but it is clear that paragraphing decisions may be more or less reader-focused, in terms of the motivation to indent. On the one hand, some paragraphing decisions are, it seems, solely related to a writer's management of the text, and should, accordingly, be considered a trace of the writing process, perhaps influenced by cognitive considerations or fatigue. These original writer-indentation patterns may or may not be changed if and when the text is revised. If indentations change, this may be for a number of reasons: the writer may believe intention is not best served by a particular indentation decision or paragraph development pattern; the writer may consider there to be a better way of formatting the message; or a writer may be influenced by page look, and accordingly, consider how to revise the text. It seems that individual writing style, degree of writing maturity, the genre type being written (and how reader-oriented it is), and the medium of composition all play a role in affecting how writers paragraph their texts. However, at the current time, the importance and effect of each of these factors on a writer's paragraphing and paragraphing revision are poorly understood.

A little more is known about how readers experience paragraphs, but as outlined in Chapter 7, this is not a simple issue: there are different ways to interpret pause and slow-down phenomena, and different reading styles affect how paragraphs are read. Further, as argued in Chapter 7, it is necessary to consider the reader's interaction with the paragraph's organization and indentation alongside six other factors which play a role in affecting the reader's experience of the text and the paragraphs within it.

In sum, it is essential to consider process elements when considering the paragraph and paragraphing. Our current state of knowledge adds something to the debate, but it must be acknowledged that highly complex multi-layered operations affect how people write and read paragraphs. Our view of the textual paragraph and paragraphing should try to incorporate process elements – albeit this can only be at a basic level at the current time, given our limited knowledge.

Three Definitions of the Paragraph

Why am I proposing three definitions of the paragraph? As mentioned earlier, some definitions of the paragraph confuse what the textual paragraph is with the writer's intention in writing it and its effect on the reader. For example, as discussed in Chapter 3, the term "unity" was used in early paragraph theorizing, but it was noted to be problematic: the concept was used in teaching paragraphing pedagogy to writers, was supposedly a characteristic of text, but may be more accurately stated to be a subjective reader judgment in response to a text. Both Angus' (1862: 401) and Crystal's (2001: 249) definitions of the paragraph seem to mix reader, writer, and textual viewpoints. With regard to a textual definition, as mentioned in Chapter 1, and as argued throughout this book, it is necessary to consider the orthographic unit's relationship to other sentential or suprasentential units within the text, be these grammatical, functional, semantic or pragmatic (e.g. stadia, blocs, episodes, and moves) not just in isolation. Turning to writer-oriented and reader-oriented definitions of the paragraph, processing considerations need to be incorporated into our definitions of paragraphing, even though these may not be well understood at the current time. Accordingly, below I propose a text-oriented definition, a reader-oriented and a writer-oriented definition of the paragraph and paragraphing to safeguard against confusing what the paragraph and paragraphing are, what writers may try to make of them, and how readers experience them. These definitions are attempts to cover the main research findings discussed throughout the book in a concise way, and while keeping product and process perspectives separate, acknowledge their inter-relatedness.

A Text-Oriented Definition of the Paragraph

A text-oriented definition of the paragraph needs to consider the textual product – both the unit and how it is linked to other paragraph units, and also how it relates to other kinds of structural, functional or semantic units within the text. Accordingly, I provide the extended definition below.

Except when it occurs as a solitary unit, or in a few kinds of marginal, non-paragraphed types of print text such as captions or various kinds of lists, a paragraph is an incomplete part of a (longer) print text, marked off from one or two other paragraphs by various conventional means (e.g. indentation, white space, pilcrow). Conventions governing indentation practices are genre specific and sanctioned by discourse community norms: practices are not universal.

When considered as an orthographic unit, the paragraph may or may not correspond to one or more recognized suprasentential structural or functional units within the text (e.g. blocs, stadia, moves, rhetorical structure). Whether mapping occurs between these entities is largely governed by genre conventions, and writer intention. Genre conventions also influence the length, function(s), development style and textual characteristics of specific paragraphs within the text. When a paragraph is composed of two or more sentences, intra-paragraph relations may be signaled by various means, including grammatical and lexical cohesive devices, metadiscourse and discourse markers, and also evident through coordination and subordination / superordination relations.

In a multi-paragraphed text, a paragraph is linked to another paragraph or paragraphs (previous or following), either by surface-textual means or implicitly through its positioning. The nature of the relationship between two or more paragraphs is largely governed by genre conventions, with some room for a writer's individual and creative decisions. The relationship between two paragraph units may be continuous or discontinuous in terms of the particular theme, episode, function, or rhetorical structure being developed at that point in text. A paragraph may be linked to another by the same cohesive means as those found operating within a paragraph, though the patterns or frequencies of signaling relations between paragraph units may be markedly different from the inter-sentential links found within the same paragraph in a particular genre.

Possible indentation functions include mapping an aspect of the textual structure of the text, framing and closing topic shift, or highlighting the importance of material within a particular paragraph (e.g. in a short paragraph) or the textual material present at the paragraph-juncture. The function of paragraph indentation at any particular time is made clear through the use of paragraph-closing and paragraph-initiating language, which may confirm, elaborate on, or disconfirm various potential paragraph break functions.

A Reader-Oriented Definition of the Paragraph

A reader-oriented definition of the paragraph will take into account how readers process paragraphs, their expectations, cognition, and reading styles.

Readers expect certain genres to be divided into paragraphs. Readers who are familiar with the formatting and textual development conventions of a particular genre are aware of the possible functions associated with a paragraph break within it, these expectations being confirmed or challenged by paragraph-final and paragraph-initial language. Reader expectations on encountering a paragraph break may extend to sensitivities concerning where certain lexis, phrases, rhetorical devices, and grammatical patterns will occur within a particular paragraph and between paragraphs.

The effect of a paragraph break on a reader is mediated by the reader's reading style, content and formal schemas, time spent on and purpose in reading the text, and whether the reader appreciates wider semantic (e.g. main point secondary point differentiation) and / or functional textual considerations (e.g. appreciating cause-effect relations between textual segments). Depending on the interactions among these variables, reader comprehension and learning from a text may be positively, neutrally, or negatively affected by a particular indentation decision or method of paragraph development. As such, one cannot make universal statements concerning how a particular indentation within text will help readers.

Part of a reader's expectation when reading a paragraph is that it will be coherent within the context of the complete text, contributing to the development of the ongoing discourse. Readers may expect certain paragraphs within a text to be more important than others, and they may focus on certain parts of particular paragraphs because of similar expectations about the importance of material in those locations. A reader may pause between paragraphs, or just after paragraph-initial material, to help manage the mental representation of the text being developed.

A Writer-Oriented Definition of the Paragraph

A writer-oriented definition of the paragraph is one which considers how indentation decisions, and paragraph development decisions are part of the writing process.

Writers may divide a text into paragraphs for four reasons. These reasons are related to: the mental processes involved in managing the production of a text; the writer's attempts, whether conscious or subconscious, to conform to genre conventions; the writer's deliberate intention to guide or manipulate the reader in some way; or for page-look, and aesthetic considerations. The latter basis for paragraphing is not arbitrary but governed by the other textual considerations.

Some paragraph breaks may best be considered to be traces of the writing process, possibly being undone in later revisions, and reflecting processes in thinking or writing. Other paragraph breaks are made for more intentional purposes. In these cases writers' motivations for indenting text are typically confirmed, elaborated upon, or weakened by their use of specific types of paragraph-initial lexis, rhetorical devices, or sentence structure / grammar. The writer may choose to map indentation decisions with one or more of the following: lexical or grammatical signals of topic or episode shift or continuity, some other aspect of the rhetorical structure of the text, a textual segment considered important, or a genre move or moves within the text. In all of these cases, such collateral mapping via multiple discourse signals and semantic or functional considerations is largely genre-governed.

When a writer makes a more considered and deliberate decision concerning mapping or non-mapping of paragraph breaks onto semantic or functional features of text, this will be done in the hope or expectation that the reader of the text will interpret an aspect of the text in a specifically intended way, although the author cannot guarantee such a response. Writers may or may not plan their paragraphs in advance of their writing, and they may or may not revise their paragraphing decisions extensively, either during their writing, or when making final edits. Factors influencing a writer's approach to and practice of paragraphing include: familiarity with the genre, the characteristics of the genre itself (e.g. in terms of its structural formulaicity and other conventions relating to paragraphing), writer style and expertise, audience considerations, and the mode of writing (pen and paper or computer).

Towards a Descriptivist Pedagogy of Paragraphing

The definitions given above may not be considered to be of particular value to writing instructors, who might question the usefulness of these definitions in an educational context, as they are not framed for pedagogical exploitation. In what follows, I consider the same points mentioned in these definitions, from an educational perspective, and seek to repackage them for use by educators. On the basis of the material covered within this book, I consider it necessary that a descriptivist pedagogy cover the following seven issues:

1. Genre sensitivity in discussing paragraphing
2. Paragraphing as a cognitive aid to the writer
3. Legitimate variation in paragraphing of the same text
4. Supra-paragraph textual units
5. The mapping or non-mapping of orthographic paragraph units and structural or functional textual units
6. Inter-paragraph cohesive linking
7. The paragraph's existence, purpose, or role within the wider text

A vehicle which may be more appreciated by teachers and learners in dealing with the above issues is the analogy. Accordingly, below I present seven analogies around a ball-and-panel image as an analogy to a text-and-paragraph image which I believe may help instructors and learners come to grips with paragraphing in a wide range of educational contexts, whether first- or second-language, school or tertiary educational contexts (see also McGee, 2016, on these points).

Genre Sensitivity in Discussing Paragraphing

Rules govern how sports are conducted; (often) unwritten rules determine how different genres are written.

The importance of locating the paragraph and paragraphing within genre conventions and discourse-community norms and purposes of designing, signposting, and organizing text cannot be overstated. General comments about paragraphs, starting with those made by Alexander Bain, had one thing in common: they tended to divorce genre conventions, writer purposes, and specific discourse communities' social goals from discussion of the paragraph unit. Once the paragraph lost its contextual grounding, it became a discrete characteristics-based entity, an entity which, in hindsight, has not been a particularly helpful one and has moreover distracted many in the educational writing community for a long time.

Balls used in sports (e.g. baseball, cricket, football, and soccer) have changed size, shape, and material according to developments in technology, and as a response to problems encountered in different sports. For example, external lacing on old soccer balls was considered something of a menace by players who would head the ball – if the lace was going to come into contact with the player's forehead he could have been cut as a result. As soon as the technology of ball production could do away with this lacing, the ball was, accordingly, adapted. Likewise, paragraphing needs to be considered a grounded phenomenon, responding to discourse community changes, purposes and goals, and the availability of new tools to effect those purposes.

Learners need to be made aware of the fact that discourse communities choose to structure texts in different ways. Such awareness might include sensitivity to the use of more or less explicit cues to structure the text at microstructural and macro-structural levels. Rather than considering paragraph structure as a given, paragraphing should be considered both as an aspect of the challenge that a novice writer faces, and also as one of the aids available to a writer for conveying a message. A speaker draws on volume, tone, stress, and speed of speech to help construct an utterance, but a writer does not have these paralinguistic aids to draw on in composing a message. However, indentation and paragraph development patterns can be used to great effect: the various potentialities of the paragraph break and structure, in collaboration with other micro- and macro-structuring devices, need to be appreciated by novice writers as they see how these are put into effect in particular genres.

Paragraphing as a Cognitive Aid to the Writer

Ball manufacturers often use panels to help make a ball; writers normally compose text with the help of paragraphs.

It seems that some early Greek paragraphing practices were for the benefit of the reader of a text: marks were put on a text, post-creation, to help in the reading out loud of a message, the paragraph marking aiding in the prosodic aspect of the oral delivery of the text. Today, paragraphing decisions are usually made while writing and revising, rather than at the very end of text production. The reasons behind paragraphing decisions are many. However, an often overlooked reason is that paragraphing helps a writer manage the complex activity of composing text. Just as panels can be stitched together to create a bigger entity, as in the sections of a baseball or football, so too, paragraphs are manageable units that a writer can stitch together to help create a complete text. The challenging task of whole text creation can be more easily managed by the writer working with a number of paragraphs. We know that some writers think in paragraphs and consider in which paragraph certain information might best be placed. We also know that many writers utilize the paragraph juncture as a place to pause for further reflection within the larger writing process, whether reviewing what has been written or planning what is to come. The reason for this pausing may be related to managing the cognitively complex writing process, and many initial (i.e. first-draft) paragraphing decisions may simply be records of a writer's thought processes. These original paragraph breaks may remain, or they may be changed at a later stage in the writing process, as the writer thinks more about the reader's reception of the text or notes a mismatch between intention and textual reality, and revises the text accordingly. However, even if the initial paragraphing decisions are undone, these initial decisions should not be considered irrelevant, but rather a necessary step on the way to the production of the final product. Learners need to be encouraged to think how paragraphs can help them in their writing.

Legitimate Variation in Paragraphing of the Same Text

A particular kind of ball can be paneled in various ways; a particular text can often be paragraphed (meaningfully) in different ways.

Because paragraphing is sometimes taught in a rather wooden and rigid way, it may not be obvious to some learners that texts may be paragraphed in different ways. In fact, there are writing exercises in some manuals and workbooks in which a learner is challenged to divide the text into paragraphs units, and there is only one correct answer. The whole rationale behind text segmentation studies seems to challenge the idea of legitimate variation: readers are assumed to be able to reparagraph a text according to the original indentation decisions. However, as argued some time ago by Scott and Denney (1895), but largely forgotten since, many texts can be paragraphed (meaningfully) in various ways.

As noted in Chapter 2, different editors of ancient Latin poet and satirist, Horace, paragraphed his work differently, and as observed in paragraph segmentation studies, readers may not agree with each other when faced with a text segmentation task. Is this a problem? Far from it. Some texts may be considered to be more predictably paragraphed, and others less so. Unpredictable paragraphs are problematic to those who have argued for the formal status of the paragraph, but it is this unpredictability and associated multifunctionality that makes paragraphing more interesting and creative than often considered. I believe that the original author of a text will (at least at times) segment a de-paragraphed version of his / her own final published text rather differently from the original paragraphing decisions. A legitimate conclusion to be drawn from such a finding would be that in spite of subject matter shift and surface level textual cues being there to help the original writer-reader identify where breaks occurred, the author is not able to retrace the original processing decisions which took place at a particular time and place, and which influenced the paragraphing of that particular text. In other words, the fact that one and the same author may not insert paragraph breaks at the same points, even in his / her own text, suggests that the factors determining paragraphing decisions are potentially variable and also that their relative importance or weight varies for reasons which have yet to be studied. At the same time, the range of variation may not be very great for some genres, or indeed for some writers.

Considering the analogy to balls in sports, soccer balls today are paneled in various ways, including hexagons, pentagons, and isolated icosahedrons. However, this is not the case with other balls in other sports, which have a more standard design: the four-panel American football, the baseball or the tennis ball for example. The range of variation in design in each case is partly a matter of ease of construction, and tradition, but also a matter of the allowable range of variation before the functionality of the ball would be affected. In the same way today, some texts are more open to varied paragraphing decisions and others are more standard and predictable. Accordingly, learners need to be aware of the freedoms they have (or do not have) when it comes to paragraphing their texts – not only in the number of paragraphs they might use, but also in the way in which paragraphs are developed.

Supra-paragraph Textual Units in Text

A number of panels on a ball may be grouped together in a series; two or more paragraphs may constitute a larger unit within a text.

Paragraphs are discrete typographic units, but it would be wrong to think this means that a paragraph is a self-contained unit: the perception of unity (howsoever defined) may turn out to be a mirage. While an individual paragraph within a text may be the only one to mention and elaborate on a particular point, that paragraph is still incomplete, in the sense that it is only part of a larger text, and its particular function may not be appreciated out of context. Two or more paragraphs may discuss and focus on one point, and these larger units may be considered to be identifiable units in the text. The use of subheadings or major topic sentences whose scope covers more than one paragraph may signal such inter-paragraph connectedness, along with certain types of inter-paragraph textual links.

There are a number of reasons why a series of paragraphs might be closely linked. Perhaps the most obvious is that a particular episode or topic is broken down into a series of smaller units to help the writer and reader manage the text: processing constraints affect both the production and subsequent reception of the final textual product. Rather than writing one large paragraph on a particular theme, a writer may choose to write three smaller paragraphs. As such, the paragraph break may or may not be a signal to a reader of topic shift: only when the reader receives or does not receive other discourse signaling cues around the paragraph juncture will paragraphs be kept together in the mind of the reader, and be considered part of a larger unit or, conversely, separated into different units. As such, it would be wrong to assume that the paragraph break is a signal to abandon a mental representation of text in SBF, or is necessarily linked to a significant functional or semantic shift in the text.

In terms of our sports ball analogy, volleyballs often contain series of three parallel panels, similarly shaped, constituting a distinct multi-panel entity on the surface of a ball which contains a total of 18 panels divided into six sets of three panels. I am not sure why the ball has traditionally been designed like this, but unlike some other balls, the series of three panels are quite obvious (particularly when colored the same way), and distinct. The analogy I am trying to make here is that in text a series of paragraphs may treat the same topic, or have the same function, and in that sense be like the series of panels on a volleyball which constitute a larger unit. In text, this linking between two or more paragraphs may be achieved through the use of a heading, but this need not be the case. Text may contain supra-paragraph structures made up of two or more paragraphs, and learners' ideas about paragraphing need to incorporate an understanding of the existence of such textual entities: learners need to think not only of paragraphs, but these larger structures, too.

The Mapping or Non-mapping of Orthographic Paragraph Units and Structural or Functional Textual Units

Panels on a ball may be similar or different in shape to each other, and might be colored differently, or carry designs or words/letters on them. Paragraphs in the same text may be similar or different in size or development, and texts contain indentation along with other discourse-managing tools.

The problem of non-mapping, or the idea that the paragraph breaks in a text do not necessarily delineate traditional formal textual units, or functions within the text, has been an issue of considerable discussion for academics and a real area of tension for educators. As noted in Chapter 1, this "problem" was responsible, at least in part, for Longacre's (1979) differentiation of the structural and orthographic paragraphing units, leading to the historic sidelining of the orthographic unit, not considered by some to be a viable unit for linguistic study. To recognize that paragraphing considerations are not just narrowly linguistically determined, but can have various potentialities is essential. If one fails to consider these various potentialities and forget reader and writer processing considerations, one cannot understand paragraphing. When all of these issues are considered together, a vibrant and robust picture of paragraphing emerges. Sometimes paragraphs do map onto linguistic structures which define the same size and type of unit, and this may be more common for some genres, and for some writers, than others.

It is only when one chooses to limit the function of the orthographic paragraph to linguistic mapping of some kind (rhetorical structure, move, bloc, etc.) that the misleading idea of correct versus deviant paragraphing emerges. This does not mean that a paragraphing decision may be poor, but a paragraph should only be termed such, when the decision works against author purpose (which may not be to make a text's orthographic structure map various linguistic units within a text).

Just as early indentation played various roles, so too does indentation function in different ways today, including: highlighting material deemed to be of importance to the writer; enforcing appreciation of some kind of textual unit; guiding a reader through difficult text; or manipulating expectations by breaking with various genre-developed conventions. The decision to indent throws up many more decisions, and many more opportunities for the writer – particularly language decisions around (i.e. before and after) the paragraph juncture. As such, indentation is best considered as having co-signaling potential, rather than having particular functions in and of itself. In the absence of paragraphing, text would be less rich and offer fewer functional opportunities for a writer to convey an intended message.

Considering the analogy to sports balls, soccer balls today may be rather plain, having no colors or adornment, just the panels. Such may be considered to be like the mixed paragraph unit mentioned in Chapter 1, a kind of mono-dimensional product, in which one sees paragraphs and at one and the same time one sees the major structural units within the text: there is no difference. However, when the textual structure and the paragraphs are non-aligned, this is like a sports ball which is paneled and yet has colors, logos, and patterns which may or may not correspond or map onto the ball panels. This is not a problem with a ball, and neither is it with a text, so long as there is a purpose-driven reason or reasons for non-alignment of different textual features and the orthographic unit. For example, a writer may decide to place a point which could have been put at the end of a paragraph, as a separate paragraph. As a consequence, the reader may consider this point to be particularly pertinent in the ongoing discourse: the material within this small paragraph has, in effect, been highlighted by the author as important. In a similar way, a particular panel on a ball may be gold colored, or fluorescent. At other times, a particular sentence within a paragraph may be particularly important within the ongoing discourse. This may be in the middle of a paragraph, and it may be profoundly important to the writer's argument, and significantly affect a reader. In such a case the language used within the paragraph itself makes a part of the paragraph important. In the analogy suggested here, this is like a logo printed across the panels, or indeed be like a letter on a particular panel on the ball. It is not the paragraph that is noticed by the reader so much as something in it. Certain writers' purposes may not be best served by simple structural or functional orthographic mapping. Poor paragraphing should not be considered to be because of non-parallelism between paragraphing and various functional or semantic units in text, but rather for failing to serve the writer's purposes, which may not be reducible to the creation of "firm precision" (see Chapter 3). It is the semantic, rather than the organizational, aspects of text which are of greater importance to most readers, and writers may choose to emphasize or de-emphasize the importance of their paragraph decisions in constructing their written messages.

Inter-Paragraph Cohesive Linking

> *The stitching between panels on a ball may be on the surface or hidden: connections between paragraphs may be achieved through specific linking language, or be left implicit.*

The paragraph's internal cohesiveness has been discussed often, though ideas of unity are problematic. Balancing this focus is a perspective I have tried to stress in this book – inter-paragraph cohesion. Probably the most important contribution of corpus-linguistic research to our understanding of the paragraph has been the identification of some of the typical links (lexical and grammatical) that connect (or indeed do not connect) paragraphs in certain genres. It is not entirely clear why certain genres utilize specific kinds of devices to link paragraphs, though as noted in Chapter 5, anaphoric shell noun usage can assist readers and writers cognitively, and the tendency not to use anaphoric pronominals across a paragraph juncture may well be linked to reader and writer psychology. Readers familiar with a genre are aware of the various ways in which a writer can signal continuity and discontinuity between paragraph units within that genre. For example, through the use of topic foregrounding, a writer can effect smooth cohesion between paragraphs in some types of text; or by introducing a new subject in paragraph-initial position, a writer can indicate a significant thematic shift.

Cricket balls are made with a raised seam, which links the two panels of leather together, covering the inner ball made of cork. This feature of the ball is functional and is exploited by cricket players (bowlers) to full effect as the ball hits the ground on or off the seam, affecting the way the ball moves accordingly. Likewise, on a baseball, the externally visible stitching affects the way the ball moves through the air, and where it ends up; and pitchers are aware of this, and utilize this knowledge in how they throw a ball. In a similar way, there are functional effects of the presence or absence of different kinds of links between paragraphs, and writers, being aware of these, may make use of such devices for desired-for functions. As suggested in Chapter 6, inter-paragraph and intra-paragraph cohesive link patterns are probably quite different for some genres. Learners need to be aware of these differences, and of the effects or functions of certain links (e.g. metadiscourse framing devices at the paragraph juncture) and how they can be employed by a writer in constructing and managing the text. The absence of obvious links also needs to be considered as a less obviously signposted way of connecting and shifting, or indeed maintaining, discourse focus.

The Paragraph's Existence, Purpose, or Role within the Wider Text

> *The ball is what matters (not the individual panel): the text is what matters (not the isolated paragraph).*

The isolated paragraph (i.e. a decontextualized unit) needs to be put in its place. Paragraphing is important, but it is possible to overdo, indeed to pervert, the role and importance of the paragraph unit, and I suggest that this has sometimes been the case historically. Because the paragraph is a visual unit, some educators have believed it to be a valid unit unto itself for theorizing and learner focus, in the sense that it has been treated as a meaningful, functionally complete unit. In focusing on the paragraph unit by itself, some educators have lost the important connections between paragraphing practices and discourse communities, genres, functions, and context – and hence to the various context-dependent potentialities of the paragraph. As made clear in the arguments throughout this book, it is sometimes quite meaningless and even false to consider the paragraph as a discrete meaningful entity, for the simple reason that it may be only part of a textual unit. Throughout the book, I have stressed the need to consider the paragraph unit's connectedness and incompleteness, alongside its internal development and coherence. As such, the paragraph is not a good focus for a pedagogy: but the complete text is. The ball is the focus in sport, not the panel. Likewise, the text is what matters, and the paragraph is only significant in terms of how it fits in with, contributes to, and completes the whole text.

As I have noted elsewhere (McGee, 2016), there are problems with the above analogies to balls in sports. While I believe the overall analogy holds for the points noted above, there are several points at which it breaks down. For example, a ball is created according to a very precise plan, but a writer may not know, when beginning to write, what exactly will be produced, and the writing process is best considered to be recursive rather than simply sequential: there may be little in the way of advance planning. In addition, a ball, unlike a text, has no beginning or end, and the panels on a ball may be linked on different edges to many other panels, not just one or two, as is the case with paragraphs in a text. Further, some paragraphs, and some parts of paragraphs, may be more important than others; but all panels on a ball are of equal importance in making up the whole. Finally, under analogy 5 above, I considered the decorative elements of the ball to be analogous to cases when the text's linguistic structure or its functions do not map on to paragraph units, or when a certain aspect of the text is highlighted in some way. The text's semantic and functional structures are best considered the more important, basic elements of text, rather than as I have considered them above, as non-essential, decorative elements.

Paragraphs in Languages other than English

While the focus of this book is the English paragraph, and the pedagogical principles I have given above are specifically formulated for the English paragraph, this book would not be complete without making some reference to issues of generalization and particularity in relation to different languages and their paragraphing practices. Accordingly, in the section below, I address this issue, primarily in order to guard against simplistic notions concerning relationships between culture, thought, discipline, genre, and paragraphing.

In Chapter 2, I made some quite detailed comments about historical Greek and Latin paragraphing practice, for the purposes of providing historical context to the genesis of early English paragraphing. However, the bulk of the research and ideas discussed in this book have come from work into the English language paragraph (with just a few exceptions as mentioned in Chapters 5 and 6). Are the principles which I have given above ones which can be applied to paragraphing in other languages? I do not know the answer to this question. The amount of research into English paragraphing far outweighs that conducted in other languages, making it difficult to make comprehensive comparisons. In this section I seek to raise awareness of some of the issues surrounding contrastive linguistic work in paragraphing, the problems inherent in such research and some of the research findings to date. I hope that other researchers will consider whether the analogies I provided in this chapter are appropriate or otherwise in other languages.

Kaplan's Early Contrastive Linguistic Work on Paragraphing

Arguably the most well-known discourse contrastive linguistic piece of work ever published was a paper that examined paragraph development patterns in different languages. Inspired by Christensen and Becker's work on the paragraph, Robert Kaplan doodled his famous paragraph development patterns (Kaplan, 1966), comparing the English deductively organized paragraph with paragraph developmental styles in other language families / ethnic groupings (Semitic, Oriental, Slavic, Romance). Kaplan (1966: 8) suggested that different "cultural thought patterns" were responsible for these varied approaches to textual development. Kaplan's paper was very important, though he himself recognized some of its shortcomings in later work (e.g. Kaplan, 1987: 9). Its ethnocentricity, in particular, was criticized, and Connor (1996, 2002) has documented the subsequent broadening of approach to contrastive studies since the first study by Kaplan.

Although Kaplan's study was very influential, his work with the paragraph was highly questionable. A key criticism of his study in light of the focus of this book, noted by Carol Severino (Severino, 1993), was his choice of the orthographic paragraph unit as the unit of comparison. For Kaplan this was not a problematic issue as he considered the paragraph to be a mixed unit (alongside Christensen and Becker). The problem is, as has been made clear throughout this book, the orthographic unit may be an inappropriate unit to analyze, because of its possible incompleteness.[1] As Severino (1993: 46) pointed out:

> Because the paragraph is often an arbitrary and artificial unit of discourse, not always intended by the writer as a unit of thought, it is less likely to reveal "cultural thought patterns" than are whole discourses.

While one might wish to quibble with the word "often" in the above quotation, it is clear that a series of paragraphs can constitute one thought, or a paragraph unit contain more than one thought, and indeed have more than one purpose. As such, the possibility of meaningful contrastive paragraphing analysis must, to a certain extent, be called into question – at least when those paragraphs are taken from the wider discourse.

Concerning Kaplan's comments, not all English paragraphing proceeds in a deductive fashion, and although he acknowledged that the pattern of development could be inductive, in what he termed the "reverse process" (Kaplan, 1966: 5), both of the typical development patterns he described were linear in nature. But are such patterns the only ways of developing text in English? Chesterman (1998: 172, 173) provided examples of English paragraphs which proceeded in parallel, spiral, digressive, scatter, and digressive manners (rather than just linear), in order to indicate the wide variety of profiles that an English paragraph may take – profiles which were considered essentially "non-English" by Kaplan. As such, the overly simplistic nature of Kaplan's work is apparent, even though there is a lot of truth in the paragraph contrasts and descriptions that he made (for some genres, and for some of the paragraphs within them).

Another weakness in Kaplan's (1966) methodological approach (again noted by Severino, 1993) was his mixing of genre types from different languages in his initial study. As mentioned in many of the chapters in this book, different genres exhibit different paragraph patternings, and cross-cultural / contrastive analyses which do not respect such differences are open to legitimate criticism.

It is not my intention to engage further with Kaplan's work, as the key issue which I wish to raise from analyzing his work has already been raised above – namely, the potentially problematic nature of paragraph-based contrastive work. Below I make reference to some post-Kaplan (1966) contrastive research, which has indicated differences between paragraphing in English and paragraphing in other languages. Relatively few research articles have focused specifically on this subject; according to Eli Hinkel, more research has focused on the possible effects of the first language (L1) in second-language (L2) paragraph writing (Hinkel, 1994). However, since interlingual and training issues play a role in L2 writing, I do not make reference to such work here, but rather comment solely on contrastive analyses of paragraphing of the same kinds of texts. The findings reported below are not intended to be comprehensive, but are rather intended to simply raise awareness of the relationship between thought, language, genre, and discipline, and the related issues of universality and particularity in writing practices in languages around the world.

French

Elisabeth Le analyzed French and English paragraphs in two corpora of academic articles in the field of international law (Le, 1999: 307). In her analyses, she differentiated five types of paragraph: single-unit (i.e. one sentence), expository (i.e. the relationship between sentences is elaboration), explanatory (i.e. the last sentence in the paragraph is more specific than the first), complex (i.e. a combination of expository and explanatory) and the combined paragraph (i.e. containing two or more of the above four types). She observed the French texts to have more single-unit sentences, and expository-style paragraphs were more common in English. Further, explanatory paragraphs were more common in French, and complex paragraphs were more common in English. Concerning the marked preference for French to use single-unit paragraphs, Le observed that these were typically structuring the argumentation (e.g. through announcing how the text would develop). As such, she believed that the French and English authors were using paragraphs in rather different ways: "it appears that English authors tend to build their argumentation within their paragraphs, while French authors use paragraphs to build their argumentation" (p. 307). Thus, she argued that "the argumentative structure of the French texts is more apparent through its segmentation into standard textual paragraphs than that of the English texts" (p. 336). Le believed that the source for this difference was in the different educational backgrounds of the writers.

Italian

Owtram (2010) demonstrated how paragraphing in English and Italian academic writing differs in terms of length and organization, and referred to other work suggesting that the paragraph was not necessarily a unit of development in Italian academic writing, and was less important in managing the rhetorical patterns, as a result. In her view: "While the role of a paragraph in an English text is to take the argument from one point to the next, Italian texts seem to privilege concepts around which paragraphs cluster" (p. 69).

Japanese

The four paragraph Japanese *ki-shó-ten-ketsu* development model has been commented on by a number of academics, including Hinds (1983, 1990) and Qi Fang (Fang, 2009). Of particular interest in the model is the third paragraph (*ten*) which Hinds (1983: 188) described as being only indirectly relevant to the argument being developed – a softening move before arriving at the conclusion, the function of which Fang (2009: 88) described as to "turn the idea to a sub-theme where there is a connection, but which is indirectly associated to the major theme." Hinds (1987) believed that Japanese (along with Thai, Chinese, and Korean) are reader-responsible languages, in the sense that they encourage reader thinking and engagement, allowing and requiring readers to "draw their own conclusions" (Hinds 1990: 99). English, on the other hand, was described by Hinds (1987) as a writer-responsible language.

Spanish

Joellen Simpson compared 20 paragraphs from Spanish humanities journals with 20 paragraphs in English journals written in the same year (Simpson, 2000). She found that English paragraphs were generally longer than Spanish ones, and contained more sentences (though the sentences contained fewer words than the

Spanish ones). She also found a difference in the way in which the paragraphs' topic structures were developed, with more repetition of key lexis in English, and cohesive relationships signaled rather differently in Spanish (e.g. with less use of lexical repetition). The Spanish paragraphs were also found to contain "different topical subjects within one paragraph" (Simpson, 2000: 305). With regard to Mexican Spanish, María Montaño-Harmon observed that conscious digression in text was common in Mexican Spanish writing of school children (i.e. through the use of markers signaling this), and one of a number of differences between English writing and Mexican Spanish writing (Montaño-Harmon, 1991: 422).

Russian

In a study of American and Russian business letters, Maria Wolfe found that the American businessmen almost always placed their thesis statement in the first paragraph of their letters, in effect noting the reason for writing up front (Wolfe, 2008). The Russian practice on the other hand was generally to defer this function – with just six of the 17 letters studied putting the thesis in the first paragraph, suggesting a rather different textual approach to persuasion.

Discussion

The above sample of studies suggests that cultural and educational backgrounds may well be behind different paragraphing practices. However, it should also be noted that some scholars, such as Chesterman (1998: 175) and Tatyana Yakhontova (Yakhontova, 2006) have argued that paragraph development patterns may be related to disciplinary practice rather than simply reflecting cultural and linguistic differences. Yakhontova (2006: 163) suggested that English and Slavic conference abstracts are different in the field of linguistics but similar in the field of mathematics because the former discipline may be more "sensitive to national contexts," whereas for mathematics the similarity in abstracts may be due to "the universality of cognitive paradigms characteristic of hard sciences."

In a rather refreshing change of viewpoint on the English paragraph, Hinkel (1994), in referring to Alfred Bloom's study of American and Chinese writers (Bloom, 1981), described the attitudes of the Chinese speakers in the study towards English argumentative style. She commented that they found the English text to be "'insufferably' redundant, cyclical, excessively detailed, forced and unnecessary" (Hinkel, 1994: 354). Reader response to textual development, and its culturally governed basis has also been mentioned by Simpson (2000: 307). Such observations serve as a rather nice balance to the idea that English linear writing style and organization is inherently superior (and recognized to be such), and the only way of (properly) doing paragraphing. While Bloom's Chinese participants would have had to learn to adapt their own writing styles to successfully communicate in English-speaking contexts – or perhaps would need to have developed a hybrid pattern, as pointed out by Joan Gregg (Gregg, 1986) – the fact remains that an outsider's view can help ensure a more realistic notion of what paragraphing can be, rather than what it should be.

Different discourse communities within societies around the world have sanctioned quite different ways of going about achieving essentially the same social purposes through the genres they have created – though as noted above, the idea that a particular discipline may be more powerful than such differences in its influence on creating universal patterns is worth much more consideration than has been given to it to date. The vast bulk of this book is concerned with how one corner of the world, a corner that uses English, has developed certain paragraphing conventions and taught them. I hope that other researchers will add to the limited contribution I make to understanding the English paragraph and paragraphing, by considering the subject from wider multi-linguistic perspectives in the future.

Areas for Future Research

As commented on throughout the book, there are some rather large research gaps in the literature, when it comes to understanding the paragraph and paragraphing. Below I consider just a few of these (under some discipline-specific heads) which I hope future researchers will consider exploring. I start with the subject area just left (i.e. contrastive linguistic studies) before moving on to technology effects, computational and corpus linguistics, reader and writer psychology, and discourse and genre.

Contrastive Linguistic Studies

Although some researchers have considered different paragraphing patterns and traditions in different languages, there is huge scope for more focused contrastive research in this area. Some possible questions to be considered might include:

- Are there languages which do not have paragraphs, and if so, do they have equivalent or non-equivalent kinds of structures to those known for English? To what extent can paragraphs in different languages and the genres in which they occur be compared?
- What additional or alternative paralinguistic devices are available for writers to manage text in other languages? What are their functions?
- Are there any common paragraphing practices across different languages? If so, for which genres or disciplines?
- To what extent have foreign paragraphing patterns been incorporated into other languages, permanently or temporarily, in different historical periods? How has the global dominance of English affected paragraphing practices in different languages and in the writing of different genres and disciplines?

- What aspects of English paragraphing might speakers of other languages struggle with most? Are these struggles logical, linguistic, or ideological?
- How similar / different are the range of indentation functions in different languages? Which functions are language-specific, if any?

Technology Effects

As noted in Chapter 8, it seems clear that the mode of communication affects how people write, whether engaging in more emergent planning, and / or revising more when using computers. Visuospatial considerations are also important factors to consider when thinking about how technology might be affecting writers' paragraphing. Some possible questions for future researchers might be:

- How do font sizes and page view in word processing packages affect paragraphing decisions?
- How are electronic versions of texts and new kinds of digital genres changing or maintaining paragraphing conventions?[2]
- How do professional writers approach paragraphing, and what kinds of development revision patterns are they engaged in, when using word processing programs?

Computational and Corpus Linguistics

Much of the computational work referred to in this book in Chapter 6 may not be considered particularly relevant or important to educators. However, I suggest that this field of research, when combined with corpus linguistic research, can yield data which may be of tremendous value, when carefully considered and thoughtfully filtered by the educational community. Researchers in these areas might explore questions such as the following:

- Can specific intra-paragraph moves or structures be identified in paragraphs, through the identification of lexical and grammatical signals?[3] What can qualitative studies of computational procedures indicate about the specific reasons for the success or failure of a particular segmentation algorithm?
- Following on from Sporleder and Lapata's (2004, 2006) work, what can genre-specific computational research reveal about paragraph-initial and paragraph-final language? Are there distinctive paragraph-initial formulaic elements in certain genres?
- For which genres is internal paragraph cohesion a meaningful concept?

Reader and Writer Psychology

Our understanding of how readers experience paragraphs and how writers construct them is, at the current time, rather basic. Some questions for further study might include:

- Can principled paragraph segmentation studies, in which reading styles, background knowledge, and genre knowledge are controlled, help differentiate text types according to the predictability or non-predictability of the paragraph break for human segmenters?
- How different or similar are writers' (as opposed to readers') segmentation decisions of their own de-paragraphed text when compared with their original decisions? How are differences accounted for by the original authors of the texts?
- Can further experimentation into the effect of paragraph decision-making control a number of variables thereby enabling researchers to consider the role of just one variable on how writers decide on their indentation decisions?
- Are pausing patterns for readers affected by certain identifiable variables, such as genre?

- How similar or different are writers' first or early and final or later paragraphing decisions? What variables affect possible variations in these decisions? Are writers able to articulate the reasons for making such changes?

Discourse and Genre

Genre analysts have largely overlooked the paragraph when considering macrolinguistic aspects of text. The paragraph needs to play a much bigger role within such studies. Specific areas of research could include:

- What is the relationship between moves and paragraphs? In which genres do paragraph and move structures tend to be mapped with one another, and so coincide? Why?
- Are there certain paragraph-internal indicators of moves within the same paragraph?
- For which genres are patterns of paragraphing primarily governed by topic, or theme, and which are more open to writer decisions and not simply linguistic unit mapping?
- In which genres is key information typically placed in paragraph-initial and / or paragraph-final positions?

Conclusion

What would text be like without paragraphs? One thing we can say with certainty is that it would be less variable and probably also less interesting than it is now. The alternatives would be pages full of unbroken text, the sentence becoming the default paragraph – as is the case in some electronic and journalistic genres today, as observed by Andy Bodle (Bodle, 2015) – or perhaps the use of some larger supraparagraph section type marker (like the traditional § mark).

On the basis of the material covered throughout this book, I believe a key word that needs to be used when discussing the paragraph and indentation is the word *potential*. Indentation has the potential to perform various functions: this potential is dependent on co-signaling textual elements, writer intention, and reader reception. The various potentialities may or may not be realized in the text, by the writer, or by the reader. A key argument of this book is the need to consider the paragraph alongside genre, alongside the linguistic and extralinguistic context, alongside the writer's process of writing and purpose, and alongside the reader's reading psychology. It is only when these factors are considered together that we can understand paragraphing. There is a long way to go before we more fully understand the interaction between these various elements; however, I believe research in recent years has at least helped us widen our appreciation of what needs to be considered to understand paragraphing.

Some pedagogical approaches to the paragraph and paragraphing have been far too narrow and limiting. As a result, the paragraph and its potential have not been appreciated by learners. I hope that this book will help linguists, writers, and educators adopt a robust notion of what the paragraph and paragraphing can be and can do, and that it will stimulate more discussion about, and research into this complex, flexible, much maligned and often-misunderstood textual feature.

Notes

1 Chesterman (1998: 152) suggested that the appropriate unit for contrastive work should be the P-unit, which he defined as "a segment of text that could be taken as an independent and self-contained text itself, which can reasonably stand in isolation from the preceding and following text." He went on to comment that this may or may not be an orthographic paragraph.

2   Just as Lewis (1894) documented changes in English paragraphing over several centuries, more modern diachronic studies can reveal much about discourse communities, changing communication patterns, and issues relating to reader and writer behavior in paragraphing.

3   Answering this question could lead to the development of a truly empirically-based formal understanding of paragraphs in different genres.

References

Adams, Heather and Quintana–Toledo, Elena (2013) Adverbial stance marking in the introduction and conclusion sections of legal research articles. *Revista de Lingüística y Lenguas Aplicadas* 8(1): 13–22.

Ädel, Annelie (2006) *Metadiscourse in L1 and L2 English.* Amsterdam / Philadelphia: John Benjamins Publishing Co.

Aguado, Teresa Marqués (2009) Punctuation practice in the antidotary in GUL MS Hunter 513 (ff. 37v–96v). *Miscelánea: A Journal of English and American Studies* 39: 55–72.

Aikman, Carol C. and O'Hear, Michael F. (1997) Main idea: Writers have always used it. *Journal of Adolescent & Adult Literacy* 41(3): 190–195.

Aktas, Rahime Nur and Cortes, Viviana (2008) Shell nouns as cohesive devices in published and ESL student writing. *Journal of English for Academic Purposes* 7(1): 3–14.

Alazzawie, Abdulkhaliq (2014) The discourse marker *wa* in Standard Arabic – A syntactic and semantic analysis. *Theory and Practice in Language Studies* 4(10): 2008–2015.

Aley, Shelley (1998) The impact of science on rhetoric through the contributions of the University of Aberdeen's Alexander Bain. In Lynee L. Gaillet (ed.) *Scottish Rhetoric and its Influences* 209–17. Mahwah, New Jersey: Lawrence Erlbaum.

Allal, Linda and Chanquoy, Lucile (2004) Introduction, revision revisited. In Linda Allal, Lucile Chanquoy and Pierre Largy (eds.) *Revision: Cognitive and instructional processes* 1–7. New York: Springer Science+Media.

Alves, Rui Alexandre, Castro, São Luis, and Olive, Thierry (2008) Execution and pauses in writing narratives: Processing time, cognitive effort and typing skill. *International Journal of Psychology* 43(6): 969–979.

American Heritage College Dictionary (2002, 4th edition). Boston / New York: Houghton Mifflin.

Angus, Joseph (1862) Handbook of the English Tongue for the Use of Students and Others. London: The Religious Tract Society.

Ariel, Mira (1988) Referring and accessibility. *Journal of Linguistics* 24: 65–87.

Ashida, Margaret E. (1968) Response to Paul Rodgers, "The stadium of discourse." *College Composition and Communication* 19(1): 30–32.

Augst, Gerhard (1992) Aspects of writing development in argumentative texts. In Dieter Stein (ed.) *Co-operating with Written Texts* 67–82. Berlin / New York: Mouton.

Baddeley, Alan D. and Hitch, Graham (1974) Working memory. In Gordon H. Bower (ed.) *The Psychology of Learning and Motivation: Advances in Research and Theory* 47–89. New York: Academic Press.

Bain, Alexander (1866) *English Composition and Rhetoric: A Manual*. New York: D. Appleton and Company.

Bain, Alexander (1890) *English Composition and Rhetoric* (enlarged edition). New York: D. Appleton and Company.

Barlow, Michael (1996) Corpora for theory and practice. *International Journal of Corpus Linguistics* 1(1): 1–37.

Barney, Stephen A., Lewis, W. J., Beach, J. A. and Berghof, Oliver (eds. and trans.) (2006) *The Etymologies of Isidore of Seville*. Cambridge: Cambridge University Press.

Baron, Naomi S. (2001) Commas and canaries: The role of punctuation in speech and writing. *Language Sciences* 23(1): 15–67.

Baumann, James F. (1986) Effect of rewritten content textbook passages on middle grade students' comprehension of main ideas: Making the inconsiderate considerate. *Journal of Literacy Research* 18(1): 1–21.

Baumann, James F. and Serra, Judith K. (1984) The frequency and placement of main ideas in children's social studies textbooks: A modified replication of Braddock's research on topic sentences. *Journal of Literacy Research* 16(1): 27–40.

Beach, Richard (1982) The pragmatics of self-assessing. In Ronald A. Sudol (ed.) *Revising: New Essays for Teachers of Writing* 71–83. Urbana, Illinois: ERIC / National Council of Teachers of English.

Becker, Alton L. (1965) A tagmemic approach to paragraph analysis. *College Composition and Communication* 16(5): 237–242.

Becker, Alton L. (1966) Contribution to the Symposium on the Paragraph. *College Composition and Communication* 17(2): 67–72.

Bell, David (2007) Sentence-initial *and* and *but* in academic writing. *Pragmatics* 17(2): 183–201.

Belletto, Steven (2011) Digression, ethical work, and Salinger's postmodern turn. *Literature Interpretation Theory* 22(1): 4–24.

Benitez-Castro, Miguel-Angel (2015) Coming to grips with shell-nounhood: A critical review of insights into the meaning, function and form of shell-noun phrases. *Australian Journal of Linguistics* 35(2): 168–194.

Bennett, Karen (2009) English academic style manuals: A survey. *Journal of English for Academic Purposes* 8(1): 43–54.

Berber-Sardinha, Anthony (1997) *Automatic Identification of Segments in Written Texts*. Ph.D. thesis. Liverpool: University of Liverpool. http://www2.lael.pucsp.br/~tony/phd/phd.htm

Berber-Sardinha, Anthony (2001) Lexical segments in text. In Mike Scott and Geoff Thompson (eds.) *Patterns of Text: In Honour of Michael Hoey* 213–237. Amsterdam / Philadelphia. John Benjamins Publishing.

Berber-Sardinha, Anthony (2002) Segmenting corpora of texts. *DELTA: Documentação de Estudosem Lingüística Teórica e Aplicada* 18(2): 273–286.

Berkenkotter, Carol and Murray, Donald M. (1983) Decisions and revisions: The planning strategies of a publishing writer, and response of a laboratory rat: Or, being protocoled. *College Composition and Communication* 34(2): 156–172.

Berlin, James A. (1984) *Writing Instruction in Nineteenth-century American Colleges*. Carbondale, Illinois: Southern Illinois University Press.

Bestgen, Yves (1998) Segmentation markers as trace and signal of discourse structure. *Journal of Pragmatics* 29(6): 753–763.

Bestgen, Yves and Vonk, Wietske (2000) Temporal adverbials as segmentation markers in discourse comprehension. *Journal of Memory and Language* 42(1): 74–87.

Biber, Douglas, Csomay, Eniko, Jones, James K. and Keck, Casey (2007) Introduction to the identification and analysis of vocabulary-based discourse units. In Douglas Biber, Ulla Connor and Thomas A. Upton (eds.) *Discourse on the Move – Using Corpus Analysis to Describe Discourse Structure* 155–173. Amsterdam / Philadelphia: John Benjamins Publishing Company.

Bloom, Alfred H. (1981) *The Linguistic Shaping of Thought: A Study in the Impact of Language on Thinking in China and the West*. Hillsdale, New Jersey: Lawrence Erlbaum Associates.

Bodle, Andy (2015) Is the writing on the wall for the paragraph? *The Guardian*, Friday 22 May 2015. https://www.theguardian.com/media/mind-your-language/2015/may/22/breaking-point-is-the-writing-on-the-wall-for-the-paragraph.

Bolinger, Dwight L. (1979) Pronouns in discourse. In Talmy Givón (ed.) *Syntax and Semantics Discourse and Syntax* 289–309. New York: Academic Press.

Bolshakov, Igor and Gelbukh, Alexander (2001) Text segmentation into paragraphs based on local text cohesion. In Václav Matoušek, Pavel Mautner, Roman Mouček and Karel Taušer (eds.) *Text, Speech and Dialogue* 4th International Conference, Železná Ruda, Czech Republic, September 11–13, 2001, Proceedings 158–166. Berlin / Heidelberg / New York: Springer.

Bond, Charles A. (1972) A new approach to freshman composition: A trial of the Christensen method. *College English* 33(6): 623–627.

Bond, Sandra J. and Hayes, John R. (1984) Cues people use to paragraph text. *Research in the Teaching of English* (1984): 147–167.

Braddock, Richard (1974) The frequency and placement of topic sentences in expository prose. *Research in the Teaching of English* 8 (3): 287–302.

Brannon, Lil, Courtney, Jennifer Pooler, Urbanski, Cynthia P., Woodward, Shana V., Reynolds, Jeanie Marklin, Iannone, Anthony E., Haag, Karen D., Mach, Karen, Manship, Lacy Arnold and Kendrick, Mary (2008) EJ Extra: The five-paragraph essay and the deficit model of education. *English Journal* 98(2): 16–21.

Branson, Mark K. (1988) What's It Going to Be, Eh? Tracing the English Paragraph into Its Second Century. Diss. North Carolina: University of North Carolina at Greensboro.

Brereton, John C. (ed.) (1995) *The Origins of Composition Studies in the American College, 1875–1925*. Pittsburgh: University of Pittsburgh Press.

Bridge, Connie A., Belmore, Susan M., Moskow, Susan P., Cohen, Sheila S. and Matthews, Patricia D. (1984) Topicalization and memory for main ideas in prose. *Journal of Literacy Research* 16(1): 61–80.

Bridwell, Lillian S. (1980) Revising strategies in twelfth grade students' transactional writing. *Research in the Teaching of English* 14(3): 197–222.

Briggs, Charles. F. (2000) Literacy, reading, and writing in the medieval West. *Journal of Medieval History* 26(4): 397–420.

Britton, Bruce K. (1994) Understanding expository text: Building mental structures to induce insights. In Morton Ann Gernsbacher (ed.) *Handbook of Psycholinguistics* 641–674. San Diego, California: Academic Press.

Britton, James, Burgess, Tony, Martin, Nancy, McLeod, Alex and Rosen, Harold (1975) *The Development of Writing Abilities. Schools Council Research Studies*. London: Macmillan.

Bronowski, Jacob (1960) *The Common Sense of Science*. New York: Vintage Press.

Brown, Gillian (1977) *Listening to Spoken English*. London: Longman.

Brown, Gillian, Currie, Karen L. and Kenworthy, Joanne (*1980*) *Questions of Intonation*. London: Croom Helm.

Brown, Gillian, and Yule, George (1983) *Discourse Analysis*. Cambridge: Cambridge University Press, 1983.

Brown, Thomas Julian (1974) Punctuation. *The New Encyclopaedia Britannica (15th edition)* Vol. 15: 274–277. London / New York: Encyclopaedia Britannica Co.

Buckley, Theodore W. A. (1857) *Treatise on Rhetoric*. London: Henry G. Bohn.

Bullokar, John (1719) *The English Expositor Improvd* (12th edition, revised R. Browne). London: W. Churchill.

Butler, Paul (2008) *Out of Style: Reanimating Stylistic Study in Composition and Rhetoric*. Logan, Utah: Utah State University Press

Butler, Shane (2000) *Litterae manent: Ciceronian Oratory and the Written Word*. Ph.D. Thesis. Columbia University.

Butler, Shane (2009) Cicero's capita. *Litterae Caelestes* 3(1): 9–48.

Cambridge Advanced Learner's Dictionary (2013, 4th edition). Cambridge: Cambridge University Press.

Cao, Feng, and Hu, Guangwei (2014) Interactive metadiscourse in research articles: A comparative study of paradigmatic and disciplinary influences. *Journal of Pragmatics* 66: 15–31.

Carrell, Patricia L. (1982) Cohesion is not coherence. *TESOL Quarterly* 16(4): 479–488.

Carroll, Ruth, Peikola, Matti, Salmi, Hanna, Varila, Mari-Liisa, Skaffari, Janne and Hiltunen, Risto (2013) Pragmatics on the page: visual text in late medieval English books. *European Journal of English Studies* 17(1): 54–71.

Chafe, Wallace (1979) The flow of thought and the flow of language. In Talmy Givón (ed.) *Syntax and Semantics Discourse and Syntax* 159–181. New York: Academic Press.

Chafe, Wallace (1992) Information flow in speaking and writing. *The Linguistics of Literacy* 21: 17–29.

Chafe, Wallace (1994) *Discourse, Consciousness, and Time: The Flow and Displacement of Conscious Experience in Speaking and Writing*. Chicago and London: University of Chicago Press.

Chambers Dictionary (2003, 9th edition). Edinburgh: Chambers Harrap Publishers.

Charolles, Michel (2005) Framing adverbials and their role in discourse cohesion, from connection to forward labelling. In M. Arnague, Myriam Bras, Anne Le Draoulec and Laure Veiu (eds.) *Symposium on the Exploration and Modelling of Meaning (SEM-05)* 13–30. Biarritz, France.

Chenoweth, N. Ann and Hayes, John R. (2001) Fluency in writing generating text in L1 and L2. *Written Communication* 18(1): 80–98.

Chesterman, Andrew (1998) *Contrastive Functional Analysis*. Amsterdam / Philadelphia: John Benjamins Publishing.

Choi, Freddy Y. Y. (2000) Advances in domain independent linear text segmentation. In *NAACL Proceedings of the 1st North American chapter of the Association for Computational Linguistics conference* 26–33. Stroudsburg, Pennsylvania: Association for Computational Linguistics.

Chomsky, Noam (1965) *Aspects of the Theory of Syntax*. Cambridge, Massachusetts: MIT Press.

Chomsky, Noam (1957) *Syntactic Structures*. The Hague: Mouton.

Christensen, Bonniejean McGuire (1970) Structures on Mrs. Johnson's strictures. *College English* 31(8): 878–881.

Christensen, Francis (1963) A generative rhetoric of the sentence. *College Composition and Communication* 14(3): 155–161.

Christensen, Francis (1965) A generative rhetoric of the paragraph. *College Composition and Communication* 16(3): 144–156.

Christensen, Francis (1966) Contribution to the Symposium on the Paragraph. *College Composition and Communication* 17(2): 60–66.

Christensen, Francis (1967) Response to Leo Rockas, "Further comments on the paragraph." *College Composition and Communication* 18(3): 186–188.

Christensen, Francis (1968) The problem of defining a mature style. *English Journal* 57(4): 572–579.

Christensen, Francis (1973) The course in advanced composition for teachers. *College Composition and Communication* 24(2): 163–170.

Christensen, Francis and Christensen, Bonniejean (2007 / 1963). *Notes Toward a New Rhetoric: 9 Essays for Teachers* (3rd edition; ed. Donald C. Stewart). Florida: Booklocker.

Coe, Richard M. (1988) *Toward a Grammar of Passages*. Carbondale, Illinois: Southern Illinois University Press.

Coe, Richard M. (1998) Generative rhetoric. In Mary Lynch Kennedy (ed.) *Theorizing Composition: A Critical Sourcebook of Theory and*

Scholarship in Contemporary Composition Studies 131–136. Westport, Connecticut: Greenwood Press.

Colby, John B. (1977) Paragraphing in technical writing. *IEEE Transactions on Professional Communication* 20(1): 20–23.

Coles, Jr., William E. (1996) Paragraph. *World Book Encyclopedia (International)* Vol. 15. London: World Book.

Coltheart, Max (1981) The MRC psycholinguistic database. *Quarterly Journal of Experimental Psychology* 33(4): 497–505.

Connor, Ulla (1984) A study of cohesion and coherence in English as a second language students' writing. *Research on Language & Social Interaction* 17(3): 301–316.

Connor, Ulla (1996) *Contrastive Rhetoric: Cross-cultural Aspects of Second Language Writing*. Cambridge: Cambridge University Press, 1996.

Connor, Ulla (2002) New directions in contrastive rhetoric. *TESOL Quarterly* 36(4): 493–510.

Connor, Ulla and Kaplan, Robert B. (1987) *Writing across Languages: Analysis of L2 Text*. Reading, Massachusetts: Addison–Wesley.

Connors, Robert J. and Glenn, Cheryl (1995) *The St. Martin's Guide to Teaching Writing*. Boston / New York: Bedford / St. Martin's.

Connors, Robert J. (1997) *Composition–Rhetoric: Backgrounds, Theory, and Pedagogy*. Pittsburgh: University of Pittsburgh Press.

Connors, Robert J. (2000) The erasure of the sentence. *College Composition and Communication* 52(1): 96–128.

Cook, Philip H. (1968) Putting grammar to work: the generative grammar in the generative rhetoric. *English Journal* 57(8): 1168–1175.

Coomber, James E. (1975) Perceiving the structure of written materials. *Research in the Teaching of English* 9(3): 263–266.

Cope, Edward Meredith and Sandys, John Edwin (1877) *The Rhetoric of Aristotle*. Vol. 2. Cambridge: Cambridge University Press.

Cornish, Francis (2003) The roles of (written) text and anaphor-type distribution in the construction of discourse. *Text – Interdisciplinary Journal for the Study of Discourse* 23(1): 1–26.

Cotter, Colleen (2003) Prescriptions and practice: Motivations behind changes in news discourse. *Journal of Historical Pragmatics* 4(1): 45–74.

Crismore, Avon, Markkanen, Raija and Steffensen, Margaret S. (1993) Metadiscourse in persuasive writing a study of texts written by American and Finnish university students. *Written Communication* 10(1): 39–71.

Crompton, Peter (2006) The effect of position on the discourse scope of adverbials. *Text and Talk* 26(3): 245–279.

Crosby, Ruth (1938) Chaucer and the custom of oral delivery. *Speculum* 13(4): 413–432.

Crossley, Scott, Dempsey, Kyle and McNamara, Danielle (2011) Classifying paragraph types using linguistic features: Is paragraph positioning important? *Journal of Writing Research* 3(2): 119–143.

Crothers, Edward J. (1979) *Paragraph Structure Inference.* Norwood, New Jersey: Ablex.

Crystal, David (2001) *A Dictionary of Language.* Chicago: University of Chicago Press.

Daiute, Colette (1986) Physical and cognitive factors in revising: Insights from studies with computers. *Research in the Teaching of English* 20(2): 141–159.

Daneš, František (1974) Functions of sentence perspective and the organization of the text. In František Daneš (ed.) *Papers on Functional Sentence Perspective* 106–128. Prague: Academia.

D'Angelo, Frank J. (1974) A generative rhetoric of the essay. *College Composition and Communication* 25(5): 388–396.

de Beaugrande, Robert (1979) Moving from product toward process. *College Composition and Communication* 30(4): 357–363.

de Moor, Johannes and Korpel, Marjo C.A. (2007) Paragraphing in a Tibero-Palestinian manuscript of the prophets and writings. In Marjo C. A. Korpel, Josef M. Oesch and Stanley E. Porter (eds.) *Method in Unit Delimitation* 1–34. Leiden: Brill.

Degand, Liesbeth (2009) Describing polysemous discourse markers: What does translation add to the picture? In Stef Slembrouck, Miriam Taverniers and Mieke Van Herreweghe (eds.) *From Will to Well. Studies in Linguistics Offered to Anne–Marie Simon–Vandenbergen* 173–184. Gent: Academia Press.

den Ouden, Johanna Neeltje (2004) *Prosodic Realizations of Text Structure.* Ph.D. Thesis. Utrecht: Utrecht University.

Department for Education and Skills (1999) *The National Strategy: Framework for English at Key Stage3.* London

Dix, Stephanie (2006) "What did I change and why did I do it?" Young writers' revision practices. *Literacy* 40(1): 3–10.

Donlan, Dan (1980) Locating main ideas in history textbooks. *Journal of Reading* 24(2): 135–140.

Duncan, Mike (2007) Whatever happened to the paragraph? *College English* 69(5): 470–495.

Durst, Russel K. (1987) Cognitive and linguistic demands of analytic writing. *Research in the Teaching of English* 21(4): 347–376.

Eco, Umberto (2007) En quoi l'usage de l'ordinateur complexifie la genèse d'un texte? In Irène Fenoglio (ed.) *L'Écriture ou le Souci de la Langue* 167–191. Louvain la Neuve: Academic Bruylant.

Eden, Rick and Mitchell, Ruth (1986) Paragraphing for the reader. *College Composition and Communication* 37(4): 416–441.

El-Awa, Salwa M. (2006) *Textual Relations in the Qur'an: Relevance, Coherence and Structure*. Oxford: Routledge, 2006.

Emig, Janet (1971) *The Composing Processes of Twelfth Graders*. Urbana, Illinois: National Council of Teachers of English.

Enkvist, Nils E. (1990) Seven problems in the study of coherence and interpretability. In Ulla Connor and Ann M. Johns (eds.) *Coherence in Writing: Research and Pedagogical Perspectives* 9–28. Alexandria, Virginia: TESOL.

Enos, Richard L. (2006) The emergence of a literate rhetoric in Greece. *Rhetoric Society Quarterly* 36(3): 223–241.

Faigley, Lester and Witte, Stephen (1981) Analyzing revision. *College Composition and Communication* 32(4): 400–414.

Fang, Qi (2009) The features of rhetorical patterns in English expository essays by Chinese EFL English majors and the pedagogical issues of teaching L2 writing at the tertiary level in China. *Asian Englishes* 12(1): 74–100.

Favart, Monik and Coirier, Pierre (2006) Acquisition of the linearization process in text composition in third to ninth graders: Effects of textual superstructure and macrostructural organization. *Journal of Psycholinguistic Research* 35(4): 305–328.

Feng-Checkett, Gayle and Checkett, Lawrence (2006) *The Write Start: Sentences to Paragraphs* (4ᵗʰ edition). Wadsworth: Cengage Learning.

Ferret, Olivier (2002) Using collocations for topic segmentation and link detection. In *Proceedings of the 19th International Conference on Computational Linguistics Taipei, Taiwan* 1–7. Stroudsburg, Pennsylvania: Association for Computational Linguistics.

Filippova, Katja and Strube, Michael (2006) Using linguistically motivated features for paragraph boundary identification. In *Proceedings of the 2006 Conference on Empirical Methods in Natural Language Processing*

267–274. Stroudsburg, Pennsylvania: Association for Computational Linguistics.

Fischer, Martin H. (2000) Perceiving spatial attributes of print. In Alan Kennedy, Ralph Radach, Dieter Heller and Joël Pynte (eds.) *Reading as a Perceptual Process* 89–117. Oxford: Elsevier.

Fischer, Steven Roger (2001) *History of Writing*. London: Reaktion Books.

Fitzgerald, Jill (1987) Research on revision in writing. *Review of Educational Research* 57(4): 481–506.

Fitzgerald, Jill (1988) Helping young writers to revise: A brief review for teachers. *The Reading Teacher* 42(2): 124–129.

Flannery, Kathryn T. (1995) The challenge of access: Rethinking Alexander Bain's reformist pedagogy. *Rhetoric Review* 14(1): 5–22.

Flower, Linda S. (1981) Revising writer-based prose. *Journal of Basic Writing* 3(3): 62–74.

Flower, Linda and Hayes, John R. (1981a) A cognitive process theory of writing. *College Composition and Communication* 32(4): 365–387.

Flower, Linda and Hayes, John R. (1981b) The pregnant pause: An inquiry into the nature of planning. *Research in the Teaching of English* 15(3): 229–243.

Flower, Linda, Hayes, John R., Carey, Linda, Schriver, Karen and Stratman, James (1986) Detection, diagnosis, and the strategies of revision. *College Composition and Communication* 37(1): 16–55.

Flowerdew, John (2009) Use of signalling nouns in a learner corpus. In John Flowerdew and Michaela Mahlberg (eds.) *Lexical Cohesion and Corpus Linguistics* 85–102. Amsterdam / Philadelphia: John Benjamins Publishing.

Folse, Keith S., Muchmore-Vokoun, April and Solomon, Elena Vestri (2010) *Great Writing 2: Great Paragraphs* (3rd edition). Boston, Massachusetts: Heinle Cengage.

Foster, John (2008) *Effective Writing Skills for Public Relations* (4th edition). London and Philadelphia: Kogan Page.

Fotheringham, Lynn S. (2007) The Numbers in the Margins and the Structure of Cicero's *Pro Murena. Greece and Rome (Second Series)* 54(1): 40–60.

Fox, Barbara A. (1993) *Discourse Structure and Anaphora: Written and Conversational English*. Cambridge: Cambridge University Press.

Francis, Gill (1986) *Anaphoric Nouns*. Birmingham: English Language Research, University of Birmingham.

Francis, Gill (1994) Labelling discourse: an aspect of nominal-group lexical cohesion. In Malcolm Coulthard (ed.) *Advances in Written Text Analysis* 83–101. Oxford: Routledge.

Fraser, Bruce (1999) What are discourse markers? *Journal of Pragmatics* 31(7): 931–952.

Garnes, Sara (1987) Paragraph perception by seven groups of readers. In Brian D. Joseph and Arnold M. Zwicky (eds.) *A Festschrift for Ilse Lehiste. Working Papers in Linguistics* 35 132–141. Columbus, Ohio: Ohio State University.

Gasparinatou, Alexandra and Grigoriadou, Maria (2013) Exploring the effect of background knowledge and text cohesion on learning from texts in computer science. *Educational Psychology* 33(6) 645–670.

Gavrilov, Aleksandr Konstantinovi (1997) Techniques of reading in classical antiquity. *The Classical Quarterly (New Series)* 47: 56–73.

Gee, James Paul (1986) Units in the production of narrative discourse. *Discourse Processes* 9(4): 391–422.

Genung, John Franklin (1891) *The Practical Elements of Rhetoric*. Boston: Ginn and Co.

Genzel, Dmitriy and Charniak, Eugene (2003) Variation of entropy and parse trees of sentences as a function of the sentence number. In *Proceedings of the 2003 conference on Empirical methods in natural language processing* 65–72. Association for Computational Linguistics.

Gernsbacher, Morton Ann (1991) Cognitive processes and mechanisms in language comprehension: The structure building framework. In Gordon H. Bower (ed.) *The Psychology of Learning and Motivation, Volume 27 Advances in Research and Theory* 217–263. San Diego, California: Academic Press.

Gernsbacher, Morton Ann (1996) The structure-building framework. In Bruce K. Britton, and Arthur C. Graesser (eds.) *Models of Text Understanding* 289–311. Hillsdale, New Jersey: Erlbaum.

Gernsbacher, Morton Ann (1997a) Two decades of structure building. *Discourse Processes* 23(3): 265–304.

Gernsbacher, Morton Ann (1997b) First mention drives how people read and comprehend language. In *Writing and Reading today: An Interdisciplinary Discussion*. Reston, Virginia: American Society of Newspaper Editors.

Gillett, Andy, Hammond, Angela and Martala, Mary (2009) *Inside Track: Successful Academic Writing*. Harlow, Essex: Pearson Education Limited.

Gillies, John (1823) *A New Translation of Aristotle's Rhetoric*. London: Cadell.

Gindin, Sergei I. (1978) Contributions to textlinguistics in the Soviet Union. In Wolfgang U. Dressler (ed.) *Current Trends in Textlinguistics* 261–274. Berlin / New York: Walter de Gruyter.

Giora, Rachel (1983a) Segmentation and segment cohesion: On the thematic organization of the text. *Text-Interdisciplinary Journal for the Study of Discourse* 3(2): 155–182.

Giora, Rachel (1983b) Functional paragraph perspective. In János S. Petöfi and Emel Sözer (eds.) *Micro and Macro Connexity of Texts*. Hamburg: Helmt Buske Verlag.

Giora, Rachel (1985) A text-based analysis of non-narrative texts. *Theoretical Linguistics* 12(1): 115–136.

Giora, Rachel (1990) Principles of segmentation in the literary text. The case of the formally unsegmented text. *Hebrew Linguistics 28–30*: 23–37.

Giora, Rachel (1996) Language comprehension as structure building. *Journal of Pragmatics* 26(3): 417–436.

Givón, Talmy (1983) Topic continuity in discourse: An Introduction. In Talmy Givón (ed.) *Topic Continuity in Discourse: A Quantitative Cross-language Study* 1–42. Amsterdam / Philadelphia: John Benjamins.

Goldberg, Amie, Russell, Michael and Cook, Abigail (2003) The effect of computers on student writing: A meta-analysis of studies from 1992 to 2002. *The Journal of Technology, Learning and Assessment* 2(1): 1–29.

Goldman, Susan R. and Saul, Elizabeth U. (1990) Flexibility in text processing: A strategy competition model. *Learning and Individual Differences* 2(2): 181–219.

Goldman, Susan R., Saul, Elizabeth U. and Coté, Nathalie (1995) Paragraphing, reader, and task effects on discourse comprehension. *Discourse Processes* 20(3): 273–305.

Gopen, George D. (2004) *Expectations: Teaching Writing from a Reader's Perspective*. New York: Pearson Longman.

Gotoff, Harold C. (1979) *Cicero's Elegant Style: An Analysis of the Pro Archia*. Urbana, Illinois: University of Illinois Press.

Goutsos, Dionysis (1997) *Modeling Discourse Topic: Sequential Relations and Strategies in Expository Text*. Westport, Connecticut: Greenwood Publishing Group.

Grady, Michael (1972) On teaching Christensen rhetoric. *English Journal* 61(6): 859–877.

Graesser, Arthur C., McNamara, Danielle S., Louwerse, Max M. and Cai, Zhiqiang (2004) Coh-Metrix: Analysis of text on cohesion and language. *Behavior Research Methods, Instruments, & Computers* 36(2): 193–202.

Graesser, Arthur C., Millis, Keith K. and Zwaan, Rolf A. (1997) Discourse Comprehension. *Annual Review of Psychology* 48(1): 163–189.

Graves, Richard L. (1981) Renaissance and reform in the composition curriculum. *The Phi Delta Kappan* 62(6): 417–420.

Gray, Jennifer P. (2014) "You can't be creative anymore": Students reflect on the lingering effects of the five-paragraph essay. *Teaching / Writing: The Journal of Writing Teacher Education* 3(2): 152–167.

Green, James L. (1969) Acrobats, plowmen, and the healthy sentence. *English Journal* 58(6): 892–899.

Gregg, Joan (1986) Comments on Bernard A. Mohan and Winnie Au–Yeung Lo's "Academic writing and Chinese students: Transfer and developmental factors." A Reader Reacts. *TESOL Quarterly* 20(2): 354–358.

Grimes, Joseph Evans (1975) *The Thread of Discourse*. The Hague: Mouton Publishers.

Grosz, Barbara J. and Sidner, Candace L. (1986) Attention, intentions, and the structure of discourse. *Computational Linguistics* 12(3): 175–204.

Gundel, Jeanette, Hedberg, Nancy and Zacharski, Ron (1993) Cognitive status and the form of referring expressions in discourse. *Language* 69: 274–307.

Guzman, Josep and Alcón, Eva (1997) The role of textual and lexical signals in paragraph recognition: implications for teaching paragraph writing. *Polifonia* 3 (3): 14–30.

Haas, Christina (1989) How the writing medium shapes the writing process: Effects of word processing on planning. *Research in the Teaching of English* 23(2): 181–207.

Haas, Christina and Hayes, John R. (1986) What did I just say? Reading problems in writing with the machine. *Research in the Teaching of English*: 20(1): 22–35.

Haberlandt, Karl (1982) Reader expectations in text comprehension. In Jean François Le Ny and Walter Kintsch (eds.) *Language and Comprehension* 239–249. Amsterdam / New York / Oxford: North Holland Publishing Company.

Halliday, Michael A. K. and Hasan, Ruqaiya (1976) *Cohesion in English*. London: Pearson Education.

Harned, Jon (1985) The intellectual background of Alexander Bain's modes of discourse. *College Composition and Communication* 36(1): 42–50.

Harris, Zellig S. (1963) *Discourse Analysis Reprints*. The Hague: Mouton.

Haslam, Andrew (2006) *Book Design*. London: Laurence King Publishing.

Hawisher, Gail E. (1987) The effects of word processing on the revision strategies of college freshmen. *Research in the Teaching of English* 21(2): 145–159.

Hayes, Elizabeth (2003) Alexander Bain's long shadow. The current traditional paragraph in the classroom. In *New Histories of Writing IV. Forms and Rhetorics*. MMLA Meeting, Chicago, Illinois.http://societyforcriticalexchange.org/includes/pageContent/Archives/Archives2003/Hayes.htm.

Hayes, John R. (1990) Individuals and environments in writing instruction. In Beau Fly Jones and Lorna Idol (eds.) *Dimensions of Thinking and Cognitive Instruction* 241–263. Hillsdale, New Jersey: Lawrence Erlbaum.

Hayes, John R. (1996) A new framework for understanding cognition and affect in writing. In Michael C. Levy and Sarah Ransdell (eds.) *The Science of Writing: Theories, Methods, Individual Differences, and Applications* 1–27. Mahwah, New Jersey: Lawrence Erlbaum Associates.

Hayes, John R. (2004) What triggers revision? In Linda Allal, Lucile Chanquoy and Pierre Largy (eds.) *Revision: Cognitive and Instructional Processes* 9–20. New York: Springer Science+Media.

Hayes, John R. and Flower, Linda S. (1983) Uncovering cognitive processes in writing: An introduction to protocol analysis. In Peter Mosenthal, Lynne Tamor and Sean A. Walmsley (eds.) *Research on Writing: Principles and Methods* 207–220. New York: Longman.

Hearst, Marti A. (1994a) *Context and Structure in Automated Full-text Information Access*. Ph.D. Thesis. University of California, Berkeley.

Hearst, Marti A. (1994b) Multi-paragraph segmentation of expository text. In *Proceedings of the 32nd Annual Meeting of Association for Computational Linguistics* 9–16. Association for Computational Linguistics.

Hearst, Marti A. (1997) TextTiling: Segmenting text into multi-paragraph subtopic passages. *Computational Linguistics* 23(1): 33–64.

Hempel, Susanne and Degand, Liesbeth (2008) Sequencers in different text genres: Academic writing, journalese and fiction. *Journal of Pragmatics* 40(4): 676–693.

Hepburn, Andrew D. (1875) *Manual of English Rhetoric*. Cincinnati: Van Antwerp, Bragg and Co.

Heurley, Laurent (1997) Processing units in written texts: Paragraphs or information blocks. In Jean Costermans and Michel Fayol (eds.) *Processing Interclausal Relationships. Studies in the Production and Comprehension of Text* 179–200. New York: Lawrence Erlbaum.

Hinds, John (1978) Levels of structure within the paragraph. In *Proceedings of the Fourth Annual Meeting of the Berkeley Linguistics Society* 598–609. Berkeley, California.

Hinds, John (1979) Organizational patterns in discourse. In Talmy Givón (ed.) *Syntax and Semantics Discourse and Syntax* 135–157. New York: Academic Press.

Hinds, John (1983) Contrastive rhetoric: Japanese and English. *Text* 3(2): 183–95.

Hinds, John (1987) Reader versus writer responsibility: a new typology. In Ulla Connor and Robert B. Kaplan (eds.) *Writing Across Languages: Analysis of L2 Texts* 141–152. Reading, Massachusetts: Addison-Wesley.

Hinds, John (1990) Inductive, deductive, quasi-inductive: expository writing in Japanese, Korean, Chinese and Thai. In Ulla Connor and Ann M. Johns (eds.) *Coherence in Writing: Research and Pedagogical Perspectives* 87–110. Alexandria, Virginia: TESOL.

Hinkel, Eli (1994) Native and nonnative speakers' pragmatic interpretations of English texts. *TESOL Quarterly* 28(2): 353–376.

Hirschberg, Julia (1993) Studies of intonation and discourse. In *Proceedings of ESCA Workshop on Prosody* 90–93. Lund.

Hirschberg, Julia and Litman, Diane (1993) Empirical studies on the disambiguation of cue phrases. *Computational Linguistics* 19(3): 501–530.

Hirst, Graeme (2002) Review of patterns of text: In honour of Michael Hoey. *Computational Linguistics* 28(4): 560–564.

Ho-Dac, Lydia-Mai and Péry-Woodley, Marie-Paule (2009) A data-driven study of temporal adverbials as discourse segmentation markers. *Discours 4 Linearization and Segmentation in Discourse (Special issue)* http://discours.revues.org/5952.

Ho-Dac, Lydia-Mai (2010) An exploratory data-driven analysis for describing discourse organization. In Aquilino Sánchez and Moisés Almela (eds.) *A Mosaic of Corpus Linguistics. Selected Approaches* 79–98. Frankfurt am Main: Peter Lang.

Hoey, Michael (1991) *Patterns of Lexis in Text*. Oxford: Oxford University Press.

Hoey, Michael (1994) Patterns of lexis in narrative: A preliminary study. In Sanna-Kaisa Tanskanen and Brita Wårvik (eds.) *Topics and Comments: Papers from the Discourse Project* 1–40. Turku: University of Turku.

Hoey, Michael (2005) *Lexical Priming a New Theory of Words and Language*. Oxford: Routledge.

Hoey, Michael and O'Donnell, Matthew Brook (2007). Death to the topic sentence: How we really paragraph. In Y.-N. Leung (ed.) *Selected Papers of the 16th International Symposium on English Teaching Taipei, Taiwan* 60–76. English Teachers' Association / ROC.

Hoey, Michael and O'Donnell, Matthew Brook (2008a) Lexicography, grammar, and textual position. *International Journal of Lexicography* 21(3): 293–309.

Hoey, Michael and O'Donnell, Matthew Brook (2008b) The beginning of something important?: Corpus evidence on the text beginnings of hard news stories. In Barbara Lewandowska-Tomaszczyk (ed.) *Corpus Linguistics, Computer Tools, and Applications–State of the Art* 189–212. Frankfurt am Main: Peter Lang

Hofmann, Thomas R. (1989) Paragraphs, & anaphora. *Journal of Pragmatics* 13(2): 239–250.

Hogan, R. Craig (1977) Self-instructional units based on the Christensen method. *College Composition and Communication* 28(3): 275–277.

Hogsette, David S. (2009) *Writing that Makes Sense*. Eugene, Oregon: Resource Publications

Horn, Vivian (1972) Response to Michael Grady, "A conceptual rhetoric of the composition." *College Composition and Communication* 23(5): 412–414.

Horning, Alice S. (1993) *The Psycholinguistics of Readable Writing. A Multidisciplinary Exploration.* Norwood, New Jersey. Ablex

Huang, Yan (2000) Discourse anaphora: Four theoretical models. *Journal of Pragmatics* 32(2): 151–176.

Hughes, Rebecca and McCarthy, Michael (1998) From sentence to discourse: discourse grammar and English language teaching. *TESOL Quarterly* 32(2): 263–87

Humes, Ann (1983) Research on the composing process. *Review of Educational Research* 53(2): 201–216.

Hunston, Susan and Francis, Gill (2000) *Pattern Grammar: A Corpus-driven Approach to the Lexical Grammar of English*. Amsterdam: John Benjamins.

Husband, Thomas Fair and Husband, Margaret Fair Anderson (1905) *Punctuation: its Principles and Practice*. London: G. Routledge & Sons, Limited.

Hwang, Shin Ja Joo (1989) Recursion in the paragraph as a unit of discourse development. *Discourse Processes* 12(4): 461–477.

Hyönä, Jukka (1994) Processing of topic shifts by adults and children. *Reading Research Quarterly* 29(1): 76–90.

Hyönä, Jukka and Lorch, Robert F. (2004) Effects of topic headings on text processing: Evidence from adult readers' eye fixation patterns. *Learning and Instruction* 14(2): 131–152.

Hyönä, Jukka, Lorch, Robert F. and Kaakinen, Johanna K. (2002) Individual differences in reading to summarize expository text: Evidence from eye fixation patterns. *Journal of Educational Psychology* 94(1): 44–55.

Hyönä, Jukka, Lorch, Robert F. and Rinck, Mike (2003) Eye movement measures to study global text processing. In Jukka Hyönä, Ralph Radach and Heiner Deubel (eds.) *The Mind's Eye: Cognitive and Applied Aspects of Eye Movement Research*: 313–334. Amsterdam: North-Holland Elsevier.

Hyönä, Jukka and Nurminen, Anna-Mari (2006) Do adult readers know how they read? Evidence from eye movement patterns and verbal reports. *British Journal of Psychology* 97(1): 31–50.

Hyland, Ken (2004) Disciplinary interactions: Metadiscourse in L2 postgraduate writing. *Journal of Second Language Writing* 13(2): 133–151.

Hyland, Ken (2005) *Metadiscourse*. London: Continuum.

Hyland, Ken and Tse, Polly (2004) Metadiscourse in academic writing: A reappraisal. *Applied Linguistics* 25(2): 156–177.

Ivanič, Roz (1991) Nouns in search of a context: a study of nouns with both open- and closed-system characteristics *International Review of Applied Linguistics in Language Teaching* 29(2): 93–114.

Ji, Shaojun (2008) What do paragraph divisions indicate in narrative texts? *Journal of Pragmatics* 40(10): 1719–1730.

Ji, Shaojun (2002) Identifying episode transitions. *Journal of Pragmatics* 34(9): 1257–1271.

Johnson, Sabina Thorne (1969) Some tentative strictures on generative rhetoric. *College English* 31(2): 155–165.

Johnson, Wendell (1946) *People in Quandaries: The Semantics of Personal Adjustment*. New York: Harper and Row.

Johnson, William A. (1994) The function of the paragraphus in Greek literary prose texts. *Zeitschrift für Papyrologie und Epigraphik* Bd.100: 65–68. Bonn: Dr. Rudolf Habelt GmbH.

Johnston, Peter and Afflerbach, Peter (1985) The process of constructing main ideas from text. *Cognition and Instruction* 2 (3–4): 207–232.

Just, Marcel A. and Carpenter, Patricia A. (1980) A theory of reading: from eye fixations to comprehension. *Psychological Review* 87(4): 329–354

Just, Marcel A., Carpenter, Patricia A. and Woolley, Jacqueline D. (1982) Paradigms and processes in reading comprehension. *Journal of Experimental Psychology: General* 111(2): 228–238.

Kaplan, Robert B. (1966) Cultural thought patterns in intercultural education. *Language Learning* 16: 1–20.

Kaplan, Robert B. (1987) Cultural thought patterns revisited. In Ulla Connor and Robert B. Kaplan (Eds.) *Writing across Languages: Analysis of L2 Text* 9–21. Reading, Massachusetts: Addison-Wesley.

Károly, Krisztina (2002) *Lexical Repetition in Text*. Frankfurt am Main: Peter Lang.

Karrfalt, David H. (1966) Contribution to the Symposium on the Paragraph. *College Composition and Communication* 17(2): 82–87.

Karrfalt, David H. (1968) The generation of paragraphs and larger units. *College Composition and Communication* 19(3): 211–217.

Kaufmann, Stefan (1999) Cohesion and collocation: Using context vectors in text segmentation. In *Proceedings of the 37th Annual Meeting of the Association for Computational Linguistics on Computational Linguistics* 591–595. Association for Computational Linguistics.

Kellogg, Ronald T. (1987) Effects of topic knowledge on the allocation of processing time and cognitive effort to writing processes. *Memory & Cognition* 15(3): 256–266.

Kellogg, Ronald T. (1988) Attentional overload and writing performance: Effects of rough draft and outline strategies. *Journal of Experimental Psychology: Learning, Memory, and Cognition* 14(2): 355–365.

Kellogg, Ronald T. (1994) *The Psychology of Writing*. Oxford: Oxford University Press.

Kellogg, Ronald T. (1996) A model of working memory in writing. In Michael C. Levy and Sarah Ransdell (eds.) *The Science of Writing: Theories, Methods, Individual Differences, and Applications* 57–71. Hillsdale, New Jersey: Lawrence Erlbaum.

Kellogg, Ronald T. (2001) Competition for working memory among writing processes. *The American Journal of Psychology* 114(2): 175–191

Kellogg, Ronald T. (2008) Training writing skills – A cognitive developmental perspective. *Journal of Writing Research* 1(1): 1–26.

Kellogg, Ronald T. and Mueller, Suzanne (1993) Performance amplification and process restructuring in computer-based writing. *International Journal of Man-Machine Studies* 39(1): 33–49.

Keseling, Gisbert (1992) Pause and intonation contours in written and oral discourse. In Deiter Stein (ed.) *Co-operating with Written Texts. The*

Pragmatics and Comprehension of Written Texts 31–66. Berlin: Mouton de Gruyter.

Kieras, David E. (1978) Good and bad structure in simple paragraphs: Effects on apparent theme, reading time, and recall. *Journal of Verbal Learning and Verbal Behavior* 17(1): 13–28.

Kilgarriff, Adam (1997) "I don't believe in word senses." *Computers and the Humanities* 31(2): 91–113.

Kinney, James (1978) Tagmemic rhetoric: A reconsideration. *College Composition and Communication* 29(2): 141–145.

Kintsch, Walter and Monk, Doris (1972) Storage of complex information in memory: some implications of the speed with which inferences can be made. *Journal of Experimental Psychology* 94(1): 25–32

Kirsch, Gesa (1991) Writing up and down the social ladder: A study of experienced writers composing for contrasting audiences. *Research in the Teaching of English* 25(1): 33–53.

Kitzhaber, Albert R. (1990) *Rhetoric in American Colleges, 1850–1900.* Dallas: Southern Methodist University Press.

Kneupper, Charles W. (1980) Revising the tagmemic heuristic: Theoretical and pedagogical considerations. *College Composition and Communication* 31(2): 160–168.

Knoblauch, Charles H. (1981) The rhetoric of the paragraph: a reconsideration. *Journal of Advanced Composition* 2(1 / 2): 53–61.

Knox, Bernard M. W. (1968) Silent reading in antiquity. *Greek Roman and Byzantine Studies* 9(4): 421–435.

Koen, Frank, Becker, Alton and Young, Richard (1969) The psychological reality of the paragraph. *Journal of Verbal Learning and Verbal Behavior* 8(1): 49–53.

Kolhatkar, Varada, Zinsmeister, Heike and Hirst, Graeme (2013) Annotating anaphoric shell nouns with their antecedents. In *Proceedings of the 7th Linguistic Annotation Workshop & Interoperability with Discourse, August 8–9, 2013, Sofia, Bulgaria* 112–121. Stroudsburg, Pennsylvania: The Association for Computational Linguistics.

Kuperman, Victor, Dambacher, Michael, Nuthmann, Antje and Kliegl, Reinhold (2010) The effect of word position on eye-movements in sentence and paragraph reading. *The Quarterly Journal of Experimental Psychology* 63(9): 1838–1857.

Labadié, Alexandre and Prince, Violaine (2008) Finding text boundaries and finding topic boundaries: two different tasks? In Aarne Ranta and Bengt Nordström (eds.) *Advances in Natural Language Processing: 6th*

International Conference, GoTAL (2008) 260–271. Berlin – Heidelberg / Springer. Note this is page 10 of the author version.

Lackstrom, John, Selinker, Larry and Trimble, Louis (1973) Technical rhetorical principles and grammatical choice. *TESOL Quarterly* 7(2): 127–136.

Lam, Clara Yin Ping (1991) *Revision Processes of College ESL Students: How Teacher Comments, Discourse Types, and Writing Tools Shape Revision*. Ed.D. Thesis. University of Georgia. Dissertation Abstracts International 52: 12, 4248A.

Larson, Richard L. (1967) Sentences in action: A technique for analyzing paragraphs. *College Composition and Communication* 18(1): 16–22.

Larson, Richard L. (1971) Toward a linear rhetoric of the essay. *College Composition and Communication* 22(2): 140–146.

Lathrop, Henry Burrowes (1920) *Freshman Composition*. New York: The Century Company.

Le, Elisabeth (1999) The use of paragraphs in French and English academic writing: Towards a grammar of paragraphs. *Text-Interdisciplinary Journal for the Study of Discourse* 19(3): 307–344.

Lehtinen, Mari (2010) The recategorization of the rheme and the structure of the oral paragraph in French and in Finnish. *Discours 7*. https://discours. revues.org/8007.

Levenston, Edward A. (1992) *The Stuff of Literature: Physical Aspects of Texts and Their Relation to Literary Meaning*. Albany: State University of New York Press.

Levy, C. Michael and Ransdell, Sarah E. (1995) Is writing as difficult as it seems? *Memory and Cognition* 23(6): 767–779.

Lewis, Edwin H. (1894) *The History of the English Paragraph*. Chicago: University of Chicago Press.

Lindemann, Erika (1995) *A Rhetoric for Writing Teachers* (3rd edition). New York: Oxford University Press.

Lindgren, Eva and Sullivan, Kirk P. H. (2006) Analysing online revision. In Kirk P. H. Sullivan and Eva Lindgren (eds.) *Computer Keystroke Logging: Methods and Applications*: 157–188. Oxford: Elsevier.

Longacre, Robert E. (1968) *Discourse, Paragraph and Sentence Structure in Selected Philippine Languages*. Dallas, Texas: Summer Institute of Linguistics Publications.

Longacre, Robert E. (1979) The paragraph as a grammatical unit. In Talmy Givón (ed.) *Syntax and Semantics: Discourse and Syntax* 115–134. New York: Academic Press.

Longacre, Robert E. (1996) *The Grammar of Discourse* (2nd edition). New York: Plenum Press.

Longman Dictionary of Contemporary English (2009, 5th edition). Harlow: Pearson Longman.

Lorch, Robert F. and Lorch, Elizabeth Pugzles (1986) On-line processing of summary and importance signals in reading. *Discourse Processes* 9(4): 489–496.

Lord, John Bigelow (1964) *The Paragraph: Structure and Style*. New York: Holt, Rinehart and Winston,

Lowth, Robert (1799) *A Short Introduction to English Grammar*. Philadelphia: R. Aitken.

Lunsford, Andrea A. (1982) Alexander Bain's contributions to discourse theory. *College English* 44(3): 290–300.

Lunsford, Andrea A. (1998) Alexander Bain and the teaching of composition in North America. In Lynee L. Gaillet (ed.) *Scottish Rhetoric and its Influences* 219–227. Mahwah, New Jersey: Lawrence Erlbaum Associates.

Lutz, Jean A. (1987) A study of professional and experienced writers revising and editing at the computer and with pen and paper. *Research in the Teaching of English* 21(4): 398–421.

MacDonald, Susan Peck (1986) Specificity in context: some difficulties for the inexperienced writer. *College Composition and Communication* 37(2): 195–203.

Mackie, Ardiss and Bullock, Chris (1990) Discourse matrix: a practical tool for ESL writing teachers. *TESL Canada Journal* 8(1): 67–76.

Mahlberg, Michaela (2009a) Local textual functions of *move* in newspaper story patterns. In Ute Römer and Rainer Schulze (eds.) *Exploring the Lexis-Grammar Interface* 265–287. Amsterdam: John Benjamins.

Mahlberg, Michaela (2009b) Lexical cohesion: Corpus linguistic theory and its application in English language teaching. In John Flowerdew and Michaela Mahlberg (eds.) *Lexical cohesion and corpus linguistics* 103–122. Amsterdam / Philadelphia. John Benjamins.

Makkonen-Craig, Henna (2011) Connecting with the reader: participant-oriented metadiscourse in newspaper texts. *Text & Talk – An Interdisciplinary Journal of Language, Discourse & Communication Studies* 31(6): 683–704.

Manchón, Rosa M. and de Larios, Julio Roca (2007) On the temporal nature of planning in L1 and L2 composing. *Language learning* 57(4): 549–593.

Mann, William C. and Thompson, Sandra A. (1988) Rhetorical structure theory: Toward a functional theory of text organization. *Text-Interdisciplinary Journal for the Study of Discourse* 8(3): 243–281.

Marcu, Daniel (2000a) The rhetorical parsing of unrestricted texts: A surface-based approach. *Computational Linguistics* 26(3): 395–448.

Marcu, Daniel (2000b) *The Theory and Practice of Discourse Parsing and Summarization*. Cambridge, Massachusetts: MIT Press.

Markels, Robin B. (1983) Cohesion paradigms in paragraphs. *College English* 45(5): 450–464.

Martín, Javier Calle and Garcia, Antonio Miranda (2005) Editing Middle English punctuation. The case of MS Egerton 2622 (ff.136–152). *International Journal of English Studies* 5(2): 27–44.

Matsuhashi, Ann (1981) Pausing and planning: The tempo of written discourse production. *Research in the Teaching of English* 15(2): 113–134.

Mauranen, Anna (1993) Contrastive ESP rhetoric: Metatext in Finnish – English economics texts. *English for Specific Purposes* 12(1): 3–22.

McCorkle, Ben (2005) Harbingers of the printed page: Nineteenth-century theories of delivery as remediation. *Rhetoric Society Quarterly* 35(4): 25–49.

McCutchen, Deborah (2011) From novice to expert: Implications of language skills and writing-relevant knowledge for memory during the development of writing skill. *Journal of Writing Research* 3(1): 51–68.

McElroy, John G. R. (1885) The *Structure of English Prose: A Manual of Composition and Rhetoric*. New York: A.C. Armstrong and Son.

McGee, Iain (2009) Traversing the lexical cohesion minefield. *ELT Journal* 63(3): 212–220.

McGee, Iain (2014) The pragmatics of paragraphing English argumentative text. *Journal of Pragmatics* 68: 40–72.

McGee, Iain (2016) Reconsidering paragraphing pedagogy: A descriptivist perspective. *English in Education* 50(3): 233–254.

McNamara, Danielle S., and Kintsch, Walter (1996) Learning from texts: Effects of prior knowledge and text coherence. *Discourse Processes* 22(3): 247–288.

McNamara, Danielle S., Kintsch, Eileen, Songer, Nancy Butler and Kintsch, Walter (1996) Are good texts always better? Interactions of text coherence, background knowledge, and levels of understanding in learning from text. *Cognition and Instruction* 14(1): 1–43.

Merriam Webster's Collegiate Dictionary (2002, 10th edition). Springfield, Massachusetts: Merriam–Webster, Inc.

Miles, Josephine (1966) Contribution to the symposium on the paragraph. *College Composition and Communication* 17(2): 80–82.

Milic, Louis T. (1967) Metaphysical criticism of style. In Martin Steinmann, Jr. (ed.) *New Rhetorics* 161–175. New York: Scribners.

Miller, Jeanette (2010) Speaking my mind: Persistence of the five-paragraph essay. *The English Journal* 99(3): 99–100.

Monahan, Brian D. (1984) Revision strategies of basic and competent writers as they write for different audiences. *Research in the Teaching of English* 18(3): 288–304.

Mones, Leon (1921) Teaching the paragraph. *The English Journal* 10(8): 456–460.

Montaño-Harmon, María Rosario (1991) Discourse features of written Mexican Spanish: Current research in contrastive rhetoric and its implications. *Hispania* 74(2): 417–425.

Moore, David W. and Readence, John E. (1980) Processing main ideas through parallel lesson transfer. *Journal of Reading* 23(7): 593–598.

Morris, Jane and Hirst, Graeme (1991) Lexical cohesion computed by thesaural relations as an indicator of the structure of text. *Computational Linguistics* 17(1): 21–48.

Morrison, Ken (1987) Stabilizing the text: The institutionalization of knowledge in historical and philosophic forms of argument. *Canadian Journal of Sociology / Cahiers Canadiens de Sociologie* 12(3): 242–274.

Murphy, James J. (ed.) (2012) *A Short History of Writing Instruction: From Ancient Greece to Contemporary America* (3rd edition). New York: Routledge.

Murray, Donald M. (1978) Internal revision: A process of discovery. In Charles R. Cooper and Lee Odell (eds.) *Research on Composing: Points of Departure* 85–103. Urbana, Illinois: National Council of Teachers of English.

Myers, Greg (1991) Lexical cohesion and specialized knowledge in science and popular science texts. *Discourse Processes* 14(1): 1–26.

Myhill, Debra (2009) Developmental trajectories in mastery of paragraphing: Towards a model of development. *Written Language & Literacy* 12(1): 26–51.

Myhill, Debra and Jones, Susan (2007) More than just error correction: students' perspectives on their revision processes during writing. *Written Communication* 24(4): 323–343.

Nash, Rose (1973) *Turkish Intonation: An Instrumental Study*. The Hague: Mouton.

New, Elizabeth (1999) Computer-aided writing in French as a foreign language: A qualitative and quantitative look at the process of revision. *The Modern Language Journal* 83(1): 81–97.

Noordman, Leo, Huntjens-Dassen, Ingrid, Swerts, Marc and Terken, Jacques (1999) Prosodic markers of text structure. In Karen Van Hoek, Andrej A. Kibrik and Leo Noordman (eds.) *Discourse Studies in Cognitive Linguistics* 133–148. Amsterdam / Philadelphia: John Benjamins.

Nunberg, Geoffrey (1990) *The Linguistics of Punctuation*. Stanford University: Center for the Study of Language and Information.

Nunes, Matthew J. (2013) The five-paragraph essay: Its evolution and roots in theme-writing. *Rhetoric Review* 32(3): 295–313.

Nystrand, Martin (1986) *The Structure of Written Communication: Studies in Reciprocity between Writers and Readers*.

Nystrand, Martin (1983) The role of context in written communication. *Nottingham Linguistic Circular* 12(1): 55–65.

Nystrand, Martin, Doyle, Anne and Himley, Margaret (1986) A critical examination of the doctrine of autonomous texts. In Martin Nystrand *The Structure of Written Communication: Studies in Reciprocity between Writers and Readers* 81–107. Orlando, Florida: Academic Press, Inc. Harcourt Brace Jovanovich.

Odell, Lee (1978) Another look at tagmemic theory: A response to James Kinney. *College Composition and Communication* 29(2): 146–152.

O'Donnell, Matthew (n. d.) The paragraph in translation studies and corpus linguistics and its application to periscope studies in ancient manuscripts. Unpublished ms.

O'Hear, Michael F., Ramsey, Richard N. and Pherson, Valli E. (1987) Location of main ideas in English composition texts. *Research in the Teaching of English* 21(3): 318–326.

Olive, Thierry (2015) Working memory in writing: Empirical evidence from the dual-task technique. *European Psychologist* 9: 32–42.

Olive, Thierry, Alves, Rui Alexandre, and Castro, São Luís (2009) Cognitive processes in writing during pause and execution periods. *European Journal of Cognitive Psychology* 21(5): 758–785.

Olive, Thierry, Kellogg, Ronald T. and Piolat, Annie (2008) Verbal, visual, and spatial working memory demands during text composition. *Applied Psycholinguistics* 29(4): 669–687.

Olive, Thierry and Passerault, Jean-Michel (2012) The visuospatial dimension of writing. *Written Communication* 29(3): 326–344.

Olson, David R. (1996) Toward a psychology of literacy: on the relations between speech and writing. *Cognition* 60: 83–104.

Ong, Walter J. (1944) Historical backgrounds of Elizabethan and Jacobean punctuation theory. *Publications of the Modern Language Association of America* 59(2): 349–360.

Ong, Walter J. (1968) Tudor writings on rhetoric. *Studies in the Renaissance* 15: 39–69.

Ong, Walter J. (1982) *Orality and Literacy: The Technologizing of the Word.* London: Routledge.

Owtram, Nicola T. (2010) *The Pragmatics of Academic Writing: A Relevance Approach to the Analysis of Research Article Introductions.* Bern: Peter Lang.

Pace, Thomas (2005) Style and the renaissance of composition studies. In T. R. Johnson and Thomas Pace (eds.) *Refiguring Prose style: Possibilities for Writing Pedagogy* 3–22. Logan, Utah: Utah State University Press.

Packard, Dennis J. (1986) A generative rhetoric. *Rhetoric Society Quarterly* 16(1–2): 59–65.

Padučeva, Elena V. (1974) On the structure of the paragraph. *Linguistics* 12(131): 49–58.

Paltridge, Eric (1978) *You Have a Point There: A Guide to Punctuation and its Allies.* London: Routledge and Kegan Paul.

Parkes, Malcolm Beckwith (1992) *Pause and Effect: A History of Punctuation in the West.* Farnham, Surrey: Ashgate Publishing Co.

Pennington, Martha C. (1996) *The Computer and the Non-native Writer: A Natural Partnership.* Cresskill, New Jersey: Hampton Press.

Perl, Sondra (1980) A look at basic writers in the process of composing. In Lawrence Kasden and Daniel Hoeber (eds.) *Basic Writing: Essays for Teachers, Researchers and Administrators* 13–32. Urbana, Illinois: National Council of Teachers of English.

Petzinger, Robert (1967) Patterns, Proportions, and Paragraphing in *Aeneid VI. The Classical World* 60(8): 313–315.

Phinney, Marianne and Khouri, Sandra (1993) Computers, revision, and ESL writers: The role of experience. *Journal of Second Language Writing* 2(3): 257–277.

Pike, Kenneth L. (1981) *Tagmemics, Discourse, and Verbal Art.* Ann Arbor: University of Michigan press.

Pike, Kenneth L. (1964) Beyond the sentence. *College Composition and Communication* 15(3): 129–135.

Piolat, Annie, Roussey, Jean-Yves and Thunin, Olivier (1997) Effects of screen presentation on text reading and revising. *International Journal of Human-Computer Studies* 47(4): 565–589.

Pitkin, Willis L. (1969) Discourse blocs. *College Composition and Communication* 20(2): 138–148.

Pitkin, Willis L. (1977) Hierarchies and the discourse hierarchy. *College English* 38(7): 648–659.

Popken, Randall L. (1987) A study of topic sentence use in academic writing. *Written Communication* 4(2): 209–228.

Porter, Stanley E. (2009) Pericope markers and the paragraph. In Raymond de Hoop, Marjo Korpel and Stanley Porter (eds.) *The Impact of Unit Delimitation on Exegesis Volume 7* 175–195. Leiden: Brill.

Prideaux, Gary D. and Hogan, John T. (1993) Markedness as a discourse management device: The role of alternative adverbial clause orders. *Word* 44(3): 397–411.

Quirk, Randolph, Greenbaum, Sidney, Leech, Geoffrey and Svartvik, Jan (1985) *A Comprehensive Grammar of the English Language*. London: Longman.

Rasekh, Abbass Eslami and Toluei, Bahareh (2009) Paragraph Boundaries: Examining Identification and Production Performance of Iranian EFL Learners. *English Language Teaching* 2(2): 30–38.

Rayner, Keith and Pollatsek, Alexander (2006) Eye movement control in reading. In Matthew J. Traxler and Morton A. Gernsbacher (eds.) *Handbook of Psycholinguistics* (2nd edition) 613–657. London: Elsevier.

Redeker, Gisela (1990) Ideational and pragmatic markers of discourse structure. *Journal of Pragmatics* 14(3): 367–381.

Reichelt, Melinda, Lefkowitz, Natalie, Rinnert, Carol and Schultz, Jean Marie (2012) Key issues in foreign language writing. *Foreign Language Annals* 45(1): 22–41.

Reid, Joy M. (1994) *The Process of Paragraph Writing* (2nd edition). Englewood Cliffs, New Jersey: Prentice Hall Regents.

Reinking, James A., Hart, Andrew W. and von der Osten, Robert (2005) *Strategies for Successful Writing: A Rhetoric, Reader and Handbook* (international edition). New Jersey: Prentice Hall.

Reynar, Jeffrey (1998) *Topic Segmentation: Algorithms and Applications*. Ph.D. thesis. Philadelphia: University of Pennsylvania.

Roberts, Carol M. (2004) *The Dissertation Journey*. Thousand Oaks, California: Corwin Press

Rockas, Leo (1964) *Modes of Rhetoric*. New York: St Martin's Press.

Rockas, Leo (1966) Further comments on the paragraph. *College Composition and Communication* 17(3): 148–151.

Rodgers, Paul C. (1965) Alexander Bain and the rise of the organic paragraph. *Quarterly Journal of Speech* 51(4): 399–408.

Rodgers, Paul C. (1966a) A discourse-centered rhetoric of the paragraph. *College Composition and Communication* 17(1): 2–11.

Rodgers, Paul C. (1966b) Contribution to the symposium on the paragraph. *College Composition and Communication* 17(2): 72–80.

Rodgers, Paul C. (1967) The stadium of discourse. *College Composition and Communication* 18(3): 178–185.

Roen, Duane H. and Willey, R. J. (1988) The effects of audience awareness on drafting and revising. *Research in the Teaching of English* 22(1): 75–88.

Roller, Cathy M. (1990) Commentary: The interaction between knowledge and structure variables in the processing of expository prose. *Reading Research Quarterly* 25(2): 79–89.

Rose, Mike (1980) Rigid rules, inflexible plans, and the stifling of language: A cognitivist analysis of writer's block. *College Composition and Communication* 31(4): 389–401.

Saenger, Paul (1997) *Space between Words: The Origins of Silent Reading.* Stanford: Stanford University Press.

Saintsbury, George (1897) *The Flourishing of Romance and the Rise of Allegory.* New York: Charles Scribner's Sons.

Salkie, Raphael (1995) *Text and Discourse Analysis.* London: Routledge.

Sanders, Ted, Janssen, Daniël, van der Pool, Els, Schilperoord, Joost and van Wijk, Carel (1996) Hierarchical text structure in writing products and writing processes. In Gert Rijlaarsdam, Huub Van den Bergh and Michel Couzjin (eds.) *Theories, Models and Methodology in Writing Research* 473–492. Amsterdam: Amsterdam University Press.

Scardamalia, Marlene and Bereiter, Carl (1983) The development of evaluative, diagnostic, and remedial capabilities in children's composing. In Margaret Martlew (ed.) *The Psychology of Written Language: Developmental and Educational Perspectives* 67–95. Chichester: Wiley.

Scardamalia, Marlene and Bereiter, Carl (1986) Research on written composition. In Merlin C. Wittrock (ed.) *Handbook of Research on Teaching* (3rd edition) 778–803. New York: MacMillan.

Schilperoord, Joost (2001) Conceptual and linguistic processes in text production. In Ted Sanders, Joost Schilperoord and Wilbert Spooren (eds.) *Text Representation: Linguistic and Psycholinguistic Aspects* 309–336. Amsterdam / Philadelphia: John Benjamins Publishing.

Schilperoord, Joost (2002) On the cognitive status of pauses in discourse production. In Thierry Olive and C. Michael Levy (eds.) *Contemporary Tools and Techniques for Studying Writing* 61–87. Dordrecht: Kluwer Academic Publishers.

Schmid, Hans-Jörg (2000) *English Abstract Nouns as Conceptual Shells: From Corpus to Cognition.* Berlin: Walter de Gruyter.

Schwartz, Joseph (1968) Review *Notes toward a new rhetoric* by Francis Christensen. *College Composition and Communication* 19(1): 41–42.

Scott, Fred Newton and Denney, Joseph Villiers (1895) *Paragraph Writing* (3rd edition, revised and enlarged). Boston: Allyn and Bacon.

Scrivener, Frederick H. A. (ed) (1873) The Cambridge Paragraph Bible of the Authorized English Version. Cambridge: Cambridge University Press.

Scrivener, Frederick H. A. (2010) *The Authorized Version of the English Bible (1611): Its Subsequent Reprints and Modern Representations.* Cambridge: Cambridge University Press.

Selinker, Larry, Todd-Trimble, Mary and Trimble, Louis (1976) Presuppositional rhetorical information in EST discourse. *TESOL Quarterly* 10(3): 281–290.

Selzer, Jack (1983) The composing processes of an engineer. *College Composition and Communication* 34(2): 178–187.

Seo, Byung-In (2007) Speaking my mind: Defending the five-paragraph essay. *The English Journal* 97(2): 15–16.

Severino, Carol (1993) The "doodles" in context: Qualifying claims about contrastive rhetoric. *The Writing Center Journal* 14(1): 44–62.

Shapire, Robert E. and Singer, Yoram (2000) BoosTexter: A boosting-based system for text categorization. *Machine Learning* 39(2): 135–168.

Simpson, Joellen M. (2000) Topical structure analysis of academic paragraphs in English and Spanish. *Journal of Second Language Writing* 9(3): 293–309.

Sinclair, John (1991) *Corpus, Concordance, Collocation.* Oxford: Oxford University Press

Sinclair, John (2004) *Trust the Text: Language, Corpus and Discourse* (ed. Ronald Carter). London: Routledge.

Skeat, Walter William (1901) *Notes on English Etymology.* Oxford: Clarendon Press.

Skorochod'ko, Eduard F. (1972) Adaptive method of automatic abstracting and indexing. In C. V. Freiman (ed.) *Information Processing: Proceedings of the IFIP Congress 71*, 1179–1182. Amsterdam: North-Holland Publishing Company.

Small, Jocelyn P. (1997) *Wax Tablets of the Mind.* London: Routledge.

Smith, Craig G. (2008) Braddock revisited: The frequency and placement of topic sentences in academic writing. *The Reading Matrix* 8(1): 78–95.

Smith, Herbert Winslow (1920) Concerning organization in paragraphs. *The English Journal* 9(7): 390–400.

Smith, Kerri (2006) In defense of the five-paragraph essay. *English Journal* 95(4): 16–17.

Sommers, Nancy (1980) Revision strategies of student writers and experienced adult writers. *College Composition and Communication* 31(4): 378–388.

Spelman Miller, Kristyan (2000) Academic writers on-line: Investigating pausing in the production of text. *Language Teaching Research* 4(2): 123–148.

Spelman Miller, Kristyan (2002a) Units of production in writing: Evidence of topic 'framing' in on-line writing research. *Reading Working Papers in Linguistics* 6: 255–272.

Spelman Miller, Kristyan (2002b) Units of production in writing: Towards a discourse perspective. In Sally Burgess (ed.) *Revista Canaria de Estudios Ingleses* 44: 115–140. Tenerife: University La Laguna.

Spelman Miller, Kristyan (2006a) The pausological study of written language production. In Kirk P. H. Sullivan and Eva Lindgren (eds.) *Computer Keystroke Logging: Methods and Applications* 11–30. Oxford: Elsevier.

Spelman Miller, Kristyan (2006b) Pausing, productivity and the processing of topic in online writing. In Kirk P. H. Sullivan and Eva Lindgren (eds.) *Computer Keystroke Logging: Methods and Applications* 131–156. Oxford: Elsevier.

Spelman Miller, Kristyan, Lindgren, Eva and Sullivan, Kirk P. H. (2008) The psycholinguistic dimension in second language writing: Opportunities for research and pedagogy using computer keystroke logging. *TESOL Quarterly* 42(3): 433–454.

Sporleder, Caroline and Lapata, Mirella (2004) Automatic paragraph identification: A study across languages and domains. In Proceedings of the Conference on Empirical Methods in Natural Language Processing 72–79. Barcelona.

Sporleder, Caroline and Lapata, Mirella (2006) Broad coverage paragraph segmentation across languages and domains. *ACM Transactions on Speech and Language Processing* 3(2): 1–35.

Stallard, Charles K. (1974) An analysis of the writing behavior of good student writers. *Research in the Teaching of English* 8(2): 206–218.

Stark, Heather A. (1988) What do paragraph markings do? *Discourse Processes* 11(3): 275–303.

Stern, Arthur A. (1976) When is a paragraph? *College Composition and Communication* 27(3): 253–257.

Stevens, David R. (1967) Concerning generative rhetoric. *College Composition and Communication* 18(3): 173–177.

Stewart, Donald C. (1978) Composition textbooks and the assault on tradition. *College Composition and Communication* 29(2): 171–176.

Stewart, Donald C. (1990) The nineteenth century. In Winifred Bryan Horner (ed.) *The Present State of Scholarship in Historical and Contemporary Rhetoric* 151–185. Columbia, Missouri: University of Missouri Press.

Stirling, Lesley (2001) The multifunctionality of anaphoric expressions: A typological perspective. *Australian Journal of Linguistics* 21(1): 7–23.

Strachey, Lytton (1924) *Queen Victoria*. London: Chatto and Windus.

Strömqvist, Sven, Holmqvist, Kenneth, Johansson, Victoria, Karlsson, Henrik and Wengelin, Åsa (2006a) What keystroke-logging can reveal about writing. In Kirk P. H. Sullivan and Eva Lindgren (eds.) *Computer Keystroke Logging: Methods and Applications* 45–72. Oxford: Elsevier.

Stubbs, Michael (2002) *Words and Phrases: Corpus Studies of Lexical Semantics*. Oxford: Blackwell Publishing.

Swerts, Marc (1997) Prosodic features at discourse boundaries of different strength. *The Journal of the Acoustical Society of America* 101(1): 514–521.

Taboada, Maite (2006) Discourse markers as signals (or not) of rhetorical relations. *Journal of Pragmatics* 38(4): 567–592.

Tebeaux, Elizabeth (2011) Technical writing and the development of the English paragraph 1473–1700. *Journal of Technical Writing and Communication* 41(3): 219–253.

Teich, Elke and Fankhauser, Peter (2005) Exploring lexical patterns in text: lexical cohesion analysis with WordNet. In Stefanie Dipper, Michael Götze, and Manfred Stede (eds.) *Heterogeneity in Focus: Creating and Using Linguistic Databases* 129–145. Universitätsverlag Potsdam.

The Concise Oxford Dictionary (2002, 10th edition). Oxford: Oxford University Press

The Shorter Oxford English Dictionary (2007, 6th edition). Oxford: Oxford University Press.

Thompson, Edward Maunde (1893) An Introduction to Greek and Latin Palaeography. New York: D. Appleton and Co.

Tibbetts, Arn, and Tibbetts, Charlene (1982) Can composition textbooks use composition research? *College English* 44(8): 855–858.

Tomitch, Lêda Maria Braga, Newman, Sharlene D., Carpenter, Patricia A. and Just, Marcel Adam (2008) Comprehending the topic of a paragraph: A Functional Imaging Study of a Complex Language Process. *DELTA: Documentação de Estudos em Lingüística Teórica e Aplicada* 24(2): 175–197.

Utiyama, Masao and Isahara, Hitoshi (2001) A statistical model for domain-independent text segmentation. In *Proceedings of the 39th Annual Meeting of the Association for Computational Linguistics* 491–498. Stroudsburg, Pennsylvania: Association for Computational Linguistics.

Vande Kopple, William J. (1985) Some exploratory discourse on metadiscourse. *College Composition and Communication* 36(1): 82–93.

van Dijk, Teun Adrianus (1981) Episodes as units of discourse analysis. In Deborah Tannen (ed.) *Analyzing discourse: Text and talk* 177–195. Georgetown: Georgetown University Press.

van Dijk, Teun Adrianus and Kintsch, Walter (1983) *Strategies of Discourse Comprehension*. New York: Academic Press.

van Silfhout, Gerdineke, Evers-Vermeul, Jacqueline and Sanders, Ted (2015) Connectives as processing signals: How students benefit in processing narrative and expository texts. *Discourse Processes* 52(1): 47–76.

Van Waes, Luuk, and Leijten, Mariëlle (2015) Fluency in writing: A multidimensional perspective on writing fluency applied to L1 and L2. *Computers and Composition* 38A: 79–95.

Van Waes, Luuk and Schellens, Peter Jan (2003) Writing profiles: The effect of the writing mode on pausing and revision patterns of experienced writers. *Journal of Pragmatics* 35(6): 829–853.

Vatri, Alessandro (2012) The physiology of ancient Greek reading. *The Classical Quarterly (New Series)* 62(2): 633–647.

Vitanza, Victor J. (1979) A tagmemic heuristic for the whole composition. *College Composition and Communication* 30(3): 270–274.

Vonk, Wietske, Hustinx, Lettica G. M. M. and Simons, Wim H. G. (1992) The use of referential expressions in structuring discourse. *Language and Cognitive Processes* 7(3–4): 301–333.

Wallwork, Adrian (2011) *English for Writing Research Papers*. New York: Springer Science & Business Media.

Walzer, Arthur E. (1991) The meanings of "purpose." *Rhetoric Review* 10(1): 118–129.

Wang, Danhua (2009) Factors affecting the comprehension of global and local main idea. *Journal of College Reading and Learning* 39(2): 34–52.

Warne, Bonnie Mary (2008) Writing steps: A recursive and individual experience. *English Journal* 97(5): 23–27.

Warner, Julian (1994) *From Writing to Computers*. London: Routledge.

Warner, Richard (1979) Teaching the paragraph as a structural unit. *College Composition and Communication* 30(2): 152–155.

Wårvik, Brita (2003) When you read or hear this story read. In Risto Hiltunen and Janne Skaffari (eds.) *Discourse Perspectives on English: Medieval to Modern* 13–55. Amsterdam / Philadelphia: John Benjamins Publishing Company.

Watson, Wilfred (2007) Unit delimitation in the Old Testament. In Marjo C. A. Korpel, Josef M. Oesch and Stanley E. Porter (eds.) *Method in Unit Delimitation* 162–184. Leiden: Brill.

Watkins, Roy Edward (1940) *A History of Paragraph Divisions in Horace's Epistles*. Iowa: University of Iowa.

Welldon, James Edward Cowell (1886) *The Rhetoric of Aristotle*. London: Macmillan.

Wendell, Barrett (1891) *English Composition: Eight Lectures Given at the Irwell Institute*. New York: Charles Scribner's Sons.

Wengelin, Åsa, Torrance, Mark, Holmqvist, Kenneth, Simpson, Sol, Galbraith, David, Johansson, Victoria and Johansson, Roger (2009) Combined eyetracking and keystroke-logging methods for studying cognitive processes in text production. *Behavior Research Methods* 41(2): 337–351.

Whaler, James (1971) *Counterpoint and Symbol*. New York: Haskell House.

Widdowson, Henry (1991) The description and prescription of language. In James E. Alatis (ed.) *Georgetown University Roundtable on Language and Linguistics 1991 – Linguistics and Language Pedagogy: The State of the Art* 11–24. Washington D.C.: Georgetown University Press.

Wingo, E. Otha (1972) *Latin Punctuation in the Classical Age*. The Hague: Mouton and Co.

Winter, Eugene O. (1977) A clause-relational approach to English texts: a study of some predictive lexical items in written discourse. *Instructional Science* 6(1): 1–92.

Winterowd, W. Ross (1973) Topics and levels in the composing process. *College English* 34(5): 701–709.

Witte, Stephen P. (1983) Topical structure and revision: An exploratory study. *College Composition and Communication* 34(3): 313–341.

Witte, Stephen P. (1985) Revising, composing theory, and research design. In Sarah Warshauer Freedman (ed.) *The Acquisition of Written Language: Response and Revision* 250–284. Norwood, New Jersey: Ablex.

Witte, Stephen P. (1987) Pre-text and composing. *College Composition and Communication* 38(4): 397–425.

Wodak, Ruth (1992) Strategies in text production and text comprehension: A new perspective. In Dieter Stein (ed.) *Cooperating with Written Texts* 493–528. Berlin: Mouton de Gruyter.

Wolfe, Maria Loukianenko (2008) Different cultures – Different discourses? Rhetorical patterns of business letters by English and Russian speakers. In Ulla Connor, Ed Nagelhout and William Rozycki (eds.) *Contrastive Rhetoric: Reaching to Intercultural Rhetoric* 87–122. Amsterdam / Philadelphia: John Benjamins Publishing.

Wolk, Anthony (1970) The relative importance of the final free modifier: A quantitative analysis. *Research in the Teaching of English* 4(1): 59–68.

World Book Dictionary (1995). Chicago: World Book.

Yakhontova, Tatyana (2006) Cultural and disciplinary variation in academic discourse: The issue of influencing factors. *Journal of English for Academic Purposes* 5(2): 153–167.

Young, Richard E. (1978) Paradigms and problems: Needed research in rhetorical invention. In Charles R. Cooper and Lee Odell (eds.) *Research on Composing* 29–47. Urbana, Illinois: National Council of Teachers of English.

Young, Richard E. and Becker, Alton L. (1965) Toward a modern theory of rhetoric: A tagmemic contribution. *Harvard Educational Review* 35(4): 450–468.

Young, Richard E. and Becker, Alton L. (1966) The role of lexical and grammatical cues in paragraph recognition. *Studies in Language and Language Behavior* 11(2): 1–6.

Young, Richard E., Becker, Alton L. and Pike, Kenneth Lee (1970) *Rhetoric: Discovery and Change*. Fort Worth: Harcourt Brace Jovanich.

Youmans, Gilbert (1990) Measuring lexical style and competence: The type-token vocabulary curve. *Style* 24(4): 584–99.

Youmans, Gilbert (n.d.) *A New Tool for Discourse Analysis: The Vocabulary-Management Profile*. https://mospace.umsystem.edu/xmlui/bitstream/handle/10355/465/A%20New%20Tool%20for%20Discourse%20Analysis.pdf?sequence=1&origin=publication_detail.

Youmans, Gilbert (1991) A new tool for discourse analysis: The vocabulary-management profile. *Language* 67(4): 763–789.

Zamel, Vivian (1983) The composing processes of advanced ESL students: Six case studies. *TESOL Quarterly* 17(2): 165–187.

Zeeman, Elizabeth (1956) Punctuation in an early manuscript of Love's Mirror. *The Review of English Studies* 7(25): 11–18.

Subject Index

CPSIA information can be obtained
at www.ICGtesting.com
Printed in the USA
LVHW10*1011201018
592471LV00002BC/9/P